THE JAPAN-U.S. TRADE FRICTION DILEMMA

To William R. Thompson

The Japan-U.S. Trade Friction Dilemma

The Role of Perception

KAREN M. HOLGERSON
Pasadena City College

Ashgate

Aldershot • Brookfield USA • Singapore • Sydney

Published by
Ashgate Publishing Limited
Gower House
Croft Road
Aldershot
Hants GU11 3HR
England

Ashgate Publishing Company
Old Post Road
Brookfield
Vermont 05036
USA

British Library Cataloguing in Publication Data
Holgerson, Karen M.
    The Japan-U.S. trade friction dilemma : the role of
perception
    1.Japan - Commerce - United States 2.United States -
Commerce - Japan
    I.Title
    382'.0952'073

Library of Congress Cataloging-in-Publication Data
Holgerson, Karen M.
    The Japan-U.S. trade friction dilemma : the role of perception /
Karen M. Holgerson.
        p. cm.
    Includes bibliographical references and index.
    ISBN 1-84014-064-X (hc)
    1. Japan--Commerce--United States--Public opinion. 2. United
States--Commerce--Japan--Public opinion. 3. Japan--Foreign public
opinion, American. 4. United States--Foreign public opinion,
Japanese. 5. Public opinion--Japan. 6. Public opinion--United
States. 7. Japan--Commerce--United States--Case studies. 8. United
States--Commerce--Japan--Case studies. I. Title.
    HF3828.U5H65 1998
    382'.0952073--dc21   97-41410
                                                                        CIP

ISBN 1 84014 064 X

Printed in Great Britain by The Ipswich Book Company, Suffolk.

Contents

List of Figures

List of Tables

Preface

On an extended stay in Japan during the summer of 1985 to do research for a seminar I was to give at the University of California – Los Angeles, I experienced more deeply the same stumbling blocks to effective communication which I had experienced with Japanese friends and acquaintances in the past. The assumption of similarities got me into trouble. I frequently misread nonverbal as well as verbal cues. Furthermore, many of my ideas about Japan – and the United States – were challenged. As a consequence, my interest in Japan and in Japan-U.S. relations began to take me in new directions, one of which was the reading and research I did in preparation for this book.

Although many books and articles have been written on Japan-U.S. relations and bilateral trade problems, this study differs from other analyses in a number of important ways. First, it is interdisciplinary, drawing on the research of anthropologists, area specialists, intercultural communication researchers, linguists, sociologists, and social psychologists as well as that of political scientists and economists. Those with interdisciplinary interests or those wishing a comprehensive approach to an old problem – conflict at the international level, in this case, between Japan and the United States over trade – should find something of interest here. However, those whose thinking is narrowly defined by a particular discipline or who believe that culture has little or no relevance to political-economic analysis, may wish to read no further. Hopefully, however, they will suspend judgment and read on.

What does each of the disciplines, in addition to political science and economics, bring to the present study? Anthropology, area studies, linguistics, sociology, and intercultural communication offer rich material for impressionistic essays on Japan-U.S. cultural and institutional differences. While no new material or approach is offered, these differences are fleshed out in broad strokes for the ultimate purposes of this study. Those who think that the *individualism-collectivism* cultural dimension has been exhausted by previous work and is now passé will find that the testing of hypotheses informed by this cultural dimension demonstrates that this is simply not the case.

Social psychology, which furnishes the theoretical framework for the present study, was also the theoretical framework for two political science studies that served as my inspirational models. These were Debra Larson's

Origins of Containment: A Psychological Explanation, published by Princeton University Press, and David Heradsveit's *The Arab-Israeli Conflict: Psychological Obstacles to Peace*, published by Univeritetsforlaget in Oslo. Other relevant social psychological analyses of political issues are listed in the bibliography. From both the political scientific and social psychological points of view, this is the first analysis of precisely this kind. As such, it bridges the two disciplines in unique ways. Additionally, the social psychological chapter functions as a critique of the somewhat culturally myopic way in which the mainstream field has developed.

A second way in which this study differs from other analyses of Japan-U.S. relations is that it both *identifies* and *measures* perceptual differences between Japanese and American opinion leaders regarding the large bilateral trade imbalances, the bilateral relationship, and national negotiating styles. Although the respondents indicate which country they believe bears the greater burden of blame for the trade friction dilemma, the writer remains impartial. Those who find themselves offended by concepts like 'Japan's relatively closed markets' or 'U.S. relative economic decline' might need to consider on which side of the Japan-U.S. perceptual divide they reside. Meanwhile, there are others who believe that diplomats are too sophisticated to fall into the misperception or biased perception 'trap' or that they simply use so-called misperceptions to camouflage real intentions and actions. This study does not deal directly with this possibility, but it is interesting to note that Bem's self-perception theory posits that often what one says is ultimately what one comes to believe.

A third way in which this study differs from other Japan-U.S. analyses is that original data were collected from completed surveys sent to 230 American and 230 Japanese opinion leaders. Selected from business, government, academia, and the media, most respondents had been involved in some way with the rice, automotive, or semiconductor sectors. Gratifyingly responsive to questions concerning bilateral trade friction and related issues, they validated what many knowledgeable Japanese and Americans have pointed out for some time – that a sizeable bilateral perceptual gap exists. Some scholars might point out that it is impossible to do a balanced job on Japan-U.S. perceptions or develop an adequate survey sample based on English language sources and English language translations of Japanese sources. On that point, my Japanese colleagues have reassured me that, in their opinion, the cultural and institutional essays as well the sample of Japanese opinion leaders are both balanced and impressive. What most impressed them was that so many highly regarded Japanese opinion leaders had actually completed questionnaires.

A fourth way in which this study is unique is that the three case studies of trade friction are representative of three differing mixes of trade friction causal factors and perceptual dynamics. The rice, automotive, and semiconductor sectors, viewed for the period of 1980 to 1992, have undergone some important changes since then. In the case of automobiles and electronics, the American industries appear to have rallied and regained their competitiveness. Some analysts point out that the United States as a whole is no longer in economic decline but has reversed the trend, while others point to the growing trade deficits and accompanying trade friction that the United States is facing not only with Japan but with countries like China.

Finally, based on the findings of this study, modest suggestions are offered on how the bilateral perceptual gap might be narrowed and trade friction diminished so that the structural and sectoral problems might more effectively be addressed. However, no new notions of fixing the trade friction dilemma have been offered. That remains the subject of another book.

In conclusion, this study should be of interest to scholars, government officials, and business leaders in Japan, the United States, and other countries in the global community who are interested in bilateral relations, international economic and political affairs, and trade friction. It should also be of special interest to social psychologists and cross-cultural scholars and researchers.

Acknowledgements

In spite of solid training in linguistics, intercultural communication, and political science, I could not have completed this book without the academic input of scholars from diverse backgrounds, most especially from economics, history, intercultural communication, Japanese area studies, political science, and social psychology. Early discussions with political scientists David Arase, Susan Sell, and Thomas Rochon, together with social psychologists Louis Medvene and Stuart Oskamp, helped me move in the direction I was eventually to take.

One of their recommendations was that I talk with social psychologist Michele Wittig, who turned out to be extremely generous with her time and expertise. She helped me think through the development of my theoretical approach, the sample of opinion leaders, and the survey instrument. Hers was academic input and encouragement I could always count on. Intercultural communication scholars George Renwick and Tapscott Steven not only contributed to my early thinking about Japan-U.S. trade friction, but they also made important suggestions during the writing process.

Research assistant Francoise Tran worked with me through long tedious hours of library research, formation of mailing lists, stuffing of envelopes, and tabulation of data as questionnaires were returned. Once the database had been set up, Francoise helped double-check all my data crunching before I ran the preliminary statistics. Later, social psychologist and statistician Elisa Grant suggested ways to organize and present the data in a logical, succinct manner. I also appreciate the indispensable assistance of the library staffs of California Institute of Technology (in particular, Janet Jenks), the Claremont Graduate School, the University of California, and the University of Southern California.

Yoshisuke Inoue, Atsuko Ishihara, Mika Nakahara, Mika Nakanishi, and Takashi Obara were more than generous with translation help and cultural input. In particular, Yoshisuke Inoue, a visiting professor from St. Andrews College near Osaka, spent an entire week working with me on the translation of the questionnaire as well as the development of a culturally appropriate cover letter. Some months later, Takashi Obara of Nihon University and Mika Nakahara helped translate comments Japanese opinion leaders had written on returned questionnaires.

Once the writing was complete, political scientist William Thompson, much admired for his fine scholarship, integrity, and laser-sharp editing skills, advised me on important final changes in the organization and presentation of the book. He was characteristically ruthless with editing suggestions. I owe him an immense debt of gratitude not only for these invaluable contributions, but also for his excellent training in World Politics, IR theory, and IPE when I was one of his doctoral students at the Claremont Graduate School.

Economist Arthur Denzau and business historian Ed Perkins, who read later versions of the manuscript, also made a number of worthy suggestions. Always professional and resourceful, Peter Banos reformatted the final manuscript and helped rework diagrams and tables into final form.

In addition to excellent academic counsel and technical support, every researcher needs a support team for encouragement. I was most fortunate – I had several. First, Pasadena City College and Claremont Graduate School colleagues and friends who contributed in a myriad of ways to the completion of the book included Rae Ballard, Pauline Crabb, Laura Davis, William Farmer, Nairy Finn, William Goldmann, Jane Hallinger, Alvar Kauti, Betty Kovacks, Inger Moen, Mike Riherd, Diana Savas, Edris Steubner, and Peter Vasilovitch.

Second, good friends from other walks of life, Al Elby, Rigoberto Enriquz, Andrea Enscoe, Barbara Gibson, George Hopkins, Eileen Kenny, Mandy King, Donna Lawrence, Nola Nordmarken, Nancy Ritnimit, Roberta Reinecke, Barbara Roofe, and Frances Steven were wonderfully understanding of their somewhat absent-minded friend, always encouraging with thoughtful words and deeds. Of these, I am especially grateful to Barbara Roofe for spiritual support, Nola Nordmarken for emotional support, and Barbara Gibson for mental support. Friends in Japan to whom I am also grateful include Yoshio and Toshie Imai, Junko and Hide Imai, Motoko Inoue, Akio Obara, and Shosuke Watanabe.

Finally, I wish to thank Ninomoya Sontoko (1787-1856) who wrote the words which kept me going day after day:

If you wish to accomplish a big job, start with a little one. Small deeds shall eventually turn into an enormous work. You harvest a ton of rice, not because each grain grew in size, but because you have a larger sum of the same tiny grains. Each strike of a hoe will add to the cultivation of a hundred acres. With a single step, you begin a thousand-mile journey. Handfuls of mud will ultimately make a mountain.

List of Abbreviations

AAMA	American Automobile Manufacturers Association
DRAMs	dynamic random access memories
EIAJ	Electronics Industry Association of Japan
EPROMs	erasable programmable read only memories
FAE	fundamental attribution error
GATT	General Agreement on Tariffs and Trade
GM	General Motors (U.S.)
HD	hypothesized cross-cultural difference
HU	hypothesized cross-cultural universal
JETRO	Japan External Trade Organization
JMAFF	Ministry of Agriculture, Forestry, and Fisheries (Japan)
LDP	Liberal Democratic Party (Japan)
MITI	Ministry of International Trade and Industry (Japan)
MOSS	Market-Oriented Sector-Selective talks
NOKYO	Association of Agricultural Cooperatives (Japan)
NUMMI	joint venture between Toyota and General Motors
RCT	realistic conflict theory
RMA	Rice Millers' Association (U.S.)
SIA	Semiconductor Industry Association (U.S.)
SII	Structural Impediments Initiative
TI	Texas Instruments
UAW	United Auto Workers (U.S.)
USDA	U.S. Department of Agriculture
USITC	U.S. International Trade Commission
USTR	U.S. Trade Representative
VERs	voluntary export restraints
ZENCHU	NOKYO's political coordinating center

List of Abbreviations

1 The Research Problem

Introduction

Over the decades since the American post-war Occupation of Japan came to an end, Japan and the United States managed to forge a close, comprehensively interdependent relationship within a Cold War context. Government leaders in both countries have generally considered the relationship an essential, vital one – politically, economically, and strategically. Yet the characteristics and terms of the relationship, as well as the global environment itself, have undergone fundamental changes. Most notably, the Cold War came to a sudden, unexpected end with the disintegration of the Soviet Union as a political entity and the move toward separate governments and market economies on the part of its former republics and satellite countries. With this shift, Japan's need for America's security umbrella diminished, and the United States found itself free to focus its full national attention on economic and trade-related issues as matters of strategic concern. These economic issues, however, would have to be addressed within a more complex, highly integrated, competitive, and far less stable global economic environment than at any previous time during the postwar era.

In addition to changes in the global economy, bilateral economic dynamics had changed radically as well. The economies of Japan and the United States, the two largest in the world, were now highly integrated through trade (as well as through capital markets), surpassing that between either nation and any of its other trading partners. At the same time, the two economies seemed to be moving in opposite directions at what was now an extremely rapid pace — a process which began to reveal itself several decades ago through bilateral and global trade imbalances.[1] Although the United States had run substantial trade surpluses with Japan every year from 1945 through 1964, this began to change in 1965. From that year through 1975, as shown in Table 1.1, modest trade imbalances in Japan's favor began to occur although trade between the two nations remained fairly evenly balanced. Then, in the late 1970s, a noticeable shift began to take place as the United States began to experience increasingly

1

Table 1.1   U.S. Merchandise Trade with Japan and the World, 1960-1993 (in billions of U.S. dollars)

	Exports to Japan	Exports to World	Imports from Japan	Imports from World	Bilateral Trade Balance	Global Trade Balance
1960	1.5	19.7	1.1	14.8	0.5	4.9
1965	2.1	26.5	2.4	21.5	-0.4	5.0
1970	4.6	42.5	5.9	39.9	-1.2	2.6
1975	9.6	107.1	11.3	98.2	-1.7	8.9
1976	10.2	114.7	15.5	124.2	-5.3	-9.1
1977	10.6	120.8	18.6	151.9	-8.0	-31.1
1978	13.0	142.1	24.5	176.0	-11.6	-33.9
1979	17.6	184.4	26.3	212.0	-8.6	-27.6
1980	20.8	224.3	31.2	249.8	-10.4	-25.5
1981	21.8	237.0	37.6	265.1	-15.8	-28.0
1982	20.7	211.2	37.7	247.6	-17.0	-36.5
1983	21.8	201.8	42.8	268.9	-21.1	-67.1
1984	23.2	219.9	60.2	332.4	-37.0	-112.5
1985	22.1	215.9	65.7	338.1	-43.5	-122.2
1986	26.4	223.3	80.8	368.4	-54.4	-145.1
1987	27.6	250.2	84.6	409.8	-56.9	-159.6
1988	37.2	320.2	89.8	447.2	-52.6	-127.0
1989	43.9	361.7	93.5	447.4	-49.7	-115.7
1990	47.8	388.7	89.6	497.6	-41.8	-108.9
1991	47.2	416.0	91.5	489.4	-44.3	-73.4
1992	47.8	448.2	96.5	532.7	-48.7	-84.5
1993	46.9	464.8	106.2	580.5	-59.3	-115.8

Source: U.S. Department of Commerce, Bureau of Statistics.

large bilateral and global trade deficits. By 1981, the American bilateral trade deficit hit the $15.8 billion mark, only to continue its rise to $17 billion in 1982, $21.1 billion in 1983, $37.0 billion in 1984, and $43.5 billion in 1985.

By 1987, the trade deficit had grown to a record high of $56.9 billion. Efforts to reduce the deficit seemed to achieve some success over the next few years as it dropped to $41.8 billion in 1990. However, as the 1990s progressed, the bilateral trade deficit once again began to edge its way upwards to $44.3 billion in 1991 and $48.7 billion in 1992. This occurred even as the U.S. global trade deficit was in the process of shrinking. As a consequence, Japan's share of the U.S. global trade deficit expanded, as shown in Table 1.2, from 35.7% in 1987 to an all-time high of 60.4% in 1991.

Table 1.2   Japan's Share of U.S. Global Merchandise Trade Deficit, 1983-1993 (in percent)

1983	32.2
1984	32.9
1985	35.6
1986	37.5
1987	35.7
1988	41.4
1989	43.0
1990	38.4
1991	60.4
1992	57.6
1993	51.0

Source: Based on data in Table 1.1.

By 1993, the bilateral trade deficit reached a new record of $59.3 billion, a 23 percent gain over the previous year. Although Japan's share of the 1993 U.S. global trade deficit of $115.8 billion had diminished slightly, it still was 51.0%. Indeed, no country has ever run deficits of the magnitude now being experienced by the United States; and, with the exception of Saudi Arabia for a year or two following the second oil shock in 1979, no other country has ever run surpluses like those of present-day Japan.[2]

Along with dramatic shifts in trade balances, Japan and the United States have increasingly found themselves at odds on a variety of bilateral trade issues. Since the 1970s, these trade issues have grown more diverse, complicated, and difficult to negotiate. In addition to agricultural products, construction materials, and services, disputed manufactured products have included textiles, steel, color television sets, automobiles, semiconductors, computers, and telecommunications equipment. As the global economic system itself has grown more complex, interdependent, and highly competitive, the timely application of costly, rapidly changing technologies to improved and ever more sophisticated products and manufacturing processes has become increasingly crucial to a nation's global competitiveness. As a result, the financial stakes have grown and are expected to grow higher as the 1990s continue to unfold.

Current bilateral contentiousness over the enormous trade imbalances and the wide array of contested products, from agricultural to high tech, appears generally more acrimonious, intense, and highly politicized than at any other time in the postwar period. For the most part, business and political leaders, as well as the press and public opinion, in both countries have tended to be more critical of the other nation's contributions to this dilemma than of its own. American business and political leaders, on the one hand, tend to blame the Japanese for much of the trade imbalance, citing unfair, predatory, or adversarial business and trade practices as well as a relatively closed Japanese domestic market. Japanese business and political leaders, on the other hand, counter these accusations with charges that Americans don't try hard enough, have been mismanaging their economy, and are now blaming Japan for their own economic and business failures.

If the enormous ongoing bilateral trade balance asymmetries and growing contentiousness over trade-related issues in a variety of sectors are not adequately addressed, the stability of the bilateral relationship, as well as that of the entire global economic system could be seriously threatened. Economist Charles Kindleberger, in the 1986 edition of his classic study, *The World in Depression: 1929-1939*, draws an analogy between the conditions in the global economy between 1929 and 1933 and those in today's global economy. A major reason for the breadth, depth, and length of the 1929 depression, he argues, was Great Britain's inability and the United States' unwillingness to assume responsibility for stabilizing the international system at a time of great instability. It was a time when 'every nation turned to protect its own national private interest, as the world public interest went down the drain, and with it the private interests of all'.[3]

According to Kindleberger, the assumption of responsibility for stabilizing the international economic system includes functions, such as maintaining a relatively open market for 'distress goods' and ensuring the coordination of macroeconomic policies. Kindleberger suggests that, as American economic leadership in the world economy 'falters' and Europe and Japan 'gather strength', a similar outcome to that of 1929 might occur, with one nation no longer able to lead and others unwilling to do so.[4] Contentiousness over the large bilateral trade imbalances and numerous sectoral disputes could trigger protectionism of the kind not experienced since 1929. Thus, it is crucial that Japan and the United States make concerted efforts to substantially diminish current levels of contentiousness so that headway might be made on bringing structural disequilibria back within acceptable ranges.

Scholars from both countries have studied the dilemma from various angles. Some political economists, concerned primarily with numbers, cite the

U.S. merchandise trade deficit itself as the major reason for growing contentiousness, while others simply see it as 'a political lightning rod for trade tensions'.[5] Although the substantial emotional impact of large trade imbalance numbers on political, business, and other opinion leaders in both countries is accounted for later, a major premise of this research effort is that this oft-cited 'major reason' is merely symptomatic of more fundamental causal factors. A second major premise is that growing contentiousness over the trade imbalances is fueled, in part, by differing bilateral perceptions regarding its probable causal factors, potential consequences, and possible cures.

Factors often identified as contributing to growing Japan-U.S. contentiousness over trade may be classified according to four broad, interrelated categorical groupings: cultural, institutional, structural, and social psychological (e.g., ingroup-outgroup perceptual dynamics). Of these, researchers focus primarily on the institutional and structural, while largely sidestepping or disregarding altogether the cultural and social psychological. A major contention of this study is that bilateral trade friction cannot be adequately explained without also accounting for cultural and social psychological factors. Understanding the impact these factors have on bilateral trade relations might help foster a negotiating environment more conducive to effectively addressing the institutional and structural discrepancies thought to be giving rise to the large trade imbalances.

The model in Figure 1.1 posits how cultural, institutional, and structural factors in Japan and the United States interact and function in tandem to produce asymmetries in bilateral economic patterns and trade norms. These asymmetries are reflected in the large bilateral trade imbalances. The model also suggests how these factors, together with large trade imbalances and other global conditions, affect the social psychological dynamics of the bilateral relationship. These dynamics, in turn, work to augment trade friction levels. Throughout this study, these factors are examined in such a way that it becomes increasingly clear that cultural and social psychological factors are important missing links in understanding and addressing the underlying causes of the bilateral trade friction dilemma.

Cultural factors, which are firmly rooted in the historically created traditions, values, and attitudes of each nation, are revealed in their respective communication, decision-making, and negotiating styles. National normative and behavioral tendencies can further aggravate and complicate already difficult bilateral trade relations. A major Japan-U.S. cultural differential is the Japanese tendency toward *collectivism* or *groupism* versus the American tendency toward *individualism*. These separate tendencies affect how individuals and groups within each society interact with one another, as well as

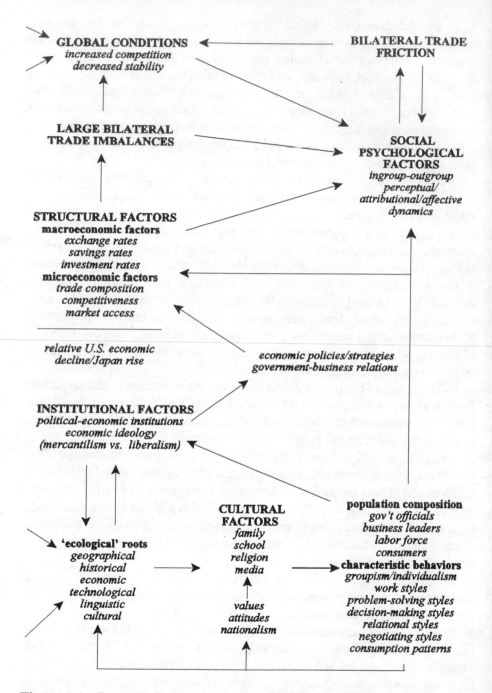

Figure 1.1   Japan-U.S. Trade Friction: The Causal Factors

how they interact with those entities in the other nation. Then, too, uniquely American and Japanese negotiating styles, as evident today as they were in the first official bilateral encounters of the 1850s, involve the Japanese preference for indirect communication versus the American preference for direct communication. These and other culturally based differences have continued to surface in the ongoing interactions and negotiated agreements between Americans and Japanese.

Institutional factors, shaped and informed by culturally based tendencies, include the differing American and Japanese political-economic and industrial organizations, their underlying economic ideologies, and their consequent macroeconomic and microeconomic strategies, policies, and practices. Japan's Ministry of International Trade and Industry (MITI) and America's Department of Commerce exemplify two very different political-economic institutional traditions, reflecting two quite different economic ideologies, and executing two substantially different economic policy agendas. MITI has played a far more active role in targeting crucial sectors, obtaining sufficient financing, and protecting the domestic market from foreign competition than has the Department of Commerce. Although both nations espouse *laissez-faire* economic ideals, the oligopolistic behavior of Japanese industrial conglomerates like the *keiretsu,* as well as the effective industrial policies of powerful governmental agencies like MITI, are more highly suggestive of a German-style mercantilism than of an American-style liberalism.

Structural factors, fostered by each nation's unique cultural legacy and institutional environment, encompass domestic macroeconomic and micro-economic dynamics in Japan and the United States and the discrepancies which exist between them. Because macroeconomic conditions within both nations affect the size of bilateral trade imbalances, many economists interested in Japan-U.S. trade friction have focused their attention on issues like national fiscal policies, savings rates, investment patterns, and currency exchange rates. Japan's national household, corporate, and government savings and investment patterns are all higher across the board than those of the United States. Most notable among the savings and investment discrepancies is America's enormous national budget deficit versus Japan's surplus.

In addition to these aggregate trade and financial dynamics, economists also focus on such microeconomic factors as sectoral competitiveness levels (e.g., quantity, quality, kind of output), composition of trade, and relative market access for imported goods. Sectoral competitiveness is determined by factors such as human inventiveness, the quality and abundance of technology, natural resources, labor, capital available for research and development, and the ability to protect new ideas. Although both nations are highly competitive in a variety of high-technology, high-value sectors, $4.5 billion of the 1992 bilateral trade imbalance consisted of compact disc players, video cameras, and numerically controlled machine tools that were either simply not produced, or no longer produced competitively, in the United States. These items continue to account for a goodly share of the chronic U.S. bilateral trade deficit as well as for its inflexibility.[6] Structural access issues are also of concern; Japan's non-tariff trade barriers, for example, are believed to contribute importantly to current trade imbalance levels.[7]

Related to these macroeconomic/microeconomic factors is the well-documented economic decline of the United States relative to Japan's rise, a topic of interest to a diverse group of international political economists. Some political theorists, such as members of the hegemonic stability school, predict growing conflict between a declining hegemon (e.g., the United States) and the challenger (e.g., Japan), leading to increased instability in the global system.[8] Yet, such theories do not adequately explain the origin and augmentation of conflictual dynamics, nor do they offer viable means of countering tendencies toward growing contentiousness and conflict. Far more adequate explanations emanate from the field of social psychology.

The social psychological approach takes into account U.S.-Japanese perceptual differences concerning what causes the large trade imbalances, as well as attributions of responsibility and blame regarding the part each nation has played in their creation and augmentation. Social psychological theory, specifically realistic conflict theory (RCT) and attribution theory, help account for contributions which cultural, institutional, and structural differences, in combination with real bilateral economic competition and conflicting national goals, make to divergences in bilateral perceptions and attributions. It helps explain the probable strain these divergences place on bilateral trade relations (intergroup relations). What social psychological theory reveals concerning the perceptual dynamics in intergroup relations sheds light on the formation and maintenance of diverging perceptions/attributions concerning the causes, consequences, and cures of large bilateral trade imbalances and other trade issues of contention. Social psychological analysis, then, addresses the main concern of this study; that is, the role perception plays in fostering, supporting, and exacerbating the currently high levels of bilateral trade friction.

Statement of the Research Agenda

Although social psychological factors draw far less attention in the literature than structural, institutional, or even culturally based factors, it is hypothesized that these contribute the most volatile, least predictable component to the calculus of factors determining future outcomes. Rather than using the social psychological factors component as a competing or rival variable, this study treats them together as an intervening variable positioned between primary causal factors (e.g., Japan-U.S. economic competition, structural discrepancies) and final outcomes (e.g., bilateral trade friction levels). The logic of this multivariate relationship also includes the trade imbalance itself as a primary independent variable which, together with other independent variables, affects the intervening social psychological variable; this, in turn, affects the dependent variable, or final outcomes. This relatively simple causal model suggests how the perceptual factor might either enflame or temper structural tensions and thereby impede or enhance bilateral efforts at finding solutions to the underlying institutional and structural factors. If it were determined that American and Japanese perceptions concerning the causes, consequences, and cures of the large bilateral trade imbalances were the same or quite similar, the null hypothesis would then be supported.

This research effort also pursues the identification, description, and examination of cultural and institutional factors and the probable contribution these make to the creation of current structural realities in Japan and the United States as reflected in the large trade imbalances. It also seeks to explain why these imbalances have captured so much public attention and have so often been identified as the major reason for currently high levels of bilateral trade contentiousness. The following diagram (Figure 1.2) presents that portion of the bilateral trade friction causal model which is the primary focus of this research effort.

Goals of the Research Agenda

This study takes an eclectic, interdisciplinary approach in the identification, description, and explanation of factors responsible for contemporary Japan-U.S. trade friction. The approach is based primarily on realistic conflict theory (e.g., Deutsch, 1973, Deutsch and Schichman, 1986) and attribution theory, especially that theory and research concerning the formation of attribution-based intergroup conflict (e.g., Pettigrew, 1979; Hewstone, 1985, 1989, 1990; Hewstone and Jaspars, 1982) and attribution-based affective tendencies (e.g., Weiner, 1982, 1985, 1986) in combination with 18 attribution-based hypotheses reflecting cross-cultural perspectives (e.g., Gudykunst, 1988; Kashima and Triandes, 1986). This theoretical combination furnishes the underlying rationale for a questionnaire addressing American and Japanese

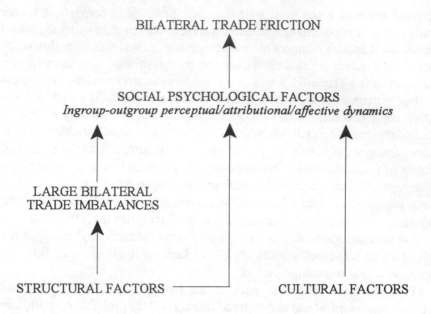

Figure 1.2   Japan-U.S. Trade Friction: A Causal Model

perceptions of, and attitudes toward, current bilateral trade relations. Surveyed issues include: (1) the relative importance of 14 commonly cited causes of the bilateral trade imbalances; (2) the country bearing greater responsibility for these imbalances; (3) the degree of domestic market openness to imports in Japan and the United States; (4) the quality of current trade relations; (5) the probable effects of a breakdown in bilateral trade relations on the prosperity of each nation; (6) the degree of expected structural change addressed in the 1990 Structural Impediments Initiative occurring in each nation by the year 2000; and (7) the national negotiation styles of Japan and the United States.

Questionnaires sent to 460 opinion leaders (230 from America, 230 from Japan) yielded a 70 percent response rate, with 61 percent of the sample actually completing questionnaires. Respondents included government officials (elected officials, bureaucrats, diplomats, trade negotiators), academics (political scientists, economists, area specialists), media specialists (publishers, editors-in-chief, journalists, reporters), and agricultural/industrial leaders from three sectors (rice, automotive, semiconductor). Most respondents were permanent residents in their respective countries during the period of data collection, except for a small number of diplomats, news correspondents, and area specialists whose work required that they be abroad.

Research expectations were that both sets of responses would correspond with their respective national positions as expressed in bilateral trade negotiations and media accounts. It was also expected that these responses would reflect the respondents' academic training and career choice. In rating the causes of the bilateral trade imbalances, economists were expected to place more importance on macroeconomic factors, political scientists more importance on institutional factors, and industrial leaders more importance on microeconomic issues. It was also expected that government and industrial leaders would tend to be more polarized in their views and more likely to place the blame for bilateral trade problems on the other nation than academic leaders, who were expected to respond with greater objectivity.

Conclusions were also to be drawn regarding American and Japanese perceptual dynamics in relationship to a set of 18 hypotheses to determine culture-universal perceptual similarities and culture-specific differences between American and Japanese respondents. Perceptual patterns of the two sets of respondents were expected to respond in similar ways to perceptual tendencies hypothesized as holding across all cultures and to reflect Japan-U.S. cultural differentials, such as that of *individualism-collectivism*. Finally, a determination was to be made concerning the extent to which the bilateral trade relationship was perceived by each set of respondents as cooperative *(win-win)* or competitive *(win-lose)*.[9] This would serve as an indicator of current levels of trade friction.

Limitations of the Research Agenda

An interdisciplinary, cross-cultural, but fundamentally social psychological approach to the question of Japan-U.S. trade friction should ideally be as unbiased as possible. Not surprisingly, financial and temporal constraints placed a number of limitations on achieving this. However, careful attention was paid to offsetting their potentially negative effects. Source materials representing both American and Japanese cultural, economic, and political perspectives were used, including those written in English as well as those translated into English from Japanese texts. Additionally, questionnaires in English were sent to Americans, whereas questionnaires translated into Japanese were sent, together with the English versions, to Japanese respondents. Furthermore, Japanese colleagues fluent in both languages evaluated the questionnaire and read the material at various stages of completion to reduce the effects of possible linguistic and cultural bias.

One major area which presented difficulty was that of social psychological theory and research on intergroup relations and attributional processes. Much of this research is Western-based and at the individual level of analysis. Even when the focus of such research is at the group level of analysis, it usually concerns ethnic or special groups within one nation or society (e.g., African-American/Caucasian-American; Chinese/Malay Singaporeans) rather than national groups from two different countries.

Because of this study's focus, it was circumscribed by a number of limitations. First, the comparative sketches of differing cultural values and behavioral tendencies and their effects on various institutional structures and functions are not intended as analyses in comparative politics in the true sense of the word. Rather, they are intended as broad overviews of diverging American and Japanese cultural, institutional, and structural tendencies, as presented in the literature. Nor is this study an analysis in public administration or bureaucratic politics, even though it acknowledges the importance of domestic pressures and constraints, political agendas, and maneuverings between and among the various branches, bureaucracies, and agencies of government. As such, it makes no attempt to unravel the complex sets of domestic political processes and political decisions in either nation. Nor does it offer a delineation or evaluation of the impact of interested persons and groups outside government on the workings and policies of the government.

Finally, to maintain its neutrality and objectivity, this analysis draws no formal conclusions concerning the rank order of trade imbalance causal factors other than those offered by respondents; nor does it propose an agenda for addressing and resolving the host of institutional and structural challenges facing American and Japanese leaders. Rather, the study's primary objectives were twofold. The first was to offer a more nuanced delineation of bilateral trade friction causal factors than has normally been the case. The second was to identify, quantify, and evaluate the perceptual and attributional differences between American and Japanese opinion leaders, between various subgroups of the sample populations, and between members of comparable subgroups in Japan and the United States regarding trade imbalances and other trade-related issues. Following the completion of these objectives, modest recommendations are made only for the reduction of perceptual and attributional differences and their likely negative effects (e.g., contentiousness, threats, retaliatory measures) on bilateral trade relations.

Organization of the Study

Besides exploring the central analytic issue, the role perception plays in the trade friction dilemma, this study also offers a cultural and institutional explanation for the creation of chronically large bilateral trade imbalances. Toward this end, the four chapters which follow describe the origins of bilateral trade conflict and summarize the basic American and Japanese positions on bilateral trade relations; discuss diverging American and Japanese cultural, institutional, and structural factors; and explore pertinent social psychological theory regarding intergroup conflict and perceptual dynamics. The three chapters following these describe the methodology and research design, present the research results together with a critique of the model and survey instrument, and offer case studies of three sectoral disputes. The last chapter presents the research conclusions and recommendations for future research. Because the approach is interdisciplinary in nature, contributions from anthropology, economics, history, intercultural communications, international political economy, political science, social psychology, and sociology are introduced and discussed as needed.

Chapter Two opens with a historical overview of Japan-U.S. trade relations from their early beginnings in the 1800s to Japan's bombing of Pearl Harbor in 1941 and the subsequent American Occupation of Japan. Discussion of the early beginnings of bilateral trade relations introduces Japan-U.S. perceptual dynamics and relational patterns occurring in the 1850s; these appear similar to those occurring in contemporary trade disputes and negotiations. Then, an abridged recap of perceptual differences and communication blunders leading up to Japan's entry into World War II, as well as a condensed account of the gradual escalation of postwar bilateral trade complaints is presented. This is followed by a broad summary of American and Japanese trade-related complaints, which points to the probable existence of a sizeable U.S.-Japanese perceptual gap and highlights the worrisome direction recent bilateral trade relations have taken.

Chapter Three follows with an interpretive essay comparing Japanese and American cultural values, attitudes, and behavioral patterns. This essay describes the pervasive effects of culture on the citizenry of Japan and the United States. It describes the probable role of cultural values and behavioral patterns in shaping distinctly American and Japanese approaches to problem-solving and decision-making, preferred patterns of communication, and favored styles of negotiation. Chapter Three also suggests how perceptual tendencies might be shaped and informed by cultural factors, which in turn are expected to foster greater distortions in the ingroup-outgroup perceptual dynamic.

Chapter Four looks at the probable roles played by divergent cultural patterns in the formulation of government institutions, industrial arrangements, and economic strategies, policies, and practices. These affect national competitiveness, import/export policies, business strategies and practices which, in turn, have an impact on trade norms. Together, the third and fourth chapters also suggest how cultural differences and their institutional and structural implications might help foster Japan-U.S. perceptual distortions and communication difficulties; however, they do not explain how and why such perceptual differences and misunderstandings occur.

Chapter Five offers a clearer understanding of these dynamics. The social psychological effects of real economic competition and conflicting national goals, in combination with cultural and institutional differences, are examined within the context of recent social psychological theory regarding the formation of intergroup competitive conflict and the perceptual dynamics that foster, support, and exacerbate such conflict. First, realistic conflict theory (Deutsch, 1973, Deutsch and Schichman, 1986) furnishes a model of intergroup conflict, specifically those competitive (malignant) processes most likely involved in the escalation of trade friction, as well as a model of intergroup cooperative (constructive) processes, which might serve as antidotes to the high levels of trade friction. Second, perceptual and attributional processes believed to be operating are also explored. Attributional theory sheds light on the formation of ingroup-outgroup attributions; how these are shaped by, and give rise to, certain emotional states; and what kinds of effects these have on intergroup relations (Pettigrew, 1979; Hewstone, 1988, 1989, 1990; Weiner, 1982, 1985, 1986). This discussion includes viable explanations for why the large trade imbalances have captured so much negative bilateral scrutiny and commentary (Fiske and Taylor, 1991; Taylor and Fiske, 1978), as well as why American and Japanese opinion leaders tend not to agree as to the causes, consequences, and cures of those imbalances. Third, the effects of cultural and academic training/career choice differences on bilateral perceptions are examined within the context of 18 hypotheses based on these theories in conjunction with cross-cultural research findings and the *individualism-collectivism* dynamic (e.g., Gudykunst, 1988; Kashima and Triandis, 1986).

Chapter Six describes and explains the methodology and research design of this research effort. Included in this discussion are the underlying rationale for the study, its objectives and procedures, the selection of 460 American and Japanese respondents, and the development of a survey instrument. The questionnaire was developed on the basis of the model in Figure 1.2 and discussions in Chapters Two through Five. The goal was to gather parallel data from American and Japanese opinion leaders for the identification, quantification, and analysis of perceptual differences regarding such topics as the ranking of factors thought to be causing or contributing to the large trade imbalances, the quality of current bilateral trade relations, the part each nation has played in the perpetuation of the trade friction dilemma, and national negotiating styles. It was hypothesized that social psychological factors (e.g., ingroup-outgroup perceptual dynamics) together function as an intervening variable between causes (e.g., bilateral structural discrepancies, large trade imbalances) and effects (e.g., high levels of trade contentiousness). In this process, intergroup perceptual dynamics might serve to exacerbate the affective and cognitive effects of trade imbalances, structural discrepancies, and cultural differences, as modeled in Figure 1.2. Finally, the 18 hypotheses proposed for testing the effects of cultural differences on bilateral perceptual dynamics within the context of the research data are also discussed.

Research findings are then presented in Chapter Seven, followed by a critique of the model and the survey instrument. Statistically significant perceptual and attitudinal differences between American and Japanese respondents are identified, as well as differences between subgroups (e.g., economists, political scientists, industry leaders) within and between the two national groups. Tendencies of American and Japanese opinion leaders to blame the other country and its constituents for the large trade imbalances are revealed through the divergent ratings of the 14 trade imbalance causal factors and responses to questions concerning relative national responsibility.

Chapter Eight then offers accounts of bilateral trade disputes involving the three very different sectors of rice, automobiles and automotive parts, and semiconductors. These sectors were chosen as generic or representative bilateral trade complaints, incidents, and agreements taking place between 1980, when U.S. bilateral and global trade deficits with Japan first began to soar, and 1993. The accounts reveal not only the degree and kind of economic competition and conflicting goals occurring between the two nations, but also the tenacity and rigidity of perceptual differences and conflicting views in both nations concerning bilateral trade. Furthermore, they suggest the interplay of bilateral economic competition and conflicts of interest; cultural and institutional differences; and perceptual discrepancies. Summaries of American and Japanese trade positions on each of the three sectors follow. Production, trade, and consumption statistics, as well as a brief comparison of the rice, automotive, and semiconductor industries in Japan and the United States, are included. Finally, implications and conclusions drawn concerning these positions and the issues raised bring each of the three sections to a close.

Together with the discussions of previous chapters and the data analysis of Chapter Seven, these case studies reveal how bilateral perceptual differences, behavioral practices, and ways of dealing with conflict, already evident in the mid-1800s, have remained fairly constant over time. In the first case, Japan's rice market best exemplifies Japan's collection of closed markets as well as those disputes over agricultural products which Japan wishes to produce herself as part of the nation's self-sufficiency programs. Rice also exemplifies Japanese industries whose products are protected from imports for reasons of cultural tradition and societal uniqueness, but whose real reasons are probably political.

The second sector, automobiles and automotive parts and accessories, is representative of those heavy industries forming the foundational source of the economic clout wielded by the United States during the war years and those immediately following. However, like the U.S. steel industry, the American automobile industry resisted the need to change standard operating procedures, thereby suffering gradual losses in competitiveness. Meanwhile, the Japanese, who built their automobile industry practically from scratch after the war, applied the most advanced thinking in efficient plant production. The result was that Japan's automotive industry eventually captured large market shares in the United States and in other world markets. Also, like the steel industry, the American automobile sector finally began to reorganize its plant and production methods in order to compete more effectively. These efforts to improve competitiveness have yielded results, for the American automotive industry recently appears to have regained much lost ground.

Meanwhile, the semiconductor industry represents those high technology, cutting-edge, high value-added industries of the future. Although semi-conductors were originally an American invention, and U.S. microelectronic firms had dominated the market until the 1980s, Japanese competitors eventually gained substantial ground. American firms have accused Japanese manufacturers of collusive activities, dumping, and other adversarial marketing procedures. They have also taken issue with the Japanese on various non-tariff barriers believed to result in a relatively closed domestic import market. Adding impetus to the urgency of the situation has been the fact that other industrial components of the Information Age, such as computers and telecommunication equipment, as well as those of the aviation and defense industries, depend on easily accessed and reasonably priced semiconductor components. Once again, the American industry appears to have gained in competitive strength since the early 1990s.

The ninth and final chapter presents a summary of research conclusions and tentative recommendations regarding the reduction of bilateral perceptual distortions and high levels of friction. These recommendations are made on the basis of the research findings in Chapter Seven and recent negotiation and conflict resolution theory and research (e.g., Axelrod, 1984; Fisher and Brown, 1988; Fisher and Ury, 1981; Pruitt, 1981; Pruitt and Rubin, 1986; Zartman and Touval, 1985). Finally, recommendations for future research complete the chapter.

Notes

1   Bersten, C. F. and W. R. Cline (1987) *The United States-Japan Economic Problem*, p. 2.
2   Ibid.
3   Kindleberger, C. P. (1986) *The World in Depression 1929-1939* (originally published in 1978) pp. 289-291.
4   Ibid., pp. 289, 304-305.
5   Bergsten, C. F. and M. Noland (1993) *Reconcilable Differences? United States-Japan Economic Conflict*, p. 55.
6   Ibid., p. 33.
7   See Bergsten and Noland (1993), pp. 179-190, for a review of recent studies assessing Japan's market-access barriers. Bergsten and Noland point out that the essentially hidden and arbitrary nature of these trade barriers poses difficult problems for economists trying to assess their impact. Consequently, there is disagreement among researchers concerning impact and potential increases in Japanese manufacturers' imports should they be completely removed. Predictions range from 7.7% (Saxonhouse, 1993) to 100.0% (Petri, 1991). More moderate estimates are 45.4-24.4% (Bergsten and Cline, 1987) and 76.0-54.3% (Lawrence, 1991). The sample period for the estimates was 1985, except for Saxonhouse, whose sample period was 1983.
8   For further reading on the hegemonic stability theory and the relative economic decline of the hegemon (world leader), see C. P. Kindleberger (1986); R. Gilpin (1975) *U.S. Power and the Multinational Corporation: The Political Economy of Foreign Direct Investment*; and S. Krasner (1976) 'State Power and the Structure of International Trade', *World Politics*, 28: pp. 317-47.
9   The terms *competitive, win-win*, and *win-lose* are used throughout the study as social psychologist, Morton Deutsch, normally uses them, rather than in the sense that economists generally do. Although Morton Deutsch acknowledges that competition is not necessarily always negative, most of his discussion on competition and competitive interests concerns negative, destructive effects (e.g., *win-lose*); while his discussion on cooperation and mutual interests concerns positive, constructive effects (e.g., *win-win*). Meanwhile, most economists view free competition as producing positive, constructive results (i.e., a *win-win* situation) for all concerned. As such, most economists, starting with Adam Smith (1937) *An Inquiry into the Nature and Causes of the Wealth of Nations*, oppose any government intervention that interferes with the workings of economic competition. Smith's fundamental economic ideology was *laissez-faire* liberalism, as it is for most economists today.

2 The Evolution of Bilateral Trade Friction

Contemporary Japan-U.S. trade relational patterns seem to display enough similarity to patterns in bilateral relations during the 1850s and throughout subsequent decades to be called continuities. In the 1800s, these relational patterns generally fostered little more than frustrating episodes of biased perceptions, mutual misperceptions, and misunderstandings. However, their cumulative effects in the 1930s, during a period of rapid global change, growing complexity, and expanding incompatibility of Japan-U.S. national goals, helped trigger Japan's entry into the Second World War with all its tragic consequences. Several decades of relative bilateral amity and tranquility followed in the postwar era.

Then, beginning in the late 1960s, and continuing to the present day, growing contentiousness over a variety of trade sectoral issues and eventually large trade imbalances signaled a reemerging bilateral rivalry complicated by familiar problematic perceptual and relational dynamics. By the 1990s, the rising tides of contentiousness over trade seemed to be threatening the very health and stability of the postwar relationship. In spite of the magnitude and complexity of recent trade disputes, the major generic American and Japanese positions on bilateral trade as gleaned from media presentations, academic and non-academic journals, and public opinion polls are summarized, following a brief review of the evolution of Japan-U.S. trade relations and the identification of some common relational patterns. Finally, the central questions are once again posed: How different are American and Japanese perceptions concerning trade imbalance causal factors and other trade issues? Do such perceptual differences really work to exacerbate Japan-U.S. trade contentiousness? Exactly what part do cultural and institutional factors play?

The Beginnings of Japan-U.S. Trade Relational Patterns

In the first half of the 1800s, expanding American and European maritime activities in the North Pacific Ocean set the stage for the termination of Japan's two and one-half centuries of self-imposed seclusion from the world. As ships and whaling vessels, especially those from the United States, increasingly sought shelter or supplies in Japanese harbors or were driven ashore by bad weather, reports of ill-treatment of crew members began to reach American ears back home. Washington, wishing to protect shipwrecked American seamen, as well as to pursue growing U.S. interest in Pacific trade, sent Commodore James Biddle to Japan in 1845 to propose the opening of Japan to trade. Even though Japanese officials soundly rejected the proposal, they correctly sensed that Biddle's petition was only a precursor of what lay ahead.[1]

Then on July 8, 1853, acting on a decision by the American government to undertake a full-scale effort to open Japan, Navy Commodore Matthew C. Perry and his squadron sailed into Uraga Harbor (outside of Edo, the site of modern-day Tokyo), with four large warships under his command. Perry's fearsome-looking ships, two with steam engines belching black smoke, had been painted black and equipped with ample cannons. Perry delivered to Japanese officials a letter from President Fillmore (and a more strongly written statement of his own) asserting that the U.S. government had friendly intentions toward Japan but was determined to secure desirable treatment for distressed American seamen and facilities for navigation and trade.[2]

From a Japanese perspective, Perry had not only violated Japanese law forbidding foreign ships from entering its coastal waters, but he had also audaciously insisted on having Japan meet his demands, not at Nagasaki, but at Edo itself.[3] The gunboats, clearly exhibiting a superior military technology, communicated a powerful message. Although Perry had made no explicit threat, one was implied in his announcement that he expected a favorable reply the following year when he returned with a larger force. The official Japanese reaction was, of course, negative, as word of the 'black ships' quickly spread through the countryside.[4]

In March of 1854, Perry returned to Japan, this time in command of eight black ships. He had little difficulty in negotiating a treaty with the Japanese despite various evasions and delays. The Japanese remained firm in rejecting the opening of trade relations, pleading that the Americans must accept gradual change; it was impossible, they said, to discard the laws and customs of three centuries all at once. Perry accepted this cultural argument with reluctance.[5] In the end, Japanese negotiators also yielded to some extent. The treaty, signed at Kanagawa in Edo Bay at the end of the month, opened the ports of Shimoda and Hakodate, in addition to that of Nagasaki. Although trade was limited to the purchase of fuel and food supplies, American consular representation in Japan was permitted.[6] Even though the Treaty of Kanagawa did not explicitly mention trade, it was enough to pierce the armor of Japanese isolation.[7] Perry's achievement was the regularization and expansion of a relationship which had previously been limited to a series of isolated contacts.[8] To the present day, Americans view Perry and his accomplishments with admiration and national pride, while Japanese view him with mixed emotions ranging from admiration, appreciation, and respect to dislike of, and indignation at, his methods.[9]

Soon Japan would be compelled to open her commercial doors to the outside world, setting the stage for the trade problems, trade disputes, and trade friction that would become part and parcel of the Japan-U.S. relationship in future decades. Additionally, a pattern in negotiations had been established, with Americans initiating a direct, aggressive set of demands and Japanese dragging their feet, but finally giving way to those demands. So also were tendencies for Japanese to respond evasively to American demands, to justify the status quo with cultural arguments, and request 'patience' from Americans wanting quicker changes than Japanese wished to make. As for Perry, he was to be the first in a long line of American officials to confront the Japanese with trade-related demands.

The Establishment of Bilateral Trade

By the early years of the twentieth century, Japan was on the move economically, diplomatically, and militarily. By 1905, a mere 50 years after Perry's bold undertaking, the once-isolated island nation of Japan had risen to the status of a major world power. Japan had defeated China in 1895, moved to create colonies in Taiwan and Sakhalin, solidified an economic and political foothold in Korea, and obtained important rights in Manchuria. She had then formed an alliance with Great Britain in 1902 and defeated Russia in 1905. In that same year, Japan's multiple gains were confirmed and extended, and foreign opposition to her control over Korea all but eliminated. In July, the United States gave its blessing to a Korea subordinate to Japan. In August, the Anglo-Japanese alliance was renewed and expanded to provide a more precise definition of Japan's hegemony in Korea. Then, in September, the Treaty of Portsmouth officially ended Japan's war with Russia, a product of Japan's desire to consolidate her position in the Korean Peninsula.[10] By 1910, Korea had been annexed outright. Once Japan had finally decided to open to the outside world, she had acted relatively quickly and effectively to establish an empire. Cautious, conservative decision-making followed by timely imple-mentation once a decision had been made would be a pattern repeated in the postwar years when Japan, following a devastating defeat, pursued the building of a strong competitive international trade base via a myriad of slow strategic decisions and relatively quick, effective implementations.

Meanwhile, the United States was also on the move in the Pacific region. Washington had annexed Hawaii in 1897 and laid claim to the Philippines as a consequence of the Spanish-American War of 1898. By 1899, the United States was beginning to proclaim an 'Open Door' policy for China, a policy which stood in direct opposition to Japan's expansionist policies and special interests in China. In the years which followed, a growing clash of national goals would increasingly undermine and poison bilateral relations and ultimately lead to the outbreak of war in the Pacific in December 1941.

After 1905, Japan's international trade, including that with the United States, sharply increased. Despite ongoing efforts to stimulate heavy industry through government subsidies and investment, and a growth rate that was impressive, the volume of Japan's industrial output remained relatively small.[11] Although agriculture remained the largest sector of her economy, with rice and raw silk her two main exportable crops, large-scale Japanese enterprises (*zaibatsu*) with wide-ranging, integrated interests developed, grew in power, and began to compete formidably.[12] The *zaibatsu*, closely linked with the Meiji government, received important government subsidies and contracts, and, in return, both supported the government financially and invested in industrial endeavors the government promoted.

The *zaibatsu* extended their operations into banking, heavy industry, shipping, and other economic activities promising large returns. In the process, they absorbed older, smaller firms and acquired yet greater wealth and power. Their webs of inter-locking financial, industrial, and commercial holdings were administered through family holding companies by extremely able managerial groups whose members often married into the founder families. Close connections with government leaders, the bureaucracy, and the imperial court made their positions impregnable. The process toward enterprises of increasing scale, of which the *zaibatsu* were notable examples, continued and would eventually come to typify Japanese economic development.[13] Although the *zaibatsu* would be disbanded under the American Occupation, they would re-emerge, although in substantially modified form, in the postwar era and be called *keiretsu*.[14]

Even though silk and cotton commodities still accounted for more than half of Japan's exports and would remain the most prominent elements of Japan trade for another two decades, the First World War afforded Japan opportunities to dramatically improve her economic situation as the Allies increasingly turned to her for supplies of munitions and other manufactures. By 1918, Japan had greatly increased her domestic production and levels of international trade.[15] However, the impact of Japan's wartime economic explosion was undermined as the United States and the European nations eventually reclaimed their former positions in world trade; as a result, Japan once again faced foreign trade deficits.[16] Then, in 1929, the devastating Great Depression followed on the heels of the U.S. stock market collapse. To protect its markets, the United States implemented the Smoot-Hawley Tariff Act in 1930, raising American tariff rates to slightly above 50 percent.[17] Even so, complaints of Japan's 'unfair competition' were heard throughout the 1930s as Japan increasingly offered reasonable facsimiles of Western products at lower prices, met demands for large quantities, and showed great skill in the conduct of business affairs.[18]

In the years following the Great Depression, Japan produced her first economic 'miracle.' Industrial output increased greatly, while heavy industry grew to represent 73 percent of total domestic output by 1942.[19] Japan also began to expand into markets in Asia, Africa, and Latin America. In hindsight, writes one analyst, the Japanese economic miracle of the postwar era would seem almost an extension of the miracle begun in this prewar era.[20] While trade with the United States increased, multilateral trade also grew within the 'yen bloc' of Korea, Taiwan, Kwantung and Manchuria to about 55 percent of total exports by 1938 and 41 percent of total imports.[21] Thus, the larger portion of Japan's foreign commerce now occurred with areas it dominated politically.

Japan further extended her political and economic control in the Pacific through the War with China (1937-1945), as the United States grew increasingly alarmed. Throughout the 1930s, however, Japan ranked as America's largest export market behind Great Britain and Canada. Although American exports to Japan peaked in 1937, they remained high until 1941 as American oil and oil products, raw cotton, metal goods, scrap steel, and machinery continued to flow across the Pacific. The two economies were largely complementary, and relations among American and Japanese business groups were good. As American exporters successfully opposed economic sanctions against Japan for most of the decade, the flourishing bilateral trade seems to have been largely unaffected by the growing estrangement between the governments of the United States and Japan.[22]

By the late 1930s, Japan had become one of the world's leading industrial and military powers. Economic tensions aggravated growing political disharmony between the United States and Japan, and these antagonisms, with racial underpinnings, contributed to an increase in military power on both sides of the Pacific.[23] As Japanese victory over China became a national goal no longer questioned publicly in Japan after 1938, a series of events occurred which further set Japan on a collision course with the United States. American hostility toward Japan's aggressive actions in China led Washington to adopt a slowly escalating program of economic sanctions that was supposed to change Japan's China policies. In the summer of 1938, Washington placed an embargo on shipments to Japan of aircraft, arms, and other war material; in July 1939, it refused to renew its commercial policy with Japan, which was due to expire the following year.

Then an embargo on all scrap-iron shipments to Japan in September 1940, and its eventual extension to iron and steel exports, seriously handicapped Japan's stockpiling of vital materials.[24] When Japan moved her troops into southern Indochina in July 1941, the United States immediately froze all Japanese assets in the United States, thereby bringing bilateral trade to a standstill. An embargo on exports of oil to Japan was also imposed, and the British and Dutch East Indian governments followed suit, thereby cutting off 90 percent of Japan's oil supplies. This sudden escalation of economic warfare was intended to deter Japan from further rashness, but in Japan, it had precisely the opposite effect. Without oil imports, Japan's war machine would have to come to a halt everywhere. As it turned out, it was the oil embargo that propelled the Japanese government inexorably toward the decision for war.[25]

Because Japanese leaders failed to appreciate the logic behind American actions, they concluded that the United States was moved by arrogance, by a sense of racial superiority, and by an intransigent hypocrisy.[26] Clearly, American and Japanese goals not only differed but were in direct conflict with one another. While Japan seemed intent on consolidating an exclusive predominance in the far East, the United States appeared determined to uphold the distribution of world political power and economic opportunity which had resulted from World War I. As Japanese leaders moved to ensure the security and growth of their empire, American statesmen worked to ensure the re-establishment of global order based on international law. This dynamic of conflicting goals set up an antagonism between the two nations which grew increasingly bitter.

Some have argued that Japan's real goal was self-sufficiency in every major respect, from food and energy to much needed natural resources, from leading exporter of strategic goods to leading exporter of more sophisticated manufactures.[27] Perhaps toward that end, Japanese war plans drawn up in November of 1941 envisioned turning the whole geographic area into a Greater East Asia Co-Prosperity Sphere, with Japan and northern China plus Manchukuo as its industrial base. The other nations would have provided raw materials and together would have formed a vast consumer market. In this way, Japan planned to build economic strength great enough to withstand any challenge or attack from outside the Sphere.[28]

From the outset, Americans were as uncomprehending of Japan's logic as the Japanese were of theirs.[29] Mutual misperceptions and misunderstandings further exacerbated growing contentiousness over incompatible interests and conflicting foreign policy goals. By 1941, mutual suspicion and hostility, aggravated by communication failures, had mounted in such a way that they fanned the flames of bellicosity.[30] In spite of last ditch efforts to avert war, a major Japanese air strike at the Hawaiian base of Pearl Harbor on Sunday morning, December 7, 1941 combined with simultaneous attacks in Wake, Guam, Midway, the Philippines, and Hong Kong, caught the United States and the world by complete surprise.[31] As the war progressed, bilateral hostilities and hatreds escalated yet further, taking on strongly racial overtones in both nations and perpetuating unrestrained violence and numerous atrocities. Permeating this horror were distorted perceptions, wartime propagandized beliefs, and rigidly nationalistic mind-sets.[32]

Historian Charles E. Neu summed up the tragedy in this way:

> The coming of war in the Pacific still evokes an overwhelming sense of sadness that two nations whose economics and cultures were so intertwined could find no peaceful escape from the impasse that they reached. Neither government wanted war, but neither could, in the end, conceive of a way to achieve its aims without one.[33]

When on September 2, 1945, Japan surrendered, radical perceptions and blind hatreds subsided and, during the Occupation period and for some years thereafter, were replaced by peaceful, apparently sympathetic bilateral relations.

The Evolution of Postwar Trade Friction

Contemporary Japan-U.S. trade relations had their early beginnings during the Occupation years (1945-1952) when a newly defeated Japan lay in ruins – her empire stripped away, her industry demolished, her economy destroyed, her governmental administration in chaos, and her people war-broken and starving. During the Occupation period, the United States aided in breaking up the *zaibatsu* firms, which resulted in the temporary dissolution of the combines into their component parts and the abolition of their central holding companies. They also designed an antitrust law to prevent such consolidations in the future and ensured the purging of nearly 200,000 persons from Japan's wartime leadership.[34] Finally, they deprived Japan of all territorial gains made since 1868.

Yet, the United States also gave Japan assistance in the form of vital shipments of foodstuffs and raw materials and aided in the successful restructuring and rebuilding of her political and economic institutions.[35] Additionally, the Americans drafted a new national Constitution for Japan aimed at creating a political system based on American political and institutional values. Kyoko Inoue, in her linguistic and cultural analysis of the postwar Japanese Constitution and its making, vividly illustrates the radically different ideas held by Japanese and American leaders concerning the roles of the government and the governed. She summarizes the evolution of the bilateral debate over the Constitution's development and the interpretation of its final version with these words:

> The Japanese often did not understand the democratic ideas on which the Americans insisted. Partly because they had little choice but to accept the democratic principles that the Americans insisted on, and partly because neither the Americans nor the Japanese realized how great the cultural differences were, the two sides rarely were able to correct each other's misunderstandings. In fact, the negotiations between the two sides were often conducted in the ambiguities of cross-cultural and cross-linguistic communication. In the end, the negotiators created and approved two versions of the Constitution, one in English and the other in Japanese, which were congenial to their respective cultural and political traditions. But neither side realized the differences in meaning between the two versions.[36]

Inoue contends that, if the Japanese had really understood the democratic ideas that the Americans intended, it would have been far more difficult and painful for them to accept. She also adds that if General MacArthur and his staff had understood precisely how the Japanese were interpreting these principles, they might have been less inclined to approve the final version of the Constitution. In her concluding remarks, Inoue writes that the cultural and linguistic barriers in communication between Americans and Japanese were a hindrance to mutual understanding but that, ironically, these same difficulties made it possible for the two sides to agree on a final document without ever agreeing on its fundamental meaning.[37] This same dynamic would seem to resurface in later trade negotiations and trade agreements, of which the Semiconductor Agreements of 1986 and 1991 are examples.

While many still argue that the United States played a major role in shaping modern postwar Japan, others, such as British historian, W. G. Beasley, view the process and final product somewhat differently:

> Once the shock (of the war) wore off and Japanese again began to take the initiative in directing their country's affairs, they gave to the new something of the flavor of the old: in society and politics a little less of America of the 1940s, a little more of Japan of the 1920s; . . . in economic development, the exploitation of wartime experience to establish a fresh industrial pattern and promote an astonishing growth. The result is that in many contexts one can trace today a far greater continuity with the past. . . than would at one time have seemed possible.[38]

The United States was instrumental, however, in creating an international environment oriented toward freer trade, one which would be more than hospitable to Japan's postwar export efforts.[39] On this U.S. contribution there is little disagreement. Furthermore, with the coming of the Korean War (1950-1952) and the onset of the Cold War, American foreign policy shifted toward actively promoting Japan's economic development as U.S. military procurement and related spending provided a major burst of demand for Japanese products.

On September 8, 1951, Japan's sovereignty was returned when Prime Minister Yoshida Shigeru signed the Peace Treaty of San Francisco with 48 other countries. Because the peace settlement was designed to be nonpunitive as well as economically supportive, these terms contributed towards bonds of bilateral friendship and alliance.[40] A year later, Prime Minister Shigeru signed the Security Treaty with America which provided the United States with military bases and Japan with cost-effective security and the opportunity to focus all her efforts on economic reconstruction, growth, and trade. In short, the two former enemies had formed a partnership of crucial importance to both nations – militarily, politically, and economically. Yet, as one bilateral team of political economists and trade analysts pointed out:

> Achieving and maintaining such a partnership has required sustained effort by leaders and officials on both sides of the Pacific, because of the ever-present potential for serious misunderstanding and disagreement.[41]

Ironically, it was to be Japan's phenomenal economic growth, without doubt the greatest unforseen success story of the postwar partnership, that was to become both the partnership's greatest challenge and its greatest nemesis in the 1980s and 1990s.

Having regained full sovereignty, and finding an environment conducive to economic expansion and growth, Japan was on her way to full economic recovery and a new 'miracle.' By the mid-1950s, Japan had attained prewar levels of productivity, national income, and personal consumption.[42] By 1957,

Japan's recovery was complete; most of her older industries had been reorganized, rebuilt, and newly equipped. Industrial production was now approximately 250 percent of prewar volumes and would continue to grow phenomenally throughout the 1960s and 1970s.[43] Trade with the United States had already begun to surpass prewar levels, as American stores sold Japanese-made pianos, sewing machines, furniture, toys, chinaware, flatware, ladies' blouses, cashmere sweaters, silks and other textiles, Christmas ornaments, and pearls.[44] The general rise in Japanese exports to the United States brought sales from an annual average of $219 million in the period of 1950-1954 to $567 million in 1955-1958 and $1,141 million in 1959-1962.[45]

In the late 1950s, during the first signs of Japan's economic resurgence, the United States began to experience stiff competition from a variety of Japanese imports. Of these, textile-related imports, which had been the subject of minor friction in prewar years, were to become the subject of one of the most contentious bilateral trade disputes of the postwar era. Although sales of Japanese-made items remained a small fraction of the overall U.S. textile market, they were concentrated in specific product lines, such as cotton cloth and cotton blouses.[46] The politically strong U.S. textile industry pushed for quota restrictions in 1955 and 1956.[47] Triggered by U.S. labor demonstrations against inexpensive Japanese blouses, a bilateral agreement was concluded in 1957, which provided for Japanese voluntary export restraints (VERs) for five years.[48] Between 1959 and 1962, the textile issue flared once again. This time the flare-up culminated in the 1962 Long-Term Arrangement on Cotton Textiles whose implementation required detailed continuous negotiations. These agreements were renewed in 1963 and 1965.[49]

During the same period, the United States was also pressing Japan to limit exports in other product lines as well, even though the basic thrust of U.S. policy was still to encourage Japan's economic expansion. Well into the 1960s, attitudes of American and Japanese officials on trade continued to run along fundamentally parallel lines. Nondiscriminatory treatment of most Japanese exports was stressed without serious expectations of Japanese reciprocity on imports.[50] Until the mid-sixties, the combination of Japan's closed door import policies and America's open door policies had made economic sense and, except for textiles, had caused few political waves.

By the end of the decade, however, both nations were beginning to adjust their trade policies to accommodate changes in their relative competitive positions as reflected in bilateral trade patterns and merchandise trade deficits. Because policy actions taken were considered isolated, self-correcting measures, little bilateral discord was expected. Then toward the end of the decade, the United States, burdened by inflation and overvaluation of the dollar, saw its once stable multilateral trade surplus shrivel. Japan's high productivity growth, governmental export incentives, and undervalued yen had combined to transform her trade deficits with the United States into regular surpluses. Although far from clear at the time, the period of American global economic hegemony was weakening and Japanese industrial power emerging.[51]

The year 1969 was, as it turns out, a watershed in Japan-U.S. trade relations. New disputes over textiles ushered in the first real signs of serious bilateral trade friction associated with Japan's export growth and low levels of imported manufactured goods occurred. In subsequent decades, a consistent pattern in bilateral behavior would become evident -- endless efforts to resolve commercial differences through *ad hoc* agreements which would ultimately fail to diminish bilateral trade disequilibria or alter structural economic conditions. Japan continued to remove formal trade barriers to manufactured imports and repeatedly responded to U.S. demands for restraints on export volumes. Nevertheless, given the minimal effects of Japan's liberalization efforts, combined with the significant impact of Japan's escalating success in the U.S. market, the Japanese were increasingly perceived as unfair traders.[52]

In 1969, the new textile disputes, this time over wool and synthetic fibers, were to elicit the first major resistance by postwar Japan to an American trade initiative and produce almost three years of acrimonious bilateral negotiations and bad press. In spite of the fact that the textile sector was an important industry for both countries but a crucial industry for neither, textiles were suddenly catapulted into prominence as a major bilateral political issue.[53] In the words of one analyst:

> Seldom has so much political capital been consumed in pursuit of the economically inconsequential. . . In a modern-day version of the Japanese capitulation to the demands made by Admiral Perry from the black ships, the government of Japan acquiesced in mid-October to a textile export restraint formula acceptable to Washington. . . . The only shared experience in the great textile dispute may have been the feeling on each side that the other was unreasonable.[54]

Problems over textiles were a harbinger of bilateral trade disputes to come. Although the products and sectors have changed, the textile negotiations established a prototype of politicizing a given trade problem and then resolving it with a political agreement negotiated between the two governments rather than within a multilateral context.[55] The trade disputes over rice, automobiles and automotive parts, as well as semiconductors, are examples of this pattern.

Yet it was not until 1971 that the term 'trade friction' first began to be heard.[56] As the imbalance in trade grew to $4 billion in Japan's favor in 1972,

Japan-U.S. tensions mounted. Later, after an upsurge in American exports to Japan closed the trade gap, bilateral tensions subsided.[57] Over the next two decades, though, a variety of products became the focus of American unhappiness. U.S. complaints included the Japanese government's subsidization of targeted industries, special government-industry arrangements, collusive practices by business enterprises, price fixing, dumping, and the numerous restraints on imports into Japan. By the 1980s, the U.S. trade deficit with Japan had mushroomed from $10.4 billion in 1980 to $37.0 in 1984 and $43.5 billion in 1985.

In response to these figures, the dollar was devalued in an attempt at macroeconomic adjustment, but this did not have the corrective impact hoped for. Additionally, a new approach to bilateral trade dialogue was initiated in 1985 with the Market-Oriented Sector-Selective (MOSS) talks. These were set up to address all identifiable trade barriers within a given Japanese industry where American companies were competitive in international markets but had poor results in Japan. Because the goal was to negotiate specific, measurable results, critics argued that this approach smacked of managed trade and was, therefore, in violation of free trade principles. It was also criticized as attempts by the United States to restructure the internal workings of the Japanese system.[58]

By 1987, the U.S. deficit had reached $56.9 billion. Although it dropped back to $52.6 billion in 1988 and $49.7 billion in 1989, American alarm over these figures had escalated and remained high. Largely for this reason, Japan and the United States began talks in 1989 under the rubric of a Structural Impediments Initiative (SII). These talks were initiated to identify and address structural problems in both countries which operated as impediments to trade and to adjustments in the balance of payments. In other words, the primary goal of the SII was the reduction of the large bilateral trade imbalances.[59]

Then, in 1990, the Bush administration published its *National Trade Estimate Report on Foreign Trade Barriers* which identified 30 Japanese trade impediments. Among those identified were high tariffs on agricultural products and leather goods; highly restrictive standards on wood products; refusal by the government to buy American-made supercomputers or satellites; export subsidies for shipbuilding; barriers to foreign ownership of Japanese corporations; and inadequate protection for patents, copyrights, and trade marks. Three years later, the *Report's* 27-page Japan section began its overview with this statement:

Many specific agreements have been reached with Japan on market access, and many of the formal government trade barriers in Japan have been eliminated or significantly reduced. Despite this, access to the Japanese market for foreign firms is still constrained by ingrained structural factors.[60]

These and other factors are summarized in the following section, are elaborated on in greater detail in the overview of institutional and structural factors of Chapter Four, and are illustrated in the discussion in Chapter Eight concerning bilateral rice, automotive, and semiconductor disputes.

A Summary of American Complaints

Once the soaring U.S. trade deficits with Japan began occurring with regularity and the commodity composition of Japanese exports to the United States began expanding into the high-quality, technologically sophisticated manufactures arena, the idea of Japan as a national economic threat gained increasing credibility. Many in the United States now viewed Japan as America's greatest economic rival and adversary. Perceptions that the Japanese were playing by different rules, that they were exploiting the international economic order without assuming responsibility for its overall health and security, also gained adherents.[61] By the late 1980s, American frustration with, and fear of, Japan had even given birth to such new American trade terms as *induced competitive advantage*, *adversarial trade*, *strategic trade theory*, *results-oriented negotiations*, and *industrial targeting*.[62] For many American business and government leaders, the bilateral trade situation had gone from bad to worse to intolerable. Americans tended to argue that all they basically wanted from Japan was reciprocity and equal market access, often expressed as 'fair play' and an 'even playing field'.

Suspicions that something was radically wrong with U.S. industrial competitiveness also grew stronger but were usually coupled with ideas that Japan's export thrust was voracious even while her own markets remained fundamentally closed. Ideas such as these gained enough credence that movements in Washington for the imposition of retaliatory measures escalated even though prewar experiences indicated that such measures taken against Japan were likely to induce undesired rather than desired results. As one American commentator has written, Commodore Perry's earlier demands to the Japanese to 'open up your market, or suffer the consequences' have continued to echo down through the years, and are as loud and clear today as they were then.[63]

The basic U.S. complaint, that Japan exports far more to the United States (especially in high-value goods), than it is willing to import from her, is grounded in beliefs that Japan's commercial successes have resulted in large measure from unfair, adversarial business and trade practices. This allegation is supported by differing but related complaints. One category of American complaints involves Japan's alleged adversarial trade practices, such as dumping and price-cutting, which are believed to create 'unfair' advantages for Japanese products in foreign domestic markets like that of the United States. Practices such as these, which serve to increase market share and weaken competitors, have been reported in Japan's automotive and microelectronic industries among others.

A second category of accusations involves the closed nature of Japan's domestic market, more in recent years because of informal rather than formal barriers. Japan has all but eliminated tariffs on industrial products, which now average only about two percent. Average rates of 12.1 percent, however, are still maintained on agricultural products.[64] Products currently subject to Japanese tariffs include petrochemicals, certain aluminum objects, semi-fabricated copper, synthetic menthol, paper, leather shoes, certain fish and fish products, distilled spirits and wine, chocolates, and cookies, pet foods, oranges, beef, poultry, pork, wood products, honey, dried egg products, and certain grain products.[65] As for quotas and bans, the best known is that of rice for which there was nearly a 100 percent ban on all imports until a Japanese rice crop failure in 1994 necessitated imports. Other numerical limits include nine global and three bilateral quotas on fish products.[66]

As for informal barriers, Japan appears to have these in abundance. Such invisible or nontransparent barriers to trade are considered extremely effective in keeping foreign imports from successfully penetrating Japan's domestic market.[67] They include product standards and certification requirements, testing, labeling, licensing, and various customs regulations on products, such as pharmaceuticals and medical devices. Among the more common non-tariff reasons for keeping imports of agricultural products and foodstuffs out of Japan's domestic markets are food additive, pesticide residue, and freshness standards. A related complaint category concerns the complex, tightly-knit Japanese distribution system along with the strong Japanese propensity toward *groupism* at all levels of society, from producers to consumers. Embedded in Japanese cultural practices and preferences and shaped by Japanese institutional formations and functions, these also serve as extremely effective informal barriers to foreign imports of products and services.[68]

A third category of U.S. complaints involves the structure and functions of Japan's governmental institutions. Japan's powerful governmental institutions and agencies, such as the Ministry of International Trade and Industry (MITI), have traditionally designed and administered Japan's industrial policy, often targeting lucrative, high technology products or industries of the future, funding research and development activities related to such products and industries, and guiding these same industries toward further enhancement of their productivity and global competitiveness. Other complaints concerning Japanese governmental functions include the lack of property protection, especially on trademarks and copyrights. Patenting procedures are extremely detailed, complicated, drawn-out endeavors which frustrate more than help the non-Japanese applicant. In short, Japan's patent system doesn't offer foreign applicants timely, effective protection for innovations and inventions. Addition-ally, American firms wishing to manufacture in Japan have often been required to license their cutting-edge technologies in order to do so (e.g., IBM, Texas Instruments).

Government procurement practices are also said to discriminate against foreign products (e.g., telecommunications equipment, satellites, computers) and services (e.g., construction, architectural, and engineering); additionally, financial services (e.g., insurance, banking, securities, accounting) face strict regulations and various market entry impediments. Furthermore, governmental policies have heavily controlled the activities of foreign multinational corporations, especially those most directly competitive with Japan's targeted industries. Finally, governmental agencies have encouraged, rather than discouraged, Japan's substantially 'closed system' of corporate networks, especially the way in which companies organize into groups called *keiretsu*, hold each other's stocks, promote linkage among critical industries, and coordinate business endeavors with governmental guidance.

Research findings generally support American allegations that Japan's import/export policies and practices are designed to promote imports of raw materials and to hinder purchases of manufactured value-added goods. American economist Edward Lincoln (1990) points out that the patterns in Japan's international trade are unique among most trading nations of the world in that her intra-industry trade is especially low in industries with high export value for both Japan and the United States. In other words, Japan accepts few imports from the United States in precisely those areas of American worldwide competitive strength.[69] Support also comes from the fact that Japan's reputation for being an unfair or adversarial trader has grown since the 1960s among her other trading partners as well, especially those which are most highly industrialized.

A Summary of Japanese Complaints

As Japan has gained in global economic power, the Japanese appear to have grown increasingly unwilling to acknowledge U.S. demands and accusations with a conciliatory attitude, often stating that the charges are simply not justified. They point out that Japan's tariff rates are now the lowest among all the industrialized nations. Earlier gratitude for postwar American assistance seems to have dissolved into irritation and disdain at the strident tones of a declining superpower that prefers complaining to self-improvement.[70] Furthermore, Japanese leaders seem to have grown ever more perplexed and dismayed by the substance of U.S trade grievances and the methods used to address them. U.S. government officials are often seen as criticizing Japanese strengths rather than remedying American failures, and American negotiating methods are generally viewed as unduly tough, confrontational, and demanding. In short, Japanese view U.S. trade complaints and demands as unwarranted and never-ending. Many Japanese have grown unsympathetic to what is perceived as hypocritical and false assertions by Americans that the U.S. market is the world's most open while Japan's is one of the most closed. They particularly take issue with notions that Japan's economic institutions are structurally, ideologically, and functionally different from those of Western industrial nations, and that these differences result in a domestic market relatively closed to imports.[71]

Japanese attribute Japan's economic success to hard work, while they tend to consider U.S. complaints as demands by a nation which prefers blaming others for its own shortcomings rather than tackling its domestic problems. The basic Japanese perspective seems to be that the United States imports far more from Japan, especially in high-value goods, than it is capable of exporting (producing and selling) to her. Additionally, the U.S. government is criticized for mismanaging the national economy. Japanese leaders often point out that the U.S. government has wasted American economic strength through unwarranted military expenditures, national deficit spending, and general misuse of funds. Additionally, American business leaders and industrial workers are criticized for not trying hard enough to improve product quality, sales, and service. High levels of American consumer spending, combined with low levels of private investment and savings, are also criticized. Finally, Japanese argue that the United States should do something about its many societal problems, such as the less-than-adequate quality of its educational and worker-training programs and its high levels of homelessness and crime. Rather than blame Japan, Japanese point out, Americans should put their own economic house in order.

Some common Japanese suggestions and advice to Americans are as follow: Americans should think more in terms of long-term goals and objectives than in short term concern for profits. Americans should invest more capital and resources in improving the quality of current products and in developing new technologies and innovations. Americans should also improve the quality of the public educational system, and, in all areas, set higher standards. Finally, American producers could improve their export levels by becoming more globally minded. In other words, products and marketing strategies should be geared to the needs and desires of customers in markets to whom Americans want to sell.

Recent research on the relative economic strength of the United States lends support to Japanese concerns about the declining health of the U.S. economy. This research, supported by all the commonly used indices of relative capability, indicates that a major change in power dynamics has taken place within the global economic system. Such indices include aggregate wealth, wealth per capita, leading sector production, proportion of world trade, financial reserves, and international lending activity. Most writers date the decline in America as beginning in the 1960s, the time during which the United States first began to experience bilateral trade deficits with Japan.[72] Some scholars have even suggested that the United States and Japan are actually in the process of reversing roles,[73] that they are literally 'trading places'.[74]

Current research efforts on hegemonic economic decline yield paradigms that describe the decline process, thereby explaining the phenomena central to all Japanese criticisms of the United States. Among the causal factors of a decline process are increased domestic resistance to change and consequent failure to continue leadership in technological innovations and leading sector performance. Scholars representing diverse approaches to the question of decline, such as Cipolla (1970) from an historian's perspective, Bousquet (1980) from the world-economy school perspective, Gilpin (1981) from structural-realism's hegemonic stability school perspective, and Rasler and Thompson (1988) from the long cycle of world leadership school perspective, concur.[75]

The Cipolla model of decline is a useful framework for conceptualizing the substance of Japanese complaints. In the decline process, technological innovations diffuse and foreign competition increases, while once productive ways of doing things become obsolete. Although these need to be updated or revised, change tends to be resisted due to growing complacency, increased conservatism, vested interests, and institutional sclerosis. Economic difficulties grow, resulting in a progressively worsening cumulative process. As the decline process continues, rising levels of public and private consumption begin to exceed the nation's productive capabilities. As the nation reaches maturity, real, perceived, or potential hostility on the part of other nations causes military expenditures to rise, even as expanded public consumption also rises. This process is further aggravated by the tendency for national prosperity to reach all levels of society, thereby causing private consumption to rise as well. The gap between rising consumption and declining productivity widens, and the decline process accelerates. Increasingly, the nation faces rising currency debasements, inflation, excessive taxation, and balance of payments difficulties. As the economic pie shrinks, group and class selfishness intensifies, cooperation and public spirit decrease. People begin to emphasize their rights as opposed to their duties; a general sense of alienation and class conflict set in as reversal of the decline process becomes ever more unlikely.

Analyses of what the United States is currently experiencing indicate a fairly good fit with the Cipolla model of decline. This model supports what indices of economic strength empirically demonstrate and the Japanese tend to point out — that the United States is in the process of economic decline. It also lends explanatory credence to Japanese complaints that Americans are not trying hard enough, are mismanaging their economy, and are now blaming Japan for their own economic and business failures.

The Causes of Bilateral Trade Friction

The preceding summaries of U.S. and Japanese complaints have been based on statements gleaned from media presentations, academic and non-academic publications, public opinion polls, and interviews with various American and Japanese opinion leaders. To what extent are these complaints reflective of views held by most opinion leaders in Japan and the United States? If such views and perceptions are indeed widely held, to what extent do they contribute to bilateral contentiousness over trade imbalances and sectoral issues? In other words, do perceptual differences, including misperceptions and biased perceptions, really work to exacerbate the Japan-U.S. trade conflict? Exactly what part, if any, do cultural and institutional differences play in bilateral conflicts? These are questions which are addressed in the chapters to come.

Notes

1   Sansom, G. (1963) *A History of Japan, 1615-1867*, pp. 232-234.
2   Beasley, W. G. (1973) *The Modern History of Japan*, pp. 57-75.

3   Ibe, H. (1992) *Japan Thrice-Opened: An Analysis of Relations between Japan and the United States* (translated by L. Riggs and M. Takechi); Neu, C. (1975) *The Troubled Encounter: The United States and Japan*, p. 8.

4   According to the editors of *Asahi Shimbun* (1972) *The Pacific Rivals: A Japanese View of Japanese-American Relations*, p. 313, the image of Perry's 'black ships' became part of Japan's folklorical language and has been used by subsequent generations of Japanese whenever conditions suggest that extreme difficulties with the United States loom ahead. This continues to be true until the present day.

5   Neumann, W. (1963) *America Encounters Japan: From Perry to MacArthur*, p. 44; Beasley, W. G. (1973) p. 60.

6   Sansom, G. (1963) p. 234.

7   Reischauer, E. (1965) *The United States and Japan* (third edition), pp. 9-10.

8   Neumann, W. (1963) p. 3.

9   Schwantes, R. (1972) 'American Relations with Japan, 1853-1895: Survey and Prospect' in E. May and J. Thompson (eds) *American-East Asian Relations: A Survey*, p. 103; for an elaboration on this point, see H. Ibe (1992).

10   Beasley, W. G. (1973) pp. 163-185; Halliday, J. (1975) *A Political History of Japanese Capitalism*, pp. 92-94.

11   Beasley, W. G. (1973) pp. 183-185.

12   Ibid., pp. 216-217.

13   Ibid., p. 216.

14   Although *keiretsu* share many similarities with *zaibatsu*, *keiretsu* are not closed, monolithic superstructures tightly held together by a single holding company, as *zaibatsu* were, nor do they operate as fully self-contained or mutually exclusive entities. For further discussion of the differences between *zaibatsu* and *keiretsu*, see M. Aoiki (1987) 'The Japanese Firm in Transition', pp. 263-288 in K. Yamamura and Y. Yashuba, *The Political Economy of Japan*, vol. I, *The Domestic Transformation*; D. Okimoto (1989) *Between MITI and the Market: Japanese Industrial Policy for High Technology*, pp. 132-142; C. Prestowitz (1988) *Trading Places: How We Allowed Japan to Take the Lead*, pp. 143, 156-171; R. Clark (1979) *The Japanese Company*, pp. 73-87; and M. Yoshino and T. Lifson (1986) *The Invisible Link: Japan's Sogo Shosho and the Organization of Trade*, pp. 30-33. For a more thorough examination of the breakup and reemergence of *zaibatsu* groups, see E. Hadley (1970) *Antitrust in Japan*, Princeton, Massachusetts: Princeton University. The *keiretsu* will be one of the primary foci of Chapter 4 (The Institutional and Structural Factors).

15   Allen, G. C. (1981) *A Short Economic History of Modern Japan* (fourth edition), pp. 95-96; Beasley, W. G. (1973) pp. 214-215.

16   Duus, P. (1976) *The Rise of Modern Japan*, pp. 173-175.

17   Neu, C. (1975) p. 127; Beasley, W. G. (1973) p. 215; see also C. P. Kindleberger (1986) *The World in Depression, 1929-1939*, p. 144, and W. Hunsberger (1972) 'Japan-United States: Patterns, Relationships, Problems' in J. B. Cohen (ed), *Pacific Partnership: United States-Japan Prospects and Recommendations for the Seventies*, p. 118.

18   Lockwood, W. W. (1954) *The Economic Development of Japan: Growth and Structural Change, 1868-1938*, p. 120.

19   See J. B. Cohen (1949) *Japan's Economy in War and Reconstruction* for a more detailed account.

20   Johnson, C. (1982) *MITI and the Japanese Miracle: The Growth of Industrial Policy,*
      1925-1975, p. 6, attributes the term, Japanese 'miracle,' to Hiromi Arisawa (1937) *The*
      Control of Japanese Industry.
21   Kindleberger, C. P. (1986) p. 282.
22   Neu, C. (1975) pp. 162-163.
23   Diebold, W. (1972) *The United States and the Industrial World: American Foreign*
      Economic Policy in the 1970s, p. 49.
24   Beasley, W. G. (1973) pp. 268-269.
25   Duus, P. (1976) p. 227; Hunsberger, W. (1972) p. 118; and Beasley, W. G. (1973)
      pp. 268-269.
26   Duus, P. (1976) pp. 224-226.
27   Barnhart, M. (1987) *Japan Prepares for Total War: The Search for Economic Security,*
      1919-1941, p. 30.
28   Beasley, W. G. (1973) p. 272.
29   Duus, P. (1976) p. 226.
30   *Asahi Shimbun* (1972) pp. 43-44.
31   Beasley, W. G. (1973) p. 271.
32   Dower, J. (1986) *War without Mercy: Race and Power in the Pacific War.*
33   Neu, C. (1975) pp. 195-196.
34   These and other U.S. contributions and changes were going to prove less influential and
      permanent than American Occupation authorities had planned.
35   Allen, G. C. (1981) pp. 187-195; Beasley, W. G. (1973) pp. 279-304; Hunsberger, W.
      (1964) *Japan and the United States in World Trade,* p. 242.
36   Inoue, K. (1991) *MacArthur's Japanese Constitution: A Linguistic and Cultural Study*
      of Its Making, pp. 266-267. This bilateral dynamic would be repeated in future trade
      negotiations and agreements. Classic examples of this dynamic occurred with the
      Semiconductor Agreements of 1986 and 1991, taken up in the next chapter.
37   Ibid., p. 270.
38   Beasley, W.G. (1973) p. 280.
39   Hunsberger, W. (1972) p. 118.
40   Destler, I.M., H. Sato, P. Clapp, and H. Fukui (1976) *Managing an Alliance: The*
      Politics of U.S.-Japanese Relations, p. 10.
41   Ibid., p. 41.
42   Neu, C. (1975) pp. 212-217.
43   Allen, G. C. (1981) p. 191.
44   Okita, S. (1990) *Approaching the 21st Century: Japan's Role.*
45   Hunsberger, W. (1964) p. 242.
46   Destler, I. M., H. Fukui, and H. Sato (1979) *The Textile Wrangle,* p. 29.
47   Destler, I. M., H. Sato, P. Clapp, and H. Fukui (1976) p. 36.
48   Ibid., p. 35-38.
49   Destler, I. M., H. Fukui, and H. Sato (1979) pp. 33, 37.
50   Destler, I. M., H. Sato, P. Clapp, and H. Fukui (1976).
51   Cohen, S. D. (1991) *Cowboys and Samurai: Why the U.S. Is Losing the Battle with the*
      Japanese and Why It Matters, p. 19.
52   Ibid., p. 51.
53   For a richly complete account of the textile dispute, see I.M. Destler, H. Fukui, and H.
      Sato (1979) *The Textile Wrangle.*

54   Cohen, S. D. (1991) pp. 19-21.
55   Okita, S. (1990) pp. 39-40.
56   Ibid., (1990) p. 40.
57   Destler, I. M., et al (1976) pp. 1-2.
58   Cohen, S. D. (1991) p. 43; Prestowitz, C. (1988) *Trading Places: How We Allowed Japan to Take the Lead*, pp. 296-299.
59   The Structural Impediments Initiative is taken up at greater length in Chapter 4 (The Institutional and Structural Factors).
60   U.S. Trade Representative (1993) *National Trade Estimate Report on Foreign Trade Barriers*, p. 143.
61   Destler, I. M., H. Fukui, and H. Sato (1979) p. 27.
62   Cohen, S. D. (1991) pp. 42-43.
63   Prestowitz, C. (1988) p. 8.
64   U.S. Trade Representative (1993) p. 146. Most of the details in the remainder of this section are taken from this source.
65   One unusual tariff is that of four million yen on each race horse brought into Japan for racing purposes.
66   In spite of this, two-thirds of all U.S. fishery exports still go to Japan.
67   See footnote 7 in Chapter 1.
68   See Chapters 3 and 4 for further discussion on these factors.
69   Lincoln, E. (1990) *Japan's Unequal Trade*. Not all economists view Japan's trade behavior in this way, however. Gary Saxonhouse (1986, 1988) is one who prefers a comparative advantage theoretical explanation. In his model, net exports (exports minus imports) are hypothesized to be the result of capital, labor, raw material, and land endowments. Using this model, Saxonhouse finds that, as a highly industrialized, high-wage nation with a high capital-to-labor ratio, Japan has a preponderance of its imports in labor-intensive industries, just as one would expect from comparative advantage theory. For a critique of Saxonhouse's application of the comparative advantage model, see E. Lincoln (1990) pp. 22-25. For an evaluation of both models, see Bergsten and Noland (1993) pp. 64-67, 179-189.
70   Cohen, S. D. (1991) p. 43.
71   Based on readings and interviews with Japanese opinion leaders.
72   See for example, M. Whitman (1975) 'The Decline of American Hegemony', *Foreign Policy*, vol. 20, pp. 138-160; C. P. Kindleberger (1981) 'Dominance and Leadership in the International Political Economy: Exploitation, Public Goods, and Free Rides', *International Studies Quarterly*, vol. 25, pp. 242-254; C. P. Kindleberger (1983) 'On the Rise and Decline of Nations', *International Studies Quarterly*, vol. 27, pp. 5-10.
73   Vogel, E. (1986) 'Pax Nipponica?', *Foreign Affairs*, 66, pp. 752-767.
74   Prestowitz, C. (1988).
75   Cipolla, C. M. (1970) *The Economic Decline of Empires*; Bousquet, N. (1980) 'From Hegemony to Competition: Cycles at the Core' in T. and I. Wallerstein (eds), *Processes of the World System*; Gilpin, R. (1981) *War and Change in World Politics*; Rasler, K. and W. Thompson (1988) 'Consumption and Decline' (unpublished paper presented at the annual meeting of the American Political Science Association, September 1988, in Washington, D.C. A later version of this paper, 'Relative Decline and the Overconsumption-Underinvestment Hypothesis', was published in *International Studies Quarterly* (1991) vol. 35, pp. 273-294).

3 The Cultural Factors

> For it is after commonalities are accounted for that politics becomes necessary.
> It is only when values, ideologies, cultures and interests clash that politics even
> begins. . . . To gloss over contradictory interests, incompatible ideologies and
> opposing cultures as sources of conflict is more than antipolitical. It is
> dangerous.
>
> Charles Krauthammer, 1983[1]

Japan and the United States have more in common than recent episodes of
bilateral trade rivalry, economic conflict, and angry rhetoric might suggest.
Both are highly industrialized, technologically advanced, economically
powerful, and highly urbanized democratic nations. Their citizenries enjoy high
standards of living; abundant educational, cultural, and international travel
opportunities; and highly sophisticated news media coverage and information
sources. Because of these and other similarities, as well as the myriad of
bilateral postwar cultural, economic, and security arrangements, the two nations
have become increasingly interdependent. Indeed, their destinies now appear
inextricably intertwined.

Yet, in much the same way that focusing on trade rivalry, economic
conflict, and angry rhetoric diminishes awareness of similarities and common
interests, so, too, does focusing on similarities and common interests result in
crucial differences being overlooked and their significance denied. Such
differences, from divergent values and behavioral patterns to dissimilar
government institutions and business arrangements, are deeply rooted in the soil
of each nation's respective cultural heritage. Over the years, clashes between
value systems and behavioral styles as well as institutions, economic ideologies,
and national priorities have contributed greatly to the mood fluctuations in
bilateral relations.[2]

One only needs to review events which took place between Japan and the
United States in the mid-1850s, and again in the 1930s and early 1940s, to
understand how the process works. In the first case, despite the assortment of
communication and perceptual problems accompanying American insistence

39

on Japan's opening to the West and Japanese resistance in doing so, these inharmonious early contacts produced results which were, in the last analysis, far more positive than negative. In the second case, however, perceptual biases, miscommunications, and foreign policy blunders aggravated already tense, contention-filled relations. These contributed to the escalation of hostilities between the two nations, hostilities which culminated in the 1941 bombing of Pearl Harbor and 'the war which should never have been fought'.[3]

Although recent trade disputes, such as those over rice, automobiles, and semiconductors, have not resulted in such unfortunate consequences, they have not improved bilateral relations either. What these disputes suggest is the chronic nature of the perceptual chasm and conflictual dynamics to which American and Japanese remain vulnerable. Also revealed is the consistent pattern of U.S. complaints and insistence that Japan make some changes coupled with Japan's prolonged resistance and often last hour accommodations. At times, the Japanese have remained unyielding in the face of continuing U.S. complaints, as with the rice issue. At other times, they have yielded, bilateral agreements have been reached, but the two parties often disagree on what their mutually acceptable agreement actually means (e.g., the 1986 and 1991 Semiconductor Agreements).[4]

Chronic perceptual distortions and communication problems tend to erode amicable relations. Because the tendency is to view reality from the vantage point of one's own national and cultural background, the motives of those from another nation and culture can be misperceived in recondite ways. Nor are those dealing directly with bilateral trade issues (e.g., government leaders, diplomats, trade negotiators) exempt from such vulnerabilities. Indeed, these are among those best-advised to move beyond their respective mindsets into those of their counterparts on the other side of the ocean.[5] Yet to do so in adequate fashion is a difficult and challenging task. The development of sufficiently accurate views of a cultural group different from one's own requires an objective examination of its cultural values and beliefs, its language and behavior, and its social patterns and institutions. It also requires an objective understanding of one's own cultural values, behavioral patterns, and institutions. Only this kind of understanding makes possible the identification of likely blind spots and distortions which prevent accurate cross-cultural readings. Yet such understanding is rare. One's own cultural values, beliefs, and attitudes are generally assumed natural, and the validity of conclusions based upon them rarely open to question.

Even anthropologists, trained to detect ethnocentric biases in their observations, fall prey to subtle cultural blind spots. The eminent American anthropologist, Ruth Benedict, who in 1944 was asked by the U.S. Office of

War Information to produce an in-depth study of Japanese culture, was skillful and meticulous in gleaning Japanese films and newsreels, books and articles, art forms, and interviews with Japanese-born Americans. Out of this great effort evolved her classic study, *The Chrysanthemum and the Sword*. For years following its publication, this work was considered an impartially and sensitively drawn portrait of the Japanese character. Recently, however, scholars have discovered subtle blind spots even in this work.

Prominent Japanese psychiatrist and sociolinguist, Takeo Doi, is one who has questioned some of Benedict's conclusions. Doi states that Benedict 'allows value judgments to creep into her ideas' and that elements of 'cultural prejudice' cause her to identify certain Japanese characteristics as culturally based rather than as prototypes of universal human behavior.[6] If observations of well trained anthropologists are vulnerable to cultural bias, then all who study and write about another culture must do so with caution. Yet Doi and numerous others concur with Benedict in asserting that American and Japanese values and behavioral patterns differ significantly.[7] These differences, often established in infancy and, therefore, 'not easily subject to conscious control . . . accent and color human behavior'. Such differences can cause trouble (e.g., bewilderment, antagonism) when people try to communicate across the emotional barriers of culture.[8]

It is within the context of these remarks and the following discussion concerning the definition, description, and parameter determination of culture that comparative sketches of American and Japanese cultural patterns (this chapter) and their effects on political institutions, economic organizations, and trade norms (next chapter) are broadly sketched. These renderings are based on *culture-specific* and *culture-comparative* studies from a number of disciplines (e.g., anthropology, business, economics, history, sociology, political science, social psychology) but augmented by *culture-interactive* perspectives (e.g., intercultural communication, sociolinguistics) wherever possible.[9] They are not intended to break new ground or explore exceptions to the rule. For the purposes of this study, a broad sweep -- a gestalt -- is what is needed and, therefore, offered. Even though culture plays an important role in many areas of interest to political scientists, it is considered by many as being of limited or residual explanatory value.[10] Despite the alleged limitations of most cultural arguments, however, culture endures as a factor meritorious of scholarly consideration. This chapter, written in its defense, serves a number of objectives.

First, it clarifies what the concept *culture* encompasses and how it relates to the purposes of this study. While no attempt is made to sort out the various lines of arguments and debate among theoretical approaches, several fundamental assumptions are drawn upon.[11] One assumption is that a culture is a system of socially transmitted behavioral patterns which relate a given human community to its ecological setting. These behavioral patterns include religious beliefs and practices as well as social, economic, and political organizations and functions. Another assumption is that a culture is a system of ideas in which language, an instrument for learning that system, is but one of its subsystems. These ideas include the concepts *(schema)* which people of a given culture have formed in their minds for organizing and interpreting new information. Yet another assumption is that, even though the ideational, behavioral, and social structural realms of culture are distinct, so closely are they interrelated that at times they appear inseparable. Since all three realms come into play when individuals, as well as collectivities, of one culture interact with those of another, the holistic cultural approach taken here addresses the content, context, and contributions of all three.

Second, it delineates culture's effects on American and Japanese national life. This is not to say that rational input, not always influenced by cultural conditioning, is nonexistent or unimportant. The argument is simply that normative and behavioral tendencies within a given cultural environment help shape, and partially account for, that society's social interactions, its political-economic institutions and functions, its business formations and practices, and even its trade norms. Third, it explores three cultural differences which can and do cause trouble in U.S.-Japanese trade relations: communication, decision-making, and negotiation styles. These can affect the bilateral trade agreement process, from negotiating and writing an agreement to interpreting it. Fourth, it suggests ways in which cultural factors can affect bilateral trade dynamics. Not only do cultural factors help shape a nation's social, political, and economic structures, functions, and processes in meaningful ways, they also affect the ways in which its leaders perceive the characteristics of their own political economy and that of another nation.

Finally, it lays the groundwork for discussing the effects of culture on ingroup-outgroup perceptual and attributional dynamics which are hypothesized to exacerbate bilateral trade friction. A basic premise of this study is that Americans and Japanese are members of national groups whose cultural differences color the substance and style of their communications, perceptions, and interactions. Cultural factors are also relevant when drawing conclusions concerning non-Western nations like Japan within the context of social psychological theory, most of which is based on Western cultural models.

Definitions of Culture and Cultural Values

One of the reasons political scientists and economists tend to dismiss cultural factors so readily is that defining *culture* is difficult. Comparative political scientists David Elkins and Richard Simeon note that the inherent characteristics of culture (or political culture) pose particular difficulties for those attempting to clearly define, describe, and measure it. First, cultural factors are difficult to disentangle from institutional, structural, and psychological factors. Second, because culture is an abstract concept, it cannot be directly seen, heard, or touched; rather, it must be inferred. Third, because culture is unconscious, inexplicit, and taken for granted by most members of a given society, researchers cannot talk directly with them about it. Finally, even though individuals participate in a culture as a collective attribute of society, culture cannot be described by merely aggregating all those individuals.[12]

Because of such difficulties, the concept of culture 'performs a largely catch-all function, its multiple meanings providing a convenient label by which to identify a variety of themes left over after all the primary explanatory variables... have been dealt with'.[13] However, Ruth Lane (1991) counters this tendency to view culture (or political culture) as little more than a residual explanatory category by proposing a 'cultural rationality' model which defines political culture as a

> complex structure of logically linked belief variables, shared by most of a group's members, about what motivates people; how the group is organized; who should get what, when, and how; what roles each person is allowed or forced to assume; and how, overall, the group is to be organized.[14]

Although an informal model of cultural rationality is one of the bases for the present analysis, the research applicability and theoretical usefulness of this or any other model of political culture is yet to achieve a consensus among political researchers.

Even among anthropologists, sociologists, and social psychologists, there seems to be no clear consensus as to the single best definition of culture. One of the broadest is simply 'the patterned ways of a people', while one of the most specific, all-encompassing is the often quoted definition of anthropologist Clyde Kluckhohn:

> Culture consists in patterned ways of thinking, feeling and reacting, acquired and transmitted mainly by symbols, constituting the distinctive achievements

of human groups, including their embodiments in artifacts; the essential core of culture consists of traditional (e.g., historically derived and selected) ideas and especially their attached values.[15]

The 'patterned ways' concept found in both definitions, and implied in Lane's cultural rationality model, is what most concerns cross-cultural researcher, Geert Hofstede. He defines cultures as 'social systems' which 'differ sufficiently from one another in patterns of thinking and behaving so as to be considered distinct'. The concept of 'social patterns' or 'social systems' is crucial because human behavior in a social context is rarely random but always, to some extent, predictable. In psychological terminology, individuals carry within them 'mental programs' which can be thought of as pertaining to one of three levels of uniqueness -- the universal, the collective, or the individual. As Figure 3.1 shows, the universal level encompasses those patterns which peoples of all cultures share, while the individual level concerns only that mental programming unique to the individual. Interposed between the two is the collective, which concerns the cultural 'programming' of an entire society's 'mind'.[16]

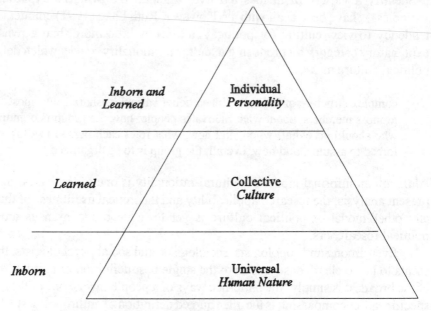

Figure 3.1   Three Levels of Uniqueness in Human Mental Programming

Source: Based on G. Hofstede (1984) *Culture's Consequences: International Differences in Work-Related Values*, p. 16, and G. Hofstede (1991) *Cultures and Organizations: Software of the Mind*, p. 6.

The cultural programming of the mind shapes the value systems of the major groups within a given population. These groups, or subcultures, are generally interdependent and share common traits within the context of the main culture. In this way, members of a given culture are recognizable to those outside as belonging to that particular society. These historically created cultural patterns are passed from one generation to the next, and even though they are subject to a certain amount of change, there is a strong tendency for stability to occur across many generations of a cultural group. The mechanisms which Hofstede suggests encourage this stability of cultural patterns are shown in Figure 3.2.

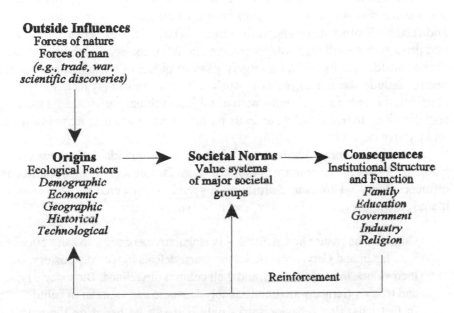

Outside Influences
Forces of nature
Forces of man
(e.g., trade, war,
scientific discoveries)

Origins ——▶ **Societal Norms** ——▶ **Consequences**
Ecological Factors   Value systems   Institutional Structure
Demographic   of major societal   and Function
Economic   groups   *Family*
Geographic   *Education*
Historical   *Government*
Technological   *Industry*
               Religion

Reinforcement

Figure 3.2   The Stabilization of Cultural Patterns
Source: Based on G. Hofstede (1984) *Culture's Consequences*, p. 22.

At the center of the figure is the system of societal norms, composed of value systems or mental programs which are shared by the major groups of a given population. The origins of these norms are rooted in a variety of 'ecological' factors, such as geography, demography, economic conditions, history, and technology, which affect a society's physical and social environment. 'Outside' influences can also give rise to, reinforce, or reshape these 'ecological' factors. The value system, which evolves as a population responds to a given set of ecological factors, creates an environment in which a particular set of social and political institutions develop and function. Once developed and functional, these institutions reinforce the societal norms which first gave rise to them.[17]

A cultural system, like other systems, may be conceptualized in terms of structure and process. As process, culture includes behavioral regularities of groups and other aggregates of individuals; as structure, it includes the supraindividual, abstract ideas, beliefs, and values. Both components of a cultural system are supported by, and manifested through, all other societal systems, including the political and economic. A society's system of fundamental values, attitudes, and beliefs about itself and the world can be viewed as central to the whole of society and its various subsystems in the same ways that a hub is central to the spokes of a wheel. In this way, culture unites and relates all subsystems one to the other. What mediates between structure and process is socialization which involves both the society and the individual. Some consider the individual a largely passive object of socialization, whose agents include the family, school, work, religion, and mass media. Others consider the individual a more active subject, taking part in and affecting socialization. In reality, all individuals within a society are both active subjects and passive objects.[18]

Changes in cultural norms result largely from 'outside' influences which can cause a shift in one or more of the ecological factors and, thereby, indirectly influence them.[19] However, cultural norms tend to resist change. As business management guru, Peter Drucker, recently expressed it:

> Culture – no matter how defined – is singularly persistent. Nearly 50 years ago, Japan and Germany suffered the worst defeats in recorded history, with their values, their institutions, and their cultures discredited. But today's Japan and today's Germany are unmistakably Japanese and German in culture. . . . In fact, changing behavior works only if it can be based on the existing 'culture'.[20]

American and Japanese cultures can be expected to change gradually and subtly, not only as a result of technological advances and changing international dynamics, but also as a result of ongoing bilateral contact. For while a culture tends toward the status quo, it is never static. Nor are its parameters easily determined even at a fixed moment in time. Particularly elusive is the extent to which collective behavior is programmed and, therefore, predictable. Also elusive is the point at which collective programming ends and another level begins. The need to further define and operationalize culture's parameters is acknowledged but not addressed at this time.

Discussed next are the major cultural values and behavioral patterns differentiating Americans from Japanese, their probable sources, and their implications for bilateral trade relations.

Divergent American and Japanese Cultural Patterns:
An Interpretive Analysis

Cultural differences between the two nations are both striking and profound. As demonstrated in Chapter Two, these can foster bilateral miscommunication and misunderstanding; they can also aggravate conflict and hostility occurring as a result of conflicting national goals and rivalry. This part of the analysis illustrates the depth and breadth of American and Japanese cultural differences. For starters, the United States has been described as a horizontal (flat) society in which individual differences like sex, age, rank, and role are acknowledged but downplayed. Meanwhile, Japan has been described as a vertical (hierarchal) society in which such differences are not only acknowledged but emphasized, institutionalized, and ritualized.[21] The national language of each nation reflects and promotes this consequential difference. While American English offers its speakers little in the way of terms, phrases, or syntactical devices to indicate or honor relative differences in position, status, or age, Japanese not only offers, but requires many. As Japanese language educator Osamu Mizutani has written:

> The Japanese show a strong consciousness of their relative relationship to the listener, and honorific forms are based on whether the listener is above or below one in position or social status. . . . Japanese society is very strict about these respect and humble forms, and those who cannot use them correctly are the target of considerable criticism.[22]

There are other important differences as well. The United States, unlike Japan, is a nation settled by large waves of immigrants who continue to arrive in large numbers. As such, it is a relatively open, nontraditional society whose population is a complex mosaic of many races, nationalities, religions, customs, and languages. It is also a society of constant geographic, social, and occupational movement in which bonds between individuals and groups are looser and more provisional than those of Japan. Relationships are largely matters of personal choice and shift with the changing interests and goals of each partner. Consequently, they tend to be less comprehensive and less durable than Japanese relationships.[23]

American journalist James Fallows writes that the United States is an 'antitraditionalist' nation and a 'culture of constant change' composed of adaptable people 'with a talent for disorder and for not knowing (their) place'.[24]

He adds:

> (America) has always been a changeable, self-defining, let's-start-over culture, in which people with talent, energy, or luck believed they could invent their own lives. . . . It is the story of people who try to bend tradition to suit their immediate needs.[25]

Not surprising, the American tendency to emphasize short-term goals over long-term goals has been shaped in part by these elements.

Unlike the United States, Japan has historically been a nation resistant to invasion from outside, including immigrants. As such, it is considered a relatively closed society whose highly homogeneous population share the same ethnicity, language, history, values, customs, and strong sense of national identification. Japan's unique history has also fostered the most noted characteristic of Japanese society, its collectivistic or group oriented structure. MITI leader and trade official, Masahisa Naitoh, sums up the view most Japanese have concerning Western influences on Japanese traditional values:

> Japan's value system has evolved out of more than one thousand years of isolation and homogeneity. The Western concept of individualism is notably absent from this value system: traditional ideology is collectivist and strongly isolationist. But Japanese society was permanently changed a century ago, when Japan's curtain of isolation was lifted. In self-defense Japan set about acquiring the technology and economic practices of the West, products of a wholly alien cultural context in which individualism and universalism were dominant.[26]

Japan's collectivist tendencies remain intact. Japanese are generally expected to accept and honor already established rules, obligations, and requirements. While the individual has little or no responsibility *for* these rules and obligations, he is completely responsible *to* them.[27] Unlike Americans, Japanese have a strong sense of one's 'proper place' and its requisite behavior; as such, Japanese tend to value predictability, tradition, and the status quo. Not surprisingly, long-term goals are favored over short-term goals.

In Japan, each person tends to function as a member of various social groups, rather than as a solitary individual. Additionally, the bonds that mean most in Japan are less a matter of choice than of birth, school, and employment.[28] Because roles are so all-important, one might say that there are only Japanese fathers and sons, students and teachers, citizens and officials, subjects and rulers, not individuals. Moreover, the Japanese tend to avoid making individual decisions and taking individual responsibility, much preferring group decisions and group responsibility.[29] Although keen competition exists in both societies, it tends to occur most between individuals in America and between groups in Japan.[30]

American and Japanese cultural differences are often presented in comparative tables similar to that of Table 3.1. While such comparisons offer useful information, they promote the idea that American and Japanese cultural patterns are merely opposite ends along a series of continua. On one major continuum, the dimension (or bundle of dimensions) called *individualism-collectivism*, Americans and Japanese are generally believed to be at opposite ends.[31] One communication scholar succinctly described this apparent polarity, when he wrote:

> In Japan the impulses and needs of the individual tend to be subordinated to the good of the group; in the U.S. any intrusion by the group on the rights of the individual is regarded as unwarranted. . . . If one (nation) is the land of the big WE, the other is the land of the big I.[32]

Table 3.1   American and Japanese Cultural Patterns

U.S.	Japan
Horizontal Society	**Vertical Society**
Equality; differences (age, role, rank) acknowledged but not emphasized. Status through achievement. Ability, experience stressed.	Hierarchy; differences (age, role, rank) outwardly acknowledged, emphasized. Status through ascription. Affiliations, roles stressed.
Non-traditionalism	**Traditionalism**
Change, spontaneity, anything goes valued.	Status quo, predictability, proper place valued.
Individualism	**Collectivism**
Individual attributes (talent, ability, experience, hard work) valued. Self-reliance stressed.	Group affiliations (family, school, work, community, nation) valued. *Amae* relations stressed.

U.S.	Japan
Goal Orientation	**Human Relations Orientation**
Accomplishment of goals stressed. Talent, ability, experience, highly valued. Facts, figures valued. Written communication, agreements honored. Varied decision-making styles.	Harmony; smooth interpersonal relations stressed. Getting along with others highly valued. Receptivity, intuition valued. Face-to-face communication, agreements honored. Consensual decision-making style.
Universalism	**Particularism**
Legalism valued.	Situational relativism valued.
Directness	**Indirectness**
Be honest and forthright. Communicate personal opinions. Explicit, verbal communication style valued. (Mean what you say; say what you mean.) Yes means yes; no means no.	Save face above all. Guard personal opinions. Implicitly, nonverbal communication style valued. (What is not said may be more important than what is said.)
Informality	**Formality**
In speech and conduct.	In speech and conduct.
Activity	**Passivity**
Be assertive; sell yourself. Take action; do something.	Be humble; be modest. Be reserved; be patient.

Source: Based on various works of D. Barnland (1989), R. Bellah (1957, 1985), R. Benedict (1970), T. Doi (1974, 1981, 1985), J. Hendry (1987, 1988), T. S. Lebra (1976), E. Stewart (1972).

Yet Geert Hofstede identifies some subtle nuances concerning this and three other cultural continua in his 1984 study of four major cultural dimensions and their strength in the dominant value systems of 40 countries. Although his findings verify the Japan-U.S. *individualism-collectivism* dichotomy, reality falls somewhat short of the expected norm. The United States placed first among all nations on the *individualism* measure (ranging from 0 to 100), with a score of 91. Meanwhile Japan placed 22nd/23rd among all nations with a score of 46. These and other findings suggest that culturally determined behavioral differences should be considered relative rather than absolute.[33] Conceptualizing cultural differences as opposing ends of continua not only tends to exaggerate U.S.-Japanese realities, but it also tends to retard the development of a holistic, integrated view of both cultures, a view which includes cultural ideals as well as cultural realities. Most comparative tables also omit the subtle interwoven connectedness of patterns and their interdependence one with the other. Elusive and deeply embedded in the psyche of a given culture are threads binding one cultural pattern to another and weaving all parts into a comprehensive whole. Identifying these threads produces a deeper, more accurate reading of a people's national character.

One of these threads must certainly be beliefs about what it means to be human. In the United States, many currently held beliefs about humankind can be traced back to the early Greeks, such as Plato and Socrates, who held that, inherent in each human being, was the ability and desire to lead a rational, productive, and moral life. They also believed that each human being was born, lived, and died alone, and that he had the right to choose whether or not to enter into relationships with others. Regardless of relationships formed, the human being remained a fundamentally separate being. A culture which holds this view would logically be one in which values enhancing the individual are stressed.

In the early 1830s, the well-known French social philosopher, Alexis de Tocqueville, kept a running journal of his travels around the United States and, in the process, coined the term *individualism* to describe what he considered the American people's most notable characteristic.[34] More than 120 years later, a team of American sociologists, with Tocqueville's work in hand, set about defining and documenting the American 'habits of the heart'. They wrote that *individualism* had 'marched inexorably through (American) history' and that Americans continued to firmly believe in the 'dignity, indeed the sacredness' of the individual. They concluded that *individualism* was still the very bedrock or core of American culture.[35]

In describing the socialization process of Americans, social psychologist Edward Stewart has written that it is 'implicitly accepted' that an American 'be encouraged to decide for himself, develop his own opinions, solve his own problems, have his own things and, in general, learn to view the world from the point of view of the self'.[36] Indeed, this process begins at a very early age when American parents first encourage their children to be independent and self-reliant. As a result of this process, an American's self-concept usually never merges with any given group. Rather the individual maintains a separate sense of self.[37] To the American, any group, regardless of size, is still no more than a collection of individuals.[38] Groups tend to be formed for specific purposes or tasks and then discarded when their usefulness is over.[39] Because Americans give little true loyalty to groups, their social groups and organizations generally have less coherence than Japanese groups and organizations.

Differing greatly from the American concept of *human being*, the Japanese concept, owing much to Confucianist and Buddhist influences, holds that a human being is, by his very nature, innately and fundamentally a person or individual (人) born connected to, or in relationship with, others (間); he does not exist alone or apart. When these two characters are combined, they produce the Japanese word *ningen* (人間), meaning *human being*. A culture holding this view of human beings would logically place emphasis on interpersonal relations in which mutual dependence, reciprocity, and cooperation played important parts. Indeed, such values are rooted in the cultural dimension called *collectivism*.[40] Japanese values concerning interpersonal relations contribute to the interconnectedness of the eight cultural patterns in Table 3.1. Japanese not only consider it 'brash' for an individual to make definitive decisions regarding himself, they expect deference to the group. Harmonious human relations are valued; nonconfrontive, face-saving communication styles encouraged; and dependency relationships fostered.[41]

Anthropologist Takie Sugiyama Lebra has identified four basic types of Japanese dependency relationships. The first, *dependency on patronage*, is found in asymmetric relationships, such as parent-child, husband-wife, employer-employee, and leader-follower, in which the weaker of the pair is considered dependent on the more powerful. The second, *dependency on attendance*, refers to the inverse of the first in which the person of superior status is dependent on a person of inferior status who serves him in some way but which also binds him in obligation. Yet the superior and the inferior can remain perfectly interdependent without either party losing his respective role status.[42]

The third type of Japanese dependency relationship, *dependency on indulgence*, or *amae*, was first identified by psychiatrist Takeo Doi. In his view, *amae* and related concepts permeate the Japanese language and culture. *Amaeru*, an intransitive verb meaning 'to depend and presume upon another's indulgence or benevolence', refers to *passive dependence*. Although there is no single English equivalent to *amaeru* or *amae*, Doi believes that the *amae* concept is not totally alien to Americans. He suggests that it might be a universal need among all human beings which the Japanese have simply been very thorough about acknowledging and building into their cultural orientation. Americans, who emphasize self-reliance and self-sufficiency, resist such 'dependency needs', as Western psychologists term it.[43] It would be difficult to envision the classic American hero, the cowboy, without conjuring up the various images of the individualistic self-reliance inherent in this heroic type. For Americans, dependency needs are considered signs of weakness and, therefore, undesirable.

Finally, the fourth type of dependence is termed *dependence on pity* or the appeal for empathy. Compared with Americans, who value independence and pursue individualism, the Japanese have less difficulty accepting help and putting themselves at the mercy of another, for the recipient is not looked on as an object of pity. Deeply embedded in the Japanese language and culture, these four types of dependency, Lebra asserts, do not exist independently of one another in real life; rather they are interdependent and fuse together.[44] Certainly a preference for dependence relationships predispose the Japanese to working well within a variety of groups and collectivities, from personal to institutional, from national to international. A predisposition toward dependence relationships also explains, in part, how bilateral trade norms have developed along certain lines. In the immediate postwar years and as late as 1965, the United States and Japan can be said to have been partners in an asymmetrical dependence relationship of the kind described. As the bilateral trade research team of I.M. Destler, Haruhiro Fukui, and Hideo Sato have expressed it:

(The postwar) asymmetrical dependence relationship was consistent with Americans' idea of their country as leader and example to the world; the United States was seen as the forgiving, postwar benefactor of a Japan democratized through American occupation. And the dependence relationship was consistent also with Japanese *amae* psychology, definable roughly as a feeling that a stronger party in a relationship has a particular obligation to protect the other. Also, the inequality of power justified for Japanese the unequal application of trade rules. Since Japan was the weak party, it was fair to seek open access to American and other foreign markets on 'free-trade' grounds, and at the same time to restrict access of others to the Japanese market on 'protectionist' grounds.[45]

Bilateral dynamics, however, have shifted radically, and the old *dependence* relationship is no longer viable. At present, Japan enjoys expanding economic power and prestige, while the United States grapples with issues of apparent economic and social decline. Japanese attitudes toward the United States and Americans seem to be leaning more toward pity and away from admiration and respect, especially when it comes to economic competitiveness and commercial prowess. Some American business and government leaders who deal directly with their Japanese counterparts have recently remarked that arrogance and condescension have begun to replace the humility and respectful politeness that was once a Japanese trademark in their dealings with Americans. Clearly, a new bilateral framework as well as new ways of relating are needed; however, somewhat incompatible communication, decision-making, and negotiating styles, resulting from two dissimilar cultural systems, impede the development of such a framework. Trade negotiations, such as the SII, suggest that perceptual discrepancies and communication barriers continue to bedevil bilateral attempts to resolve the divisive structural and sectoral discrepancies.

A major communication barrier involves attitudes toward the use of language. Americans generally use linguistic skills to clarify, compare and contrast, and test the relative merits of differing views. While they respect the power of words and respond well to eloquent expression, Japanese place far less faith in verbal style and expression, especially when complex and elusive realities are involved. While the preferred speaking and writing style among Japanese is indirect, implicit, and veiled, the preferred style among Americans is direct, explicit, and concise. When Americans want to make a point, they tend to make it at the beginning of a statement, followed by some kind of explication. Japanese, in contrast, generally offer a somewhat lengthy discussion before actually stating the main point, usually at the end of the complete statement.

While Americans are generally uncomfortable with verbal ambiguity, preferring issues 'spelled out in black and white', Japanese feel relatively comfortable with ambiguity, often attaching greater importance to what is implied or left unsaid. Even negative responses are couched in ambiguity; one Japanese linguist has identified at least sixteen ways in which Japanese actually avoid saying *no* directly.[46] While Americans have little trouble with a firm *no* response, they have some difficulty understanding an indirect negative. It has even been suggested that intuition is the instrument of understanding favored by Japanese, and intellect the instrument favored by Americans.[47]

In group decision-making processes, Americans tend to identify, confront, and discuss differences of opinion, a process they believe ultimately yields the best decisions. Whereas Americans tend to favor 'a rhetoric of exclusion', in which differences of opinion are emphasized, Japanese tend to favor 'a rhetoric of inclusion', in which similarities of viewpoint are stressed. Japanese tend to avoid verbal confrontation as group consensus is quietly and methodically pursued.[48] Furthermore, while Japanese prefer formality, understatement, and modest or self-deprecatory remarks, Americans tend toward informality, overstatement, and self-congratulatory remarks. Not surprisingly, approaches to disputes are also distinctive. When difficulties arise, Americans tend to call them to everyone's attention, explain and justify their own behavior, and ask others to be equally frank. Once sources of conflict are identified and responsibility admitted, a compromise acceptable to everyone is sought. Although equally sensitive to difficulties, Japanese tend to promote indirect ways of diffusing such situations without embarrassing or confronting anyone.

Japanese, masters at 'enigmatic utterances' and 'soliloquies of silence',[49] often frustrate Americans who want 'all cards laid on the table'.

The Japanese communication style often leads Americans to conclude that the Japanese are deceptive. Commodore Perry was perhaps the first American to record this impression when he wrote: 'A Japanese. . . never takes offence at being charged with disingenuousness or even with duplicity. One would suppose that they consider it a compliment to be thought tricky and deceitful.'[50] Perry also considered the Japanese masters of polite evasion, foot-dragging, meaningless objections, and extreme preoccupation with and attention to trivia.[51] Americans today still tend to find the Japanese attention to minute detail bothersome. Meanwhile, American attention to broad universal principles, sometimes in conflict with pragmatic and workable solutions, is bothersome to the Japanese. Whereas Americans tend to find Japanese evasive and purposely vague, Japanese find Americans confrontational, abrasive, abrupt, and arrogant.[52]

Americans prefer negotiating in a fairly straightforward, direct fashion. Negotiation sessions are generally viewed as problem-solving exercises, with 'problems the dragons that Americans take joy in slaying'.[53] In the process, Americans tend to gloss quickly over areas of mutual agreement in order to concentrate on each problem or area of disagreement one at a time. Unlike Americans, Japanese prefer to spend more time discussing areas of common agreement before addressing differences. They take an indirect approach to negotiations, often employing pre-negotiating techniques to avoid conflict and direct confrontation within the negotiating session itself.[54]

Michael Blaker, a specialist on the Japanese negotiating style, suggests that distinctive Japanese bargaining habits have remained fairly constant over time. He argues that they 'were not broken by the Japanese surrender, the demise of the emperor system, or the creation of a constitutionally based system of parliamentary democracy'. Indeed, the Japanese have 'displayed a distinctive and enduring negotiating style under widely varying domestic and international conditions'.[55] From Perry to the present, he asserts, the Japanese negotiation approach has been dominated by risk minimization and confrontation avoidance. Japanese generally prefer doing nothing when it is relatively safe to do nothing, acting only when the pressure of events forces them to do something. Because of this 'passive mentality', they often appear hesitant and indecisive to Americans,[56] who much prefer 'taking the bull by the horns', 'taking action', and 'making a change for the better'.

Sources of Divergent American and Japanese Cultural Patterns

Communication, decision-making, and negotiating styles, as well as other behavioral patterns, are absorbed through the home environment, educational system, and religious traditions of the community. In most societies, the family is where members of a given culture first learn how to interact with others and the world at large. A recent study on childrearing practices determined that cultural differences between American and Japanese babies are already observable at the age of three or four months. These become more pronounced and deeply entrenched as children grow into adulthood.[57]

In the case of Japan, it has also been suggested that the traditional *ie*, best translated as *house* or *household*, continues to be a functional model in modern Japanese life. The *ie*, which included the house, property, resources, family members, and even ancestral graves, was a unit of continuity stretching from the distant past to the present. Because the *ie* was considered far more important than the individuals living in it at any given time, it was considered natural for the personalities of individual members to be ignored or sacrificed, if necessary, for the good of the *ie* as a whole.[58] Asymmetrical dependency relationships of the type discussed earlier were part of traditional *ie* life. The expression, *oyabun/kobun*, or *parent-part/child-part*, best describes such relationships in which one more powerful offers benevolence in exchange for the loyalty of one less powerful. *Oyabun/kobun* relationships, found throughout Japanese life, resemble the bond between parent and child. Once such relationships are established, they are normally expected to last for life. The beneficiary is expected to seek out and consult with his benefactor, while the benefactor looks out for and gives advice to the beneficiary. A similar relational pattern, that of *mentor-mentoree*, is often found in Japanese companies between older, more experienced managers and younger, less experienced employees.[59]

New *ie* branches were usually established by younger sons of the household; these remained loyal to, and interconnected with, the primary *ie*. Together they functioned as a legal, political, and economic unit, but with an element of master-servant subordination between the original *ie* and its branches.[60] Finally, the *ie* occupied a certain position in the village status system. As such, Japanese village community life was hierarchical as opposed to the 'flat' village communities of the West, and community solidarity was interwoven with this stratification system. The existence of resources over which the community had a monopoly made cooperative effort necessary. In this sense, traditional Japanese villages can be considered communities of a corporate kind, producing not only relations of dominance between superior and inferior, but also relations of mutual assistance among all community members.[61] Indeed the *ie* system is often used as an analogy for the modern Japanese business enterprise and its network of interconnections with other companies and close relationship with government agencies; it is a system which some believe has affected trade norms with the United States and other industrialized nations.

Not only are cultural values and behavioral patterns learned in the home but also at school. A comparison of American and Japanese educational systems reveals many contrasts. The Japanese educational system is conformist, universally standardized, and highly centralized, whereas the American system tends to be decentralized, diverse, and largely under local jurisdiction. The student body in Japan is largely homogeneous, while, in the United States, it often tends toward heterogeneity in racial composition, religious preference, and cultural-linguistic background. The central values taught in a Japanese school (e.g., playing one's proper role, conformity, group consensus, group harmony, frugality, self-denial, reciprocity) are quite different from those taught in American schools (e.g., expression of one's individuality, equality, equal opportunity, respect for diversity, competitiveness, self-reliance, self-fulfillment). Communication styles learned at home are also reinforced in the schools. In the United States, the ability of every person to act as one's own advocate, to articulate personal opinions persuasively, is cultivated throughout the educational process. The constant encouragement to express one's self, to be heard and felt, promotes a certain assertiveness and propensity for overstatement.[62] Meanwhile, in Japan, modesty of speech and conduct are encouraged, and students are trained to listen to and follow the guidance of their teachers.

At school, Japanese children learn to work harmoniously together in groups, to respect and honor those who are older or of higher rank, and to act with modesty and reserve. Another important concept first learned at home and then reinforced in school, is that of *uchi-soto*, roughly translated as *inside-outside*. *Uchi-soto* includes such references as *our-their*, *our house-their house*, and *ingroup-outgroup*. Japanese children, from early on, learn to associate feelings of security with their particular school, study group, and class. This *uchi-soto* reference (the family, the school, and later on, the workplace) will be life-long. This is not so for Americans, whose connections at school and at work are generally less pronounced, less profound, and less permanent. In Japan, the values learned at home are similar to those learned at school; in the United States, the values learned at home may vary substantially from those learned at school.

The values learned first at home and later in school are also part of each group's religious legacy. The Judeo-Christian tradition unifies major segments of the American population and provides underlying premises that shape U.S. social structure, institutions, laws, and economic system. Out of this ideological heritage comes a deep respect for the independent, self-realizing individual, faithful to one's own inner truth, as the ideal.[63] The American work ethic is often credited to a combination of individualism and activism, legacies of the so-called Protestant work ethic.[64] Some Japan scholars maintain that the role of Confucianism has been the most crucial element in shaping modern Japanese social ethics and economic behavior. Economist Michio Morishima is one who argues that Confucianism is what makes Japanese capitalism different from, and more dynamic than, Western forms of capitalism.[65] Confucianism promotes the ideal of a rational natural world order in which man is but a harmonious element who lives according to principles of loyalty to one's ruler, filial piety to one's father, and adherence to behavior appropriate to one's proper role in society.

Others argue that Confucianism is simply the most apparent or accessible of religious/ethical factors. One of the foremost authorities on Japanese history and culture, sociologist Robert Bellah, takes a more comprehensive approach when he argues that religious/ethical movements of the Tokugawa period (e.g., Kokutai, Mito, Hotoku, Shinshu, and Shingaku), whose core values were already part of the *samurai* code of honor, helped set the stage for Japan's future economic success. Core values of these religious movements, derived from a synthesis of Confucianism, Shintoism, and Buddhism, included absolute loyalty to one's leader, selfless devotion to interests of the polity, frugality, industry, and fulfillment of one's social determined obligations. These religious groups were responsible for spreading the core values to the rest of Japanese society. The Hotoku movement was instrumental in spreading them to the peasants, while the Shingaku movement spread them to the merchant class.[66]

The spread of Tokugawa religious/ethical thought enabled Japan to adopt Western-style industrialization far more readily than China because, unlike China, Japan already possessed strong central political values by the time industrialization became an option. While loyalty was as important a value in China as it was in Japan, it did not permeate the whole of society as it did in Japan. In Japan loyalty was an ideal which came to be shared by all classes and was directed to the polity as a whole, whereas in China it remained confined to smaller groups, such as the family or local community. The spread of Tokugawa religious/ethical thought also contributed to Japan's political and economic rationalization. Not only was there a high commitment to the polity, there was also a commitment to 'this-world' asceticism and frugality, commitments which have continued into the present time. Thus Tokugawa religions provided both the motivation and the ethic which made possible the high rate of accumulation and sacrifice that Japan's economic modernization was to require; that is, high production and low consumption rates. In this way, argues Bellah, the Japanese religions served as the functional equivalent of Weber's Protestant ethic.

Finally, a number of scholars have observed that the mass media in highly developed countries like the United States and Japan have tended to take over socialization functions formerly fulfilled by the family, the school, and the religious community. Indeed the mass media, especially television, may now be regarded among the most important contributors to a society's general knowledge and understanding of issues as well as to the building of a consensus. In other words, the media play key roles in shaping the attitudes, perceptions, and opinions of the populace in their country of operation, which are generally in keeping with the cultural values and norms of each society.

Implications of Divergent Cultural Patterns

Culture has been defined and described, comparative sketches of American and Japanese normative and behavioral tendencies presented, and their sources summarized. Just as cultural factors shape American and Japanese values and behavioral tendencies; these in turn, influence national organizational, investment, productivity, and consumer patterns, which ultimately affect bilateral economic and trade dynamics. The next chapter builds further on this discussion by describing how cultural factors have both shaped, and been shaped by, differing American and Japanese political-economic institutions, business enterprise organizations and arrangements, and government-industry relational dynamics. Also described is the likely impact these have on bilateral trade norms and trade imbalances. Because the Structural Impediments Initiative (SII) addresses these issues, a summary of what occurred during the SII talks concludes the discussion. The SII reveals the complexity of institutional and structural differences between Japan and the United States and suggests the likely existence of Japan-U.S. perceptual and attributional discrepancies.

Notes

1   Krauthammer, C. (1983 August 15) 'Deep Down, We're All Alike, Right? Wrong', *Time*, p. 32.

2   Naitoh, M. (1980) 'Overview: The Bases for Conflict and Cooperation in U.S.-Japanese
     Relations', Chapter 1 in D. Tasca (ed) *U.S.-Japanese Economic Relations: Cooperation,
     Competition, and Confrontation*, pp. 1-17. Masahisa Naitoh, educated as an attorney,
     served in various capacities within MITI, played a major role in bilateral negotiations in
     the mid- to late 1970s, and has written numerous articles on Japanese industrial policy
     and bilateral relations.

3   Cohen, J. B. (1949) *Japan's Economy in War and Reconstruction*, p. 80; for detailed
     accounts of misperceptions, miscommunications, deleterious foreign policies, and events
     which culminated in World War II, see D. Borg and S. Okamoto (eds) (1973) *Pearl
     History as History: Japanese-American Relations, 1931-1941*.

4   The rice, automotive, and semiconductor sector disputes are discussed in greater detail
     in Chapter 8.

5   Fisher, G. (1988) *Mindsets: The Role of Culture and Perception in International
     Relations*; Glen Fisher, an experienced former Foreign Service Officer, academician, and
     researcher, argues that culturally-based mindsets – ways of perceiving, reasoning and
     viewing the world – determine how events are evaluated and decisions made in
     international relations. Fisher also offers suggestions for diminishing mindset rigidities
     and their unintended negative effects.

6   Doi, T. (1981) *The Anatomy of Dependence* (English translation of *Amae no Kozo* (1971)
     by J. Bester), pp. 48-50. Doi points out, for example, that 'it is evident that when she
     (Benedict) states that the culture of guilt (the United States) places certain emphasis on
     inner standards of conduct whereas the culture of shame (Japan) places emphasis on
     outward standards of conduct she has the feeling that the former is superior to the latter'.
     He goes on to show how shame and guilt are not mutually exclusive but often occur
     simultaneously. What is characteristic about the Japanese sense of guilt, Doi writes, is
     that it shows itself most sharply when the individual suspects his behavior or action will
     result in betraying or hurting the group to which he belongs. He concludes on p. 50 that
     'the Japanese sense of guilt, thus, shows a very clear cut structure, commencing as it does
     with betrayal and ending in apology; it represents, in fact, the very prototype of the sense
     of guilt, and Benedict's failure to see this can only be attributed to her cultural
     prejudice'.

7   See also T. Doi (1986) *The Anatomy of Self: The Individual Versus Society* (English
     translation of *Omote to Ura* (1985) by M. Harbison); W. Caudill (1973) 'The Influence
     of Social Structure and Culture on Human Behavior in Japan and America', *Journal of
     Nervous and Mental Disorders*; J. Hendry (1987) *Understanding Japanese Society*; T.
     S. Lebra (1976) *Japanese Patterns of Behavior*; H. Nakamura (1964) *Ways of Thinking
     of Eastern Peoples*; E. Stewart (1972) *American Cultural Patterns: A Cross-Cultural
     Perspective*.

8   Caudill, W. and H. Weinstein (1974) 'Maternal Care and Infant Behavior in Japan and
     America' in T. S. Lebra and W. Lebra (eds) *Japanese Culture and Behavior*, pp.
     225-276. The mechanism of the ingroup-outgroup affective response to cultural
     differences is taken up in Chapter Five.

9   *Culture-specific* studies focus on a single culture, *culture-comparative* studies focus on
     the similarities and differences between two or more cultures, and *culture-interactive*
     studies examine what occurs when members of two or more cultures come into contact
     with one another. Of the three, *culture-interactive* studies are the most comprehensive,
     for they build on the first two by contributing a dynamic cross-cultural, interrelational

perspective.

10 Chalmers Johnson, an expert on Japan's industrial policies, is one of many political economists who argue that, while it is probable Japanese basic values differ from American values, explanations of social behavior in terms of basic cultural values and tendencies should be reserved only for the 'residue of behavior that cannot be explained in more economical ways'. Johnson argues that cultural arguments are 'overgeneralized' and tend to 'cut off rather than advance serious research'. See C. Johnson (1982) *MITI and the Japanese Miracle: The Growth of Industrial Policy, 1925-1975*, pp. 8-9.

11 For more thorough discussions of major theoretical approaches to culture, see M. Singer (1968) 'Culture', *International Encyclopedia of Social Science*, vol. 3, pp. 527-543; R. Keesing (1974) 'Theories of Culture', *Annual Review of Anthropology*, vol. 3, pp. 73-97.

12 Elkins, D. and R. Simeon (1979) 'A Cause in Search of Its Effect, or What Does Political Culture Explain?' in *Comparative Politics*, pp. 137-138.

13 Walker, R. (1990) 'The Concept of Culture in the Theory of International Relations' in J. Chay (ed) *Culture and International Relations*, p. 8.

14 Lane, R. (1992) 'Political Culture: Residual Category or General Theory?', *Comparative Political Studies*, vol. 25, 3, pp. 364-365.

15 Kluckhohn, C. (1951) 'The Study of Culture' in D. Lerner and H. Lasswell (eds) *The Policy Sciences*, p. 86.

16 Hofstede, G. (1984) *Culture's Consequences: International Differences in Work-Related Values*, pp. 14-16.

17 Ibid., pp. 22-23.

18 Ibid.

19 Ibid.; for a discussion of a political cultural model of change, see H. Eckstein (1988) 'A Culturalist Theory of Political Change', *American Political Science Review*, vol. 82, 3, pp. 789-803.

20 Drucker, P. (1992) *Managing for the Future*, p. 192.

21 For a discussion of horizontal and vertical societies and groups, see C. Nakane (1973) *Japanese Society*, pp. 23-38.

22 Mizutani, O. (1981) *Japanese: The Spoken Language in Japanese Life*, pp. 121-122.

23 Barnland, D. (1989) *Communicative Styles of Japanese and Americans*, pp. 30-39.

24 Fallows, J. (1989) *More Like Us: Making America Great Again*, pp. 48-66. Perhaps herein lies the reason for the apparent dearth of precise, well-documented cultural analyses of the United States. It is simply too large, diverse, and mutable to analyze with as much qualitative precision as Japan. Therefore, analyses of American culture usually take one of three basic forms: demographic statistical studies, anecdotal accounts based largely on interviews, and interpretive essays.

25 Ibid., p. 51.

26 Naitoh, M. (1980) p. 3. Notable in this quotation is Naitoh's choice of words (e.g., *in self-defense* and *wholly alien*).

27 Reischauer, E. (1965) *The United States and Japan*, p. 150.

28 Barnland, D. (1989) p. 32.

29 Reischauer, E. (1965) p. 150.

30 Barnland, D. (1989) pp. 38-39; the author also points out that the rewards accrue to the group rather than the individual.

31   Dore, R. P. (1987) *Taking Japan Seriously: A Confucian Perspective on Leading Economic Issues*, p. 245.

32   Barnland, D. (1989) p. 32.

33   Hofstede, G. (1984) pp. 148-175. According to G. Hofstede (1991) *Cultures and Organizations: Software of the Mind*, p. 261, *individualism* describes any society in which the ties between individuals are loose and everyone is expected to look after oneself and one's own immediate family only.

34   Tocqueville, A. de (1945) *Democracy in America*, vol. 2.

35   Bellah, et al. (1985) *Habits of the Heart: Individualism and Commitment in American Life*, p. 142.

36   Stewart, E. (1972) *American Cultural Patterns: A Cross-Cultural Perspective*, p. 70.

37   Caudill, W. and H. Weinstein (1974) pp. 225-276.

38   Stewart, E. (1972) p. 70.

39   Austin, L. (1975) *Saints and Samurai: The Political Culture of the American and Japanese Elites*, pp. 139-140.

40   According to G. Hofstede (1991) pp. 260-261, *collectivism* describes any society in which people from birth onwards are integrated into strong, cohesive ingroups that, throughout people's lifetimes, continue to protect them in exchange for unquestioning loyalty. Such ingroups provide their members with a sense of identity.

41   Stewart, E. (1972) p. 34. It is important to note that while harmonious relationships is a Japanese cultural ideal, it is not always a reality. For an excellent discussion of harmony versus conflict in Japanese society, see Krauss, E., T. Rohlen, and P. Steinhoff (1984) 'Conflict and Resolution in Postwar Japan' in Krauss, et al (eds) *Conflict in Japan*, pp. 377-397.

42   Lebra, T. S. (1976) *Japanese Patterns of Behavior*, pp. 50-66.

43   Doi, T. (1981) pp. 28-35; Doi argues that lexical items constituting the nucleus of the *amae* concept reflect the mentality of the Japanese. Takeo Doi (1985) acknowledges in *The Anatomy of Self: The Individual Versus Society* (English translation of *Omote to Ura*) that his view is based on the Sapir-Whorf hypothesis in linguistics.

44   Lebra, T. S. (1976) p. 66.

45   Destler, I. M. et al (1979) *The Textile Wrangle: Conflict in Japanese-American Relations, 1969-1971*, p. 25.

46   Ueda, K. (1974) 'Sixteen Ways to Avoid Saying 'No' in Japan', J. Condon and M. Saito (eds) *Intercultural Encounters with Japan: Communication-Contact and Conflict*, pp. 186-189. See also M. Imai (1981) *16 Ways to Avoid Saying No* and (1975) *Never Take Yes for an Answer*.

47   Barnland, D. (1989) p. 42.

48   Ibid., pp. 32-33; Graham, J. and Y. Sano (1984) *Smart Bargaining: Doing Business with the Japanese*, pp. 13-14.

49   Barnland, D. (1989) p. 191.

50   Pineau, T. (ed) (1968) *The Japanese Expedition 1852-1854: The Personal Journal of Commodore Matthew C. Perry*, p. 214.

51   Ibid., pp. 174-240.

52   Holland, H. (1992) *Japan Challenges America: Managing an Alliance in Crisis*, pp. 190-202.

53   Fisher, G. (1980) *International Negotiation: A Cross-Cultural Perspective*, p. 18.

54   The Japanese negotiation style shares similar ground with the negotiation approach proposed by R. Fisher and W. Ury (1981) *Getting to Yes: Negotiating Agreements Without Giving In* and R. Fisher and S. Brown (1988) *Getting Together: Building Relationships As We Negotiate.*

55   Blaker, M. (1977b) 'Probe, Push, and Panic: The Japanese Tactical Style in International Negotiations' in R. Scalapino (ed), *The Foreign Policy of Modern Japan*, p. 56. For further discussion of Japan's postwar negotiation style, see the cited article; for an examination of Japan's prewar patterns, see M. Blaker (1977a) *Japanese International Negotiating Style.*

56   Ibid., pp. 98-99. Recently, it should be noted, some Japanese negotiators have begun to deal with American negotiators in a more direct, confrontive style, thus breaking with cultural expectation.

57   Caudill, W. and H. Weinstein (1974) pp. 264-265; for more detailed information on pre-school Japanese children, see J. Hendry (1986) *Becoming Japanese: The World of the Pre-School Child.*

58   Fukutake, T. (1989) *The Japanese Social Structure: Its Evolution in the Modern Century* (translation and foreword by R. Dore (1981) *Nihon Shakai no Kozo*) p. 28.

59   Hendry, J. (1988) *Understanding Japanese Society*, pp. 21-35.

60   Ibid.

61   Fukutake, T. (1989) pp. 6, 35-36.

62   Barnland, D. (1989) p. 38.

63   Ibid., p. 37.

64   Naitoh, M. (1980) 'American and Japanese Industrial Structures: A Sectoral Comparison' in D. Tasca (ed) *U.S.-Japanese Economic Relations: Cooperation, Competition, and Confrontation*, pp. 73-74.

65   See M. Morishima (1978 June) 'The Power of Confucian Capitalism', *The Observer.* Morishima, trained at Kyoto and Oxford, is an economist affiliated with the London School of Economics and Political Science. For a more comprehensive discussion of this perspective, see Dore, R. (1987) *Taking Japan Seriously: A Confucian Perspective on Leading Economic Issues.*

66   Bellah, R. (1957) *Tokugawa Religion: The Cultural Roots of Modern Japan.*

4 The Institutional and Structural Factors

From a structural perspective, the current friction in U.S. economic relations, can be described as a *grinding of gears*.[1]

Ellen L. Frost

Culture has been identified by some as the internal organizational, unifying factor of the nation-state.[2] It might also be considered the internal organizational, unifying factor of national political economy.[3] For just as a nation-state's cultural assumptions are by necessity deeply imbued with economic and political motives and conditions, so conversely is its political economy shaped by cultural assumptions and tendencies.[4] Not only is a nation's political economy significantly shaped by culture, but it must also operate according to the inherent logic of the particular cultural milieu in which it continues to evolve and function. As such, culture both informs and lends integrity to a nation's political-economic institutions, business arrangements, and commercial policies and practices. In other words, culturally determined assumptions, values, and behavioral tendencies can be considered foundational ingredients of a nation's industrial organization, management style, and workforce characteristics as well as the formation of relational arrangements between and among its business enterprises, banking institutions, and governmental agencies.

Many economists downplay the role of culture, preferring instead to emphasize the importance of rational choice in explaining individual and group economic behavior. Others, most notably anthropologists, assert the primacy of culture in providing a fundamental framework for all social action, including economic behavior. Still others, particularly political scientists and sociologists, tend to stress the importance of institutions in setting the parameters for political and economic behavior. However, all three – rational choice, culture, and institutional structure – are important and 'coexist in an interwoven relationship of complexity'.[5] As political economist Daniel Okimoto (1989) points out,

Culture conditions rational choice and permeates institutional structure; rationality and institutional structures, in turn, give contextual shape to the ways in which individuals and groups draw upon and enact cultural values. The complexity of the interaction means that. . . culture plays a central role in political-economic behavior.[6]

Because American and Japanese cultural assumptions, normative tendencies, and behavioral patterns have differed so profoundly, the 'internal organizational, unifying factor' of culture has logically yielded two substantially divergent approaches to political economic development. The role of culture in Japan's political-economy is especially noteworthy, not only because of 'differences in the configuration of values from those found in most Western capitalist countries', but also because of the way Japanese culture 'reinforces the maze of delicately meshed, interdependent institutions without leading to costly rigidities and economic inefficiencies'.[7] Concerning Japan's government bureaucracies and administrative elite, another analyst has written that 'one sees in the Japanese record a powerful confirmation of the tenacity of culture over structure'.[8] In yet another study, this time on Japan's influential trading companies, the *sogo shosha,* culture has been used as a 'major artifact of analysis'. Although the *sogo shosha* system has deep roots in the culture and society of Japan, this cultural heritage has been carefully adapted to serve the needs generated by its own business situation.[9] And so it is with other institutions and organizations of Japan's political-economic system – they are all shaped to some extent by Japanese culture and society as they also shape and mold this legacy to serve their own objectives and needs.

Perspectives such as these underpin the contents of this chapter on institutional and structural factors. The early sections of the chapter deal with how the cultural soils in which American and Japanese political-economic institutions and business enterprise arrangements have taken root, developed, and matured, have likewise supported diverging national economic ideologies and approaches to economic planning and policy-making. Together with the cultural tendencies of their respective populations, these have nurtured the formation of structural discrepancies and trade asymmetries, which underlie the chronic trade imbalances.

The model in Figure 4.1 suggests how each nation's cultural and institutional factors interact and function in tandem so as to generate asymmetrical bilateral trade dynamics and structural discrepancies (e.g., divergent national savings and investment rates, differing import market structures).[10] This dynamic, ongoing process is both subtle and pervasive. It begins with the normative and behavioral characteristics of each nation's

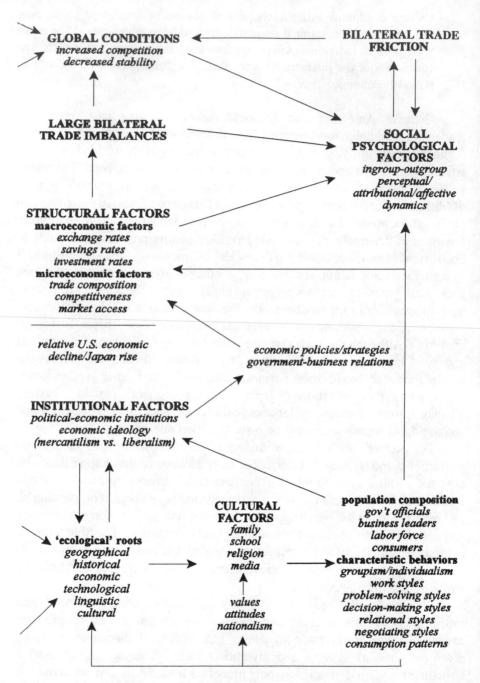

Figure 4.1   Japan-U.S. Trade Friction: The Causal Factors

population, since it is ultimately the people of a nation who pursue a national economic ideology; develop government institutions; create and carry out economic plans and policies; organize, manage, and work within business enterprises; innovate and control product quality; spend, invest, and save money. Conversely, the characteristic tendencies of each nation's population are also shaped or reinforced by the prevailing national economic ideology; political-economic institutions and policies; and organizational, managerial, and functional styles and norms of the domestic workplace.

As a result of these differing national realities, American and Japanese leaders and their respective constituencies tend to perceive the same reality in somewhat incompatible ways. American and Japanese academic analyses, media accounts, and opinion poll statistics all suggest that a bilateral perceptual gap concerning the causes, consequences, and cures of trade problems exists, and that it is both wide and deep.[11] On the one hand, Japanese writers tend to emphasize the macroeconomic causes of large trade imbalances, especially U.S. economic policy and decline issues. They cite the failures of American business in areas like productivity and quality control. On the other hand, American writers tend to focus on Japanese business practices, both internal and external, and the structural barriers to Japan's import markets.[12] In response to allegations of closed markets, Japanese writers often bring up episodes of U.S. protectionism while downplaying their own.[13] As these diverging perspectives might suggest, differing economic institutions and traditions and their perceptual consequences can 'work to exacerbate what are already extremely complicated diplomatic relations'.[14]

The final section of the chapter overviews the 1989-1990 Structural Impediments Initiative (SII), a series of bilateral talks during which Japanese and American leaders identified, and pledged to address, the institutional and structural issues thought to be causing the large trade imbalances. The SII offers an opportunity not only to witness the complexity of institutional-structural issues involved in bilateral economic relations but also to observe how each nation's institutional realities complicate bilateral diplomatic efforts to resolve real issues. The SII suggests how politics and economics overlap and influence each other as well as how cultural tendencies shape and inform both.[15] What is not clear is the extent to which the participants are aware of this and merely use it to their advantage.

Economic Ideologies and Approaches to Economic Development

Both countries claim to be democratic, capitalistic nation-states; their respective national leaders espouse similar *laissez-faire* economic principles and ideals. Additionally, successful American and Japanese business ventures both reveal entrepreneurial initiative, vim, and vigor at home and an aggressively competitive spirit abroad, behaviors in keeping with the principles of economic liberalism.   However, the oligopolistic behavior of Japanese industrial conglomerates like the *keiretsu,* the application of strong industrial policies of governmental agencies like MITI, the collection of relatively closed domestic markets (e.g., rice, automotive, semiconductor) in combination with aggressive trade practices abroad (e.g., automotive, semiconductor) are much more highly suggestive of a German-style mercantilism than of an American-style liberalism.[16]

Even though Japan and the United States share certain goals and values as democratic capitalistic systems, they approach the problems of industrial development from opposite directions, most especially because of conflicting perspectives regarding questions of individual freedom *(individualism)* and social harmony *(collectivism).* This difference would logically give rise to contrasts between the two political-economies, between the American bias in favor of freely operating market forces and the Japanese preference for economic planning and goal setting through the mechanism of consensus.[17] Differences in industrial structure are founded in the divergent social values of the two cultures, especially Japan's emphasis on collectivistic values and America's emphasis on individualistic values.[18]

Japan scholar Ronald Dore has named the United States an 'extreme exemplar of the genus *individualist Western economy*'. Meanwhile, Dore writes, Japan demonstrates how very efficient economic organizations can also be built along 'very unindividualist lines'.[19] Acknowledging that Japan's economic success is due in part to intervention by an increasingly developmentalist state to improve international competitiveness, Dore also credits Japan's national tendencies toward a hierarchy of enterprises and the 'meritocracy' hiring of employees according to hierarchical rankings of schools and universities attended. In addition to the economic and social importance of not allowing market forces alone to determine allocation or outcome, he also credits culturally shaped mechanisms which promote strong interpersonal relations and greater economic efficiency as well. The Japanese ability to develop compromise mechanisms, for example, is not a late-development effect according to Dore. Rather, as the result of long-standing preferences for obligated, trustful relationships, it is a cultural effect.[20]

Industrial policy and relatively closed import markets can be considered natural extensions of Japan's historical experience in much the same way that America's lack of industrial policy and relatively open markets are extensions of the U.S. experience. These foster national predispositions for pursuing a particular economic orientation, developing certain political-economic institutions, and developing and pursuing specific economic plans, policies, and procedures. This difference should not be surprising given the island-contained, resource-limited national experience of Japan versus the expansive, resource-abundant national experience of the United States. Early in their long history, Japanese learned to live and work cooperatively and harmoniously with others to ensure their own and their community's survival in an often hostile, unpredictable physical environment.[21]

Meanwhile, the relatively open, nonrestrictive physical and social environment of the United States, whose national experience is rooted in economic abundance and individualistic effort, would be expected to give rise to organizational tendencies in which bonds between entities of all sizes would be relatively loose and provisional. In the United States, individual effort combined with a minimum of governmental interference has generally been considered the best means of achieving economic success and prosperity.[22] Indeed, U.S. political culture 'frowns upon close ties between government and any interest group – including business'.[23] While culture is not an 'explanatory panacea', the political economies of Japan and the United States are clearly informed by 'a complex of historical, social, and geographical factors' in such a way that they differ substantially and importantly.[24]

Government Institutions, Government-Business Relations, and Policy-Making

As far as economic policy-making entities are concerned, American government institutional structures and functions have been characterized as relatively weak and fragmented, while Japan's have been viewed as relatively strong and cohesive. Japan has followed a tradition in which government has had a far greater and more substantial influence over microeconomic policies and decisions than has been the case in the United States. In Japan, government intervention in market-related matters has generally been viewed as necessary and, therefore, legitimate; in the United States, however, it has generally been viewed as unwanted and, therefore, unwarranted. The Japanese government's greater disposition to act on the basis of anticipated outcomes sets it apart from the American government, which has tended to deal primarily with failures only after they have occurred. Some political analysts have characterized Japan's economic policy as more proactive, integrated, and focused on the market success of specific industrial sectors than U.S. economic policy, which they have characterized as more reactive, *ad hoc*, and market-failure focused, but with little reference to specific industry goals.[25]

While government-business relationships in Japan tend to be collaborative, those of the United States tend to be adversarial. Perhaps because it 'carries heavier ideological and institutional baggage' than Japan, the U.S. government until recently has tended to function more as 'regulator of business behavior' than as 'booster of commercial success'. At times, American government bureaucracies with greater power to influence the commercial aspects of certain sectors, especially those related to defense and agriculture, have pursued objectives unrelated to the international commercial success of American industries.[26] The two key commerce-related governmental entities, Japan's Ministry of International Trade and Industry (MITI) and America's Department of Commerce, exemplify two very different political economic institutional traditions, shaped by and representing two very different political economic ideologies, and executing two very different kinds of economic policy agendas. Differing from Chalmers Johnson (1982) and other writers who emphasize the vision and power of MITI as the central explanation for Japan's 'economic miracle' and competitive challenge to the United States, Daniel Okimoto (1989) casts MITI in the broader context of the complex system within which it operates. The characteristics of Japan's industrial organization, distinctive cultural factors, and the LDP-dominated political system are all relevant to understanding how and why Japanese capitalism differs from that which developed in the United States.[27]

Okimoto writes that the Japanese government's power seems 'embedded' in the public-private sector's extensive 'structure of interdependence.' Its varied but crucial functions within this interdependent structure include communication, coordination, collective goal-setting, resource mobilization, conflict resolution, and interest aggregation. MITI has achieved what it did with industrial policy by consulting widely with private sector groups, taking their views and interests fully into account, and arriving at a carefully crafted consensus. The Japanese government's power, therefore, has emerged more out of a complex network of interrelationships and 'voluntary' arrangements than out of a framework of legal authority or the threat of coercive sanctions as tends to be the case in the United States.[28] MITI has played a far more active role in targeting crucial sectors, getting sufficient financing for those sectors, and protecting the domestic market from foreign competition than the Department of Commerce. MITI has encouraged the substantially 'closed system' of corporate networks, particularly the way in which companies organize into groups (e.g., *keiretsu*), condone intercorporate stockholding, allow close banking-business ties, promote linkage among critical industries, and 'guide' various kinds of business endeavors.[29] Indeed, much of what is viewed as standard operating procedures in Japan would probably be disallowed under U.S. antitrust laws.

In choosing which industries to emphasize at a particular time, MITI's objective has always been to move to industries with high technology content and potentially large mass markets. A second objective has been to promote industries that have ripple effects on other sectors of the economy, while a third has been to favor industries that lead to further increases of knowledge.[30] While historically the U.S. government has placed greatest importance on promoting industries which enhance American military dominance and space exploration, the Japanese government, particularly through the efforts of MITI, has placed greatest priority on promoting industrial structures which enhance Japan's global economic competitiveness. These cooperative, some would say collusive, arrangements have worked toward limiting U.S. access to those markets in Japan while, at the same time, promoting Japanese penetration of foreign markets.[31]

Although the American Occupation gave Japan its Fair Trade Commission, neither this agency nor Japan's antitrust laws have ever functioned the way U.S. authorities had envisioned that they would. To restrain excessive competition, Japan developed an elaborate set of measures which necessitated close cooperation between industry and government. Policy was set and then implemented with the constant participation of, and consultation with, the private sector. The Japanese government has promoted the stable, solid structure of Japanese industry and has worked to ensure its success, most especially by reducing risk and lowering the cost of capital. Some have even argued that, for Japanese government agencies, especially MITI, trade has been *the* national security issue, whereas for U.S. agencies, trade traditionally has been secondary to national security issues.[32] Japan's industrial policies have also controlled the activities of foreign multinational corporations, especially those which would directly compete with key targeted industries, an activity which the U.S. government participates in only under conditions of perceived national security threat. Although MITI's efforts have often been hampered by the frequent opposition of other ministries jealous of their own jurisdictions, MITI has arguably been the most powerful, influential economic policy institution in the world, with the possible exception of the European Commission.[33]

While trade policy is fragmented in most countries, it is unusually dispersed in the United States, with rival political parties often controlling different parts of the trade apparatus. The trade policies of most major trading states are driven, to a certain degree, by *laissez-faire* principles, but few are to the extent of the United States, where government-business relations have been, until recently, uneasy at best, adversarial at worst. The trade policies of many countries have an *ad hoc,* 'muddle-through' aspect, but rarely has government policy been more reactive and driven by random events than in the United States.[34]

Unlike the United States, the official Japanese attitudes towards trade were from the very first those of restriction and control.[35] The strength and cohesiveness of Japan's trade policy-making versus the weakness and fragmented quality of its American equivalent can be explained on the basis of institutional structural and functional differences. In Japan, MITI is perhaps the single unifying power, while a total of eleven government bodies play important roles in the making U.S. trade policy. These are the Congress; the U.S. Trade Representative; the Council of Economic Advisers; the National Security Council; the Departments of Agriculture, Commerce, Defense, State, and the Treasury; the U.S. Embassy in Tokyo; and even the Central Intelligence Agency. Neither the Department of Commerce nor the Office of Trade Representative is involved in such important matters as currency exchange rates (the domain of the Treasury Department); economic summit meetings (attended only by the President, Secretary of State, and Secretary of the Treasury); antitrust issues; and National Security Council deliberations.[36]

The Department of Commerce, however, controls many of the tools which an integrated U.S. trade strategy would require. Responsible for administering much of America's trade policy, such as antidumping and antisubsidy laws, it staffs the commercial sections of U.S. embassies, licenses exports of high technology goods, recommends to the President which industries should be protected for purposes of national security, and promotes U.S. exports. However, its tools to promote exports are limited. Although the U.S. Trade Representative is responsible for developing trade policy, the Department of Commerce is responsible for administering much of it. The development of a comprehensive U.S. trade policy agenda is made more difficult by this dispersion of authority. Little coordination occurs because of the splintering of responsibility and the limited coordinator role of the U.S. Trade Representative. In addition to the frequent 'turf battles', as each agency tries to make its own trade policy, enormous amounts of time and effort are consumed in maneuvering among the various agencies.[37]

The conflicts among U.S. agencies also reflects the 'disarray' of Congress and the lack of coherence in the American approach to trade. Congress lacks any concept of trade as part of an integrated economic policy aimed at ensuring the long-term American prosperity and power; it thus organizes itself to deal with the parts, not the whole. At least seven Congressional committees have some kind of trade oversight authority. While one committee writes a law assigning responsibility for trade promotion to the Department of Commerce, another gives trade policy authority for developing trade policy to the U.S. Trade Representative, and little effort is made to link the two.[38]

Even though Japanese ministries and American departments are both staffed by career civil servants, the top U.S. positions go to approximately 3,000 political appointees, whereas in Japan most top positions are held by senior career officers. One of the disadvantages of the American staffing practice is that the average term of office is about two years and, as a result, U.S. officials are always 'in training'. This is a disadvantage in negotiations with Japanese professionals whose tenure is far longer. A second disadvantage is that internal communication, *esprit de corps,* and policy coordination suffer as members compete for supremacy in policy-making, a tendency exacerbated by the limited tenure of office. Third, the institutional memory bank is either short or non-existent; this produces a lack of continuity. Finally, ignorance and division among personnel is reportedly rampant.[39]

Because of the dispersal of U.S. trade authority, American negotiating strength is weakened because Japanese have often played on the divisions between the various U.S. agencies in often successful efforts to divide and conquer. Japanese agencies have turf battles, too, and sometimes on a far greater scale than American agencies because of the greater power of Japan's ministries. In trade negotiations, however, the Japanese side is generally more united than the American side. This occurs largely because responsibilities, which in the United States are divided among many agencies, are usually united under the single umbrella of MITI. Last but not least, the Japanese negotiator has had no overriding national security concerns as the American negotiator so often has had.[40]

Industrial Organizations and Functions

Modern business enterprises are generally complex entities composed of investors, managers, workers, banks, and unions that depend on managerial strategies for effective use of capital, technology, workforce, and marketing strategies. A company's success or failure is determined by the ways in which these elements are combined in response to a given competitive environment. Levels of risk and return are established that either encourage or discourage investment and economic growth. Business enterprises tend to manifest organizational and management patterns, decision-making processes and work habits, and business practices in keeping with the cultural tendencies of their countries of origin. In other words, a business enterprise is not an isolated phenomenon but operates within the cultural context of a particular nation. Japanese enterprises exhibit considerable uniformity in their organizational pattern, a pattern which differs substantially from that of American enterprises. Although Japanese companies, labor unions, government agencies, and financial institutions have all been influenced by Western models, Japan's own national legacy has determined the degree and kind. It is difficult to determine exactly where the Japanese contribution ends and the Western begins, for the Western influences are soon adapted to Japanese purposes. The Japanese business enterprise exemplifies the myriad of ways traditional patterns of meaning can vigorously endure and remain vitally operative in the present.[41]

In Japan, individual discipline, conformism, and hard work, together with group effort, harmony, and reciprocity, have produced a workforce which is cost-effective, committed, and well trained. Consequently, Japanese workers are highly productive and put out items of generally high quality. The tendency toward group work and group study as well as strong intra-company, inter-company, and government-business linkages and collaborations in the workplace are believed to have increased Japan's economic competitiveness and clout. National preplanning and societal cohesiveness are also believed to have contributed to Japan's economic success.[42]

Part of this cohesiveness is fostered by Japan's *keiretsu* system. When W. W. Lockwood (1954) described the prewar *zaibatsu* system, he might just have well been writing about the postwar *keiretsu*:

> Corporate action came naturally to Japanese. The great combines employed all the latest financial devices for concentrating business power, but their prominence in modern Japan was itself an expression of old traditions of authority and teamwork. So, too, were their close and mutually dependent relations with the government.[43]

Just as a Japanese company is composed of various work units and sections, each having its place within a hierarchical scheme, so the company has its place in the hierarchy of companies belonging to a particular industry. Each member enterprise functions as a unit within the nation's industrial and commercial activities. Each tends to be narrowly specialized, engaging in a particular line or a few closely related ventures. This differs from the large American firm, which tends to be less specialized and more diversified than its Japanese counterpart. Japanese industrial organization, or 'society of industry', circumscribes the organization and administration of each company holding a position within the 'society of industry' hierarchy.[44]

Nor do Japanese banks and investors function like their American counterparts either. Japan, known for its high rate of household savings, redirects such funds to business enterprises. Not only have companies often relied heavily on bank loans to meet their need for capital, but banks have also bought stock in companies to which they have made loans. Therefore, the relationships between banks and businesses have been close and interdependent. Such interrelationships not only include same-industry networking, but also intercorporate stockholding and subcontracting networks. In this way, the various organizations of the 'banking-industrial complex', work interdependently to reduce risks and uncertainties, make smooth adjustments to fluctuations in business cycles, and foster solidly long-term relationships. This arrangement helps give the Japanese economy its stability, flexibility, and dynamism.[45]

Macroeconomic and Microeconomic Patterns

Structural factors, which are fostered by each nation's unique cultural legacy and institutional environment, include discrepant national macroeconomic and microeconomic realities. Because fluctuating macroeconomic conditions within both economies affect bilateral economic relations, many economists interested in Japan-U.S. trade friction have focused on issues like exchange rates and national savings and investment patterns.[46] These are also said to affect national production, trade, and consumption volumes, which ultimately contribute to a nation's trade balance. Japan's national savings and investment rates, composed of household, corporate, and government savings and investment patterns, are higher than those of America. Most notable among the savings and investment discrepancies is America's enormous national budget deficit.

In addition to aggregate trade and financial dynamics, other economists focus on microeconomic factors, such as sectoral competitiveness levels (e.g., output quantity, quality, and kind), composition of trade, and market access. Sectoral competitiveness is determined by factors like the quality and abundance of technology, natural resources, labor, and capital available for research and development. Although Japan and the United States are highly competitive in a variety of high-technology, high-value sectors, approximately $4.5 billion of the 1992 bilateral trade imbalance consisted of compact disc players, video cameras, and numerically controlled machine tools that are simply no longer produced in the United States. These items continue to account for about 3 percent of the U.S bilateral trade deficit and its inflexibility.

Yet other items (e.g., semiconductors, computers, telecommunications equipment, satellites) are sectors in which the United States is still highly competitive. Structural access issues for these are of concern, as they are for other sectors (e.g., agricultural, automotive), because Japanese non-tariff trade barriers are believed to contribute importantly to current trade imbalance levels.[47]

Many analysts believe that Japan's competitive advantage in world markets has been attained by the concerted efforts of Japanese government and industry, together with failures by U.S. business and government to respond.[48] Indeed, the Japanese competitive challenge has been systematic in a specific set of industries, as Japan's policies and industrial structure have shaped the environment within which Japanese firms have developed their competitive strengths and strategies. Thus, the removal of constraints and the creation of opportunities associated with challenging American technical and market leadership have paved the way for the international success of Japanese firms.[49]

Although Japanese tariffs and quotas are now generally low if exceptions like rice are ignored, subtle impediments remain. Although these and other informal barriers are extremely difficult to quantify, American companies do experience real problems in exporting to Japan. Although some progress has been made in negotiating away these nontariff barriers, many still remain quietly, but powerfully, intact.[50] By comparing import-penetration ratios (ratio of imports to domestic consumption) in the manufacturing sector, some analysts have determined that informal trade barriers (including all transparent border measures that directly or indirectly limit imports), have been in effect in Japan.[51] Informal barriers include administrative guidance; customs proceedings; standards, testing, and certification requirements (e.g., automobiles, pharmaceuticals, foodstuffs); public procurement practices (e.g., construction, high technology products); defense of depressed industries (e.g., soda ash, paper); promotion of high technology industries (e.g., semiconductors, telecommunications); regulation of intellectual property (e.g., patents, trade marks); and distribution channels (e.g., automobiles, automotive parts, retail efforts). Japan has improved import procedures and reduced the number of products subject to standards, but informal barriers remain in other areas.[52]

As this discussion suggests, a country's trade patterns are, to a great extent, conditioned by its industrial structure and government policies.[53] American and Japanese governments, industrial systems, companies, and markets simply do not operate according to the same rules and assumptions.[54] The U.S. market is relatively easy to enter; regulations are fairly transparent and guarantee the same rights and protections to foreign corporations as they do to domestic corporations. While the Japanese have found it relatively easy to enter the U.S. market, Americans have found it relatively difficult to enter Japan's market.[55] The Japanese distribution system, a system difficult for foreign and domestic newcomers alike to enter, further complicates the situation.[56]

Then there are issues of adversarial Japanese pricing. Dumping (selling products below fair value) can be used to export unemployment or gain market position; this is illegal under U.S. trade law as well as under international rules of the GATT, but it occurs with some frequency in Japan.[57] As a former trade negotiator for the United States has written:

> U.S. demands that (dumping) be halted did not allow for the fact that Japan's industrial structure and competitive dynamics made dumping inevitable.[58]

The combination of these various microeconomic factors, in conjunction with the macroeconomic factors discussed earlier, has helped give rise to chronic bilateral trade imbalances as well as to the relative U.S. economic decline-Japan rise dynamic. After years of frustrating, time-consuming bilateral trade sector disputes and mounting trade contentiousness, a new approach to trade imbalances and other Japan-U.S. trade problems was initiated under the Structural Impediments Initiative.

The Structural Impediments Initiative

The Structural Impediments Initiative (SII) process, involving three years of bilateral discussions, was launched by President Bush and Prime Minister Uno in July 1989 with the aim of identifying and resolving structural factors in both countries which functioned as impediments to reciprocal trade. The purpose of the SII was to stem the rising resentment in both countries by moving the debate over bilateral trade from narrow sector disputes toward more systemic factors and fundamental policy issues. As such, these talks were designed to complement more traditional efforts of diminishing trade imbalances and opening relatively closed markets. In short, they were meant to dampen any threats of a trade war.[59]

Specifically, the series of SII discussions were held for the purpose of identifying the features of each economy, more fundamental than tariffs and quotas, that were thought to give rise to and sustain the large bilateral trade imbalances. In other words, the SII process was geared to addressing the institutional and structural factors that acted to impede the reciprocal flow of trade and which fostered large merchandise trade and current account imbalances. These highly complex, systemic features, deeply entrenched throughout the two economies, cut across many sectors. Included were government policies and procedures as well as economic practices, patterns, and preferences, at all levels of American and Japanese societies, from consumers and workers to business and government leaders. Clearly, these issues would take time to identify, address, and correct.

The SII process can be considered an unprecedented, historic undertaking between two sovereign governments. Its occurrence was a reflection of the interdependence of the two national economies, an indication of the increased concern over trade imbalances, and a demonstration of greater visibility of structural impediments to desirable bilateral trade patterns. The SII process was also unique in the large number of government agencies that were involved from both countries: ten government agencies from the U.S. and almost twenty from Japan. To achieve success, the SII effort necessitated substantial cooperation among the participating members of each side, an element not particularly common in either government or between the two national groupings of agencies.

In early 1990 Prime Minister Kaifu and President Bush themselves met in Palm Springs to discuss the various structural impediments, resulting in a document with commitments to act, rather than commitments to execute specific mutually agreed-upon actions. Then on June 28, 1990 the Working Group, consisting of delegations from both countries, issued a Joint Report containing a wide range of concrete complaints and commitments by both governments, with implementation to take place in 1990, 1991, and beyond. The Working Group met at regular intervals to discuss the progress of measures both sides had agreed upon. They held three follow-up meetings in the first year after the Joint Report and two meetings in the two years thereafter. In October 1990, a two day follow-up meeting was held in the United States, while, in January 1991, a two day follow-up meeting took place in Tokyo.

During the course of the SII process, the United States identified 240 issues concerning Japan, and Japan identified 80 items concerning the United States. The American government asked the Japanese government to encourage changes in national savings and investment patterns, revise land use policy, crack down on exclusionary/collusive business practices, improve antitrust enforcement, strengthen civil litigation and commercial arbitration systems, propose new laws enhancing transparency in government, streamline customs and clearing house procedures, reform pricing practices, boost spending on public works, reform the distribution system, crack down on bid-rigging by large Japanese corporations, revise restrictive policies toward direct foreign investment, and reform patent procedures. Meanwhile, the Japanese government asked the American government to reduce the U.S. national budget deficit; improve the overall competitiveness of the U.S. economy with more corporate (and individual) savings and investments, together with increases in expenditures on workforce education and training and on research and development; expand production capacity; improve the kind and quality of products; reform the practice of corporate raiding; encourage businesses to focus more on long-term planning than on short-term profits; provide incentives for higher national savings and investment rates; discourage the high levels of national consumption; improve the national educational system and worker training programs; and promote exports more aggressively.

Including everything from macroeconomic policy and practices to market-openness and national competitiveness issues, the SII process revealed how virtually everything within, and between, the two nations affected bilateral trade norms and trade imbalances. It also revealed a substantial and telling difference between the two sets of national objectives. American complaints focused on issues related to Japan's limited market access for imports and chronic external surpluses, while Japan's complaints concentrated on U.S. macroeconomic policy and competitive shortcomings. Concerning the SII process, two trade policy analysts have recently written that

> If there is one insight that the SII process has afforded its more astute participants, it is that Japan and the U.S. do differ, that those differences give rise to conflict, and that the current rate of convergence between the U.S. and Japan is too slow to avert a continuing series of explosive confrontations.[60]

Just as diverging national goals, economic ideologies, political-economic institutions, and economic policies logically give rise to structural asymmetries, so also would they be expected to yield important perceptual discrepancies. These perceptual differences would arguably contribute the most dangerous component of the bilateral trade friction equation.

A bilateral team of trade specialists has identified three sources of potential Japan-U.S. perceptual discrepancies. The first is the particular set of conflicting interests that divide the two nations. A second source is the collection of differences in political and institutional structures and functions. Misperceptions may occur, for example, when leaders in one nation fail to recognize the existence of bureaucratic and broader political divisions and struggles within the other nation and view the target government as if it were a unified, rational actor making a series of carefully calculated decisions. Misperceptions may also occur when officials recognize the other country's domestic political complexities and divisions but then interpret these in terms of the particular features of their own political system. A third source of perceptual discrepancies are simply those divergent cultural values and styles peculiar to each nation that are often misconstrued by the other.[61] Other trade analysts have argued that the Japan-U.S. perceptual gulf is especially wide and difficult to bridge because each side believes its form of economic organization is superior to that of the other.[62]

The potential impact of these alleged perceptual differences would be less crucial if so much were not at stake. In spite of the SII process, both sides have failed to agree on the diagnoses of the problem and have failed to create effective, mutually acceptable policies and approaches to the problem. Not only have the SII Accords and numerous trade sector agreements not corrected the primary sources of friction, but they have also not bridged the apparent bilateral perceptual and communication gaps. Before effective remedial action can be taken, each nation must acknowledge and face its own role in the trade friction dilemma. The economic disputes between Japan and the United States are not merely the result of economic structural asymmetries; they are more fundamentally the result of 'a cultural clash of societies with different national priorities, social values, and domestic structures'.[63] As one astute observer recently wrote,

> The underlying source of tensions . . . is the rapid shift in the relative wealth of Japan and the United States. In relation to each other, Japan has gotten richer and the United States poorer. Adjusting to this transition alone would strain any partnership, let alone one that seeks to transcend differences in race, language, and culture, memories of World War II, and the world's largest body of cold water.[64]

The one missing factor in this quotation concerning the galaxy of conflict sources is the apparent perceptual gap between Americans and Japanese on such topics as trade imbalance causal factors and other trade-related issues. Without such perceptual differences, the currently high levels of bilateral contentiousness over trade imbalances and sectoral issues would likely be lower. Although this study does not empirically determine how much of the trade friction dilemma is traceable to economic rivalry, how much to cultural and institutional differences, or how much to the existence of perceptual discrepancies, it does argue that without the subjective awareness or perception of objective reality (e.g., economic positional reversal), little contentiousness or conflict between Japan and the United States would be occurring. It also argues that American and Japanese subjective realities are shaped and informed by cultural and institutional differences. Finally, and most importantly, it argues that significant perceptual differences between Americans and Japanese regarding trade imbalance causal factors and other trade issues as well as the assignment of blame to the other side do exist and probably work to exacerbate the trade friction dilemma. Adequately addressing the subjective realities as well as the objective realities is crucial to averting the constant danger of economic conflict turning into political conflict. Social psychological theory, which sheds light on how, when, and why intergroup conflict is likely to occur, is taken up in the next chapter.

Notes

1   Frost, E. (1987) *For Richer, for Poorer: The New U.S.-Japan Relationship*, p. 39.

2   Kumon, S. (1987) 'The Theory of Long Cycles Examined' in G. Modelski (ed) *Exploring Long Cycles*, p. 62.

3   In this research effort, the cultural roots of American and Japanese political economies are emphasized together with the political and economic domains of trade friction. However, political economists, depending on their academic affiliation, tend to emphasize either the political or economic domain of political economic issues while disregarding altogether the relevant cultural factors. Not surprisingly, there is little agreement on what the term *political economy* actually means. For one of the best discussions regarding the difficulties and challenges of defining the term, see Robert Gilpin (1987) *The Political Economy of International Relations*, pp. 8-11. Observing that the term is 'fraught with ambiguity', Gilpin argues that a unified methodology or theory of political economy would require a general comprehension of the process of social change, including the ways in which the social, economic, and political aspects of society interact. Yet he does little in the way of incorporating the cultural domain into discussions in his otherwise excellent volume.

4   Miyoshi, M. (1991) *Off Center: Power and Culture Relations between Japan and the United States*, p. 62; Masao Miyoshi, a Japan-U.S. cultural and diplomatic relations scholar, declares this proposition 'indisputable, even trite'.

5   Okimoto, D. (1989) *Between MITI and the Market: Japanese Industrial Policy for High Technology*, p. 237.

6   Ibid., pp. 237-238.

7   Ibid., p. 238. Although this line of reasoning is one of the underlying premises of the present study, the ultimate need to explain the diverging perceptions of American and Japanese opinion leaders necessitates a greater elaboration of the cultural factor and its effects on institutions and rational choices than would otherwise have been warranted.

8   Koh, B.C. (1989) *Japan's Administrative Elite*, p. 266.

9   Yoshino, M. and T. Lifson (1986) *The Invisible Link: Japan's Sogo Shosha and the Organization of Trade*, pp. 93-94. Numbering about nine in all and including Mitsubishi, Mitsui, and C. Itoh, these highly powerful, uniquely Japanese institutions play a key role in Japan's economy. Coordinating a vast array of business functions that range from the procurement of raw materials to the fabrication of manufactured goods and the sales of finished products both in Japan and abroad, they control about half of all Japan's imports and exports.

10   The terms *institutional* and *structural* require some defining. *Institutional* may be used to refer to a significant practice; a long established custom; a relationship or set of relations; or an established organization, corporation, or group in a society or culture. In this study, the term *institutional factor* encompasses governmental bodies, departments, ministries, and agencies; industrial/business organizing arrangements; and the various government-business interrelationships, policies, standard operating procedures, and underlying economic ideologies. Meanwhile, *structural* can be used to refer to any arrangement or organizational pattern of parts into a whole as well as to the relatively stable character of that whole. In this study, *structural factor* is used to refer to bilateral macroeconomic patterns (e.g., exchange rates, national savings rates, national investment patterns) as well as microeconomic tendencies (e.g., trade composition, product competitiveness, market access issues). It is also used to describe the relative U.S economic decline-Japan rise dynamic as well as the chronic bilateral trade imbalances. Because *structural* can be used to refer to any factor or situation persisting over a prolonged period, the institutional factor is often subsumed within the structural factor (e.g., the Structural Impediments Initiative).

11   For recent public opinion polls on Japan-U.S. economic relations, see *Business Week* (1989 August 7) 'Business Week/Harris Poll: What Americans Think of Japan'; *Time* (1992 February 10) 'Japan in the Mind of America' and 'America in the Mind of Japan'; W. Holstein (1990) 'Appendix A' in *The Japanese Power Game: What It Means for America*. For further references, see *American Public Opinion Index* (various years) and *The Gallup Poll: Public Opinion* (various years).

12   For further discussion concerning divergent national views, especially those of economists, see E. Lincoln (1990) *Japan's Unequal Trade*, pp. 5-6, 25-29. Edward Lincoln, who argues that Japan's trade patterns are strikingly different from those of other industrial nations, remarks that Japan's macroeconomic argument 'neatly transfers the blame for the problem and the responsibility for its solution from Japan to the United States'. He adds that the largely macroeconomic analyses of American economists, such as C. Fred Bergsten, William Cline, and Gary Saxonhouse, furnish Japanese analysts with ample American support for their views.

13   Ibid., p. 25. For a fairly typical example of the Japanese view of bilateral trade conflict, see Kazuo Ogura (1982) *Trade Conflict: A View from Japan* (Chapters 1-7 of Nichi-bei Keizai Masatsu [U.S. Japan Economic Conflict]). As a member of Japan's Foreign Ministry since 1962, Mr. Ogura's arguments fall into line with those of most Japanese analysts but are expressed in somewhat livelier, more vivid style. American writers, especially those who share views such as those of so-called *Japan-bashers* James Fallows (1989), Chalmers Johnson (1982), and Clyde Prestowitz (1988) would take strong issue with his views. Japanese writers, especially those who share views such as those of so-called *America-bashers* Shintaro Ishihara (1991), Hajime Karatsu (1990), and Akio Morita (1987) would express the same opinions except in somewhat more vehement terms.

14   Saxonhouse, G. and K. Yamamura (eds) (1986) *Law and Trade Issues of the Japanese Economy: American and Japanese Perspectives*, p. ix. As an amusing aside, one of Kazuo Ogura's monographs on international political-economic affairs bore the English title, 'How the Inscrutables Negotiate with the Inscrutables'.

15   The domains of *politics* (state, power) and *economics* (market, wealth) have fundamentally and importantly been divorced from one another in most theory if not in reality. For theory to catch up with reality, it will be necessary to bridge the gap between the disciplines of economics and politics by fully exploring the interface between the two. Fortunately, public choice and political economy are currently two approaches that are attempting to do exactly that.

16   Chalmers Johnson (1982) *MITI and the Japanese Miracle: The Growth of Industrial Policy, 1925-1975,* pp. 7-9; 17-20, is one who has forcefully argued that Japan's political economy falls *precisely* in the line of descent from the German Historical School, otherwise known as *economic nationalism* or *neomercantilism.* He points out that, shortly after the Meiji Restoration of 1868, Japan had already evolved as a strong, 'developmental, plan-rational state' whose economic orientation was keyed to industrial policy. Johnson's argument echoes one made earlier by A. Gerschenkron (1962) *Economic Backwardness in Historical Perspective* concerning the Germany-style *late* industrial development which occurred in various 19th century European states. Gerschenkron argued that such late development (rapid, sizable, and different in character than that of *early* British-style industrial development) occurred largely as a result of the application of certain 'institutional instruments' within a particular intellectual climate. Other factors conducive to successful late development included the availability of a stable, reliable, and disciplined workforce and a backlog of technological innovations as well as an emphasis on larger-sized plants and production and the simultaneous building of infrastructure, such as roads and railroads.

17   Tasca, D. (ed) (1980) *U.S.-Japanese Economic Relations: Cooperation, Competition, and Confrontation,* p. xi.

18   Naitoh, M. (1980a) 'American and Japanese Industrial Structures: A Sectoral Comparison' in D. Tasca (ed) *U.S.-Japanese Economic Relations: Cooperation, Competition, and Confrontation,* p. 72.

19   Dore, R. (1987) *Taking Japan Seriously: A Confucian Perspective on Leading Economic Issues,* pp. 226-227.

20   Ibid., p. 227.

21   Boyd, R. (1987) 'Government-Industry Relations in Japan: Access, Communication, and Competitive Collaboration' in S. Wilks and M. Wright (eds) *Comparative Government-Industry Relations: Western Europe, the United States, and Japan,* p. 63. Boyd offers a concise summary of the cultural argument for Japan: 'The coincidence of an acute scarcity of resources (food, energy, and raw materials), physical density (born in the first instance of the pressure of a large population on a small land mass, and exacerbated by the mountains and forests which make much of the land unusable), and a harsh and unforgiving environment of natural disasters (typhoons, earthquakes, volcanoes, tidal waves, floods, and mud-slides) has taught the Japanese to view the world in Darwinian terms: to triumph over inherent weakness and manage adversity. These physical and geographical characteristics reinforce a social history of groupism, a profound sense of mutual interdependence (reinforced by the exigencies of rice cultivation), which has made debt and obligation critical values. Not least of which is the consequence that the search for consensus and a harmonious resolution of conflict is seen as imperative: an imperative widely acknowledged to be of significance in the formation and implementation of industrial policy in contemporary Japan.'

22   Steve Krasner (1978) 'United States Commercial and Monetary Policy', p. 64, in P. Katzenstein (ed) *Between Power and Plenty: Foreign Economic Policies of Advanced Industrial States,* has written that it can be said that national economic abundance is conducive to a democratic system which diffuses rather than centralizes power and authority. This remark builds on a quotation from David Potter (1954) *People of Plenty: Economic Abundance and the American Character,* p. 112, that 'economic abundance is conducive to political democracy'.

23   Vogel, D. (1987) 'Government-Industry Relations in the United States: An Overview' in S. Wilks and M. Wright (eds) *Comparative Government-Industry Relations: Western Europe, the United States, and Japan,* pp. 92-96.

24   The phrases in quotation marks are taken from R. Boyd (1987), p. 63.

25   This view is expressed by D. Okimoto (1989) pp. 11-12, S. Krasner (1978), and J. Hart (1992) *Rival Capitalists: International Competitiveness in the United States, Japan, and Western Europe.*

26   Howell, T. and A. Wm. Wolff (1992) 'Introduction' in A. Wm. Wolff and T. Howell (eds) *Conflict among Nations: Trade Policies in the 1990s,* pp. 9-12.

27   Okimoto, D. (1989) pp. 235-237.

28   Ibid., pp. 48-50.

29   The term *keiretsu* refers to Japan's industrial groupings whose 'loose' affiliations are based on prewar conglomerates (*zaibatsu*), financial ties (*kin'yu keiretsu*), or vertical integration (*kigyo keiretsu*). Most of the leading Japanese electronics companies, such as NEC, Fujitsu, Hitachi, and Toshiba, belong to a major *keiretsu* (Ibid., pp. 132-133). For excellent discussions concerning the *keiretsu,* see D. Okimoto (1989), pp. 132-142 and 145-150; M. Gerlach (1989) 'Keiretsu Organization in the Japanese Economy: Analysis and Trade Implications' in C. Johnson, L. Tyson, and J. Zysman (eds) *Politics and Productivity: How Japan's Development Strategy Works.*

30   Prestowitz, C. (1988) *Trading Places: How We Allowed Japan to Take the Lead,* p. 129. Considered a bilateral trade guru by many in the United States but a Japan-basher by many in Japan, Prestowitz, a former U.S. trade negotiator, has much of value to say to both sides. Although his content is rich and well-researched, his manner and style of delivery are confrontive and his rhetoric inflammatory. His 'us versus them' comparisons and contrasts, especially his tendency to view Japanese political economy and industrial development as deviants of Western normality can be interpreted as biased criticism. Therefore, whenever his material is used in this study, his manner, style, and rhetoric are modified.

31   Pugel, T. (ed) (1986) 'Introduction' in *Fragile Interdependence: Economic Issues in Japanese Trade and Investment,* p. 3. The Very Large Scale Integrated Circuit (VLSI) project of the late 1970s is a typically cited example of the allegedly unfair advantages which Japanese firms gained by participating in these projects. J. Halliday (1975) *A Political History of Japanese Capitalism,* p. 281, wrote that the most logical, rational course for Japanese capitalism would be towards knowledge-intensive, high technology, low resource-consuming industries and away from labor-intensive, highly polluting industries that consumed high quantities of natural resources per unit of output. Japan has been highly successful in doing exactly that.

32   Prestowitz, C. (1988) pp. 141, 257.

33   Howell, T. and A. Wm Wolff (1992) p. 7.

34   Ibid., pp. 11-12.

35   Beasley, W. G. (1973) *The Modern History of Japan*, p. 77. With these words, Beasley was describing the period of 1860 to 1868.

36   See J. Hart (1992) pp. 224-238; C. Prestowitz (1988) pp. 268-271.

37   Ibid.

38   Prestowitz, C. (1988) pp. 254-257.

39   Ibid.

40   Ibid., pp. 64, 256-257.

41   Clark, R. (1979) *The Japanese Company*, see pp. 221-222 for a comparison of Japanese and Western-style companies. For more on the relationship between culture and organization, see W. Evan (1975) 'Culture and Organizational Systems', *Organization and Administrative Sciences* 5; G. Hofstede (1978) 'Culture and Organization: A Literature Review Survey', *Enterprise Management* 1; G. Hofstede (1991) *Cultures and Organizations: Software of the Mind*. As M. Yoshino and T. Lifson (1986), p. 89, write: 'Culture does affect organization in many ways, large and small'.

42   Ezra Vogel, E. (1986) 'Pax Nipponica', *Foreign Affairs*, vol. 64, pp. 752-767 and (1979) *Japan as Number One: Lessons for America*. See also J. Abegglen (1984) *The Strategy of Japanese Business*; J. Abegglen, and G. Stalk (1985) *Kaisha: The Japanese Corporation*.

43   Lockwood, W. W. (1954) *The Economic Development of Japan: Growth and Structural Change, 1868-1938*, p. 586.

44   Clark, R. (1981) p. 95.

45   Rohlen, T. (1988) *For Harmony and Strength: White-Collar Organization in Anthropological Perspective*.

46   For macroeconomic analyses of the bilateral economic problem, see B. Balassa and M. Noland (1988) *Japan in the World Economy*; C. F. Bergsten and W. Cline (1987) *The United States-Japan Economic Problem*; G. Saxonhouse (1986) 'Japan's Intractable Trade Surpluses in a New Era', *World Economy*, vol. 9, 3, pp 239-258.

47   For the tariff-equivalents of Japanese nontariff barriers on approximately 500 product categories, see Y. Sazanani, S. Urata, and H. Kuwai (1993) 'Trade Protectionism in Japan' in G. Hufbauer, and K. Elliott (eds) *Comparing the Costs of Protectionism: American and Japanese Perspectives*.

48   For an excellent review of current theories explaining Japan's 'excessive' industrial competition, see D. Okikmoto (1989) pp. 38-48.

49   Borrus, M. (1988) *Competing for Control: America's Stake in Microelectronics*, pp. 4-5.

50   Rapp, W. (1986) 'Japan's Invisible Barriers to Trade' in T. Pugel and R. Hawkins (eds) (1986) *Fragile Interdependence: Economic Issues in U.S.-Japanese Trade and Investment*.

51   Balassa, B. and M. Noland (1986) *Japan in the World Economy*, pp. 51-52. Between 1975 and 1986, these ratios increased from 7.0 to 13.8 percent in the United States, from 17.9 to 26.7 percent in France, from 24.3 to 37.2 percent in Germany, and 22.0 percent to 31.2 percent in Great Britain. In Japan, however, they declined from 4.9 percent to 4.4 percent (p.183).

52   Ibid., pp. 56-57, 183.

53   Naitoh, M. (1980) p. 67.

54   Prestowitz, C. (1988) p. 70.

55   Ibid., pp. 43-44.

56   For an overview of Japan's distribution system, see H. Laumer (1986) 'The Distribution System: Its Social Function and Import-Impeding Effects' in M. Schmiegelow (ed) *Japan's Response to Crisis and Change in the World Economy.*

57   Ibid., pp. 38-39. For an informative assessment of Japanese dumping prior to the 1980s, see G. C. Allen (1978) *How Japan Competes: An Assessment of International Trading Practices with Special Reference to 'Dumping'.*

58   Prestowitz, C. (1988) p. 58.

59   Much of the information included here on the SII is taken from articles from the *Los Angeles Times, The New York Times*, and *The Wall Street Journal* during the 1989-1991 period. Another source is the *United States-Japan Economic Relations: Structural Impediments Initiative* (Hearings before the Asian and Pacific Affairs and International Economic Subcommittees of the House of Representatives' Foreign Affairs Committee on February 20 and April 19, 1990).

60   Howell, T. and A. Wm. Wolff (1992) p. 27.

61   Destler, I. M., H. Sato, P. Clapp, and H. Fukui (1976) *Managing an Alliance: The Politics of U.S.-Japanese Relations*, pp. 89-90.

62   Howell, T. and A. Wm. Wolff (1992) p. 28.

63   Gilpin, R. (1987) p. 377.

64   Frost, E. (1987) p. ix.

5 The Social Psychological Factors

As long as groups are in conflict, the casting of blame by either side will lead to a vicious circle of recriminations.

Muzafer Sherif, 1966[1]

American and Japanese worldviews and economic goals have grown increasingly incompatible in the past several decades. Moreover, the ways in which the two sets of national leaders have addressed incompatible goals and their consequences are not always consistent or mutually reinforcing. As a team of American and Japanese trade specialists wrote several years ago,

> If views of the world in Washington and Tokyo are similar or at least compatible, if the preferred means for coping with that world are consistent or mutually reinforcing, then there exists a strong basis for cooperation. If, however, world views are mutually inconsistent or if the ways leaders in one country seek to cope with the world are threatening to the other, then the prospect for conflict is heightened.[2]

Indeed, heightened Japan-U.S. conflict over trade has been a reality for some time now, as evidenced by difficult trade negotiation proceedings and angry rhetoric over trade imbalances and sectoral issues. Apparent differences in interpreting agreement intent and content as well as frequently divergent expectations concerning outcomes suggest that Japan-U.S. perceptual differences are also at work.[3] Might these and other perceptual differences exacerbate tendencies toward mutual recriminations and blame? If they do, this would further heighten the prospect for increased bilateral contentiousness over trade issues. A social psychological perspective offers theoretical insights into why this might be so.

A Social Psychological Perspective on Intergroup Conflict

Various analyses of international conflict or foreign policy decision-making by political scientists (e.g., Axelrod, 1976; George, 1979; Heradsveit, 1979; Holsti, 1962, 1976; Janis, 1982; Jervis, 1976; Larson, 1985; Lebow, 1981) and social psychologists (e.g., Chilstrom, 1984; Deutsch, 1983; Kelman & Cohen, 1986; Mack, 1985; Pruitt & Rubin, 1986; Tetlock & McGuire, 1986; White, 1986) have utilized social psychological paradigms and approaches. Common foci of their research have been Cold War/nuclear arms race dynamics and Arab-Israeli disputes. Yet rarely has this social psychological analytical tradition been extended to international economic conflicts generally or to international trade conflicts specifically.[4]

This study attempts to address this deficiency by employing hypotheses from two major social psychological approaches to intergroup conflict in the identification, quantification, and analysis of likely interactional dynamics and perceptual processes involved in the ongoing Japan-U.S. trade conflict dilemma. One of these approaches is realistic conflict theory (RCT) which argues that conflict between groups arises as a result of objective (real) or subjective (perceived) competition over limited resources. While most RCT theorists tend to focus more on objective than on perceived competitive conditions, they generally acknowledge that diverging perceptions of the same event can contribute powerfully to a climate of intergroup conflict.

Morton Deutsch, a prominent RCT researcher, is one who argues cogently for the important role that perception plays in intergroup conflict. Furthermore, he contends that, while it is important to depict the objective state of affairs in any intergroup conflict as well as the state of affairs as perceived by the conflicting parties, it is also important to depict the interdependence between the objective and perceived realities.[5] This is a tall order, but it is one that this research effort makes an effort to address both qualitatively and quantitatively. It does so in the model presented in Figures 1.2 and 6.1 together with accompanying remarks. It does so through the commentary of Chapter Seven in which collected data on American and Japanese perceptual differences concerning trade imbalances and related issues are identified, quantified, and analyzed. Finally, it does so in Chapter Eight in which bilateral disputes over rice, automotive, and semiconductor trade issues are discussed in relation to real and perceived economic competition between Japan and the United States as well as diverging cultural, institutional, and structural patterns.

Perhaps the single most appropriate theoretical tool for examining the conditions and catalysts which give rise to differing bilateral perceptions is a collection of hypotheses contained under the single rubric of attribution theory.

Specifically, attribution theory accounts for how human beings arrive at causal explanations of events and situations, including how responsibility, either credit or blame, is assigned. It should provide answers to questions such as:

(1) Why has bilateral trade contentiousness escalated in recent years?

(2) Why do many American and Japanese opinion leaders tend to view the currently large trade imbalances as the most important reason for growing bilateral trade friction and yet differ as to which factors are most important in causing these imbalances?

(3) Why does each set of national leaders tend to assign responsibility or blame for these imbalances and other trade-related problems to the other?

No doubt Morton Deutsch would argue that RCT best explains when, where, and how intergroup conflict begins but agree with intergroup specialist Miles Hewstone's contention that 'the attributional approach seems most valuable in underlining how conflict is supported, even exacerbated'.[6]

Caveats, Concerns, and Considerations

The existence of conflictual relations between all kinds and sizes of groups, including national and cultural groups, is a pervasive feature of human society. Social scientists of various persuasions (e.g., anthropology, sociology, political science) have tried to understand the underlying dynamics of intergroup conflict and to establish effective methods for diminishing it. Attitudes, perceptions, attributions (causal perceptions), emotions, motivations, and overt actions of individuals, all of which come into play in inter-group/international conflictual contexts, are part of social psychology's domain. As expected, one of social psychology's major goals has been to determine how such behaviors influence relations between groups as well as how they, in turn, are affected by these relations.[7]

Yet the individual-group distinction is not as clear-cut as it might seem. On the one hand, the group has no real existence apart from the individuals who compose it. In this view, the group is an 'artifact' and its individual members, with their human motives and behavior, the group's 'composers' and 'creators'.[8] On the other hand, the individual is influenced by his context and, as a member of a group, does not really act alone. As much influenced by group consensus as by his own perception, a person's individual psychology is operative even in response to the influence of his group. However, he has been inculcated with the point of view and reinforcements of his culture.[9]

Still, one would logically expect intergroup relations to be a central topic of social psychological research. However, the paucity of pertinent articles in key social psychology journals and the weak showing of the topic in most tables of contents of major social psychology texts indicate that this is simply not the case.[10] The minimal interest in attributions at the group level of analysis has occurred in spite of the sustained interest in attribution theory within social psychology[11] and rather forceful early statements on its behalf.[12]

When groups are discussed at all, the focus tends to be exclusively on small, closed groups (e.g., work-related or therapeutic groups) rather than on more open, fluid groups occurring naturally within society.[13] Furthermore, the focus of such research has generally been more on why particular individuals hold certain views than on why an entire society shares such views.[14] The evasive 'individualistic ideology' of North America, where most of the theory formation and research has been conducted, is often cited as a major cause for this discrepancy.[15] Perhaps it is largely because of this bias that comparatively little comprehensive theory formation and research in intergroup and cross-cultural social psychology have been completed to date.[16] Indeed, much of the important theory formation and research on intergroup dynamics completed thus far, especially that involving attributional tendencies, appears to be European in origin.

Additional caveats and words of concern are in order at this time. First, relationships between and among various social psychological theoretical approaches are not always clear even though they generally appear complementary rather than conflictual. Often these theories generate somewhat parallel hypotheses which can be used compatibly in certain analyses. Such is the case at hand in which Morton Deutsch's realistic conflict theoretical approach offers the larger context within which to view the Japan-U.S. trade friction dilemma, while hypotheses from attribution theory at the individual level of analysis (e.g., Jones, Kelley, Weiner) and group level of analysis (e.g., Hewstone, Pettigrew) shed light on apparent bilateral perceptual/attributional discrepancies concerning trade imbalances and other trade issues.

Second, because most social psychological theory and research is based on intra- and interindividual rather than on intra-, intergroup, and cross-cultural processes, individual-based findings are often extrapolated to higher levels. While valid parallels may exist, it is more than likely that individual, intergroup, and cross-cultural processes differ in some respects from one another. Due to the lack of attention paid to intergroup and cross-cultural dynamics, potentially valuable questions and hypotheses may not always have been considered. Yet Morton Deutsch is one who defends extrapolations from research findings at one level of analysis to conclusions pertaining to another. He and a colleague recently wrote that what can be studied in the social psychology laboratory has 'conceptual relevance for the understanding of large-scale conflict processes'.[17] Their assumption of a correspondence in social processes across different types of social units is justified in this way:

> We are in much the same position as the astronomers. It seems unlikely that we shall ever be able to conduct true experiments with large-scale social events. However, if we are able to identify the conceptual similarities between the large scale and the small, as the astronomers have between the planets and Newton's apple, we may be able to understand, predict, and possibly control what happens in large-scale sociohistorical processes by investigating what occurs in interpersonal and intergroup situations with which we can experiment.[18]

A similar theoretical position is adopted in this dissertation. However, research findings at the group level of analysis, when available, take precedence over those at the individual level of analysis; selected research findings from cross-cultural approaches complete the offering.

A third issue of concern is that the relationship between cognitive (thinking) and emotional (feeling) states to behavior is yet to be clearly delineated and the interplay of both adequately explained. Indeed, some social psychologists take a purely cognitive approach, while others pursue a largely affective one. The former argue that emotion is, in many ways, prior to and more fundamental than cognition, while the latter argue the reverse. Those pursuing an affective approach, such as Howard Leventhal, argue that how individuals feel about something is ultimately more important in determining their appraisals than cognitive factors.[19] Leventhal is one who recognizes, however, that to assign emotion priority in time or in importance over cognition as determining behavior is to treat emotional and cognitive processes as unitary events. Although the two processes are partially independent and parallel, emotionally provocative situations can give rise to both strong feelings and specific perceptions which become intertwined and mutually dependent to such a degree that their later separation seems artificial and sensible only for purposes of theory construction.[20] Although he proposes that emotional impulses may often be more important as determinants of behavior than complex reasoning, he notes that 'some kind of perceptual process is always active along with – if not prior to – emotion', that some kind of cognition is 'intimately involved in the generation of emotion'.[21]

Most cognitive social psychologists, including attribution theorists, focus solely on the thinking process without addressing the part emotion plays in fostering various kinds of behavior. Bernard Weiner's attributional theory of motivation and emotion addresses this lack. Although Weiner emphasizes, as do other attribution theorists, that how people think powerfully influences how they feel, he acknowledges that emotions may be elicited without any intervening thought processes, such as in the case of hormonally induced depression or certain cases of conditioned fear.[22] However, Weiner insists that cognitions quite typically precede and determine most affective reactions, but he concurs with Leventhal that no fixed demarcation exists between a 'hot' affect and a 'cold' cognition even though each is a distinctly different process.

Emotions, which Weiner defines as a complex syndrome or composite of many interacting factors, are presumed to have positive or negative qualities (hedonistic direction) as well as a certain level of intensity. Weiner contends that general positive or negative emotions are instigated following a positive or negative event. As outcomes are evaluated as either good or bad, these evaluations give rise to more clearly defined outcome-related emotions. Then, if an attribution for the outcome is made, the attribution selected elicits yet more differentiated emotions based on the perceived cause of the outcome and the perceived properties of that cause. In other words, Weiner conceives of emotions as coming at a juncture between behavioral events, since they summarize reactions to the past and instigate actions in the future. Such features, Weiner points out, are not characteristics of cold cognitions. Weiner argues that these associations between causal thinking and feeling (see Figure 5.1) form well-established and robust laws.[23] Once again, however, the use of Weiner's theory necessitates extrapolations from the individual level of analysis to that of the group.

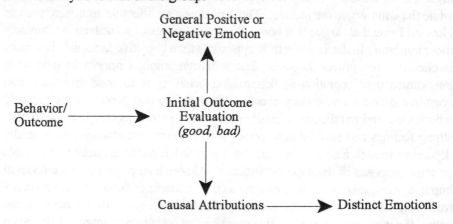

Figure 5.1   The Cognition-Emotion Process
Source: Based on B. Weiner (1986) *An Attributional Theory of Motivation and Emotion*, p. 122.

Because Weiner's cognitive-affective model addresses the probable role emotion plays in the attributional process, it may help account for increases and decreases in bilateral trade-related contentiousness as well as suggest how certain actions and reactions quite naturally occur as a result of those fluctuations. Quite simply, it might be argued that causal perceptions (attributions) on the part of American and Japanese opinion leaders give rise to negative or positive emotional reactions, which result in increased or decreased levels of bilateral trade contentiousness.[24] Although this relationship is not tested in the present study, it is assumed that negative outgroup attributions elicit negative emotions which, ultimately, give rise to negative ingroup reactions toward the outgroup.

A final concern is the definition of key terms, such as *group, intergroup relations, conflict, competition, cooperation,* and *attribution,* which are used in keeping with definitions and uses in the theory and research upon which this chapter is based. Because differences of opinion over definitions of terms exist among the social psychologists cited, as well as among scholars of different disciplines, discrepancies are identified and clarified as the need arises.[25]

Realistic Conflict Theory

Unlike most theoretical approaches to intergroup relations, realistic conflict theory (RCT) addresses relations between groups of relatively equal power and prestige. It also addresses the three major issues in intergroup relations: how intergroup conflicts arise, what courses such conflicts take, and how they might be resolved. An essentially economic theory of intergroup behavior, RCT is based on three central assumptions concerning human behavior. First, people are fundamentally selfish and try to maximize their own rewards. Second, intergroup conflict occurs as a result of incompatible group interests and competition over limited or scarce resources; these can be either concrete (e.g., geographical territory, wealth) or abstract (e.g., power, prestige, status). Third, the social psychological aspects of intergroup behavior are largely determined by (rather than determinants of) the compatibility or incompatibility of group interests. In other words, misattributions, biased perceptions, and negative or stereotyped attitudes that one group's members have concerning those of another are thought to emanate from incompatible interests or competition over scarce resources.[26]

While strict RCT functionalists like Muzafer Sherif agree that the objective or real competition between groups for scarce resources leads to negative intergroup perceptual and attitudinal biases, RCT researcher Morton

Deutsch places greater emphasis on the role played by perceptual differences, including those which may not be the result of real competition, in fostering and exacerbating intergroup competition and conflict.[27] Deutsch argues that the objective state of affairs does not 'rigidly determine' the presence or absence of conflict.[28] In his view, misperceptions and biased perceptions not resulting from real competition can of themselves lead to the development of a conflict as well as to its intensification and escalation.[29] Since a central premise of this study is that bilateral perceptual discrepancies, those caused by cultural and institutional differences, in addition to those caused by economic rivalry and conflicting national goals, foster, support, and exacerbate Japan-U.S. trade friction, Deutsch's version of RCT, then, is the theoretical framework within which this problem was initially conceptualized.

After extensively reviewing various usages of the term *group*, Morton Deutsch settles on the 'intuitive' notion of the group as an entity consisting of people aware of being psychologically bound together by mutually linked interests or goals.[30] This psychological linkage has certain cohesive features to it. Members of a group, for example, perceive that in certain respects they either sink or swim together.[31] Deutsch notes that an assemblage of cooperating people qualifies as a group only if it is composed of members who are aware of themselves as an entity; in other words, a group is conscious of itself.[32] In order for intergroup relations to occur, distinctions between *ingroup* and *outgroup* must be both 'visible' and 'distinguishable' and some form of contact between the two groups must exist.[33] A most adequate definition of intergroup behavior is Muzafer Sherif's succinct, often quoted one:

> Whenever individuals belonging to one group interact, collectively or individually, with another group or its members in terms of their group identification, we have an instance of intergroup behavior.[34]

Although not all interactions between individuals of two groups are necessarily examples of intergroup behavior, in the case of Japan-U.S. trade friction, perceptual and behavioral dynamics by necessity involve national group membership: for Japanese and Americans are well aware of being members of two distinctly different cultural and national 'groups', and identifiable patterns of competitive intergroup behavior are plainly evident.[35]

While contact between two clearly distinguishable groups are necessary conditions for intergroup conflict to occur, they are not sufficient. Yehuda Amir (1969), the first researcher to determine that even the best-intended contact could foster tensions, prejudices, and hostilities between groups, identified the following contact conditions as producing negative intergroup feelings: those which lowered the status of one of the groups; those which were unpleasant, frustrating, or tension-laden; and those which produced intergroup competition. He found that such contact conditions could even lead to the formation and entrenchment of outgroup scapegoating.[36] The Japan-U.S. trade friction dilemma exhibits all three contact conditions, with perhaps some degree of outgroup scapegoating. Clearly, the U.S. position as the world's preeminent economic power is being seriously challenged by Japan, and trade relations have grown increasingly tension laden of late.

However, the horizon of conditions both necessary and sufficient for conflictive intergroup dynamics to occur is broadened by Deutsch's summary of three major social psychological perspectives on conflict:

> Almost all scholars include the real conflicts of interest that arise from the competition for such scarce resources as wealth, power, prestige, and territory. Others also stress the opposition that arises from ideological and cultural differences, differences in beliefs and values about what is universally true and right. Still others would indicate that it is not the *real* conflict of interest, or *real* ideological differences that create opposition but rather the *perception* of such conflict.[37]

In addition to perceptual distortions natural to the competitive process, other distortions can occur in the course of intergroup interaction.[38] Deutsch argues that these, too, can transform a situation into a competitive struggle even if it did not originally evolve out of a competitive relationship. Some distortions occur because of cultural differences, especially when mutual awareness or understanding of these differences is lacking.[39] Other distortions occur as a result of the 'properties' of the communication system between the two groups; in fact, communication systems of themselves can be conflict-enhancing.[40] Yet other distortions can occur during periods of rapid social change. Finally, the effects of stress of themselves can cause perceptual distortions to occur.[41]

Deutsch also describes how a competitive process, once set in motion, can escalate as stress-related perceptual effects add fuel to the fires of growing contention. To begin with, a competitive intergroup process tends to create an environment in which impoverished communication, hostile attitudes, and oversensitivity to differences thrive. These, in turn, work to reinforce preexisting orientations and negative expectations. Then, too, conflict-induced stress further impairs the 'notoriously underemployed and underdeveloped' ability in most humans to place oneself in another's shoes.[42] It also reduces the intellectual resources available for discovering new ways of coping with, or resolving, the conflict. As cognitive rigidity sets in, a shift of focus to the immediate, rather than to the overall consequences of perceived alternatives, takes place. Often the perceived scope of contentious issues expands in such a way that the conflict becomes a matter of general principle no longer confined to one particular issue at a given time and place.

Finally, simplistic, polarized thinking impels both parties to view their alternatives as being limited to either victory or defeat (a *win-lose* orientation) as simplistic precepts of one extreme or another (e.g., good/bad, right/wrong, fair/unfair) become entrenched. In keeping with this tendency, members of each group perceive their motives and actions as being more legitimate and benevolent than those of the other group. This, in turn, leads to stereotyped responses, increases each side's susceptibility to fear and defensiveness, and fosters the use of coercive processes to change the other's behavior. The conflict intensifies, and as it does, yet higher levels of stress and tension are induced. The conflict further escalates, increasing in significance as each side's emotional involvement intensifies.[43] This might be an apt description of the bilateral scenario occurring in the decade preceding Japan's entry into the Second World War. It also suggests what might occur today if both nations do not effectively address the structural and sectoral issues involved in the bilateral trade friction dilemma.

Deutsch writes that the existence of either competition or cooperation is revealed most especially through the quality and kinds of communication, perceptions and misperceptions, attitudes, and task orientations occurring between members of the two groups. While a competitive intergroup process entails communication which is often purposefully misleading or lacking altogether, a cooperative process involves open, honest communication of relevant information between the two sets of participants, each of whom clearly demonstrates an active interest in informing and being informed by the other. Whereas a competitive process tends to increase sensitivity to differences and promote the formation of diverging intergroup perceptions, a cooperative process serves to increase sensitivity to similarities and common interests, minimize the salience of differences, and foster the convergence and conformity of beliefs and values. While a competitive process gives rise to suspicious, hostile attitudes and a readiness to respond negatively to the other group's requests, a cooperative process leads to trust and friendly attitudes, and the willingness to respond positively to the needs and requests of the other. Finally, while a competitive process fosters the view that solutions to a conflict can only be imposed by one side or the other, with the objective of enhancing one's own power and reducing the other's, a cooperative process leads to the goal of enhancing mutual power and resources, recognizing both parties' interests as legitimate, defining conflicting interests as problems to be solved through collaborative efforts, and seeking solutions responsive to the needs of both.[44]

In other words, competitive processes foster win-lose dynamics, while cooperative ones foster *win-win* dynamics. That is, the experience of competitive conflict will induce a 'vicious spiral of intensifying competition' while the experience of cooperation will bring about a 'benign spiral of increasing cooperation'.[45] Although both processes tend to be self-confirming, various restraints operate to limit the spiraling effect of either process. Perhaps the most important is each side's simultaneous involvement in numerous other situations and relationships which work to prevent or contain the obsessive intensification of any particular relationship.[46] Restraints operating to prevent the spiraling of intergroup competitive conflict include the number and strength of existing cooperative bonds, common allegiances, and memberships among conflicting parties as well as the existence of values, institutions, procedures and groups that are organized to help limit and regulate conflict.[47] Yet warns Deutsch,

> If these conflict-limiting factors are weak, it may be difficult to prevent a competitive conflict from expanding in scope. Even if they are strong, misjudgment and the pressures arising out of tendencies to be rigidly self-consistent may make it difficult to keep a competitive conflict encapsulated.[48]

The Japan-U.S. trade friction case appears to be one in which real conflicts of interest; cultural and institutional differences; and perceptions of their existence are all part of the calculus of factors causing bilateral contentiousness. This study has addressed the first two conflict-producing factors. The real conflicts of interest over economic gain, power, and prestige within the global economy were a central focus of Chapter Two, while sources of probable opposition arising from cultural and institutional differences were discussed in Chapters Three and Four. In this and subsequent chapters, the perceptual significance of large bilateral trade imbalances, the attributional bases of intergroup (Japan-U.S.) conflict, and the effects of cultural factors on perceptions are the focus. On the basis of the preceding discussion concerning RCT, it is hypothesized that:

> Significant perceptual differences exist between American and Japanese opinion leaders regarding the causes of the bilateral trade imbalances.

> American and Japanese opinion leaders place greater responsibility or blame for the large trade imbalances with the other country and its constituents than with their own.

American and Japanese opinion leaders view bilateral trade relations with more of a win-lose orientation than a win-win orientation.

The nation with the larger trade deficit (U.S.) should view the bilateral trade relationship more in win-lose terms than the other nation (Japan).

The Social Psychological (Cognitive) Significance of Large Bilateral Trade Imbalances

What is it about the chronically large bilateral trade imbalances that, more than any other issue, have become the focus of so much intense scrutiny, publicity, and commentary by American and Japanese opinion leaders? Why is it so often cited as the major cause of bilateral trade contentiousness? Cognitive psychology offers a number of answers. Perhaps the most succinct is one offered by Susan Taylor and Shelley Fiske (1978). After integrating evidence from various studies, they concluded that most perceivers seek a single, sufficient, and salient explanation for events or behavior.[49] In other words, most people look for explanations that are uncomplicatedly adequate yet perceptually notable or important.

What exactly determines whether or not a piece of information (a stimulus) is salient or notably important? Fiske and Taylor (1991) point out that salience depends on whatever catches the perceiver's attention. They suggest that the term *relative* is key, for the information must be distinctive in relation to other factors in the perceiver's context for it to be salient. To begin with, an unexpected piece of information is generally more salient than one that is expected. Additionally, an extreme stimulus tends to be more salient than one that is moderate. Finally, a negative stimulus appears to be more salient than one that is positive. Not surprisingly, highly salient information tends to trigger strong reactions in the perceiver.[50]

Exactly how does the process work? Fiske and Taylor (1991) explain that social information or stimuli (e.g., large bilateral trade imbalances) external to a person (e.g., American or Japanese opinion leader) must be represented in the mind before the information can be used cognitively. Therefore, attention and encoding are first steps in all social information processing. During the encoding process, perceived external stimuli (which have first drawn the perceiver's attention) are transformed into internal representations (consciousness) which influence both memory and inference.[51] Perceptually salient information is 'over-represented' in the perceiver's mind and shapes subsequent causal explanations (attributions).[52] Certainly the large trade imbalance figures are highly salient information for both

Americans and Japanese – for Americans, because of the negative national economic implications and, for Japanese, because of the inevitable U.S. complaints and accusations.

It is also hypothesized that vividness and accessibility of stimuli also work to capture the perceiver's attention.[53] Vividness, a phenomenon related to salience, refers to qualities inherent in the stimulus itself. A piece of information is vivid to the extent that it is concrete and proximate in a sensory, temporal, or spatial way. It also has emotional impact.[54] Vivid information is predicted to be more persuasive than more pallid information of equal or greater validity simply because it comes more easily to mind and, therefore, has a greater or disproportionate impact on the perceiver's judgments and explanations.[55] The trade imbalance numbers qualify as vivid, concrete information; for they are graphically simple, yet evocatively powerful symbols of the highly competitive nature of bilateral trade relations as well as of the relative U.S. economic decline-Japan rise dynamic in process.

Finally, accessible (or readily available) information, especially those 'chronically encountered categories' which have been recently and frequently activated, comes more easily to mind than information which has not been so frequently activated.[56] Bilateral trade imbalance data qualify as 'chronically encountered categories'. They have appeared again and again in print; have frequently been reported and discussed on television news and business news programs; and have often been the focus of academic research efforts, forums, and seminars. In other words, these numbers have high accessibility, in addition to high salience and vividness. Although symptomatic of far more complex underlying causes, these large figures offer American and Japanese perceivers that single, sufficient, and salient explanation for the currently high levels of bilateral trade friction.

A related question concerns the apparent lack of bilateral, as well as cross-disciplinary, consensus as to the causes, consequences, and cures of the large trade imbalances. Part of the answer lies in the tendency of people to be influenced by their own 'small' corner of experience, including the kind of data most salient and accessible to them. Consequently, opinion leaders and analysts would be expected to emphasize factors falling within their own areas of expertise. Economists would logically tend to emphasize economic factors, while political scientists would be expected to place greater focus on institutional factors. The situation of opinion leaders and analysts, then, can be said to be analogous to that of the blindfolded men who, when asked to identify and describe the object in front of them (an elephant), were able to describe only that portion immediately before them. To have fully identified and described the object, the blindfolded men would have had to share observations. By integrating these observations or viewpoints into a set of hypotheses, the essence of the observed might finally have become known to all. On the basis of the preceding discussion, it is hypothesized that:

> The causal perceptions of both American and Japanese opinion leaders tend to be shaped by their academic training and career choice.

Opinion leaders and analysts, like members of the general public, are also likely to be influenced to some extent by their respective nation's government and media statements. As a result, American and Japanese opinion leaders would logically be expected to differ somewhat in their perspectives according to their national group identity. Yet, this is only the tip of the iceberg. The major part of the answer is more than likely found in the tendencies of ingroup constituents to favor ingroup members over outgroup members when evaluating behavior, outcomes, and events and arriving at causal explanations.

The Attributional Bases of Intergroup Conflict

Attribution theory sheds light on those intergroup perceptual dynamics, including distortions and biases, which Deutsch has argued can escalate a latent conflict into an active (veridical) one. In so doing, light is shed not only on why American and Japanese leaders so often seem to disagree as to the causes, consequences, and cures of the trade imbalance, but also why each side seems to place greater responsibility or blame for this and other trade issues of contention with the other side. While the human attributional process is far from logical or thorough, attributions (causal perceptions) offer people viable explanations for behavior, outcomes, and events. Attributions influence how people perceive themselves and others, in contexts ranging from the individual to the international. They not only shape attitudes, opinions, and perceptions, but they also give rise to certain emotions. Due to the complexity of most real world events, attributions are often not completely accurate. Not only does the complexity of events mitigate against perfectly accurate attributions, but attributors often attempt to meet conflicting goals.[57]

Attribution theory, then, describes how people infer motives and attitudes, determine causes of outcomes and events, and assign responsibility (credit or blame). It also explains how *schema* (prior knowledge structures) influence the *encoding* (interpreting and taking in) of new information, the accessing of memory for old information, and the making of inferences in cases where information is missing.[58] Although competing theoretical models may differ somewhat in how these cognitive processes and outcomes are described, all assume the human tendency to form causal explanations.

All theoretical approaches to the attributional process stem from Fritz Heider's (1944, 1958) seminal analyses of how people perceive and explain the actions of others.[59] These furnished a conceptual framework and a 'brilliant pastiche of provocative ideas' for the more systematic, explicit, testable statements on attributional processes that were to follow.[60] One provocative concept is that people search for the causal structures of events through attributions to either the environment *(external)* or something in the person(s) involved in the event *(internal)*. External causes are said to comprise environmental or situational influences, pressures, and constraints, while internal causes encompass any dispositional characteristics of the observed individual(s), such as personality, character traits, abilities, attitudes, motives, and emotional states. In determining an internal locus, observers are believed to take three factors into consideration: the actor's ability, intention, and exertion. Ability is evaluated in relation to the difficulty of the task at hand, and exertion by observing the person's apparent effort. Intention, however, is more difficult to assess largely because an actor's behavior or actions could have both intended and unintended consequences.

Harold Kelley (1967) expanded on this internal-external classification by arguing that people generally consider three factors or conditions in deciding whether to make a dispositional or situational attribution about a behavior or an outcome. These factors are *distinctiveness, consistency,* and *consensus.* First, people are likely to make dispositional rather than situational attributions when the behavior differs from what is expected (high distinctiveness). Second, a dispositional attribution is more likely when the actor is known to engage frequently in the observed behavior (high consistency). Finally, a dispositional attribution is more likely when the same kind of behavior occurs in various situations involving different stimuli (high consensus).[61]

If Kelley's model were applied to the trade imbalance question, a simple causal explanation involving responsibility or blame might be one of the following:

Japan is at fault (internal to Japan; external to U.S.).
The U.S. is at fault (internal to U.S.; external to Japan).
Japan and the U.S. are both at fault (internal to both).
Neither Japan nor the U.S. is at fault (external to both).

A person concluding that Japan is more responsible might have used the following criteria:

Japan is the only industrialized nation to have large trade surpluses with the U.S. (high distinctiveness).

Japan has had chronically large trade surpluses with the U.S. for many years (high consistency).

Japan has large trade surpluses with most other industrial nations (high consensus).

Someone arriving at the opposite conclusion, that the United States is more responsible, might have used these criteria:

The U.S. is the only industrialized country to have such large trade deficits (high distinctiveness).

The U.S. has had chronically large trade deficits with Japan for many years (high consistency).

The U.S. has large trade deficits with most other industrialized countries (high consensus).

However, someone concluding that both nations are at fault might have used both sets of criteria, while a person concluding that neither is at fault might have found that distinctiveness, consistency, and consensus were low or would have focused on other criteria (e.g., global economic conditions).

In the same year, Jones and Harris (1967) described a *self-serving* or *egocentric bias* which accounted for people's apparent tendency to assume more credit for success than for failure.[62] This together with the *actor-observer effect* (describing people's tendency to favor more dispositional factors in explaining others' behavior while favoring more external factors when explaining their own) formed the basis of what became known as the *fundamental attribution error* (FAE). The FAE describes the observer's tendency to explain an actor's behavior or part in a negative outcome by overestimating the importance of dispositional factors while downplaying or underestimating the situational factors. Moreover, the observer tends to make such dispositional inferences even when presented with ample evidence of strong external pressures on the person observed. However, an actor tends to attribute his own failures or shortcomings to situational requirements or constraints, even while attributing the very same failures or shortcomings to someone else's internal or dispositional characteristics.[63]

As for a parallel bias at the group level of analysis, Allport (1954), in his study on prejudice, first described the group-serving or ethnocentric tendency of people to infer the traits and attitudes of an entire social group on the basis of one group member's behavior.[64] Then Jones and Nisbett (1972) described a *group-serving error* grounded in the 'actor-observer' fallacy.[65] Finally, Pettigrew (1979) identified a group-level phenomenon similar to the individual-level actor-observer discrepancy and the fundamental attribution error (FAE) which he termed the *ultimate attribution error*.[66] There is substantial evidence that biases favoring the ingroup over the outgroup are quite prevalent in intergroup relations.[67]

As shown in Table 5.1, the ultimate attribution error occurs when members of a group attribute negative or undesirable behavior and outcomes to external (situational) causal factors for the ingroup and internal (dispositional) causes for the outgroup. The pattern reverses for positive or desirable behavior and outcomes, that is, attributions to internal (dispositional) causes for the ingroup and external (situational) influences, as well as exceptional effort, for the outgroup. Clearly this has implications for why Americans and Japanese leaders might tend to hold the other more accountable for trade imbalances and sectoral problems. It is hypothesized that each national group tends to blame the other nation's internal (domestic) tendencies or fundamental national 'character' for such problems rather than acknowledge their own contributions; that is, their own internal, domestic, or national characteristics and tendencies.

Table 5.1   The Ultimate Attribution Error

Behavior/Outcomes	Actor/National Group Member	
	Ingroup	Outgroup
Positive	Internal	External
Negative	External	Internal

Source: Based on M. Hewstone (1988) 'Attributional Biasis in Intergroup Conflict' in W. Stroebe, A Kruglanski, D. Bar-Tal and M. Hewstone (eds), *The Social Psychology of Inter-group Conflict: Theory, Research and Applications*, p. 49.

In a variant of the ultimate attribution error, Allison and Messick (1985) have found that people also tend to use a group decision, judgment, or outcome as the basis for forming inferences about outgroup members' attitudes. This assumption of a decision-attitude correspondence can lead to an attribution error since group decisions are determined not only by members' attitudes, but also by the structural properties of groups and by the decision rules groups employ. In exactly the same way that people fail to properly weigh external constraints on individual behavior, people also fail to account properly for structural constraints on group decisions.[68]

Hewstone (1990) reviewed nineteen studies concerning three paradigms of the ultimate attribution error: causal explanations for positive and negative outcomes, for success and failure, and for group differences. He reports that the evidence is strongest for three general findings: (1) More internal attribution for positive behavior or events and less internal attribution for negative behavior and events by ingroup members than by outgroup members; (2) More attribution of outgroup failure to lack of ability than ingroup failure and the 'explaining away' of outgroup success to good luck, high effort, or ease of task; (3) A preference for ingroup-serving over outgroup-serving attributions for group differences.[69] Concerning implications of the ultimate attribution error for intergroup conflict and its resolution, Hewstone (1988) proposes that internal attributions for outgroup behaviors that confirm negative expectancies increase the likelihood of a continued conflict, while internal attributions for outgroup behaviors which disconfirm negative expectancies reduce the likelihood of continued conflict.[70] Clearly these findings have relevance for U.S.-Japan relations. On the basis of the discussion in this section, the following hypotheses regarding Japan-U.S. perceptions and attributions are offered:

> American and Japanese opinion leaders attribute the large bilateral trade imbalances more to factors external to their own nation (but often internal to the other nation) than to factors internal to their own nation.

> American and Japanese opinion leaders perceive the other nation as blaming their nation for the trade friction dilemma more than they perceive their nation as blaming the other for the dilemma.

> Both sets of opinion leaders view their own national negotiating style in a more positive light (i.e., more ingroup serving attributions) than the other nation's negotiating style.

Concerning the future of Japan-U.S. relations, it might also be hypothesized that

> If American and Japanese opinion leaders make more negative internal attributions for outgroup contributions to trade imbalances, and other issues of contention thereby conforming negative expectancies of the outgroup, trade friction (conflict) can be expected to continue.

What role do *schema*, or cognitive structures representing organized knowledge about a given stimulus, play in the attributional process? Not only do people impose structure and meaning on new incoming information by matching situations and people to *schemas* already stored in memory, but they also tend to adjust and twist incoming information to fit such *schemas*, even when presented with opposing data.[71] *Schemas* generally guide cognitive processes toward information relevant to prior knowledge as speed, efficiency, predictability, and generalization win out over accuracy.[72] This includes stereotypes, which Hamilton (1979) views as *schemata* or 'structural frameworks' that affect information-processing related to a given national group.[73] Though useful in simplifying complex reality, stereotypes are overly simple, somewhat inaccurate evaluations generally containing a kernel or two of truth. Resistant to change, they are often derived from faulty perceptions, from mass media, or from direct teachings. In response to new information bringing into question a given stereotype, a schema about an individual is more likely to change than a *schemata* or stereotype about a whole social group. People often explain *schema*-consistent behavior of members of an ethnic or national group in keeping with stereotyped dispositional factors without ever considering other factors.[74]

Further, it has also been hypothesized that people tend to perceive an outgroup as being more homogeneous in composition than their own group and to evaluate outgroup members in terms of extremes (polarized attributions).[75] One clear example of this tendency is the popular American concept of Japan as a single, gigantic, monolithic 'company' known as *Japan Inc.* As Rodney Clark (1979) has written concerning the reality behind this concept:

> The idea of *Japan, Inc.* is partly an extension from persons to institutions of the ill-informed judgement that all orientals look the same. It is also partly a rationalization of Japanese commercial success, which becomes attributable to an advantage no Western businessman enjoys: the unconditional support of a sympathetic government. It is an absurd over-simplification. Neither the Japanese government nor Japanese business are unitary bodies. The government party is split into factions. Different ministries publicly adopt opposing policies and privately work to defeat each other. Business interests do not coincide.[76]

Other examples of the human tendency to harbor polarized views concerning an outgroup's members as well as concepts of the outgroup as being more homogeneous than one's own group are currently popular Japanese perceptions concerning the United States. In a nutshell, the United States is perceived as a declining noncompetitive society with a violent, drug- and crime-ridden population that is illiterate and unwilling to work hard.[77] Obviously, there is sufficient data and news coverage to support such views; yet the United States and its citizens are far more than the sum of these parts, and far more diverse.

Finally, scapegoating, another product of the group-serving attributional bias, also has wide implications for intergroup behavior and conflict. Attributing negative outcomes or events to an outgroup or its members and then blaming them as scapegoats exonerates members of the ingroup from any responsibility or blame for their conditions and thereby prevents the lowering of self-esteem of the group membership.[78] Although it is hypothesized that a certain amount of mutual scapegoating is occurring, the extent to which this may be so is not tested at this time.

A Postscript from Cross-Cultural Social Psychology

Although many have argued that theory should be concerned with the universal logic and processes underlying the acquisition of social knowledge,[79] it is more than likely that linguistic and associated cultural meaning systems influence the causal inference process in varied and subtle ways. While the concept of the person as a separate, distinct entity that can be set apart from others in a given environment is central to most attribution theorizing, and appropriate in studies dealing with American subjects, cross-cultural researchers argue that attribution theory must take cultural variabilities into account before claiming universality. One variability of substantial cultural significance, that of the importance and meaning of group affiliations, is crucial to fully understanding the way in which people construe the causality of behavior.[80] As William Gudykunst (1988) has written,

> Given the importance of the ingroup-outgroup distinction for intergroup behavior and the fact that culture influences how this distinction is made, future research cannot afford to ignore culture as a theoretical variable in explaining intergroup behavior. . . .[81]

One example of research findings which questions the universality of the self-serving bias is that of Yoshihisa Kashima and Harry Triandis (1986) which determined that Japanese students placed a higher value on amount of effort expended and rather less importance on actual outcomes, either success or failure, than American students. The researchers concluded that the self-serving bias, an individual coping strategy, was not as likely to occur in societies like Japan, in which collective coping was the norm. In Japan, mutual support and effort toward group aims tend to be given greater importance than individual achievement, whereas in the United States, an individualistic culture in which self-reliance and individual competition are highly valued, individual achievement is generally given greater importance than group accomplishments.[82]

Concerning the effect of culture on intergroup processes, Gudykunst (1988) proposes 28 hypotheses: 20 deal with cultural differences (HD) and eight with cross-cultural universals (HU). Taken together, these hypotheses emphasize the necessity of taking cultural variability, such as the *individualism-collectivism* dimension, into consideration when examining intergroup processes. Three of the twenty hypotheses dealing with differences across cultures have implications for Japan-U.S trade relations. One concerns the degree of influence group memberships have on an individual's self-concept:

> Group memberships are a more important part of the self-concept in collectivist cultures than in individualistic cultures.[83]

Consequently, it is expected that being Japanese and belonging to certain Japanese organizations and groups is more important to a Japanese person's self-concept than being American and belonging to certain American organizations and groups is to an American person's self-concept.

Yet another hypothesis concerning the effects of cultural variability on the attributional process states that:

> Group membership is a more salient aspect of perceptions of social episodes involving intergroup behavior in collectivistic cultures than in individualistic cultures.[84]

The implication here is that being Japanese, as well as working for a particular organization or company, is a more salient aspect of Japanese perceptions concerning bilateral trade issues than of American perceptions. Another implication is that Japanese purchases of products such as rice, automobiles, automotive parts, and semiconductors are more likely to be based on factors of country of origin or company of origin than American purchases.

Yet another hypothesis concerning the effects of cultural differences on the attributional process is that:

> When group membership is salient, stronger and more confident attributions about members of an outgroup who cause a negative outcome are made in collectivistic cultures than in individualistic cultures.[85]

Since nationality is salient in the Japan-U.S. trade friction dilemma, and since group membership is more important in Japan than in the United States, Japanese are expected to form stronger, more confident attributions concerning Americans in regard to trade imbalances, sector disputes, and accompanying friction than Americans concerning Japanese contributions.

Three of Gudykunst's eight hypotheses concerning universals also have implications for U.S.-Japan trade relations. One hypothesis states that:

> Ingroup self-judgments are more favorable than judgments about outgroups across cultures.[86]

This supports the earlier discussion of the ultimate attribution error; that is, that both American and Japanese are expected to make more favorable judgments about themselves and their country than about the other country and its constituents.

Two additional hypotheses concerning universals have implications for this research effort. The first is that:

> The greater the dissimilarities between the ingroup and the outgroup, the greater the anxiety associated with, and difficulty of, intergroup interaction across cultures.[87]

Because the dissimilarities between American and Japanese are substantial, bilateral interactions potentially involve more anxiety and difficulty than bilateral interactions between two nations with far more in common.

Yet, on the other hand, Gudykunst hypothesizes that:

> Dissimilarities between the ingroup and the outgroup increase uncertainty less as the intimacy of an intergroup encounter increases across cultures.[88]

Concerning American and Japanese relations, this means that the effects of cultural dissimilarities should have fewer anxiety-producing difficulties as bilateral encounters grow more intimate and mutual transparency and understanding increase. Gudykunst concludes his analysis with a statement concerning the resolution of conflict. Gudykunst argues that cultural differences relating to such basic dimensions as *individualism-collectivism* significantly determine the decision rules used by groups for the resolution of competing interests.[89]

The existing evidence from cross-cultural social psychology, though scanty, generally supports the view that similar attributional processes are involved across cultures in producing the group-serving bias. However, the group-serving bias appears to be influenced by cultural variabilities, of which the *individualism-collectivism* dimension is but one dimension likely to be an influential factor in the Japan-U.S. trade friction dilemma. On the basis of the preceding discussion concerning the effects of the *individualism-collectivism* dimension on attributional processes, it is hypothesized that:

Japanese perceptions of American contributions to trade imbalances and other trade problems are generally more negative than American perceptions of Japanese contributions.

Japanese perceptions of Japanese contributions to trade imbalances and other trade problems are generally less negative than American perceptions of American contributions.

Japanese perceptions and their perceptions of other Japanese perceptions generally show less variation than American perceptions and their perceptions of other American perceptions.

Japanese perceptions of the Japanese negotiating style are generally more positive than American perceptions of the American negotiation style.

Japanese perceptions of the American negotiating style are more negative than American perceptions of the Japanese negotiation style.

Perceptions based on national group membership loyalties supersede perceptions based on academic training and career choice more for Japanese opinion leaders than for Americans.

Concerning a potential breakdown in bilateral trade relations, it is hypothesized that

American and Japanese view a breakdown in bilateral trade relations as seriously affecting the prosperity of both countries,

but that

American and Japanese opinion leaders believe that Japan's prosperity would be more adversely affected by a breakdown in bilateral trade relations than the United States would be.

However, given Japan's traditional sense of vulnerability and insecurity (e.g., small size, scarce national resource endowments, foodstuff shortages), in combination with America's traditional sense of confident autonomy and strength (e.g., large size, abundant national resource endowments, plentiful foodstuff supplies), it is hypthosized that:

> Japanese opinion leaders believe that the prosperity of both countries would be adversely affected by a breakdown in bilateral trade relations to a greater extent than American opinion leaders do.

It has been hypothesized that Japan-U.S. attributional tendencies, leading ultimately to mutual recriminations and blame, continue to increase the prospect for heightened bilateral contentiousness over large trade imbalances and sectoral issues. Aided by insights into the why and how of intergroup conflict which have been gleaned from social psychological theory and research, the next chapter discusses the methodology and research design used to identify and quantify trade-related bilateral perceptual differences and to test the hypotheses proposed in this chapter.

Notes

1   Sherif, M. (1966) *Group Conflict and Co-operation: Their Social Psychology*, p. 115.
2   Destler, I. M., H. Fukui, and H. Sato (1979) *The Textile Wrangle: Conflict in Japanese-American Relations, 1969-1971*, p. 22.
3   The Semiconductor Agreements of 1986 and 1991, examples of these tendencies are discussed in Chapter Eight.
4   John Conybeare (1985, 1987) employs a gaming theoretical approach in his analysis of trade wars throughout history. His analysis shows that trade wars have sometimes begun as a result of mistaken beliefs or perceptions and that cognitive factors can and do play important roles in whether cooperative efforts to resolve such conflicts are successful. A comprehensive search of major data bases conducted in May, 1994 located no other research of major significance conducted in the past decade in which a social psychological approach was used to analyze economic or trade conflicts. Terms such as trade conflict, economic conflict, and Japan-U.S. trade relations were combined with terms such as social psychology, realistic conflict theory, attribution theory, and the names of leading realistic conflict and attribution theorists. Data bases included PAIS (Public Affairs Information Service), Psychological Abstracts, Sociological Abstracts, Dialog, Nexus Lexus, CARL (Colorado Alliance Research Libraries), Business Index, Eureka Business Data Base, Periodical Abstracts, and Dissertation Abstracts.
5   Deutsch, M. (1969) 'Conflicts: Productive and Destructive', *Journal of Social Issues*, vol. 25, 1, pp. 8-9.
6   Hewstone, M. (1988) 'Attributional Bases of Intergroup Conflict', Chapter 3 in W. Stroebe, A. Kruglanski, D. Bar-Tal, and M. Hewstone (eds) *The Social Psychology of Intergroup Conflict: Theory, Research, and Applications*. As early as 1977, J. Horai 'Attributional Conflict', *Journal of Social Issues*, 33, pp. 88-100, had argued that

differing attributions for the same set of events were critical supports for intergroup conflict, while in 1979, J. Cooper and R. Fazio 'The Formation and Persistence of Attitudes That Support Intergroup Conflict' in W. G. Austin and S. Worchel (eds) *The Social Psychology of Intergroup Relations*, p. 149, wrote that one of the important bases of intergroup conflict could be found in the 'motivated misuse of attributional rules' and that attributions thus formed served to 'further sustain and nurture the conflict'.

7   Taylor, D. and F. Moghaddam (1987) *Theories of Intergroup Relations: International Social Psychological Perspectives*, p. 3.

8   Horrocks, J. (1966) 'Editor's Foreword' in M. Sherif, *Intergroup Conflict and Co-operation: Their Social Psychology*, p. ix.

9   Ibid.

10   Taylor, D. and F. Moghaddam (1987) p. 3.

11   See, for example, the literature reviews of J. H. Harvey and G. Weary (1984) 'Current Issues in Attribution Theory and Research', *Annual Review of Psychology*, vol. 35, pp. 427-459; J. Jaspars, M. Hewstone, and F. Fincham (1983) 'Attribution Theory and Research: The State of the Art' in J. Jaspars, F. Fincham, and M. Hewstone (eds), *Attribution Theory and Research: Conceptual, Development, and Social Dimensions*; H. Kelley and J. Michela (1980) 'Attribution Theory and Research', *Annual Review of Psychology*, vol. 31, pp. 457-501; M. Ross and G. Fletcher (1985) 'Attribution and Social Perception' in G. Lindzey and E. Aronson (eds), *The Handbook of Social Psychology*. See also the two editions of *Social Cognition* by S. Fiske and S. Taylor (1984, 1991).

12   See footnote 6 of this chapter.

13   Taylor, D. and F. Moghaddam (1987) p. 3.

14   Even when social psychologists, such as Morton Deutsch (1973) in *The Resolution of Conflict*, refer to culturally related misperceptions, they generally do so without clearly specifying what the cultural component encompasses. See the preceding chapter for discussion on the difficulties of determining boundaries between the individual (personality), the collective (culture) and the universal (human nature) levels of mental programming.

15   Taylor, D. and F. Moghaddam (1987) p. 4.

16   For further discussion on this shortcoming and proposals to remedy it, see S. Bochner (1982) 'The Social Psychology of Cross-Cultural Relations' in S. Bochner (ed) *Cultures in Contact: Studies in Cross-Cultural Interaction* (International Series in Experimental Social Psychology, vol. 1) pp. 5-44; G. Fletcher and C. Ward (1988) 'Attribution Theory and Processes: A Cross-Cultural Perspective' and other pertinent articles in M. Bond (ed) *The Cross-Cultural Challenge to Social Psychology*; M. Bond (1983) 'A Proposal for Cross-Cultural Studies of Attribution' in M. Hewstone (ed) *Attribution Theory: Social and Functional Extensions*, pp. 145-148.

17   Deutsch, M. and S. Shichman (1986) 'Conflict: A Social Psychological Perspective' in M. Hermann (ed) *Political Psychology: Contemporary Problems and Issues*, pp. 219-220.

18   Ibid., p. 220.

19   Leventhal, H. (1980) 'Toward a Comprehensive Theory of Emotion' in L. Berkowitz (ed) *Advances in Experimental Social Psychology*, vol. 13, pp. 192-193.

20   Ibid., p. 193.

21   Ibid.

22   Weiner, B. (1986) *An Attributional Theory of Motivation and Emotion*, p. 119.

23   Ibid., pp. 154-155; see also B. Weiner (1982) 'The Emotional Consequences of Causal Attributions' in Clark M. and S. Fiske (eds) *Affect and Cognition: The 17th Annual Carnegie Symposium on Cognition* and B. Weiner (1985) 'An Attributional Theory of Achievement Motivation and Emotion', *Psychological Review*, vol. 92, pp. 548-573.

24   An appealing implication of Weiner's approach, is that people can be 'reasoned' out of affective states since emotions (e.g., anger, pride, pity, fear) are only appropriate when particular causal attributions are made; this would have important implications for the resolution of conflict.

25   For example, see footnote 9 in Chapter 1 for a discussion concerning the difference between Morton Deutsch's use of the term *competitive* and that of economists.

26   Taylor, D. and F. Moghaddam (1987) pp. 34-35.

27   For further discussion, see M. Sherif (1966) and M. Deutsch (1969, 1973). The intellectual roots of the functional approach to intergroup relations as well as interest in intergroup relations itself can be traced back to sociologist William Sumner's (1906) writings on the basic state of conflict between the ingroup ('we group') and outgroups ('other-groups'). Sumner viewed intergroup biases, which he believed resulted from intergroup competition and functioned to preserve ingroup solidarity and to justify the exploitation of outgroups, as 'ethnocentrism'. See especially pp. 12-13 of W. Sumner's (1906) *Folkways*.

28   Deutsch, M. (1969) p. 9.

29   Deutsch, M. (1973) p. 352.

30   Ibid., pp. 48-49.

31   Ibid., p. 49.

32   Ibid., p. 60.

33   Ibid., pp. 67-68.

34   Sherif, M. (1966) p. 62.

35   As G. Allport (1958) *The Nature of Prejudice*, p. 115, wrote that 'it is possible to slice mankind by nations. . . (or national group) and ask what differences exist among them. The concept 'national character' implies that members of a nation, despite ethnic, racial religious, or individual differences among them, do resemble one another in certain fundamental patterns of belief and conduct, more than they resemble members of other nations'. Possible exceptions to clear-cut national group membership might be those American citizens born and raised in Japan who now live permanently in the United States. Depending on the circumstances in which they found themselves, such persons might feel -- or be perceived -- simultaneously as members of both groups, as members of only one group, or as members of neither group.

36   Amir, Y. (1969) 'Contact Hypothesis in Ethnic Relations', *Psychological Bulletin*, vol. 71, 5, pp. 338-339.

37   Deutsch (1973) p. 70-71.

38   Ibid., p. 354.

39   Ibid.

40   Ibid., p. 71. For potential conflict-producing properties of the Japan-U.S. communication system, see Chapter IV.

41   Ibid., pp. 354-355.

42   Ibid., p. 353.

43   Ibid., p. 355.

44   Ibid., pp. 29-31.

45 Ibid., p. 31.
46 Ibid.
47 Ibid., p. 352. Examples of such institutions include the OECD and the GATT.
48 Ibid.; consequently, one major bilateral goal should be the continued strengthening of such organizations.
49 Taylor, S. and S. Fiske (1978) 'Salience, Attention, Attribution: Top of the Head Phenomena' in L. Berkowitz (ed) *Advances in Experimental Psychology*, vol 11, pp. 249-288.
50 Taylor, S. and S. Fiske (1991) 'Social Encoding: Attention and Salience' in *Social Cognition*, second edition, pp. 249-250; for further discussion concerning salience, see L. McArthur (1981) 'What Grabs You? The Role of Attention in Impression Formation and Causal Attribution' in E. Higgins, et al (eds) *Social Cognition: The Ontario Symposium*, vol. 1, pp. 201-246. For a review concerning this and other heuristic errors, see R. Nisbett and L. Ross (1980) *Human Inference: Strategies and Shortcomings of Social Judgment*.
51 Fiske, S. and S. Taylor (1991) pp. 245-254.
52 Hewstone, M. (1988) p. 56.
53 Fiske, S. and S. Taylor (1991) pp. 254-257.
54 Nisbett, R. and L. Ross (1980) p. 45.
55 Ibid., pp 43-51.
56 Fiske, S. and S. Taylor (1991) pp. 257-260, 266; see also A. Tversky and D. Kahneman (1973) 'Availability: A Heuristic for Judging Frequency and Probability', *Cognitive Psychology*, vol. 5, pp. 207-232.
57 Fiske, S. and S. Taylor (1991) pp. 117-118.
58 Ibid., pp. 23-24; 553-554.
59 Heider, F. (1944) 'Social Relations Perceptions and Phenomenal Causality', *Psychological Review*, vol. 51, pp. 358-374, (1958) *The Psychology of Interpersonal Relations*.
60 Fletcher, G. and C. Ward (1988) p. 230; see also M. Bond (1983) pp. 145-148.
61 Kelley, H. (1967) 'Attribution Theory in Social Psychology' in D. Levine (ed) *Nebraska Symposium on Motivation*, vol. 15, pp. 192-240.
62 Jones, E. E. and V. Harris (1967) 'The Attribution of Attitudes', *Journal of Social Psychology*, vol. 3, pp. 1-24.
63 For further discussion, see E. E. Jones and R. Nisbett (1972) 'The Actor and the Observer: Divergent Perceptions of the Causes of Behavior', pp. 79-94 in E. E. Jones et al (eds) *Attribution: Perceiving the Causes of Behavior*, see also E. E. Jones (1979) 'The Rocky Road from Acts to Dispositions', *American Psychologist*, vol. 34, pp. 107-117.
64 Allport, G. (1954) *The Nature of Prejudice*.
65 Jones, E. E. and R. Nisbett (1972) pp. 79-94.
66 Pettigrew, T. (1979) 'The Ultimate Attribution Error: Extending Allport's Cognitive Analysis of Prejudice', *Personality and Social Psychology Bulletin*, vol. 5, pp. 461-476. The identification of an ultimate attribution error actually built on an earlier experiment by D. Taylor and V. Jaggi (1974) 'Ethnocentrism in a South Indian Context', *Journal of Cross-Cultural Psychology*, vol. 5, pp. 162-172, in which the same basic intergroup attributional bias was demonstrated. This bias was later elaborated on by M. Hewstone and C. Ward (1985) 'Ethnocentrism and Causal Attribution in Southeast Asia', *Journal of Personality and Social Psychology*, vol. 48, pp. 614-623.

67   See M. Brewer (1979) 'The Role of Ethnocentrism in Intergroup Conflict' in W. G. Austin and J. Worchel (eds) *The Social Psychology of Intergroup Relations*; H. Tajfel (1978) 'Social Categorization, Social Identity and Social Comparison' in H. Tajfel (ed) *Differentiation between Social Groups: Studies in Intergroup Behavior*, J. C. Turner (1981) 'The Experimental Social Psychology of Intergroup Behaviour' in J. C. Turner and H. Giles (eds) *Intergroup Behaviour*.

68   Allison, S. and D. Messick (1985) 'The Group Attribution Error', *Journal of Experimental Social Psychology*, vol. 21, pp. 564-565.

69   Hewstone, M. (1990) 'The 'Ultimate Attribution Error'? A Review of the Literature on Intergroup Causal Attribution', *European Journal of Social Psychology*, vol. 20, pp. 311-335.

70   Hewstone, M. (1988).

71   Nisbett, R. and L. Ross (1980) pp. 228-381.

72   Fiske, S. and S. Taylor (1991) pp. 553-554.

73   Hamilton, D. (1979) 'A Cognitive-Attributional Analysis of Stereotyping', pp. 53-84 in L. Berkowitz (ed) *Advances in Experimental Social Psychology*, vol 12; see also D. Hamilton (1981), *Cognitive Processes in Stereotyping and Intergroup Behavior*.

74   Pysczynkki, T. and J. Greenberg (1981) 'Role of Disconfirmed Expectancies in the Instigation of Attributional Processing', *Journal of Personality and Social Psychology*, vol. 40, pp. 31-38.

75   Park, B. and M. Rothbart (1982) 'Perception of Out-Group Homogeneity and Levels of Social Categorization: Memory for the Subordinate Attributes of In-Group and Out-Group Members', *Journal of Personality and Social Psychology*, vol. 42, pp. 1051-1068.

76   Clark, R. (1979) *The Japanese Company*, pp. 6-7. For an early example, *Business Week* (1970 March 7) 'Japan Inc'.

77   For examples, see L. Helm (1991 October 25) 'In Japan, Scorn for America', C. Chipello and U. Lehner (1992 February 4) 'Miyazawa Calls U.S. Work Ethic Lacking', *The Wall Street Journal*, and G. Fukushima (1993 August 8) 'Japan Sticks Third-World Label on U.S.', *The Los Angeles Times*.

78   Park, B. and M. Rothbart (1982) p. 1052.

79   See, for example, A. Kruglanski (1979) 'Causal Explanation, Teleological Expansion: On the Radical Particularism in Attribution Theory', *Journal of Personality and Social Psychology*, vol. 37, pp. 1447-1457.

80   Bond, M. (1983) 'A Proposal for Cross-Cultural Studies of Attribution' in M. Hewstone, (ed) *Attribution Theory: Social and Functional Extensions*, p. 146; see also, M. Hewstone and J. Jaspars (1982) 'Intergroup Relations and Attribution Processes' in H. Tajfel (ed) *Social Identity and Intergroup Relations* and W. Gudykunst (1988) 'Culture and Intergroup Processes' in M. Bond (ed) *The Cross-Cultural Challenge to Social Psychology*.

81   Gudykunst, W. (1988) p. 181.

82   Kashima, Y. and H. Triandis (1986) 'The Self-Serving Bias in Attributions as a Coping Strategy: A Cross-Cultural Study', *Journal of Cross-Cultural Psychology*, vol. 17, pp. 83-97.

83   Gudykunst, J. W. (1988) p.169 (HD1).

84   Ibid., p. 177 (HD17).

85   Ibid., p. 177 (HD18).

86   Ibid., p. 172 (HU3).

87 Ibid., p. 176 (HU7).
88 Ibid., p. 176 (HU8).
89 Ibid., p. 195.

6 Methodology and Research Design

The Rationale

The differing perceptions, mutual misunderstandings, and concomitant tensions first observed in 1853 have been recurring events, fluctuating in intensity and significance, in Japanese-American relations ever since. During the 1930s they nourished Japan's eventual decision to bomb Pearl Harbor which, in turn, 'inspired an immediate commitment to a vengeful war without mercy'.[1] Yet in the postwar years, a security alliance crucial to both was formed and a highly complex, mutually lucrative, interdependent trade relationship created. Since the 1970s, however, bilateral trade disputes have grown in scope and intensity. By the 1980s, the large U.S. trade deficit with Japan had become the focal point of bilateral contentiousness as leaders of both nations appeared unable to agree as to its causes and cures. As Americans grew ever more critical of Japanese for what were perceived as unfair business practices and closed import markets, Japanese increasingly responded with irritation and criticism regarding American economic and business laxities and shortcomings.

Even though both sets of national leaders seem to place greater responsibility or blame for the trade friction dilemma with the other nation than with their own, they continue to pursue workable solutions. Within the context of the 1989-1990 Structural Impediments Initiative, negotiators developed a document in which factors believed to contribute to the large trade imbalances were identified and elaborated on. Although an agenda for addressing these factors was set, leaders of both nations focused more on what the other nation should do than on what their own should do. The apparent perceptual gap, as reflected in much of the recent bilateral dialogue on issues from trade imbalances to sectoral complaints, has been the impetus for this study on the role perception plays in the Japan-U.S. trade friction dilemma. Although many have referred to a perceptual gap, this is perhaps the first research effort to attempt a systematic measurement and analysis of it.

Most would agree with a former chief economist of the U.S.-Japan Trade Council who recently wrote:

116

Beliefs and perceptions are difficult to quantify. The dividing line between politics and economics is inevitably blurred, and the addition of cultural factors exacerbates methodological problems.[2]

Yet the quantification of bilateral perceptual differences regarding Japan-U.S. trade is precisely the goal of this research effort, and social psychological theory furnishes the appropriate framework for accomplishing it. The probable roles played by culturally based factors in the creation and augmentation of Japan-U.S. perceptual differences were explored in Chapters Three through Five, while the difficulties of defining the extent of culture's domain and of determining the dividing line between economics and politics were discussed in Chapters Three and Four, respectively.

This is also a study in public opinion; that is, an expression by many individuals (in this case, opinion leaders selected from particular segments of American and Japanese society) of sentiments, cognitions, evaluations, and beliefs about certain societal issues (in this case, Japan-U.S. trade relations). Not only are studies of the public's views valuable and interesting in their own right, but they also have 'implications for attitude and attribution theories, for our understanding of intergroup relations, and for the role that events alongside different socializing agents play in the formation of people's cognitions'.[3]

Socializing agents, such as the family, neighborhood, school, and workplace, as well as a nation's institutions and political system, promote certain social beliefs and perceptions, as discussed in Chapters Three and Four. These 'derive from, and interact with, the environment which, though it gave rise to the beliefs, does not operate independently of them'.[4] The environment not only affects perceptions and beliefs but is also affected by them 'in a cycle of mutual dependence'.[5] Although the cultural and institutional components are major factors in shaping public perceptions and opinions, it is the set of social psychological factors discussed in Chapter Five that serves as the mechanism or agent giving rise to and supporting these perceptions and beliefs.

The current chapter on research methodology and design first offers an overview of the model, research objectives, and hypotheses. It then delineates the development of comparable samples of American and Japanese opinion leaders. Next it explains the research procedures, beginning with the selection of the survey method for the gathering of data on perceptual differences, the development of the survey instrument, the pilot tests, and the collection and tabulation of data. Finally, it describes the year-long evolution of a questionnaire whose purpose was to gather parallel data from American and Japanese opinion leaders for the identification and quantification of bilateral perceptual similarities and differences regarding bilateral trade relations, large trade imbalances, and national negotiating styles. It also describes and explains the questionnaire's final content, sequencing, and format; and reviews each of the questions and its intended purpose.

The Objectives

The basic premise on which this research effort rests is that social psychological factors serve as catalytic agents in the creation and augmentation of bilateral trade friction. While conventional wisdom holds that trade friction has occurred largely because of the immensity of bilateral trade imbalances in conjunction with the often complicated, drawn-out sectoral disputes, it is hypothesized here that social psychological factors (e.g., ingroup-outgroup perceptual discrepancies) act together as an intervening variable between causes (e.g., large bilateral trade imbalances) and effects (e.g., high levels of trade contentiousness). In this way, intergroup perceptual dynamics might serve to exacerbate the psychological effects of trade imbalances, structural discrepancies, and cultural/institutional differences, as modeled in Figure 6.1. Although this model is not fully tested in the current study, the existence of bilateral perceptual differences regarding trade imbalances, mutual attributions of blame, and the influence of cultural differences on perceptions are.

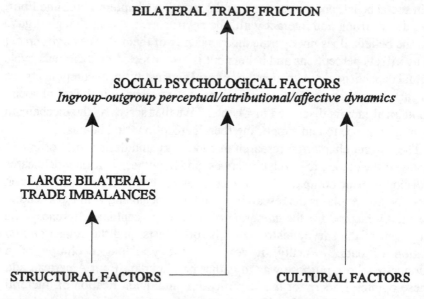

Figure 6.1   Japan-U.S. Trade Friction: A Causal Model

A perceptual gap, especially one involving differing attributions of the same event, are likely to occur to some extent between members of any two interacting groups. However, the size of the gap is expected to increase or decrease depending on the importance each side attaches to particular conflicts of interest, competitive dynamics, and their outcomes. The perceptual gap is also expected to be affected by the scope and significance of their cultural, institutional, and ideological differences. Identifying relevant perceptual distortions occurring between members of two interacting groups (in this case, Japan and the United States) can aid in the selection and application of appropriate means and mechanisms for diminishing their incendiary effects. Such understanding can also shed light on intergroup dynamics in general, and attributional tendencies in particular, by testing the veracity of pertinent social psychological theory.

In keeping with the objectives of this study, the first major task was the development of equivalent samples of American and Japanese opinion leaders. The second was the design of an appropriate survey instrument. The third was the collection and tabulation of quantifiable American and Japanese perceptual differences concerning trade imbalances and other aspects of the bilateral trade relationship, while the fourth was the evaluation of quantified perceptual differences within the context of relevant hypotheses based on realistic conflict theory (RCT), attribution theory, and cross-cultural research. In general, expectations were that the data would verify the alleged tendency of both sides to perceive the importance of trade imbalance causal factors differently and to place greater blame for trade imbalances and other trade problems with each other than with their own national group. Expectations were also that each side would view its own national negotiating style in a more positive light than that of the other side. More specifically, a determination would be made concerning the extent to which research findings lent support to the following set of hypotheses based on the theoretical models and research findings presented in the preceding chapter.

The first hypothesis (HD1) establishes the existence of bilateral perceptual differences in regard to large bilateral trade imbalances:

HD1 Significant perceptual differences exist between American and Japanese opinion leaders regarding the causes of large bilateral trade imbalances.

In addition to identifying, quantifying, and evaluating perceptual differences between American and Japanese opinion leaders, the same was to be done with responses of subgroups within and across the two sets of respondents. It was expected that a respondent's academic training and career choice would affect how the fourteen trade imbalance factors were ranked:

> **HU2** The causal perceptions of both American and Japanese opinion leaders tend to be shaped by their academic training and career choice.

This hypothesis suggests that economists would tend to rank macroeconomic factors as more important than institutional factors, while political scientists would tend to rank institutional factors higher than economists. Morever, American rice, automotive, and semiconductor sectoral leaders would be expected to place greater importance on microeconomic and institutional factors than on macroeconomic factors.

Although American and Japanese economists would both be expected to rank macroeconomic factors as being of greatest causal importance, they should each also exhibit the internal-external intergroup attributional tendency hypothesized in (HU4). However, Japanese would be expected to show this tendency to a greater extent than Americans:

> **HD3** Perceptions based on national group membership loyalties supersede perceptions based on academic training and career choice more for Japanese opinion leaders than for Americans.

This means that Japanese economists were expected to rate U.S. macroeconomic factors higher than Japanese macroeconomic factors to a greater degree than American economists rated Japanese macroeconomic factors higher than U.S. macroeconomic factors. Furthermore, Japanese economists would also be expected to rate the microeconomic factor of *superior Japanese product quality,* a positive internal to Japan factor, as high or higher than any single U.S. macroeconomic factor. Meanwhile, Japanese sectoral leaders would be expected to rate *superior Japanese product quality* as more important than American sectoral leaders would rate *relatively closed Japan domestic markets* or *unfair Japanese trade practices* as more important.

The fourth hypothesis (HU4), based on Pettigrew's ultimate attribution error, addresses the universal tendency of members of interacting groups to attribute negative outcomes to factors external to themselves or their group, while, at the same time, attributing the same or similar negative outcomes to factors internal to the other group and its members:

> **HU4** American and Japanese opinion leaders attribute the large bilateral trade imbalances more to factors external to their own nation (but often internal to the other nation) than to factors internal to their own nation.

The fifth hypothesis (HU5) builds on (HU4) by specifically addressing the group-serving tendency to place responsibility or blame with the other group rather than with one's own group. It, therefore, stresses the blame syndrome connected with intergroup competitive proceses described by Deutsch:

> **HU5** American and Japanese opinion leaders place greater responsibility or blame for the large trade imbalances with the other country and its constituents than with their own.

Although each side was expected to place greater responsibility or blame for negative bilateral outcomes with the other, the sixth hypothesis (HU6) suggests that both groups of opinion leaders would perceive that their nation is being blamed for negative bilateral outcomes by the other nation more than they perceived that their nation was blaming the other nation.

> **HU6** American and Japanese opinion leaders perceive the other nation as blaming their nation for the trade friction dilemma more than they perceive their nation as blaming the other nation.

The seventh and eighth hypotheses (HD7, HD8) are based on Gudykunst's hypothesized effects of the *individualism-collectivism* cultural dimension in which the salience of group membership is proposed to be stronger among members of collectivistic cultures than among members of individualistic cultures. As a result, stronger, more confident group-serving attributional tendencies are expected from members of collectivistic cultures than from members of individualistic cultures, while stronger self-serving attributional tendencies are expected more from members of individualistic cultures than from members of collectivistic cultures. On the one hand,

> **HD7** Japanese perceptions of American contributions to trade imbalances and other trade problems are generally more negative than American perceptions of Japanese contributions,

while, on the other hand,

> **HD8** Japanese perceptions of Japanese contributions to trade imbalances and other trade problems are generally less negative than American perceptions of American contributions.

In other words, (HD7) expresses the expectation that Japanese respondents would place greater responsibility or blame for the large trade imbalances with the United States than American respondents would place with Japan. Meanwhile, (HD8) expresses the expectation that Japanese respondents would place less responsibility or blame for the imbalances with Japan than American respondents would place with the United States.

Once again, an individual's sensitivity to the group's opinions, attitudes, and perceptions as well as susceptibility to the group's influence on one's opinions, attitudes, and perceptions are expected to be stronger among members of collectivistic cultures than among members of individualistic cultures. Consequently, it would be expected that:

> **HD9** Japanese perceptions and their perceptions of other Japanese perceptions generally show less variation than American perceptions and their perceptions of other American perceptions.

This means that comparisons of American and Japanese opinions with their perceptions of what best represents the opinions of most Americans and Japanese, respectively, should reveal that the gap between Japanese opinions and their perceptions of other Japanese opinions are substantially smaller than the gap between American opinions and their perceptions of other American opinions.

In the context of Deutsch's cooperative *win-win* intergroup dynamic versus competitive win-lose dynamic, it is hypothesized that

> **HU10** American and Japanese opinion leaders view bilateral trade relations with more of a *win-lose* orientation than a *win-win* orientation.

The extent to which each side viewed the trade relationship as *win-lose* might serve as a measure of current trade friction levels.

In keeping with realistic conflict theory's premise that real conflicts of interest are of great importance in the creation of perceptions of conflict, it would be expected that the United States, the nation with the large trade deficits, would be inclined to view the bilateral trade relationship in *win-lose* terms to a greater extent than Japan, the nation with the large trade surplus:

> **HD11** The nation with the larger trade deficit (U.S.) should view the bilateral trade relationship more in *win-lose* terms than the other nation (Japan).

Given the interdependence of the two economies, it would be expected that Americans and Japanese would both view a breakdown in bilateral trade relations as seriously affecting the prosperity of both countries:

> **HU12** American and Japanese opinion leaders view a breakdown in bilateral trade relations as seriously affecting the prosperity of both countries.

Furthermore, perceived vulnerability should be considered higher for Japan than for the United States among both sets of respondents, given the two countries' relative geographical sizes, natural resources, and histories:

> **HU13** American and Japanese opinion leaders believe that Japan's prosperity would be more adversely affected by a breakdown in bilateral trade relations than the United States would be.

However, given the expected effects of Japan's history and socialization processes on the thinking of Japanese opinion leaders and the effects of America's history and socialization processes on the thinking of American opinion leaders, a breakdown in trade relations should be viewed as more serious for both Japan and the United States by Japanese opinion leaders than by their American counterparts.

> **HD14** Japanese opinion leaders believe that the prosperity of both countries would be adversely affected by a breakdown in bilateral trade relations to a greater extent than American opinion leaders do.

Concerning national negotiation styles, the internal-external intergroup attributional tendencies of the ultimate attribution error were expected to be in full operation. Therefore, it is hypothesized that

> **HU15** Both sets of opinion leaders view their own national negotiating style in a more positive light (i.e., more ingroup serving attributions) than the other nation's negotiating style.

(HU15) expresses the expectation that each group's responses would reveal a preference for positive descriptions of their own national negotiating style (e.g., *fair, flexible, cooperative*) over negative descriptions (e.g., *unfair, rigid, uncooperative*) as well as a preference for negative descriptions of the other's national negotiating style over positive descriptions. However, given expectations of stronger group-serving tendencies among members of collectivistic cultures than among members of individualistic cultures, it would be expected that

HD16 Japanese perceptions of the Japanese negotiating style are generally more positive than American perceptions of the American negotiation style.

It would also be expected that

HD17 Japanese perceptions of the American negotiating style are more negative than American perceptions of the Japanese negotiation style.

In other words, Japanese opinion leaders would be expected to show a stronger preference for negative descriptions of the American national negotiating style than Americans would exhibit regarding the Japanese national negotiating style.

Concerning the implications of the ultimate attribution error for intergroup conflict and its resolution, Hewstone (1988) proposed that internal attributions for outgroup behaviors that confirm negative expectancies increase the likelihood of a continued conflict, while internal attribution for outgroup behaviors which disconfirm negative expectancies reduce the likelihood of continued conflict. Based on these proposed implications, it is hypothesized that

HU18 If American and Japanese opinion leaders make more negative internal attributions for outgroup contributions to trade imbalances and other issues of contention, thereby confirming negative expectancies of the outgroup, trade friction (conflict) can be expected to continue.

Although (HU18) cannot be tested at this time, the other seventeen hypotheses are now tested in Chapter Seven. Based on the results, conclusions are drawn concerning the extent to which bilateral perceptual differences and attributional biases are in operation. Conclusions are also drawn as to the nature and kind of these perceptual differences. Although American and Japanese rankings of imbalance factors are not evaluated as to their validity, Chapter Nine offers modest suggestions for the reduction of perceptual discrepancies. However, no specific proposals are made for addressing or resolving the host of structural and institutional challenges facing the two nations.

The Respondents

In order to test these hypotheses, nonprobability (or purposive) sampling was employed in selecting respondents on the basis of the following requirements.

First, respondents had to be opinion leaders who, because of their position, prestige, and power, had the ability to influence the opinions of others. Second, they had to be persons who were likely to have an inside story concerning Japan-U.S. trade relations because of the professional world in which they moved. Their opinions were expected to be more informed than those of the general public, and recent public opinion poll findings were expected to be largely reflections of what had already been expressed by persons of the calibre and type selected for inclusion in the sample. Third, the composition of the two sets of respondents had to be comparable in function and prestige within their respective countries. Potential respondents were chosen from among those holding leadership positions within the government, academic, media, and business sectors. Fourth, all had to be residents in their respective countries during the data collection period, except for selected diplomats, news correspondents, and area specialists whose work took them abroad.

Although it would have been preferable for each of the major groups to have had the same number of subgroups and respondents, it soon became clear that the ideal would be nearly impossible to accomplish, given the reality of the subject, the characteristics of the two populations, and the constraints of limited research time and money. Candidates for inclusion in the four groups of respondents were selected from an extensive list of persons compiled from numerous sources over a three-year period. Some had been published, quoted, or referred to in publications of various kinds. Some had been interviewees or participants in radio, television, or public seminars, programs, and forums. Others had been mentioned during interviews and informal telephone conversations with members of American and Japanese governmental agencies and private sector organizations. Still others were selected from various membership lists and business directories.[6] Final decisions to include potential respondents in the samples were made on the basis of whether or not professional positions held in one country had comparable counterparts in the other.

The list of potential respondents was easier to compile for some subgroups than for others. Among the easiest was the subgroup of American rice producers who were largely selected from annual business publication listings.[7] They were listed alphabetically along with names, addresses, phone numbers, amount of annual sales, and crops grown, in addition to rice. However, the most difficult subgroup was its Japanese counterpart. Reasons for this difference were partly the structural differences between the two domestic industries and their differing political significance. Another reason was the resistance of officials from the JMAFF, JETRO, and Japanese embassies, together with the resistance of Japanese agricultural promotional and lobbying groups in the United States, to offer significant assistance or suggestions in the development of a list of Japanese respondents from the rice sector.[8] In all other respects, government agencies, both American and Japanese, were generally helpful. Consequently, the development of the parallel samples was a challenging, pleasant enough activity, even while it was also tedious, painstaking, and time-consuming. The final composition of parallel American and Japanese samples is provided in Table 6.1.

Table 6.1   The American and Japanese Respondents - Questionnaires Sent/Returned/Completed

	Americans	Japanese	Total
Government Totals	**83 / 53**	**83 / 42**	**166 / 95**
Executive branch	10 / 1	10 / 0	
Legislative branch	15 / 7	15 / 5	
National bureaucracies			
Agriculture/JMAFF	8 / 6	8 / 3	
Commerce/MITI	18 / 14	18 / 10	
State/Foreign Affairs	12 / 8	12 / 9	
Miscellaneous[a]	10 / 8	10 / 5	
State level bureaucracies			
State/prefecture	10 / 9	10 / 10	
Academic Totals	**32 / 27**	**32 / 19**	**64 / 46**
Political Scientists	13 / 12	13 / 4	
Economists	11 / 7	11 / 10	
Area specialists	8 / 8	8 / 5	
Media Totals	**32 / 15**	**32 / 21**	**64 / 36**
Newspapers	13 / 9	13 / 8	
Magazines	11 / 5	11 / 7	
Television	8 / 1	8 / 6	
Industry Totals	**83 / 52**	**83 / 53**	**166 / 105**
Rice	25 / 17	25 / 13	
Automobiles	25 / 12	25 / 18	
Semiconductors	25 / 16	25 / 15	
Miscellaneous[b]	8 / 7	8 / 7	
Total questionnaires sent	**230 (100%)**	**230 (100%)**	**460 (100%)**
Response rate	**180 (78%)**	**143 (62%)**	**323 (70%)**
Completed questionnaires	**147 (64%)**	**135 (59%)**	**282 (61%)**
Additional comments	41 (23%)	66 (46%)	107 (33%)
Requests for summary	96 (53%)	125 (87%)	220 (68%)

Legend: [a]   Includes various national government agencies/organizations.
          [b]   Includes various trade-related private organizations.

A total of 460 questionnaires were sent out to 230 Americans and 230 Japanese. As shown in Table 6.1, the actual response rate was 70 percent (78 percent for Americans, 62 percent for Japanese), while those actually completing the questionnaires was 61 percent (64 percent for Americans and 59 percent for Japanese). A response rate of at least 60 percent is generally considered *good*, while 70 percent is considered *very good*.[9] Given the respondents' heavy work schedules and responsibilities, the response rate in this case has to be considered very good.[10] Those making additional comments included 46 percent of all Japanese and 23 percent of all Americans actually completing questionnaires.[11] Those requesting research summaries included 87 percent of the Japanese and 53 percent of the Americans who completed questionnaires.[12]

The group of 166 (83 American, 83 Japanese) government leaders involved seven subgroups of elected and appointed officials from comparable branches, departments, and agencies of each government. Specifically, these subgroups embodied members from each executive branch; elected senators; representatives or dietmen from each legislative branch; and career officials from each nation's agricultural, commercial, and diplomatic bureaucracies. A total of 53 American and 42 Japanese government officials actually completed questionnaires.

The bureaucratic subgroup was composed of career bureaucrats from America's Department of Agriculture (USDA) and Japan's Ministry of Agriculture, Forestry, and Fisheries (JMAFF), from the U.S. Department of Commerce and Japan's Ministry of International Trade and Industry (MITI) and from Japan External Trade Organization (JETRO), from the U.S. Department of State and Japan's Ministry of Foreign Affairs, and from various other national bureaucracies and agencies of each country. On the American side, these included the Department of the Treasury, the Department of Defense, the Department of Labor, the Federal Trade Commission, the International Trade Commission (ITC), and the Export-Import Bank. On the Japanese side, these included the Ministry of Finance (MOF), the Ministry of Posts and Telecommunications, the Ministry of Labor, the Economic Planning Agency (EPA), and the Fair Trade Commission. As Table 6.1 shows, the U.S. Departments of Agriculture and Commerce made stronger showings than Japan's JMAFF and MITI, while the two diplomatic bureaucracies contributed about equally.[13]

The last subgroup was composed of trade specialists from ten of the 50 state levels of government and ten of the 47 prefectural levels of government. The ten states and ten prefectures were chosen largely on the basis of whether or not the rice, automotive, or semiconductor sectors were important local industries. A second consideration was the overall economic importance of each state/prefecture to the nation as a whole. A third consideration was the inclusion of as many diverse geographical locations as possible. A final consideration was the difficulty, time, and cost of obtaining the appropriate mailing addresses and their verification. Getting American information was achieved through telephone operators and calls to the seats of state governments. Obtaining Japanese information proved considerably more difficult. Telephone calls to Japanese telephone operators and seats of perfectural governments were prohibitively expensive as well as logistically and temporally problematic. Therefore, verification was done by cross-referencing available sources in print with calls to pertinent offices in the United States.

The ten American states selected were Arkansas, California, Illinois, Massachusetts, Michigan, Mississippi, Missouri, New York, Ohio, and Texas. California, for example, was chosen largely because of its importance both as a semiconductor and a rice producer, whereas Michigan was chosen for its centrality in the American automotive industry. Futhermore, both states are among the most economically important to the country as a whole. The ten Japanese prefectures selected were Hiroshima, Hokkaido, Kanagawa, Miyagi, Nagano, Niigata, Osaka, Shizuoka, Tokyo (metropolitan area), and Yamagata. Other prefectures that might have been chosen included Aichi because of its automotive and rice production, Ibakari for its rice production, and Saitama, directly north of Tokyo, for both its automotive and semiconductor production. However, difficulties in obtaining information ultimately excluded them. Meanwhile, Tokyo and Osaka were chosen because of their centrality in Japan's automotive and semiconductor industries. They were also chosen because they include two of the most economically powerful cities in Japan. Meanwhile, the prefecture of Miyagi was chosen solely for its importance in rice production.

The group of 64 (32 American, 32 Japanese) academics and researchers from various universities and research institutes, as well as independent scholars, included political scientists, economists, and area specialists. Most members of the academic sample had done research and been published in topics relevant to the international political economy, trade, business, history, or intercultural communication. Additionally, they had all concentrated to some extent on Japan-U.S. relations in general or bilateral economic/trade relations specifically. The group of area specialists was composed of historians, intercultural communication specialists, and nonaffiliated writers who had published or were working in some area of bilateral relations. As Table 6.1 indicates, American political scientists and Japanese economists were the largest contributors to the data base from the academic group.

The group of 64 (32 American, 32 Japanese) media leaders selected were divided according to three subgroups: newspapers, magazines and journals, and television. Each national group included publishers, editors-in-chief, and well-known journalists of leading news and business news dailies, prominent weekly news, business news, or economic magazines/journals with large circulations. It also included eight producers, directors, or leading reporters for major television network news or business news programming in each country.

The final group of respondents was composed of 166 (83 American, 83 Japanese) leaders. These represented 25 each from the agricultural (rice), heavy industrial (automotive), and high technology (semiconductor) sectors and ten American and ten Japanese trade-related organizations. Industrial leaders in the automotive and semiconductor sectors included chairmen of the board, presidents, CEOs, and other executive officers or persons appointed or designated by the initially contacted persons to complete the questionnaires on their behalf. While the American rice sector sample was composed of managers or owners of large farms, the Japanese rice sector sample ended up being composed largely of politically active farmers or their ZENCHU and NOKYO representatives.

The Procedures

A survey method was used in this study not only because it was the best way to collect data on Japan-U.S. perceptual differences, but because it was the only way. It also meets the various requirements of social science.[14] The survey instrument developed for this study, a four page questionnaire developed over a year's time, was shaped by a number of research decisions, requirements, and constraints. These were of great importance in determining the questionnaire's content, length, style, format, and sequencing. The first decision was to compare parallel samples of American and Japanese opinion leaders, most of whom resided on a relatively permanent basis in their country of origin and citizenship. Because a major research goal was a meaningful but accurate identification and quantification of perceptual differences between these two sample populations, great care was taken in conceptualizing and designing a questionnaire that would both answer the needs of the research agenda and be relevant and interesting to respondents. Specifically, the questionnaire's purpose was to pinpoint areas of American and Japanese perceptual differences concerning the bilateral trade relationship, the factors causing the large trade imbalances, the roles each nation played in the perpetuation of the trade friction dilemma, and other aspects of the bilateral trade relationship, including national negotiation styles.

Because a decision was also made to use the same survey instrument for all respondents, the questionnaire content, style, and format, therefore, had to accommodate all members of both samples, from political scientists to economists, from government leaders to editors, and from industrialists to rice farmers. Because the questionnaire had to be sufficiently generic for all to answer, questions specific to any particular sample subgroup were eliminated. Instead, respondents were invited to add any comments or opinions they cared to make at the end of the questionnaire. A related goal was to achieve as high a return rate of completed questionnaires as possible. Because members of both samples were likely to be extremely busy people, it was decided that the questionnaire had to be short, concise, and accessible enough to be answered in 15 minutes or less. Therefore, greatly detailed or nuanced questions were avoided as was an overly academic format and question style. Response scales also had to be user-friendly.

Finally, the questionnaire had to be both a valid and reliable research instrument. Because the content, wording, and sequencing of questions affect the validity and reliability of attitude and opinion scales, care was taken to eliminate ambiguity and bias and to increase the degree of their cultural neutrality and appropriateness by having five American and five Japanese academic leaders (e.g., business, cross-cultural communication, international education) read and critique them. Up until the first pilot test, the questionnaire employed funnel sequencing, in which broad, open-ended questions preceded more limited questions focusing on more specific (narrow) aspects of the topic.

Pilot Testing

In the first of two preliminary tests, 28 ethnically mixed members of an American business-service organization first answered and then critiqued the questionnaire in a controlled group setting. In the process, several questions were identified as either biased or ambiguous, while broad, open-ended questions were found to be unnecessarily time-consuming, frustrating, or inhibiting for respondents. Additionally, responses to such questions were found difficult to precisely categorize and quantify. Consequently, it was decided to forfeit a higher degree of validity for a higher response rate. As a result, open-ended questions were eliminated altogether, including one that asked which single factor was thought to cause the currently high levels of bilateral trade friction. Results from the first pilot test, in which this question had been used, indicated that 21 of 28 respondents cited the trade imbalance. This result lent support to the research assumption that most informed persons were likely to cite the trade imbalance as a major cause, if not *the* major cause. This assumption was then incorporated into the underlying logic of the final questionnaire.

Remaining questions were rewritten in a simpler, more succinct form. Cumbersome, potentially confusing negative and double negative grammatical structures as well as passive voice and subjunctive mood (unreal conditions) verb structures were also eliminated to avoid confusion. Additionally, care was taken to rewrite several 'double-barreled' questions (questions in which more than one idea was expressed). Terms or phrases which members of the first pilot group thought biased or unclear were also modified.

Once the questionnaire had been carefully revised, a second pilot test was conducted, this time informally over a two month period with thirty carefully selected American and Japanese educators, business people, and government officials. Members of this second group were far more representative of the final target populations than members of the first group. The tabulation and analysis of data from this group revealed many of the hypothesized American and Japanese perceptual differences and attributional bias tendencies. Respondents from the second group were then asked on an *ad hoc* basis to critique the questionnaire's content and format. As a result of this input, the questionnaire was once again shortened and minor ambiguities eliminated.

It was during the second pilot test that efforts were also made to check the reliability of the questionnaire as a research instrument. Ten persons from the second group were selected to respond to the same questionnaire one to two weeks after their first response.[15] The second set of answers revealed slight discrepancies from the first. Follow-up interviews with each of the ten respondents revealed that fluctuations in responses had probably resulted from something read, heard, or seen prior to filling out the questionnaire. Because the overall response tendency of the ten respondents appeared relatively consistent, it was assumed that the questionnaire's reliability was sufficiently high to discount the need for further changes.

Additional changes were made during the week-long process of translating the survey instrument into Japanese. The primary translator, a Japanese professor and former industrialist who had lived in the United States for three extended periods of time, made suggestions concerning format and sequencing that he felt would make the questionnaire more appealing to Japanese respondents. Consequently, the question on the bilateral trade imbalance causal factors was placed first and the sequence of the remaining questions changed slightly. Secondly, the wording of several questions was adjusted to permit a smoother translation into Japanese and to eliminate instances of translation ambiguity. As a result, final American and Japanese versions of the questionnaire were thought to be as nearly equivalent as was possible.

The initial American and Japanese cover letters, however, were not. The American cover letter, which began with an attention-grabbing opening,

> Quite rare is the American two dollar bill. Far more rare is the enduring
> friendship between two nations,

would be accompanied by a $2 bill enclosure. Meanwhile, the Japanese cover
letter was rewritten in a more culturally appropriate style (e.g., polite, modest,
somewhat apologetic). Rather than a $2 bill, it would include an American
version of the questionnaire, in addition to the Japanese version. In the same
way that the letter in English was written to appeal to American respondents to
achieve a higher response rate, so the letter in Japanese was written to appeal
to Japanese respondents. As a result, there were striking differences in content
and style between the American and Japanese cover letters. Versions of both
are included in Appendix B.

Data Collection and Tabulation

After completion of the pilot testing and translation process, questionnaire
packets were sent to a total of 460 opinion leaders, 230 Americans and 230 of
their Japanese counterparts. Expectations were that American and Japanese
responses would tend to correspond with the national positions of their
respective countries as expressed in bilateral trade negotiations, media
accounts, and public opinion polls. An initial distribution of 230 packets to
American opinion leaders included a personalized cover letter, a two dollar bill,
a questionnaire, a self-addressed return envelope with the appropriate return
postage, while 230 packets to Japanese opinion leaders included a personalized
cover letter in Japanese, a questionnaire in Japanese, a questionnaire in English,
and a self-addressed envelope with the appropriate return postage. Follow-up
mailings were conducted two to three weeks later, and a limited third American
mailing was sent by registered mail to 65 American respondents three weeks
after the second mailing. While a third mailing would probably nudge a few
more Americans to respond, a third mailing would have been counterproductive
in the case of Japanese respondents.

In order to identify which subgroup each respondent belonged to, different
postal stamp combinations on the return envelopes were used for each subgroup
of both sample populations. Additionally, different sets of stamp combinations
were used on the return envelopes for each subsequent American mailing. This
provided information necessary for subgroup data tabulations and quantifica-
tions. As it turned out, because most Japanese respondents requested a
summary of research results, names, titles, and addresses were included on the
returned questionnaires. However, in the case of American respondents, the
postage stamp scheme became crucial since requests for research summaries

were less frequent.

Data processing involved the development of a coding method, a codebook or dictionary, and a method of inputting the data so that it could be manipulated to yield the appropriate quantified data. To ensure accuracy, computer entries were double-checked with the help of an assistant. Once all questionnaire data were received and tabulated, statistical differences in bilateral responses were identified and patterns in perceptions determined. Conclusions were then drawn regarding American and Japanese perceptual tendencies concerning the bilateral relationship and the relative importance of factors causing the bilateral trade imbalance. Conclusions were also drawn concerning national tendencies toward attributional blame regarding which country was more responsible for the creation of large trade imbalances as well as perceptions regarding solutions and probable outcomes if the dilemma were not resolved. A final determination was made concerning the extent to which the bilateral trade relationship was perceived as primarily cooperative *(win-win)* or competitive *(win-lose)*. This is taken up in the next chapter on results.

The Instruments

The equivalent American and Japanese versions of the questionnaire began with the bilateral trade imbalance question for which respondents were asked to rank fourteen commonly cited causal factors. Then questions concerning relative import market openness, economic competitiveness, and tendencies to blame the other nation for trade problems followed. The next question asked whether the current bilateral trade relationship was best described as cooperative *(win-win)* or competitive *(win-lose)*, followed by questions concerning how seriously a breakdown in bilateral trade relations would affect the prosperity of each country and the extent to which changes suggested in the Structural Impediments Initiative were expected to take place in each country by 2000. Respondents were then asked to select terms which best described typical American and Japanese negotiation styles. Both versions of the questionnaire concluded with questions asking respondents to identify their current occupation, give their names and addresses if they wished to receive a summary of research results, and add any remarks they cared to make. (See Appendix A for the American and Japanese versions of the questionnaire.)

Each section of the questionnaire and its questions are now described as to intent and purpose, especially as they relate to the hypotheses concerning bilateral perceptual/attributional tendencies. Part A concerns the ranking of fourteen factors often cited as causes of the large bilateral trade imbalances between Japan and the United States. These fourteen factors can be divided into two categorical groups. The first includes four categories of causal factors: macroeconomic, microeconomic, institutional, and cultural. The first category, that of macroeconomic factors, includes numbers 1, 4, 6, 7, 9, 12, 13, and 14. Of these, 7 and 13 can be included in the category of microeconomic causal factors as well, along with 2, 8, and 10. The institutional category includes numbers 3 and 5, while the single cultural factor is number 11. These will be useful in examining the types of factors each national group and various subgroups of opinion leaders (e.g., government officials, sectoral leaders, economists, political scientists) place greatest emphasis on. Furthermore, they will be useful in setting an effective agenda for tackling the trade imbalance problem. They will also offer insight into how respondents' academic training and career choices might affect the tendency to emphasize certain factors over others.

Part A (Trade Imbalance)

Please rate the following factors below as to their relative importance in causing the enormous bilateral trade imbalances of the 1980s and early 1990s.

Not a factor	. . . .	1
Minor factor	. . . .	2
Somewhat important factor	. . . .	3
Very important factor	. . . .	4
Unfamiliar	. . . .	U

1.	Currency misalignment	1	2	3	4	U
2.	Superior Japanese product quality	1	2	3	4	U
3.	Differing political-economic ideologies	1	2	3	4	U
4.	Low U.S. national savings rate	1	2	3	4	U
5.	Differing government/business relations	1	2	3	4	U
6.	U.S. national budget deficit	1	2	3	4	U
7.	Global economic conditions	1	2	3	4	U
8.	Unfair Japan trade practices	1	2	3	4	U
9.	Japan macroeconomic policies	1	2	3	4	U
10.	Relatively closed Japan domestic markets	1	2	3	4	U
11.	Differing negotiating styles	1	2	3	4	U
12.	High Japan national savings rate	1	2	3	4	U
13.	Declining U.S. competitiveness	1	2	3	4	U
14.	U.S. macroeconomic policies	1	2	3	4	U
15.	_____	1	2	3	4	U

(Insert your own/topic/idea here)

The second categorical grouping of the fourteen factors concerns the internal-external attributional dimension. This also yields four basic categories: positive internal attribution for Japan, negative internal attribution for Japan, negative internal attribution for the United States, and neutral or external attribution for both Japan and the United States. The single positive internal attribution for Japan is *superior Japanese product quality*. The second category includes three negative internal attributions: *unfair Japan trade practices, Japan macroeconomic policies,* and the *relatively closed Japan domestic markets*. Another factor, *Japan's high savings rate,* is a positive internal attribution for Japan from a Japanese perspective but a negative internal attribution for Japan from an American perspective. The two factors of *differing political-economic ideologies* and *differing government/business relations* appear to be neutral, but they are both factors which Americans tend to cite when discussing how different Japan is from other highly industrialized democracies and why she 'doesn't play by the rules'. To these, Japanese are expected to react negatively. The third category, negative internal attributions for the United States, is composed of four factors: *low U.S. national savings rate, U.S. national budget deficit, declining U.S. competitiveness,* and *U.S. macroeconomic policies.* The fourth and final group involves factors either neutral or external to both nations. These are *currency misalignment, global economic conditions,* and *differing negotiating styles.*

The data are expected to show that both American and Japanese opinion leaders attribute large bilateral trade imbalances more to factors external to their nation (often internal to the other nation) than to factors internal to their nation (HU4). A strong verification of this hypothesis would be interpreted as demonstrating that both sets of opinion leaders blame the other country and its constituents for the large trade imbalances more than they blame their own nation and its constituents. It would also suggest that negative affect levels related to bilateral trade relations were high among both sets of opinion leaders and that, as a consequence, bilateral trade friction levels were also elevated.

Viewing the factors more carefully in terms of both sets of categorical groups, it would appear that factors 2, 8, 10, and 13 are most likely to be the largest bones of bilateral contention. First, superior *Japanese product quality, unfair Japan trade practices,* and *relatively closed Japan domestic markets* are not only all microeconomic factors, but they can also be considered culturally and institutionally based factors as well. Given the current bilateral trade competition, which the United States appears to be losing, American respondents are expected to rate these much higher than Japanese respondents. Secondly, *declining U.S. competitiveness* can be thought of as both a macroeconomic factor and a microeconomic factor as well as culturally and institutionally based factors. Japanese respondents can be expected to rate this much higher than American respondents. Additionally, all four indicate the occurrence of real (objective) bilateral trade competition; a strong verification of (HU10) would indicate the occurrence of high levels of perceived (subjective) trade competition.

Part B of the questionnaire includes questions meant to identify an assortment of perceptions about the bilateral relationship itself.   Topics concerned which country was considered more responsible or to blame for the bilateral trade imbalance (B1), the extent of relative openness of American and Japanese domestic markets to imports (B2, B3), possible explanations for why Japan exports more to the United States than Japan imports from the United States (B4, B5), and what American producers might do if they want to increase their exports to Japan (B6). Also included were questions concerning the extent to which each country was blaming the other so that it did not have to face its own part in the trade friction dilemma (B7, B8) and the extent to which each national group was skilled at promising changes but in avoiding substantive implementation (B9, B10). Of great perceptual consequence was the question (B11) concerning the extent to which the current Japan-U.S. trade relationship was best described as cooperative (win-win) or competitive (win-lose). Finally, the last questions in Part B (B12, B13) asked respondents how seriously they believed a breakdown in the bilateral trade relationship would affect the prosperity of each nation; in other words, which nation was more vulnerable to an interruption of bilateral trade.

Part B (Perceptions)

Directions: Please place an *X* in a blank along the continuum underneath each question which best represents your *personal* opinion. Then place an *A* and a *J* in the blanks which you believe best represent the opinions of most Americans and Japanese, respectively.

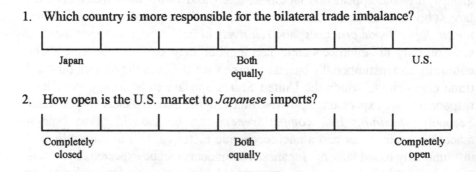

1. Which country is more responsible for the bilateral trade imbalance?

| Japan | | | Both equally | | | U.S. |

2. How open is the U.S. market to *Japanese* imports?

| Completely closed | | | Both equally | | | Completely open |

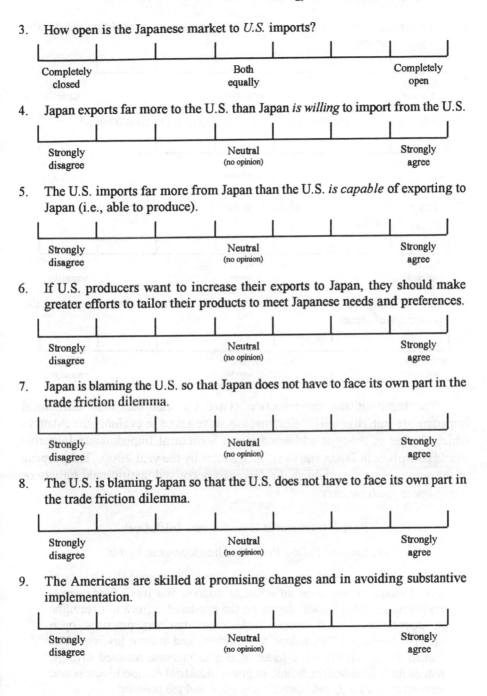

3. How open is the Japanese market to *U.S.* imports?

Completely   Both   Completely
closed   equally   open

4. Japan exports far more to the U.S. than Japan *is willing* to import from the U.S.

Strongly   Neutral   Strongly
disagree   (no opinion)   agree

5. The U.S. imports far more from Japan than the U.S. *is capable* of exporting to Japan (i.e., able to produce).

Strongly   Neutral   Strongly
disagree   (no opinion)   agree

6. If U.S. producers want to increase their exports to Japan, they should make greater efforts to tailor their products to meet Japanese needs and preferences.

Strongly   Neutral   Strongly
disagree   (no opinion)   agree

7. Japan is blaming the U.S. so that Japan does not have to face its own part in the trade friction dilemma.

Strongly   Neutral   Strongly
disagree   (no opinion)   agree

8. The U.S. is blaming Japan so that the U.S. does not have to face its own part in the trade friction dilemma.

Strongly   Neutral   Strongly
disagree   (no opinion)   agree

9. The Americans are skilled at promising changes and in avoiding substantive implementation.

Strongly   Neutral   Strongly
disagree   (no opinion)   agree

10. The Japanese are skilled at promising changes and in avoiding substantive implementation.

Strongly disagree | | | Neutral (no opinion) | | | Strongly agree

11. How would you describe the current U.S.-Japan trade relationship?

Cooperative (*win-win*) | | | Neutral (no opinion) | | | Competitive (*win-lose*)

12. How seriously would a breakdown in the bilateral trade relationship affect the prosperity of the U.S.?

Not at all seriously | | | Neutral (no opinion) | | | Very seriously

13. How seriously would a breakdown in the bilateral trade relationship affect the prosperity of Japan?

Not at all seriously | | | Neutral (no opinion) | | | Very seriously

The topic of the third section (Part C) was the 1990 Structural Impediments Initiative (SII). Respondents were asked to evaluate the extent to which change of the type addressed in the Structural Impediments Initiative would take place in Japan and the United States by the year 2000. The purpose of the question was to establish the degree of perceived institutional rigidity or flexibility in each country.

Part C (Structural Impediments Initiative)

Directions: Follow the same directions as in Part B.

In 1990 President Bush and Prime Minister Kaifu signed the *Structural Impediments Initiative* in an effort to address the more fundamental trade-related policy issues. Japan, on the one hand, agreed to streamline its distribution system, reduce exclusionary business practices, open *keiretsu* business relationships to outsiders, and reform pricing. The United States, on the other hand, agreed to increase national savings, reduce its federal budget deficit, improve industrial competitiveness and long-term planning, and upgrade education and job training.

1. A great deal of the change addressed in this agreement will have taken place in Japan by the year 2000.

Strongly disagree   Neutral (no opinion)   Strongly agree

2. A great deal of the change addressed in this agreement will have taken place in the U.S. by the year 2000.

Strongly disagree   Neutral (no opinion)   Strongly agree

The fourth section (Part D) concerned perceived negotiating styles of American and Japanese. Respondents were asked to circle words from a list of 19 adjectives which they believed best described the typical American and Japanese negotiation styles. The list included neutral, positive, and negative adjectives which would indicate neutral, positive, and negative internal national characteristics. Part D is as follows:

Part D (Trade Negotiations)

Directions: Answer the questions below, and write in any words or items not mentioned which you believe should be included.

1. Circle the words which best describe *American* negotiation styles. Write in any other words you would like to add.

1. Direct	2. Indirect	3. Legalistic	4. Vague
5. Detailed	6. Fair	7. Unfair	8. Honest
9. Deceptive	10. Flexible	11. Rigid	12. Effective
13. Ineffective	14. Cooperative	15. Uncooperative	16. Confrontational
17. Modest	18. Arrogant	19. Goal-oriented	

2. Circle the words which best describe *Japanese* negotiation styles. Write in any other words you would like to add.

1. Direct	2. Indirect	3. Legalistic	4. Vague
5. Detailed	6. Fair	7. Unfair	8. Honest
9. Deceptive	10. Flexible	11. Rigid	12. Effective
13. Ineffective	14. Cooperative	15. Uncooperative	16. Confrontational
17. Modest	18. Arrogant	19. Goal-oriented	

Attributes considered neutral are (1) *direct* and (2) *indirect*. Those considered positive include (6) *fair*, (8) *honest*, (10) *flexible*, (12) *effective*, and (14) *cooperative*. Those considered negative include (7) *unfair*, (9) *deceptive*, (11) *rigid*, (13) *ineffective*, (15) *uncooperative*, (16) *confrontational*, (17) *modest*, and (18) *arrogant*. Finally, the remaining characteristics might be considered either neutral or a mixture of both positive and negative attributes, depending on one's perspective: (3) *legalistic*, (4) *vague*, (5) *detailed*, and (19) *goal-oriented*.

In the fifth and final section (Part E), respondents were asked to respond to several miscellaneous questions:

Part E (Miscellaneous)

1. What is your current occupation?

2. If you would like to receive a summary of research results, please fill out your name and address below.

3. If you have any comments you would like to make, please use the following space.

The American and Japanese versions of this questionnaire are found in Appendix A.

Notes

1   Dower, John (1986) *War without Mercy: Race and Power in the Pacific War*, p. 181.
2   Cohen, S. D. (1991) *Cowboys and Samurai: Why the United States Is Losing the Battle and Why It Matters*, pp. 14-15.
3   Himmelweit, H. (1990) 'The Dynamics of Public Opinion' in C. Fraser and G. Gaskell (eds) *The Social Psychological Study of Widespread Beliefs*, pp. 79, 82.
4   Ibid., p. 96.
5   Ibid.
6   A list of sources used to develop the intended sample mailing list is found in Appendix C where they are arranged according to sector. Also included are the Japanese telephone directories.
7   See Appendix C for directories, indexes, guides, and yearbooks used to compile the list of political respondents.

8   After months of phone calls to Japanese government offices and agricultural organizations in the United States, not to mention the numerous letters complying with requests to explain research goals and requirements as well as to verify researcher credentials, the information received in return was generally vague, minimal, or out-of-date. Additionally, delays and requests for further information were endless and the reasons offered repetitively evasive.

9   Babbie, E. (1990) *Survey Research Methods*, Second Edition, p. 182.

10   Of 23 Americans and eight Japanese not completing questionnaires, 12 Americans gave no reason, four followed a 'don't-fill-out-questionnaires policy', and four cited the volume of questionnaires received. Two Americans and one Japanese were under heavy time constraints, two Americans and one Japanese felt the request should have gone to another agency, three Americans were abroad at the time, two Americans and one Japanese could not get clearance, one American and one Japanese wanted to remain impartial, and two Japanese had left their positions. Finally, two Americans and one Japanese found they could not express their opinions within a questionnaire format, one American did 'not feel well enough versed' on the topic, and one Japanese felt the Japan-U.S. trade imbalance 'was not as unfair as some think' and, therefore, declined the request to fill out a questionnaire.

11   Not only were Japanese respondents more likely to complete the questionnaires than American respondents, but they tended to do it with greater care and thoroughness. Contrary to this tendency, a number of Americans offered especially thoughtful, well-constructed comments, while several even wrote letters expressing opinions on trade relations or offering critiques of the survey instrument.

12   Some might say that this bilateral difference lends support to the idea that Japanese opinion leaders tend to be more interested than their American counterparts in understanding the bilateral trade friction dilemma. However, Americans might argue that it shows what assiduous collectors of information the Japanese are, while some Japanese might say that it offers yet another example of Americans not making enough effort.

13   In the same way that it was difficult to get names and addresses of persons involved in Japanese rice production or marketing, it was extremely difficult obtaining responses from officials in the Japanese government involved with the rice sector or other agricultural commodities.

14   According to survey research methodologists like Earl Babbie (1990) *Survey Research Methods* (Second Edition) pp. 40-44, a survey method is, first of all, guided by *logical* constraints and the careful implementation of logical understanding. Second, it pursues a clear and rigorous elaboration of a logical model, and can be used to clarify the *deterministic* system of cause and effect. Third, it is often conducted to determine and understand the leanings of the larger population (i.e., the results obtained are *generalizable*). Fourth, it can determine the relative value of a given set of variables in a relatively *parsimonious* fashion. Finally, the survey method is *specific* in that it clearly and cleanly meets the research need to conceptualize and measure variables accurately.

15   Only two respondents from the second pilot study (one Japanese and one American, both with extensive experience in both cultures) were included in the final data collection and tabulation.

7 Research Results and Discussion

While conventional wisdom holds that currently high levels of Japan-U.S. trade friction have occurred largely because of immense bilateral trade imbalances, underlying structural asymmetries, and strong sectoral competition, the argument presented here is that ingroup-outgroup perceptual dynamics serve to intensify the cognitive and affective consequences of real causes. In other words, Japan-U.S. perceptual dynamics act as an intervening variable between real causes (e.g., large bilateral trade imbalances) and effects (e.g., high levels of trade contentiousness). Diverging political-economic institutional systems and cultural patterns not only contribute to the creation of real causes, but also inform the perceptual processes of both Americans and Japanese.

A perceptual gap, especially one involving differing attributions of the same event, is likely to occur to some extent between members of any two competing groups. However, the perceptual gap increases or decreases depending on the scope and significance of competitive dynamics; real outcomes; diverging national goals; and cultural, institutional, and ideological differences between members of one group and those of another. Identifying crucial perceptual differences occurring between members of two interacting groups, in this case Japanese and Americans, can aid in the selection and application of appropriate means and mechanisms for diminishing their incendiary effects. Such understanding can also shed light on intergroup dynamics in general and attributional tendencies in particular by testing the veracity of pertinent social psychological theory. The evaluation of quantified Japan-U.S. perceptual differences within the context of 18 hypotheses based on realistic conflict theory (RCT) and attribution theory as well as research on the cultural dimension of *individualism-collectivism* was expected to verify the apparent tendency of American and Japanese opinion leaders to differ over the relative importance of factors believed to be causing the large bilateral trade imbalances. Additionally, the data were expected to support the hypothesis that Americans and Japanese place greater blame for trade imbalances and other issues of contention with the other nation than with their own. Expectations were also that each national group would tend to view its own national

142

negotiating style in a more positive light than that of the other side, but that academic training and career choice were expected to affect the perceptions of both sets of respondents.

Causes of the Large Bilateral Trade Imbalances

This section examines the extent to which the research data support the first and second hypotheses (HD1, HD2) that posit the existence of significant bilateral perceptual differences regarding trade imbalance causal factors between national groups (Americans, Japanese) and occupational groups (economists, political scientists, industrial leaders). It also examines the extent to which loyalties to national group membership supersede the perceptual effects of academic training and career choice more for Japanese than for Americans (HD3). The first hypothesis posits that

> **HD1** Significant differences exist between American and Japanese opinion leaders regarding the causes of large bilateral trade imbalances,

while the second proposes that

> **HU2** The causal perceptions of both American and Japanese opinion leaders tend to be shaped by their academic training and career choice.

As shown in Tables 7.1a and 7.1b, Japan-U.S. differences in perceptions regarding factors thought to be causing the large bilateral trade imbalances of the 1980s and early 1990s are extensive. Furthermore, a Spearman Rho correlation coefficient of -.1824, p> .05, indicates there was a low correlation between American and Japanese rankings. The American respondents' first ranked factor, *relatively closed Japanese domestic markets* (3.33), is followed by *differing government/business relations* (3.29), and *Japan macroeconomic policies* (3.21). The Japanese respondents' first ranked factor, *superior Japanese product quality* (3.57), is followed by *declining U.S. competitiveness* (3.33) and *U.S. national budget deficit* (3.19). The American top ranked factor (3.33) is ranked eleventh (2.31) by Japanese, while the top-ranked Japanese factor (3.57) is ranked seventh (3.05) by Americans. In keeping with the second hypothesis, economists were expected to rank macroeconomic factors as more important causes for trade imbalances than political scientists who were expected to place greater emphasis on institutional factors. Additionally, American rice, automotive, and semiconductor sector leaders were expected to

Table 7.1a   Relative Importance of Trade Imbalance Causal Factors: Total U.S. Mean Scores in Ranked Order Compared with Japan Results and Rankings

Causal Factors	Americans		Japanese	
Relatively closed Japan domestic markets	(1)	3.33	(11)	2.31
Differing government/business relations	(2)	3.29	(9)	2.39
Japan macroeconomic policies	(3)	3.21	(7)	2.53
Differing political-economic ideologies	(4)	3.09	(12)	2.25
U.S. macroeconomic policies	(5)	3.08	(4)	3.10
Unfair Japanese trade practices	(6)	3.08	(14)	1.83
U.S. national budget deficit	(7)	3.06	(3)	3.19
Superior Japanese product quality	(8)	3.05	(1)	3.57
Low U.S. national savings rate	(9)	2.96	(5)	3.07
High Japan national savings rate	(10)	2.85	(6)	2.67
Currency misalignment	(11)	2.82	(10)	2.34
Declining U.S. competitiveness	(12)	2.59	(2)	3.33
Global economic conditions	(13)	2.41	(8)	2.47
Differing negotiating styles	(14)	2.25	(13)	2.08

Legend: 4 = Very important factor   2 = Minor factor
          3 = Somewhat important factor   1 = Not a factor

Table 7.1b   Relative Importance of Trade Imbalance Causal Factors: Total Japan Mean Scores in Ranked Order Compared with U.S. Results and Rankings

Causal Factors	Japanese		Americans	
Superior Japanese product quality	(1)	3.57	(8)	3.05
Declining U.S. competitiveness	(2)	3.33	(12)	2.59
U.S. national budget deficit	(3)	3.19	(7)	3.06
U.S. macroeconomic policies	(4)	3.10	(6)	3.08
Low U.S. national savings rate	(5)	3.07	(9)	2.96
High Japan national savings rate	(6)	2.67	(10)	2.85
Japan macroeconomic policies	(7)	2.53	(3)	3.21
Global economic conditions	(8)	2.47	(13)	2.41
Differing government/business relations	(9)	2.39	(2)	3.29
Currency misalignment	(10)	2.34	(11)	2.82
Relatively closed Japan domestic markets	(11)	2.31	(1)	3.33
Differing political-economic ideologies	(12)	2.25	(4)	3.09
Differing negotiating styles	(13)	2.08	(14)	2.25
Unfair Japanese trade practices	(14)	1.83	(5)	3.08

Legend: See Table 7.1a.

place greater importance on microeconomic factors (e.g., relative openness of Japan's markets to imports) and institutional factors than on macroeconomic factors. The data in Tables 7.3a through 7.3f indicate that this is generally the case.

In order to look for significant differences, based on both nationality (HD1) and occupational group (HU2), scales of three of the major factors were created. The scales are macroeconomic (containing factors 1, 4, 6, 9, 12, 14), microeconomic (containing factors 2, 8, 10), and institutional (containing factors 3, 5). The reliabilities on the scales are macroeconomic (.70), microeconomic (.64), and institutional (.68), all of which are good reliabilities. Using two-way ANOVA, significant differences were looked for based on the different occupational groups (government, media, academic, and industrial) and nationality (Americans, Japanese) as to the major causes of trade imbalances. Results are shown in Tables 7.2a through 7.2e. For macroeconomic causes, significant differences were found (F (nationality) = 7.046, $p < .01$ and F (occupational group) = 4.43, $p < .01$); there were no interaction effects. Overall, Americans rated macroeconomic causes as more important than did Japanese, while academics generally rated macroeconomic factors as the most important. Regarding microeconomic causes (F (national group) = 173.19 $p < .01$; F (occupational group) = 2.94, $p > .01$; F (interaction effect) = 6.34, $p < .01$), Americans rated these as more important than Japanese respondents did. This is a particularly interesting finding given the fact that Japanese respondents overwhelmingly rated the microeconomic factor *superior Japanese product quality* above all other factors. Regarding institutional causes (F (nationality) = 82.74, $p < .01$), Americans generally rated these as more important than Japanese did. Regarding cultural causes (F (nationality) = 5.83, $p > .01$; F (occupational group) = 3.906, $p < .01$), there were no significant differences between Americans and Japanese, but media respondents generally rated these as more important than the government, academic, or industry respondents did. There were no interaction effects.

Table 7.2a   Means of Macroeconomic Causes

	Government	Academic	Media	Industry	All
Americans	2.89	3.30	2.86	2.73	2.95
Japanese	2.77	2.77	2.51	2.61	2.67
All	2.83	3.03	2.69	2.67	

Table 7.2b   Means of Microeconomic Causes

	Government	Academic	Media	Industry	All
Americans	2.68	2.54	2.49	3.03	2.69
Japanese	1.68	2.02	2.10	1.80	1.90
All	2.18	2.28	2.30	2.41	

Table 7.2c   Means of Institutional Causes

	Government	Academic	Media	Industry	All
Americans	3.12	2.77	3.27	3.32	3.12
Japanese	1.77	2.50	3.38	2.28	2.48
All	2.45	2.64	3.33	2.80	

Table 7.2d   Means of Cultural Causes

	Government	Academic	Media	Industry	All
Americans	2.25	1.82	2.62	2.27	2.24
Japanese	1.45	2.12	2.43	2.10	2.03
All	1.85	1.97	2.50	2.19	

Table 7.2e $\underline{F}$ - Values for Macroeconomic, Microeconomic, Institutional, and Cultural Causes

Causes	Nationality (American, Japanese)	Occupational Group	Interaction Effects
Macroeconomic	7.046**	4.43**	None
Microeconomic	173.19**	2.94	6.34**
Institutional	82.74**	2.769*	3.48*
Cultural	5.83	3.906**	None

Legend: * $\underline{p} < .05$
         ** $\underline{p} < .01$

A comparison of mean scores in Tables 7.2a to 7.2d indicates that, while Americans tended to rate all four groups of causes as important, they rated institutional causes as most important. Meanwhile, Japanese respondents rated macroeconomic causal factors highest. This national comparison suggests that Japanese respondents tend to be more discriminating in their ranking of factors than Americans. In general, all government officials as well as all academics ranked macroeconomic causes as most important, while all media respondents rated institutional causes as most important.

However, breaking the data down into smaller subgroups, as shown in Tables 7.3a through 7.3f, lends further support to the contention (HU2) that causal perceptions of both American and Japanese opinion leaders tend to be shaped by their areas of academic training and career choice. As expected, American economists rated macroeconomic factors more highly than all others, while American leaders from the rice, automotive, and semiconductor sectors rated Japanese microeconomic factors and institutional factors highest. One anomaly among these generally supportive findings was the set of responses from the twelve American political scientists, who rated macroeconomic factors more highly than all other factors. Another anomaly was the set of responses from Japanese economists, who rated the microeconomic factor *superior Japanese product quality* above all other factors. This ranking was followed by the expected high rankings of macroeconomic factors.

Furthermore, a comparison of responses of American and Japanese economists was expected to show that both groups generally ranked macroeconomic factors as being of greater causal importance than other factors, yet exhibit both the internal-external and group-serving attributional tendencies hypothesized in (HU4). As such, it was expected that all groups of Japanese respondents, even economists, would rate *superior Japanese product quality* more highly than they rated any other single factor. Therefore, it was hypothesized that

HD3 National group membership loyalties supersede academic training and career choice more for Japanese opinion leaders than for Americans.

As shown in Tables 7.3a through 7.3f, the data support the hypothesis (HD3) that loyalties to national group membership supersede the perceptual effects of academic training and career choice more for Japanese than for Americans. All Japanese groups fell into line with this expectation, while only American political scientists deviated from expectations when they ranked macroeconomic factors above all others and institutional factors in the lower half. Meanwhile, Japanese political scientists rated *superior Japanese product quality* in first place according to the expectation of (HD3), but *differing government/business relations* in second according to (HU2) expectations.

Table 7.3a   Relative Importance of Trade Imbalance Causal Factors: Political Scientists (Mean Scores)

	Causal Factors	U.S.	Japan
1.	Currency misalignment	3.17 (3)	2.40
2.	Superior Japanese product quality	3.17 (3)	3.60 (1)
3.	**Differing political-economic ideologies**	**2.83**	**3.00**
4.	Low U.S. national savings rate	3.33 (2)	3.00
5.	**Differing government/business relations**	**2.83**	**3.40 (2)**
6.	U.S. national budget deficit	3.67 (1)	3.00
7.	Global economic conditions	2.75	2.60
8.	Unfair Japanese trade practices	2.58	1.75
9.	Japan macroeconomic policies	3.00	2.00
10.	Relatively closed Japan domestic markets	2.92	3.20 (3)
11.	Differing negotiating styles	1.75	2.00
12.	High Japan national savings rate	2.83	2.60
13.	Declining U.S. competitiveness	2.75	3.00
14.	U.S. macroeconomic policies	3.17 (3)	2.25

Legend:

4 = Very important factor	2 = Minor factor
3 = Somewhat important factor	1 = Not a factor

Institutional factors in **bold**.
Sample: 12 American and 5 Japanese political scientists.

Table 7.3b   Relative Importance of Trade Imbalance Causal Factors: Economists (Mean Scores)

	Causal Factors	U.S.	Japan
1.	**Currency misalignment**	**3.38 (4)**	**2.44**
2.	Superior Japanese product quality	2.75	3.55 (1)
3.	Differing political-economic ideologies	2.50	1.22
4.	**Low U.S. national savings rate**	**3.63**	**3.44 (2)**
5.	Differing government/business relations	2.50	2.11
6.	**U.S. national budget deficit**	**3.63 (1)**	**3.44 (2)**
7.	Global economic conditions	2.25	1.44
8.	Unfair Japanese trade practices	2.63	1.67
9.	**Japan macroeconomic policies**	**3.00**	**3.00**
10.	Relatively closed Japan domestic markets	2.75	2.00
11.	Differing negotiating styles	1.63	1.33
12.	**High Japan national savings rate**	**3.63 (1)**	**3.11**
13.	Declining U.S. competitiveness	1.88	3.22 (4)
14.	**U.S. macroeconomic policies**	**3.52 (3)**	**3.22 (4)**

Legend:

4 = Very important factor	2 = Minor factor
3 = Somewhat important factor	1 = Not a factor

Macroeconomic factors in **bold**.
Sample: 8 American and 9 Japanese economists.

Table 7.3c   Relative Importance of Trade Imbalance Causal Factors: Rice Sector Respondents (Mean Scores)

	Causal Factors	U.S.	Japan
1.	Currency misalignment	2.86	2.31
2.	**Superior Japanese product quality**	**3.00**	**3.79 (1)**
3.	Differing political-economic ideologies	3.00	2.58
4.	Low U.S. national savings rate	2.33	2.77
5.	Differing government/business relations	3.65 (2)	2.92 (4)
6.	U.S. national budget deficit	2.75	3.38 (2)
7.	Global economic conditions	2.76	2.55
8.	**Unfair Japanese trade practices**	**3.71 (1)**	**2.00**
9.	Japan macroeconomic policies	3.57 (3)	2.31
10.	**Relatively closed Japan domestic markets**	**3.53 (4)**	**2.14**
11.	Differing negotiating styles	2.71	2.07
12.	High Japan national savings rate	2.27	2.71
13.	Declining U.S. competitiveness	3.00	3.14 (3)
14.	U.S. macroeconomic policies	3.00	2.55

Legend: 4 = Very important factor   2 = Minor factor

3 = Somewhat important factor   1 – Not a factor
Microeconomic factors in **bold**.
Sample: 14 American and 13 Japanese rice sector respondents.

Table 7.3d   Relative Importance of Trade Imbalance Causal Factors: Automotive Sector Respondents (Mean Scores)

	Causal Factors	U.S.	Japan
1.	Currency misalignment	2.50	2.61
2.	**Superior Japanese product quality**	**3.08**	**3.47 (2)**
3.	Differing political-economic ideologies	3.33 (5)	2.47
4.	Low U.S. national savings rate	2.42	2.73
5.	Differing government/business relations	3.58 (2)	2.65
6.	U.S. national budget deficit	3.00	3.28 (3)
7.	Global economic conditions	2.00	2.94 (5)
8.	**Unfair Japanese trade practices**	**3.58 (2)**	**1.72**
9.	Japan macroeconomic policies	3.42 (4)	2.82
10.	**Relatively closed Japan domestic markets**	**3.67 (1)**	**2.39**
11.	Differing negotiating styles	2.67	2.25
12.	High Japan national savings rate	2.58	2.53
13.	Declining U.S. competitiveness	2.17	3.56 (1)
14.	U.S. macroeconomic policies	2.67	3.24 (4)

Legend: 4 = Very important factor   2 = Minor factor

3 = Somewhat important factor   1 = Not a factor
Microeconomic factors in **bold**.
Sample: 12 American and 18 Japanese automotive sector respondents.

Table 7.3e   Relative Importance of Trade Imbalance Causal Factors: Semiconductor Sector Respondents (Mean Scores)

	Causal Factors	U.S.	Japan
1.	Currency misalignment	2.53	2.36
2.	**Superior Japanese product quality**	**2.81**	**3.73 (1)**
3.	Differing political-economic ideologies	3.44 (3)	1.93
4.	Low U.S. national savings rate	2.75	2.80 (5)
5.	Differing government/business relations	3.50 (2)	2.07
6.	U.S. national budget deficit	2.88	2.93 (4)
7.	Global economic conditions	2.06	2.54
8.	**Unfair Japanese trade practices**	**3.31 (5)**	**1.43**
9.	Japan macroeconomic policies	3.44 (3)	2.71
10.	**Relatively closed Japan domestic markets**	**3.75 (1)**	**2.20**
11.	Differing negotiating styles	2.13	2.07
12.	High Japan national savings rate	2.44	2.33
13.	Declining U.S. competitiveness	2.75	3.73 (1)
14.	U.S. macroeconomic policies	3.06	3.14 (3)

Legend: 4 = Very important factor   2 = Minor factor

3 = Somewhat important factor   1 = Not a factor
Microeconomic factors in **bold**.
Sample: 15 American and 14 Japanese semiconductor sector respondents.

Table 7.3f   Relative Importance of Trade Imbalance Causal Factors: All Rice, Automotive, and Semiconductor Industry Sector Respondents (Mean Scores)

	Causal Factors	U.S.	Japan
1.	Currency misalignment	2.65	2.50
2.	**Superior Japanese product quality**	**2.94**	**3.62 (1)**
3.	Differing political-economic ideologies	3.26	2.29
4.	Low U.S. national savings rate	2.66	2.82
5.	Differing government/business relations	3.58 (2)	2.55
6.	U.S. national budget deficit	2.88	3.25 (3)
7.	Global economic conditions	2.29	2.61
8.	**Unfair Japanese trade practices**	**3.50 (3)**	**1.74**
9.	Japan macroeconomic policies	3.41 (4)	2.65
10.	**Relatively closed Japan domestic markets**	**3.62 (1)**	**2.26**
11.	Differing negotiating styles	2.44	2.16
12.	High Japan national savings rate	2.58	2.61
13.	Declining U.S. competitiveness	2.67	3.43 (2)
14.	U.S. macroeconomic policies	2.94	3.06 (4)

Legend: 4 = Very important factor   2 = Minor factor

3 = Somewhat important factor   1 = Not a factor
Microeconomic factors in **bold**.
Sample: 48 American and 52 Japanese rice, automotive and semiconductor sector respondents.

However, they ranked the microeconomic factor, *relatively closed Japan markets*, in third. The responses of both American and Japanese industrial groups generally lent strong support to (HU2) and (HU3). Except for political scientists, each set of responses fell into line with research expectations and national norms.

Internal-External Attributions and Blame

The data have supported the first hypothesis (HD1) which proposed that significant Japan-U.S. perceptual differences regarding large bilateral trade imbalances and other trade-related issues are in operation. These findings set the stage for the testing of the fourth hypothesis (HU4) which addresses the universal tendency of members from interacting groups to attribute negative outcomes to factors external to themselves and their national group while, at the same time, attributing the same or similar negative outcomes to factors internal to the other group and its members. Therefore, it is hypothesized that

> HU4 American and Japanese opinion leaders attribute the large bilateral trade imbalances more to factors external to their own nation (but often internal to the other nation) than to factors internal to their own nation.

The fourteen factors listed in Part A of the questionnaire included one positive factor for Japan *(superior product quality)* and four negative factors *(relatively closed domestic markets, adverse macroeconomic policies, unfair trade practices, high national savings rate)*. Two additional factors *(differing government/business relations, differing political-economic ideologies)* are considered negative regarding Japan because the implication is that Japan does not follow political-economic norms and policies similar to those of other nations in the West (the United States, European Economic Community) or in keeping with the ideals of economic liberalism and an open trading system. The list also included four negative American factors *(adverse macroeconomic policies, the national budget deficit, low national savings rate, declining national competitiveness)* as well as three factors neutral in regards to Japan and the United States, or external to both. These are *currency misalignment, global economic conditions, differing negotiating styles.*

A comparison of mean scores in Table 7.4 lends support to the fourth hypothesis. The one exception seems to be *superior Japanese product quality*, a factor which is positive internal to Japan and which Japanese respondents favored above all others.[1] To formally test this hypothesis for statistical

Table 7.4   Bilateral Trade Imbalances: The Internal-External Dimension (Means of Each Factor With Their Rankings)

Causal Factors	Americans		Japanese		t-values
Internal to Japan+					
Superior Japanese product quality	(8)	3.05	(1)	3.57	-5.21**
Internal to Japan; External to the U.S.					
Relatively closed Japan domestic markets	(1)	3.33	(11)	2.31	10.03**
Differing government/business relations	(2)	3.29	(9)	2.39	8.01**
Japan macroeconomic policies	(3)	3.21	(7)	2.53	6.35**
Differing political-economic ideologies	(4)	3.09	(12)	2.25	6.37**
Unfair Japanese trade practices	(5)	3.08	(14)	1.83	11.87**
High Japan national savings rate	(10)	2.85	(6)	2.67	1.39
Internal to the U.S.; External to Japan					
Declining U.S. competitiveness	(12)	2.59	(2)	3.33	-6.87**
U.S. national budget deficit	(7)	3.06	(3)	3.19	-1.08
U.S. macroeconomic policies	(6)	3.08	(4)	3.10	-.14
Low U.S. national savings rate	(9)	2.96	(5)	3.07	-.94
Neutral; Internal to both the U.S. and Japan					
Currency misalignment	(11)	2.82	(10)	2.34	4.39**
Differing negotiating styles	(14)	2.25	(13)	2.08	1.39
External to both the U.S. and Japan					
Global economic conditions	(13)	2.41	(8)	2.47	-.45

Legend:	** $p < .001$
	+ Positive 'internal to Japan' factor
	4 = Very important factor
	3 = Somewhat important factor
	2 = Minor factor
	1 = Not a factor

significance, a scale of items negative 'internal to the United States' was created (reliability = .57) together with a scale of negative 'internal to Japan' was created (reliability = .57).[2] Negative 'internal to the U.S.' contained factors 4, 6, 13, 14 and negative 'internal to Japan' contained factors 3, 5, 8, 9, 10, 12. Using two-way ANOVA, with the scale (internal to Japan), the main effect of nationality was $F = 128.06$, $p < .01$. Overall, Americans rated these higher than Japanese. Thus, Americans perceived negative causes internal to Japan to be more important than Japanese did. Examining the scale, 'internal to the U.S.', $F = 4.89$, $p < .05$ (main effect of nationality), indicates that Japanese tended to rate these higher than Americans. Likewise, Americans and Japanese both rated negative causes internal to their own nation as less important than did the other country. Consequently, these results strongly support the fourth hypothesis. A comparison of t-values in Table 7.4 reveals statistically significant differences between American and Japanese respondents regarding two microeconomic factors *(unfair Japanese trade practice, relatively closed Japan domestic markets)*, two institutional factors *(differing government/business relations, differing political-economic ideologies)* and one macroeconomic-microeconomic factor *(declining U.S. competitiveness)*. In trade negotiations, these five factors are likely to cause the greatest amount of bilateral disagreement and contentiousness and should, therefore, be approached with the highest degree of diplomatic care.

This strong verification of (HU4) lays the groundwork for the fifth hypothesis (HU5) which addresses the group-serving tendency to place responsibility or blame with the other group rather than with one's own group. This hypothesis proposes that both sets of opinion leaders blame the other country and its constituents more than their own for the large trade imbalances.[3]

HU5 American and Japanese opinion leaders place greater responsibility or blame for the large trade imbalances with the other country and its constituents than with their own.

Then, as shown in Table 7.7, hypothesis (HU5) was tested using a t-test ($t = -7.75$, $p < .01$) for question B1 which once again supported the hypothesis that Americans and Japanese are more likely to blame the other nation than blame their own. Americans had a mean score of 3.20, while Japanese had a mean score of 4.43, as shown in Table 7.9. Although both scored near the mid-point, these scores showed that Americans more highly blamed the Japanese than Japanese blamed the Americans.

Further evidence of important perceptual differences between American and Japanese opinion leaders concerning underlying trade imbalance causal factors and the country bearing greater blame or responsibility is found in Tables 7.5a and 7.5b. These list the causal factors which respondents themselves contributed as write-ins and rated 'somewhat important' or 'very important'. Although Americans and Japanese responded in relatively similar fashion regarding linguistic or cultural differences and global realities, they once again revealed perceptual differences regarding domestic market openness, government policies, business management, product quality, and consumer practices.

Table 7.5a   American Written-In Additions to Trade Imbalance Causal Factors

(6)   CULTURAL DIFFERENCES (CD) (e.g., individualism-collectivism)

Differing business and social cultures
Effects of (CD) on business arrangements and practices
Effects of (CD) on lifestyle and consumer practices
Cultural and economic patterns peculiar to Japan

(4)   LANGUAGE DIFFERENCES

Lots of words—little communication; therefore, no results
Translation difficulties impede constructive bilateral change
Japanese communication style: (1) obfuscation of issues; (2) pursue *own* agenda with focus; (3) resist agreement until the end

(5)   ETHNOCENTRISM

General ignorance of each other's system
Refusal to see each other's perspective
Willingness to blame the other fellow
Both lack imagination to see future cooperative golden age
Japanese belief in Japanese uniqueness

(3)   GLOBAL REALITIES

Failure to complete Uruguay Round of the GATT
Defense burdens, foreign policy overhead
Demographics

(5)   GENERAL BILATERAL ECONOMIC FACTORS

Changes in comparative advantage
Producer economics in Japan/consumer economics in U.S.
Japanese investment barriers
Japanese greed: Japan a capitalistic, money-hungry nation of insensitive businessmen and giant conglomerates

(3)   BILATERAL TRADE PATTERNS

Automotive sector's large share of overall U.S.-Japan trade
Japan must run surpluses with developed countries to offset expenditures on raw material imports

continued

Table 7.5a *continued*

(11)   DOMESTIC MARKETS

Large U.S. import market
Japan's protected domestic markets
Japanese trade impediments/barriers
Japanese distribution system*
High costs of entering Japanese market
High costs of doing business in Japan compared to other markets

(19)   GOVERNMENT ECONOMIC, INDUSTRIAL, AND TRADE POLICIES

Japanese industrial/technical/trade policies/strategies*
Orchestrated efforts by Japanese business/government
Japanese business-government collaboration*
No Japanese enforcement of antitrust Japanese intellectual property
    improprieties
U.S. geopolitics: underemphasis on economics
U.S. gives low priority to trade policy goals
Abundance of U.S. political appointees who participate in negotiations
    with the Japanese
Intergovernmental policies for export controls

(29)   BUSINESS MANAGEMENT, PRODUCTIVITY, AND PRODUCTS

Japanese *keiretsu*/monopolies**
Large size of *keiretsu* have inherent competitive advantage over
    smaller U.S. firms
Japanese corporate insular attitudes
Japanese manufacturers use Japanese suppliers in Japan and U.S.
Japanese prefer to do business with their own
Japan business strategies and (mercantilistic) practices
Japanese dumping and other adversarial business practices
Insufficient U.S. export effort/expertise*
Short-sighted U.S.industrial management (low investment in capital
    equipment and technology)
Poor U.S. business practices (short-term oriented, legalistic, inflexible,
    difficult to work with)
U.S. companies often unwilling to adapt their products or marketing
    techniques as needed for Japanese market
Insufficient U.S. products for export
No U.S. source for certain products
Insufficient U.S. product quality

continued

Table 7.5a *continued*

(7)   CONSUMER PRACTICES

U.S. customers are accustomed to buying high quality Japanese goods
Japanese preference for own goods*
A 'buy Japanese' mentality

Legend: Figures in parentheses before each category indicate the number of
American respondents contributing to this category. All factors listed
were ranked as 'somewhat important' or 'very important'.
*Five or more respondents.
**Ten or more respondents.

Table 7.5b   Japanese Written-In Additions to Trade Imbalance Causal Factors

(4)   CULTURAL DIFFERENCES (CD) (e.g., groupism-individualism)

(1)   LANGUAGE DIFFERENCES

(7)   ETHNOCENTRISM

General ignorance of each other's system
Japanese closed-mindedness
Japanese lack of international mentality
Japanese insist on Japan's uniqueness

(4)   GLOBAL REALITIES

End of the Cold War
Changes in structure of international political economy
U.S. economy now 100% integrated into global economy

(6)   GENERAL BILATERAL ECONOMIC FACTORS

Changes in comparative advantage
U.S. large with abundant resources, but Japan not
Japanese investment patterns
Differences in business cycles
Japanese greed: Japan stronger than she thinks

continued

Table 7.5b *continued*

(6)   BILATERAL TRADE PATTERNS

Multinational corporations: international production/markets
U.S. move operations abroad and sell from abroad
Japan runs surpluses to offset expenditures on energy

(5)   DOMESTIC MARKETS

Large U.S. market (well-developed, self-sufficient)
Large U.S. consumer market for Japan's high tech products
Japanese distribution system
Japan local foreign market unsophisticated

(10)   GOVERNMENT ECONOMIC, INDUSTRIAL, AND TRADE POLICIES

Differing economic policies
Japanese financing of U.S. national debt
Japan must change (e.g., increase income taxes)
U.S. protectionism only (e.g., dumping accusations)

(37)   BUSINESS MANAGEMENT, PRODUCTIVITY, AND PRODUCTS

Differences in industrial structures
Differences in corporate management styles*
Differences in export mindedness*
Differences in trade manufacturing and marketing effort
Good Japanese trade strategy and effort
Insufficient U.S. export effort/expertise**
Insufficient U.S. products/product quality*
Short-sighted U.S. industrial management*
U.S. enterprises breaking up and leaving manufacturing
Relative source availability

(8)   CONSUMER PRACTICES

U.S. prefers large, abundant; Japan small, economical (e.g., autos)
Japanese preference for Japanese goods
Excessive U.S. consumption*

Legend: Figures in parentheses before each category indicate the number of American respondents contributing to this category. All factors listed were ranked as 'somewhat important' or 'very important'.
*Five or more respondents.
**Ten or more respondents.

Regarding the relative openness of domestic import markets, more than five American respondents identified Japan's distribution system as a major causal factor, while only one Japanese respondent did. Regarding government policy factors, five Americans identified Japan's industrial, technical, or trade policies as major causes, and five cited Japanese business-government collaboration. Regarding business management, more than ten Americans identified the Japanese *keiretsu* as causal factors, while five Japanese identified short-sighted American industrial management, five cited bilateral differences in corporate management styles, and five pointed to bilateral differences in export-mindedness. While more than five Americans acknowledged insufficient U.S. export effort or expertise, more than ten Japanese identified this as a major factor, and ten cited insufficient American products or product quality. Concerning consumer practices, more than five Americans identified a Japanese preference for Japanese goods, while more than five Japanese cited excessive U.S. consumption. Clearly, a blame-the-other-nation tendency is in operation on both sides of the Pacific.

Although each side places greater responsibility or blame for negative bilateral trade balance outcomes with the other, the sixth hypothesis (HU6) proposes that each group of opinion leaders perceives its own nation as being blamed by the other nation more than they perceive their own nation as blaming the other. The hypothesis states that

> **HU6** Japanese and American opinion leaders perceive the other nation as blaming their nation to avoid facing its part in the trade friction dilemma more than their nation blames the other to avoid facing its own contribution to the same.

American and Japanese responses to the seventh and eighth questions of Part B of the questionnaire verifies that this is indeed the case. Table 7.6 reveals that Americans moderately agree (5.07) while Japanese somewhat more strongly disagree (2.42) with the statement that Japan is blaming the United States. On the one hand, Americans somewhat agree (4.58) while Japanese agree more strongly (5.50) that the United States is blaming Japan. In both cases, the differences in responses between the two groups are statistically significant, as shown in Table 7.7. Regarding the first statement (B7), $t = 15.60$, $p < .01$; for the second statement (B8), $t = -5.08$, $p < .01$. Although American respondents perceived both Japan and the United States as blaming the other, they found Japan to be blaming the United States more than the United States was blaming Japan. On the other hand, Japanese respondents perceived Japan as not blaming, but being blamed, by the United States. These were the perceptions even though Table 7.8 reveals that Japanese respondents were blaming the United States nearly as much as American respondents were blaming Japan.

Table 7.6 National Tendencies to Blame the Other Country, Questions B7, B8 (Means)

Statements	Respondents	Own Personal Opinion	Perceived American Opinion	Perceived Japanese Opinion

Japan is blaming the U.S. so that Japan does not have to face its own part in the trade friction dilemma.

| | Americans | 5.07 | 6.07 | 2.29 |
| | Japanese | 2.42 | 5.71 | 2.08 |

The U.S. is blaming Japan so that the U.S. does not have to face its own part in the trade friction dilemma.

| | Americans | 4.58 | 2.74 | 6.04 |
| | Japanese | 5.50 | 2.19 | 5.92 |

Legend: 1 = Strongly disagree   4 = Neutral   7 = Strongly agree

Table 7.7 T-Values for Questions B1 - B13

Question #	T-Values	Question #	T-Values	Question #	T-Values
B1	-7.75**	B6	-5.22**	B11	4.18**
B2	3.61**	B7	15.60**	B12	-2.91**
B3	-8.76**	B8	-5.08**	B13	-7.29**
B4	1.98*	B9	.30		
B5	-7.26**	B10	10.54**		

Note: For complete text of Part B questions (B1-B13), refer to Appendix, pages 268-270.

Legend: * $p < .05$
  ** $p < .01$

Table 7.8 Country More Responsible for Bilateral Trade Imbalance, Question B1 (Means)

Respondents	Own Personal Opinion	Perceived American Opinion	Perceived Japanese Opinion
Americans	3.20	1.88	5.49
Japanese	4.43	1.81	5.13

Legend: 1 = Japan   4 = Both equally   7 = U.S.

Current Bilateral Trade Relations

Because the salience of group membership is likely to be stronger among members of collectivistic cultures than among members of individualistic cultures, stronger, more confident group-serving attributional tendencies can be expected from Japanese than from Americans; meanwhile, stronger, more confident self-serving attributional tendencies can be expected from Americans than from Japanese. Concerning Japanese perceptual tendencies compared with American perceptual tendencies, the seventh hypothesis (HD7) proposes that

> **HD7** Japanese perceptions of American contributions to trade imbalances and other trade-related problems are generally more negative than American perceptions of Japanese contributions.

while the eighth hypothesis (HD8) proposes that

> **HD8** Japanese perceptions of Japanese contributions to trade imbalances and other trade problems are generally less negative than American perceptions of American contributions.

In other words, Japanese are expected to be more critical of the United States than Americans are of Japan, while Japanese are expected to be less critical of Japan than Americans are of the United States. As shown in Table 7.8 above, research findings regarding (HD7) are mixed and, therefore, inconclusive; however, the mean scores support (HD8). This data suggests that both national groups hold the other nation more responsible for the bilateral trade imbalances than their own or those of the other group. However, American respondents place somewhat greater responsibility with Japan than Japanese respondents place with the United States.

Because an individual's sensitivity to the group's opinions, attitudes, and perceptions as well as the group's influence on its members' opinions, attitudes, and perceptions are expected to be stronger among members of collectivistic cultures than among members of individualistic cultures, it can also be expected that

> **HD9** Japanese perceptions and their perceptions of other Japanese perceptions generally show less variation than American perceptions and their perceptions of other American perceptions.

The descriptive statistics in Table 7.9 demonstrate that both groups generally view public perceptions as more polarized than their own. However,

Table 7.9   Comparing Personal Opinions with Perceived Opinions, Questions B1-B13 (Means/Standard Deviations)

Question/Respondents	Own Personal Opinion (P) Means / S.D.		Perceived American Opinion (A) Means / S.D.		Perceived Japanese Opinion (J) Means / S.D.	
B1. Which country is more responsible for the bilateral trade imbalance?						
Americans	3.20	1.51	1.88	1.25		
Japanese	4.43	1.05			5.13	1.24
B2. Openness of the U.S. market to Japanese imports.						
Americans	5.73	1.15	6.31	1.31		
Japanese	5.22	1.07			5.30	1.07
B3. Openness of the Japanese market to U.S. imports.						
Americans	2.77	1.12	2.02	1.36		
Japanese	4.05	1.27			4.44	1.16
B4. Japan exports far more to the U.S. than Japan *is willing* to import from the U.S.						
Americans	5.40	1.65	6.38	1.11		
Japanese	4.89	1.84			4.63	1.77
B5. The U.S. imports far more from Japan than the U.S. *is capable* of exporting to Japan.						
Americans	2.62	1.85	2.33	1.72		
Japanese	4.24	1.85			4.18	1.73
B6. If U.S. producers want to increase their exports to Japan, they should make greater efforts to tailor their products to meet Japanese needs and preferences.						
Americans	5.63	1.31	4.64	1.39		
Japanese	6.40	1.06			6.60	.78
B7. Japan is blaming the U.S. so that Japan does not have to face its own part in the trade friction dilemma.						
Americans	5.07	1.44	6.07	1.07		
Japanese	2.42	1.39			2.08	1.18
B8. The U.S. is blaming Japan so that the U.S. does not have to face its own part in the trade friction dilemma.						
Americans	4.58	1.67	2.74	1.46		
Japanese	5.50	1.14			5.92	1.18
B9. The Americans are skilled at promising changes and in avoiding substantive implementation.						
Americans	3.68	1.77	2.75	1.58		
Japanese	3.70	1.49			4.06	1.36

continued

Table 7.9 *continued*

B10.   The Japanese are skilled at promising changes and in avoiding substantive
        implementation.

Americans	5.68	1.31	6.35	.93		
Japanese	3.75	1.68			3.42	1.51

B11.   The extent to which U.S-Japan trade relations are viewed as win-win (cooperative)
        or lose-lose (competitive).

Americans	5.07	1.54	6.14	.99		
Japanese	4.22	1.73			4.53	1.63

B12.   Effects of breakdown in bilateral trade relations on the prosperity of the United
        States.

Americans	5.38	1.54	4.00	1.60		
Japanese	5.92	1.34			5.60	1.30

B13.   Effects of breakdown in bilateral trade relations on the prosperity of Japan.

Americans	6.09	1.13	5.67	1.34		
Japanese	6.49	1.87			6.27	1.06

the American group's personal opinions (P) and perceived American opinions
(A) generally showed substantially more divergence than the Japanese groups's
personal opinions (P) and perceived Japanese opinions (J). American responses
generally show greater variation across the board than Japanese responses, as
indicated by comparing the standard deviations in Table 7.9 of American
perceptions of American opinions and Japanese perceptions Japanese opinions.

Testing for statistically significant Japan-U.S. perceptual differences
regarding question B4 revealed that American respondents believe more
strongly than Japanese respondents that Japan exports far more to the United
States than Japan *is willing* to import ($t = 1.98$, $p< .05$). This is shown above
in Table 7.7. Meanwhile, testing for such differences regarding Question B5
showed that Americans strongly disagree, while Japanese slightly agree, that the
United States imports far more from Japan than the United States *is capable* of
exporting ($t = -7.26$, $p< .01$). However, concerning Question B6, both groups
of respondents believe that, if American producers want to export more to
Japan, they should make greater efforts to meet Japanese needs and preferences.
The relative strength of their agreement (6.40 for Japanese, 5.63 for Americans)
as shown in Table 7.9, yields yet another significant difference ($t = -5.22$, $p <$
.01), as shown above in Table 7.7.

Concerning whether Americans and Japanese are perceived as being
skilled at promising changes and in avoiding substantive implementation
(Questions B9, B10), both sets of respondents were in close agreement

concerning Americans ($\underline{t}$ = .30, $\underline{p}$> .05), but in strong disagreement regarding the Japanese ($\underline{t}$ = 10.54, $\underline{p}$ <.01). While Japanese respondents evaluated their compatriots at about the same level (3.75) as they evaluated the Americans (3.70), American respondents demonstrated moderately strong agreement (5.68) concerning the statement about the Japanese and slight agreement (3.68) regarding the statement about their fellow Americans.

In the context of Morton Deutsch's cooperative *(win-win)* intergroup dynamic versus competitive *(win-lose)* intergroup dynamic (B11), it was hypothesized that

> **HU10** American and Japanese opinion leaders view bilateral trade relations with more of a win-lose orientation than a win-win orientation.

A chi-square test of significance suggests that both sets of opinion leaders perceive the current bilateral trade relationship as a *win-lose* rather than a *win-win* situation (X^2 = 54.06, $\underline{p}$< .01). Americans perceive current bilateral trade relations as more win-lose than win-win at 5.07 (with 4.0 signifying neutral), while Japanese respondents gave a rating of 4.22, or almost neutral. For both groups, answers were skewed towards *win-lose*. Expectations had been that both sets of respondents would rate the relationship as *win-lose* to an even greater extent than they did. The probable reason for why they did not was the phrasing of the question itself, which equated *win-win* with cooperative and *win-lose* with competitive, in the same way as Deutsch does. Respondents trained as economists are likely to have found that phraseology objectionable or confusing.[4]

In keeping with Deutsch's RCT premise that real conflicts of interest are of great importance in the creation of perceptions of conflict, it would be expected that the United States, the nation with the large trade deficit, would be more inclined to view the bilateral trade relationship in win-lose terms than Japan, the nation with the large trade surplus. Therefore, hypothesis nine (HD9) proposes that

> **HD11** The nation with the larger trade deficit (U.S.) should view the bilateral trade relationship more in win-lose terms than the other nation (Japan).

This hypothesis is supported by the data from Table 7.10 which shows a significantly higher American win-lose rating of 5.07 compared to the Japanese rating of 4.22, with a $\underline{t}$ value of 4.18, $\underline{p}$< .01, as shown in Table 7.7.

Table 7.10   Perceptions of Current Japan-U.S. Trade Relations, Question B11 (Means)

Respondents	Own Personal Opinion	Perceived American Opinion	Perceived Japanese Opinion
Americans	5.07	6.14	4.29
Japanese	4.22	6.06	4.53

Legend: 1 = Cooperative (*win-win*)
              4 = Neutral
              7 = Competitive (*win-lose*)

Given the interdependence of the two economies, it would be expected that Japanese and American respondents would both tend to view a breakdown in bilateral trade relations as having potentially serious effects on the prosperity of both countries (B12, 13). Therefore, it is hypothesized that

> **HU12** Japanese and Americans view a breakdown in bilateral trade relations as seriously affecting the prosperity of both countries.

Results from chi-square tests of independence indicated that Americans and Japanese both perceived a breakdown in bilateral trade relations as having a significant impact on their countries ($X^2 = 216.00$, $p < .01$ for the effects on the U.S.; $X^2 = 481.74$, $p < .01$ for effects on Japan). Thus, results were highly skewed towards the belief that a breakdown in bilateral trade relations would have a major negative impact on the prosperity of both nations.

However, vulnerability should be perceived as higher for Japan than for the United States among both sets of respondents, given the two country's relative geographical size, natural resources, and histories. Therefore it is hypothesized that

> **HU13** American and Japanese opinion leaders believe that Japan's prosperity would be more adversely affected by a breakdown in bilateral trade relations than the United States would be.

The results from a matched t-test revealed that Americans and Japanese both perceived a breakdown in trade relations as affecting Japan more seriously than the United States, $t = -7.29$, $p < .01$, as shown above in Table 7.7.

Furthermore, given the expected effects of Japan's history and socialization processes on the thinking of Japanese opinion leaders, a breakdown in trade relations should be viewed as more serious for both Japan and the United States by Japanese opinion leaders than by their American counterparts. Therefore, it is hypothesized that

HD14 Japanese opinion leaders believe that the prosperity of both countries would be adversely affected by a breakdown in bilateral trade relations to a greater extent than American opinion leaders do.

T-tests were used to analyze significant differences between Americans and Japanese. Japanese perceived that a breakdown in bilateral trade relations would have a more adverse effect on the United States than Americans did (t = -2.91, p< .01); they also perceived that it would have a greater adverse effect on Japan than Americans did (t = -2.94, p< .01). This is shown above in Table 7.7.

Therefore, (HU12), (HU13), and (HD14) are all supported by the research data. First, both national groups view a breakdown in bilateral trade relations as having quite serious effects on the prosperity of both nations. Second, both national groups perceive Japan's economic prosperity as being more adversely affected by a trade breakdown in trade relations than that of the United States. Finally, Japanese respondents perceive that the prosperity of both nations would be more adversely affected by a breakdown in trade than American respondents.

Table 7.11 reveals that both groups believe that less change of the type addressed by the Structural Impediments Initiative will take place in the United States by the year 2000 than will take place in Japan. Americans are relatively neutral (4.08) on whether a great deal of change will occur in Japan, but disagree to a slight degree (3.63) that such change will occur in the United States. Meanwhile, Japanese somewhat disagree (3.28) that a great deal of change will occur in the United States but somewhat agree (4.89) that such change will occur in Japan. In other words, mean scores indicate that Japanese respondents tend to believe to a greater extent than American respondents that Japanese institutions are more flexible than American institutions in making significant changes, while neither group has much faith in the flexibility of American institutions.

American and Japanese Negotiation Styles

Table 7.12 reveals how Americans and Japanese perceive national negotiating styles. While styles have little to do with causing trade imbalances, they have much to do with the maintenance of cordial bilateral relations and effective

Table 7.11   Degree of Agreement with the Statements in Questions C1, C2 (Means)

Statements	Respondents	Own Personal Opinion	Perceived American Opinion	Perceived Japanese Opinion
C1.	A great deal of the change addressed in this agreement will have taken place in Japan by the year 2000.			
	Americans	4.08	2.71	5.26
	Japanese	4.89	3.31	4.56
C2.	A great deal of the change addressed in this agreement will have taken place in the U.S. by the year 2000.			
	Americans	3.63	4.38	2.68
	Japanese	3.28	4.19	3.00

Legend: 1 = Strongly disagree
4 = Neutral
7 = Strongly agree

Table 7.12   Words Best Describing Negotiation Styles (Percentage of Times Chosen)

Words	American style — American Response	American style — Japanese Response	Japanese style — Japanese Response	Japanese style — American Response
Direct	77.5%	80.6%	2.2%	7.1%
Indirect	2.1%	.0%	59.0%	75.2%
Legalistic	59.2%	37.3%	17.2%	17.7%
Vague	9.2%	2.2%	54.4%	45.6%
Detailed	39.4%	20.9%	14.2%	22.7%
Fair	31.0%	11.2%	4.5%	7.1%
Unfair	.0%	11.2%	2.2%	10.6%
Honest	32.4%	9.7%	8.2%	7.8%
Deceptive	2.1%	9.0%	64.2%	29.8%
Flexible	30.3%	1.5%	23.1%	14.9%
Rigid	8.5%	39.6%	14.9%	27.7%
Effective	11.3%	9.0%	2.2%	33.3%
Ineffective	29.6%	6.7%	17.9%	5.0%
Cooperative	21.8%	2.2%	31.3%	14.2%
Uncooperative	.0%	6.0%	2.2%	19.9%
Confrontational	40.1%	75.4%	.7%	4.3%
Modest	9.2%	.0%	23.1%	17.0%
Arrogant	17.6%	46.3%	3.0%	17.0%
Goal-oriented	57.7%	59.7%	6.0%	31.9%

negotiating and problem-solving. Respondents were asked to circle words best describing the negotiating style of Americans and Japanese. The percentages given below indicate how often respondents chose or didn't choose a given word. To describe the American negotiating style, 77.5 percent of the American respondents chose *direct*, 59.2 percent *legalistic*, 57.7 percent *goal-oriented*, 40.1 percent *confrontational*, and 39.4 percent *detailed*, while 80.6 percent of the Japanese respondents chose *direct*, 75.4 percent *confrontational*, 59.7 percent *goal-oriented*, 46.3 percent *arrogant*, and 39.6 percent *rigid*. To describe the Japanese negotiating style, 64.2 percent of the Japanese respondents chose *deceptive*, 59.0 percent *indirect*, 54.4 percent *vague*, and 31.3 percent *cooperative*, while 75.2 percent of the American respondents chose *indirect*, 45.6 percent *vague*, 33.3 percent *effective*, 31.9 percent *goal-oriented*, and 29.8 percent *deceptive*. Concerning the concept *deceptive*, the Japanese equivalent, unlike the American concept, suggests nothing about motive or intent; instead it focuses more on unintended result.[5]

Concerning national negotiation styles, the internal-external intergroup attributional tendencies are expected to be in full operation. Therefore, it is hypothesized that

HU15 Both sets of opinion leaders view their own national negotiating style in a more positive light (i.e., more ingroup serving attributions) than the other nation's negotiating style.

However, given expectations of stronger group-serving tendencies among members of collectivistic cultures than among members of individualistic cultures, it would be expected that

HD16 Japanese perceptions of the Japanese negotiating style are generally more positive than American perceptions of the American negotiation style.

It would also be expected that

HD17 Japanese perceptions of the American negotiating style are more negative than American perceptions of the Japanese negotiation style.

The list of nineteen adjectives describing national negotiating styles is composed of neutral (=), positive (+), and negative (-) terms, many of which are paired, as shown in Table 7.13. The terms *direct* and *indirect* can be considered neutral. Meanwhile, the terms *fair, honest, flexible, cooperative,* and *modest* can be classified as positive, and *unfair, rigid, uncooperative,*

Table 7.13   The Cumulative Values of Positive and Negative Terms Describing National Negotiation Styles (Percentage of Times Chosen)

	American style		Japanese style	
Words	American Response	Japanese Response	Japanese Response	American Response
Fair+	31.0%	11.2%	4.5%	7.1%
Honest+	32.4%	9.7%	8.2%	7.8%
Flexible+	30.3%	1.5%	23.1%	14.9%
Cooperative+	21.8%	2.2%	31.3%	14.2%
Modest+	9.2%	0.0%	23.1%	17.0%
Unfair-	0.0%	11.2%	2.2%	10.6%
Rigid-	8.5%	39.6%	14.9%	27.7%
Uncooperative-	0.0%	6.0%	2.2%	19.9%
Arrogant-	17.6	46.3%	3.0%	17.0%
Confrontational-	40.1%	75.4%	0.7%	4.3%

Legend: Terms of positive value (+)
                      Terms of negative value (-)

arrogant, and *confrontational* can be considered negative terms. The terms *legalistic*, *detailed*, and *goal-oriented* are relatively neutral or negative, depending on one's perspective. Then, too, *effective* and *ineffective*, which at first appear to be positive and negative terms, respectively, are not always interpreted as such. Sometimes respondents circled *effective* but their written comments indicated a negative meaning. The Japanese equivalents for *vague*, *indirect*, and *deceptive* can all be grouped together as characteristics of the Japanese negotiation style which Japanese respondents realize prevent them from being easily or accurately understood by non-Japanese. As such, these Japanese equivalents can be interpreted as being either neutral or mildly negative. Meanwhile, Americans perceive that the American negotiating style is confrontational (40.1%) compared with the Japanese negotiation style (4.3%).

   Comparing the percentages of times that positive and negative descriptive words were chosen supports (HU15)'s contention that both national groups view their own negotiation style in a more positive light than they view that of the other nation's negotiation style. It also supports (HD16)'s contention that Japanese perceptions of the Japanese negotiation style are generally more positive than American perceptions of the American negotiation style and (HD17)'s contention that Japanese perceptions of American negotiation style are more negative than American perceptions of the Japanese negotiation style. No tests of statistical significance, however, were run.

Similar conclusions can be drawn from the Japanese and American written-in responses to this question as shown in Table 7.14a and 7.14b. Once again, Japanese were far more critical of the American negotiating style than Americans were of the Japanese style, while Japanese appear less critical of the Japanese style than Americans were of the American style. Other differences in responses between the two sets of respondents were also illuminating. While only one Japanese indicated that he couldn't respond to the question because he didn't understand the American negotiating style, eight Americans indicated that they were 'not qualified' to respond because they had had no direct experience with bilateral trade negotiations. One of two Americans writing that both sides were 'rigid' had this to say: 'Both sides are rigid — they only want what they want'. Another American commented that in order to identify negotiating styles, one needed 'to look beyond style to content and purpose' and added that 'the U.S. wants to achieve specific results; Japan wants to avoid committing to giving anything up'.

Japanese write-in comments concerning national negotiating styles were more numerous and illuminating than American write-ins. One Japanese respondent wrote that 'the U.S. demands, pushes, pressures, and uses threats, and Japan says wait, wait, and wait'. Another found both styles goal-oriented but commented that trends were shifting: 'The U.S. was goal-oriented but general (e.g., free trade, open markets) but is now becoming quantitative (e.g., what percent of a given market)'. Meanwhile, he continued, 'The Japanese style used to be specific (e.g., how many branch licenses must we grant?), but they are now resisting quantified targets'. Several wrote that the members of government and industry had different styles and, therefore, made different agreements. Several Japanese respondents wrote that 'the U.S. thinks of short-term victory rather than of long-term relationship' while another commented: 'Results first; logic comes later'. The comment of yet another Japanese, that 'the United States demands change from others without changing itself' was echoed by another's that 'Americans argue reciprocity but don't practice it'.

Finally, based on Hewstone's hypothesis that internal attributions for outgroup behaviors which confirm negative expectancies increase the likelihood of a continued conflict, it was predicted that:

HU18 If American and Japanese opinion leaders make more negative internal attributions for outgroup contributions to trade imbalances and other issues of contention, thereby confirming negative expectancies of the outgroup, trade friction (conflict) can be expected to continue.

Table 7.14a American Written-In Terms Describing Negotiation Styles

The American Negotiation Style

> Goal-oriented; results-oriented*
> Short-term oriented approach*
> Rapid, quick, get to the point fast
> Open, transparent
> Fragmented; lack of continuity
> Institutionally fragmented
> Dominated by interest groups
> Ill-prepared; incompetent
> Lack of follow-up, follow-through
> Inconsistent
> Likely to state bottom line at the beginning
> Moralistic; argue on principles (e.g., fair play)
> Naive
> Not motivated to own interests

The Japanese Negotiation Style

> Process-oriented
> Personal relationship oriented
> Group-interest based, oriented
> Long-term oriented approach*
> Slow, tedious, lengthy*
> Obsessed with, obfuscates with irrelevant detail
> Closed, not open, opaque, inscrutable*
> Well-prepared
> Unified approach
> Well-coordinated
> Well-rehearsed
> Evasive
> Difficult to pin down when not to their advantage
> Effective at not coming to a firm agreement
> Foot-dragging
> Grudging in making concessions
> Stubborn
> Passive
> No fall-back position
> Pragmatic
> Lack broad, long-range set of objectives

Legend: *   Five or more respondents
           **   Ten or more respondents

Table 7.14b Japanese Written-In Terms Describing Negotiation Styles

The American Negotiation Style

Goal-oriented, results-oriented*
Short-term oriented*
Fast-paced
Straight-forward, purposeful, intentional
Demanding; demands change of others without changing itself*
Pressure-oriented; pushes, pressures, threatens*
Contract-oriented; lawyer-attorney approach
Ill-prepared; rough; not clearly thought out; not specific in approach
Blames others; blames Japan even when Japan is not to blame
Selfish; self-centered, only thinks of U.S.; not reciprocal**
Only interprets from own point-of-view
Closed-minded; dogmatic*
Stubborn
Inconsiderate
Unreasonable; not pursuing reasonable arguments*
Emotional; not rational; not logical*
Unprincipled
Untrustworthy; not in good faith
Misguided; misdirected
National superiority complex

The Japanese Negotiation Style

Relational
Team play
Long term oriented*
Slow, gradual; careful; slow to respond*
Status-quo oriented
Evasive; footdragging
Resistive
Passive
Defensive, passive-defensive, protective
Apologetic: 'Please try to understand'
Too accepting; more accepting than should be
Circumstantial; speak only to the occasion
Not good at promoting self, country
Lack of leadership
Japan doesn't say what it should say
Compromising, conceding, 'combine and split'
Opportunistic; unprincipled
Inefficient
Incremental
Unclear
Inconsistent

Legend: *   Five or more respondents
                 **   Ten or more respondents

Research findings suggest that bilateral trade friction can be expected to continue; however, this cannot be tested at this time. A replication of this study at some later date might confirm whether or not these expectations had been met.

Discussion

Summary of Research Findings

The data verify the existence of pervasive bilateral perceptual differences regarding trade imbalance factors and other issues related to Japan-U.S. trade relations. The analysis of quantified bilateral perceptual differences generally support the set of eighteen hypotheses based on the social psychological models and precepts of Chapter Five. It was determined that statistically significant perceptual differences exist between Japanese and American opinion leaders regarding the relative importance of trade imbalance causal factors. The data also verify that American and Japanese opinion leaders attribute bilateral trade imbalances more to factors external to their own nation (but often internal to the other nation) than to factors internal to their own. The one exception was *superior Japanese product quality* factor, which Japanese generally rated as most important. Additionally, it has been determined that American and Japanese opinion leaders place greater responsibility or blame for the large trade imbalances with the other country and its constituents than with their own. Yet each side perceives that its own nation is being blamed more by the other nation than its own nation is blaming that nation.

Other perceptual differences have been identified and quantified regarding the country bearing greater responsibility for the imbalance; the relative market openness in each country; the quality of bilateral trade relations; the probable outcomes if the dilemma is not resolved; the degree of change expected in each country by the year 2000; and national negotiating styles. Since both groups of opinion leaders hold far more negative internal attributions for outgroup contributions to trade imbalances and other issues of contention, thereby confirming negative expectancies of the outgroup, trade conflict is expected to continue.

In keeping with expectations that the salience of group membership is likely to be stronger among members of collectivistic cultures like Japan than among members of individualistic cultures like the United States, the data also verify that Japanese perceptions of American contributions to trade imbalances and other trade-related problems are generally more negative than American perceptions of Japanese contributions, but that Japanese perceptions of Japanese contributions to trade imbalances and other trade problems are less negative than American perceptions of American contributions. In other words, Japanese respondents have been found to be more critical of the United States and Americans than Americans are of Japan and the Japanese. Also in keeping with these same expectations, it has been found that Japanese perceptions and their perceptions of other Japanese perceptions show far less variation than American perceptions and their perceptions of other American perceptions. While both national groups tend to view public perceptions as more polarized than their own or those of the other group, American perceptions and their perceptions of American opinions generally show substantially more divergence than do the Japanese groups's personal opinions and perceived Japanese opinions.

The question using Deutsch's cooperative *win-win* and competitive *win-lose* terminology have yielded data that lend a support to the hypothesis that American and Japanese opinion leaders perceive bilateral trade relations as more *win-lose* than *win-win*. The data also support the hypothesis that American respondents tend to view the relationship in win-lose terms to a greater extent than Japanese respondents. In keeping with expectations related to the strong interdependence of the two economics, the research data verify that both American and Japanese view a breakdown in bilateral trade relations as seriously affecting the prosperity of both nations, but that both sets of respondents tend to believe Japan's prosperity would be more adversely affected than that of the United States. It has also been found that Japanese opinion leaders tend to believe the prosperity of both countries would be adversely affected by a breakdown in bilateral trade relations to a greater degree than American opinion leaders.

Patterns of negative ingroup attributional tendencies regarding outgroup internal characteristics were also found to be in operation during the selection of national negotiating style attributes. It was found that each set of opinion leaders view its own national negotiating style in a more positive light than the other nation's. However, in keeping with expectations of stronger group-serving tendencies among members of collectivistic cultures than among members of individualistic cultures, Japanese perceptions of the Japanese negotiating style were found to be generally more positive than American perceptions of the American negotiation style. Japanese perceptions of the American negotiating style were also found to be more negative than American perceptions of the Japanese negotiation style.

Furthermore, the research data also verify the tendency for both groups of respondents to emphasize trade imbalance causal factors in keeping with their own areas of academic training and career choice. The one group that deviated most from the norm were American political scientists whose aggregated responses are more similar to those of American economists. The data also verify that national group membership loyalties supersede the influence of academic training and career choice more for Japanese opinion leaders than for Americans.

Based on these findings, modest recommendations have been made in the final chapter regarding ways in which these perceptual differences might be diffused so that real headway can be made on the structural issues underlying the trade imbalances and the various ongoing sectoral disputes, such as those involving rice, automotive, and semiconductor issues.

Critique of the Model and Research Design

Although the survey instrument has accomplished what it was designed to do, a critique of its structure and content is now in order. Of the many favorable comments from respondents, three Americans and six Japanese remarked on how easy and quick it was to complete, three Americans and four Japanese mentioned that it was 'interesting', two American and five Japanese wrote that 'this type of research is useful, especially in negotiations', and four Japanese commented on the high level of translation from English to Japanese. One of the less favorable comments was that the questions were too general and allowed little room for expressing nuances and complexities or for establishing differences between and among sectors. Yet others remarked that the questions were too specific. Five Americans and four Japanese found survey methods to be generally 'inaccurate', 'misleading', 'ineffective', 'simplistic', or 'potentially dangerous'. Three Americans and five Japanese thought this particular survey polarized issues unnecessarily, while seven Americans and four Japanese had reservations concerning the researcher's political agenda, the motives of her employer or funding agency, and the ultimate application of findings. The variety of these responses indicate that no survey instrument is likely to please all respondents. On the whole, the questionnaire accomplished its purpose; that is, the collection of perceptual data on American and Japanese opinion leaders regarding the bilateral trade relationship and national negotiating style.

Comments which respondents made on particular questions were especially helpful, both for evaluating results as well as for making changes in the questionnaire since a replication of the study is planned. An American economist wrote that beginning the questionnaire with a set of questions about what caused the large bilateral trade imbalances incorrectly implied that the imbalance itself was the major part of the perceived trade problem. He proposed that it might have been far more revealing to begin with a question concerning what people actually perceived 'the problem' to be. This had been the original intent; however, the difficulty of tabulating responses ruled that out as discussed in the preceding chapter. In the same economist's view, the trade problem lay far more in dissatisfaction at the microeconomic level (e.g., concerns about the status of market access) than the bilateral trade imbalance *per se*, a comment in keeping with his responses to the question and with his own publications on the topic. Two Japanese respondents found the ranking system of Part A 'difficult', while eight Japanese took issue with the *unfair Japan trade practices* factor. Japanese comments concerning this factor included: 'N/A', 'too vague', 'who decides fair or unfair?', and 'what are your criteria for 'unfair'?' These responses further verify the conclusions reached concerning the greater tendency for Japanese respondents to make group-serving attributions than American respondents.

The American economist mentioned earlier correctly noted that the focus on trade imbalances was also reflected in the wording of a number of questions in Part B, especially the fourth question concerning whether Japan exported more to the United States than Japan was willing to import from the United States. As explained in Chapter Six, that was the intent. The economist, however, pointed out that answering the question with a 'strongly disagree' did not mean that there was no perceived connection between the size of exports to the U.S. market and imports in Japan, but simply that Japan was unwilling to import as much as it exported and that something other than Japan's 'willingness' accounted for the trade imbalances. Seven Japanese respondents also took issue with the fourth question, as well as the fifth, for similar reasons. Japanese comments included: 'N/A', 'strange asking-style', 'imports and exports are two different issues', 'inappropriate', 'misleading', 'no meaning', and 'translation not quite right'. These are definitely issues to consider when revising the questionnaire for replication of the study. The revised fourth and fifth questions might read, 'How open is the Japanese market to high technology imports?' and 'How competitive are U.S. high technology products with those of Japan?'.

The ninth and tenth questions in Part B, concerning the extent to which each national group was skilled at promising changes but in avoiding substantive implementation, also received comments. Seven Japanese wrote they couldn't understand the meaning or intent of the question, and one American wrote that the wording of the questions was 'not quite accurate'. The American respondent noted that, during the SII process, American negotiators included statements about what the United States ought to do, but no promises were made to change anything. The critical word was 'promise' and what was believed to constitute a promise. The original intent of this pair of questions was to quantify American and Japanese perceptions regarding institutional rigidity/flexibility in each nation for making needed changes for the good of the bilateral relationship. For a replication of this research effort, this pair of questions would be rewritten. Questions C1 and C2 concerning how much change addressed in the SII agreement could be expected to take place in each nation by the year 2000 would also be incorporated into this pair of questions.

To the eleventh question in Part B, concerning whether the current U.S.-Japan trade relationship was best described as cooperative *(win-win)* or competitive *(win-lose)*, seven Japanese and three American respondents disagreed with the pairing of concepts. One American wrote that no economist could ever agree with the characterization of competitive as *win-lose* and cooperative as *win-win*. As he and a number of other economists correctly pointed out, the essence of economic theory is that the process of economic competition is considered a win-win situation for all those involved. He suggested that it might have been better to simply have used win-win and *win-lose* without the cooperative and competitive terminology. His comment further supports the earlier discussion to do exactly that in a future replication of this study. Results would be expected to show a much greater bilateral perceptual gap. This could serve as a measure of Japan-U.S. trade friction levels.

The last two questions in Part B asked respondents how seriously they believed a breakdown in the bilateral trade relationship would affect the prosperity of each nation, that is, which nation was more vulnerable to an interruption of bilateral trade. One American found the question 'naive', while two Japanese opinion leaders simply remarked, 'No breakdown will occur'.

Regarding the Structural Impediments Initiative (SII) question of Part C, respondents were asked to evaluate the extent to which the SII would result in change in Japan and the United States by the year 2000. To this question, which attempted to get at the degree of perceived institutional rigidity or flexibility in each country, five Japanese wrote that Japanese negotiators had agreed only to principles, not to any specific changes or to any due dates. Again, these might be revised to read, 'To what extent will Japan make internal changes of the kind recommended by the U.S. during the SII talks?' and 'To what extent will the U.S. make internal changes of the kind recommended by Japan during the SII talks?'. Finally, the question in Part D on perceived negotiating styles also yielded strong evidence of intergroup perceptual discrepancies as did the collection of write-in comments.

In a replication of this study, some changes would be made in the samples of academic and media opinion leaders. The academic samples would include equivalent numbers of political scientists, economists, and area specialists to those of the business sector's rice, automobile, and semiconductor leaders. The same would be done for the media samples, thereby including equivalent numbers of TV reporters, newspaper journalists, and editors/publishers of books on Japan-U.S. relations.

Notes

1   The date in Table 7.4 also indicates that both national groups ranked factors considered neutral or external to both no higher than midway between 'somewhat important factor' and 'minor factor'. These included *currency misalignment, outside global economic conditions,* and *differing negotiating styles.* Another factor not awarded a high ranking by either group was *high Japan national savings rate.*

2   These reliabilities are considered acceptable.

3   It also suggests that levels of negative affect related to bilateral trade relations have been running high among both sets of opinion leaders and that, consequently, bilateral trade friction levels are also somewhat elevated.

4   See footnote 9 in Chapter One.

5   What was completely unexpected was *deceptive's* being chosen so often by Japanese respondents as representing their national negotiating style. Also surprising was the relatively low rating given to *indirect.* This issue is discussed in the critique of the model and survey instrument section of this chapter.

8 Three Sectoral Disputes: 1980-1992

Introduction

It has been argued in preceding chapters that Japan-U.S. cultural, institutional, and perceptual differences, in addition to bilateral economic competition, have played important roles in creating and supporting currently high levels of bilateral trade friction. This chapter attempts to determine the relative importance of each of the four causal factors in the context of bilateral contentiousness over trade in the rice, automotive, and semiconductor sectors. An examination of these cases offers a clearer understanding of the contributions and interplay of trade friction causal factors in three very different sectors.

The rice, automotive, and semiconductor sectors were selected as case studies for four fundamental reasons. First, all three had been the focus of fairly recent trade disputes involving substantially high levels of bilateral trade contentiousness. Second, they represent three quite different sectoral groupings: agriculture, heavy industry, and high technology. As such, they function at, and depend on, three quite different levels of technological sophistication which can be classified, respectively, as low, medium, and high. Third, they each reflected varying levels of relative American and Japanese competitive strength. While the American rice sector is clearly more competitive than its Japanese counterpart, the Japanese automotive industry had been, for a period, more competitive than the American industry. Meanwhile, the competitive strengths of the American and Japanese semiconductor industries, now considered relatively comparable, had shifted when the Japanese industry had, for a time, moved ahead of the American industry as global front-runner. Fourth, these three sectors were expected to reveal a differing proportional mix of trade friction casual factors. In other words, what functioned as a primary casual factor in one sector might function as a secondary factor in another. Although all three sectors seemed to involve Japan-U.S. perceptual differences, it was likely that other trade friction factors were of greater importance. For rice, such factors were cultural and, perhaps, institutional differences; for automobiles and semiconductors, they were institutional differences and strong

178

bilateral economic competition. The following sectoral discussions suggest to what extent these impressions were valid.

Each sectoral discussion is developed in the same format. First, pertinent statistics regarding trade, production, and consumption levels for the period 1980-1992 are offered. This is followed by a brief account of recent bilateral trade friction over trade in the given sector. Then, summaries of both nations' basic positions on trade problems are presented, followed by descriptions of each nation's industry within the context of its particular domestic realities. Findings and implications regarding the relative importance of bilateral trade friction factors wrap up each section.

At the end of the chapter, conclusions regarding the relative importance of trade friction factors in the three sectoral disputes are summarized and an estimation of each sector's relative importance in the overall bilateral trade friction dilemma is given.

A   The Rice Sector

Rice was selected as one of the sectoral case studies for the following reasons. First, rice has long been the subject of Japan-U.S. trade disputes and bilateral contentiousness. Secondly, it is representative of agricultural products and basic foodstuffs whose production requires relatively low levels of technological sophistication. As such, it is also more labor intensive than automotive and semiconductor production. Third, the American rice sector is indisputably more competitive than the Japanese rice sector, as are most American agricultural product sectors compared with their Japanese counterparts. Fourth, rice has historically played a central role in Japan's economy, has been a mainstay of the national diet, and has formed the basis for Japanese societal development. Therefore, it was expected that cultural differences would be an important factor in rice sectoral trade friction. The main issue of bilateral contention over rice had been Japan's restricted domestic import markets; this has likewise been the main issue for other agricultural products and foodstuffs which Japan would like to produce herself. Unlike the restricted markets of most agricultural items, Japan's rice market had been completely closed to imports, until 1994. This was largely the result of government policies. As a result, institutional differences were also expected to be a major trade friction causal factor in this sector.

Bilateral Trade in Agricultural Commodities and Rice

Trade in agricultural commodities has been, and continues to be, an important component of the Japan-U.S. trade relationship. Not only is Japan the world's largest national importer of agricultural products, it is (and has been since 1964) the single largest national market for U.S. agricultural products, followed by Canada and Mexico. The United States, whose agricultural commodities accounted for 10 percent ($42.4 billion) of its total exports and approximately 20 percent ($8.4 billion) of its exports to Japan in 1992, has been Japan's single largest national supplier.[1] Tables 8A-1, 8A-2, and 8A-3 reveal the continued importance of Japan as a prime market for American agricultural goods, while Tables 8A-4, 8A-5, and 8A-6 reveal the continued strength of the United States as Japan's most important provider of such goods.

Since Japan became America's first billion-dollar market for agricultural products in 1970, the Japanese market has accounted for annually between 14 percent and 21 percent of U.S. agricultural exports. As shown in Table 8A-1, these exports were worth $6.1 billion in 1980, $8.1 billion in 1990, and $8.4 billion in 1992.

Table 8A-1　Japan's Share of U.S. Agricultural Exports: 1980-1992

	Value of Exports (Millions of $)	Japan's Share (%)
1980	6,117	14.6
1981	6,570	15.0
1982	5,551	15.0
1983	6,246	17.1
1984	6,762	17.7
1985	5,404	18.2
1986	5,141	19.6
1987	5,723	19.3
1988	7,640	20.6
1989	8,164	20.4
1990	8,104	20.6
1991	7,729	19.7
1992	8,437	19.7

Source:　USDA Economic Research Service, *Foreign Agricultural Trade of the United States (FATUS)*, various years.

Japan's shares of selected American agricultural exports in 1992 were, as in previous years, substantial. As shown in Table 8A-2, these shares included 15.2 percent of soybeans, 26.1 percent of feed grains, and 12.0 percent of wheat as well as 46.7 percent of meat and meat products, 17.6 percent of cotton, 24.3 percent of fruit, 22.4 percent of tobacco, and 14.1 percent of vegetables.

Table 8A-2 Japan's Share of Selected U.S. Agricultural Exports: 1988, 1990/91, 1992 (Given in Percent)

Products with 1992 Rankings as Major U.S. Agricultural Exports	1988	1990/91	1992	(Value in millions of $)
Total exports	11.7	12.3	10.5	N/A
Total agricultural exports	20.4	20.4	19.8	(8,383)
Feed grains(1)	28.9	23.8	26.1	(1,783)
Soybeans(2)	13.9	16.7	15.2	(903)
Wheat(3)	8.5	11.5	12.0	(543)
Meat and meat products(4)	51.5	48.7	46.7	(1,774)
Vegetables(5)	20.6	14.8	14.1	(394)
Fruits(6)	30.9	24.4	24.3	(677)
Cotton(7)	25.7	20.6	17.6	(386)
Tobacco(8)	20.3	19.8	22.4	(351)
Rice(13)	0.0	0.0	0.0	(0)

Note: Product rankings are given in parentheses. Source: USDA Economic Research Service *Foreign Agricultural Trade of the United States (FATUS)*, various years.

　　　Japan continues to be either the first- or second-ranked market in each of the major U.S. agricultural commodity export groups (i.e., exports exceeding $1 billion). These include soybeans, feed grains, wheat, meat and meat products, cotton, fruits, tobacco, and vegetables. Rice, which ranked 12th in 1990/91 and 13th in 1992 among all American agricultural commodity exports and accounted for approximately 2.0 percent ($789 million) of such exports in 1990/91 and 1.8 percent ($75 million) in 1992, continued to encounter a completely closed market in Japan until 1994, a year during which Japan experienced partial rice crop failures.[2] This pattern is shown in Table 8A-3. The United States also continues to be Japan's largest single supplier of most major agricultural commodity imports. As indicated in Table 8A-4, American products accounted for 33 percent of all Japanese agricultural imports (36 percent, if products such as cotton and soybeans are included).[3]

Table 8A-3   Rankings of Japan as a Market for Selected U.S. Agricultural Exports: 1988, 1990/91, 1992

	1988	1990/91	1992
Total agricultural products	1	1	1
Feed grains	1	1	1
Soybeans	2	1	1
Wheat (and flour)	4	2	2
Meats and meat products	1	1	1
Vegetables	2	2	2
Fruits	1	2	2
Cotton	1	1	1
Tobacco	1	1	1
Rice	-	-	-

Source: USDA Economic Research Service *Foreign Agricultural Trade of the United States (FATUS)*, various years.

Table 8A-4   U.S. Share of Japan's Agricultural Imports: 1986 to 1990

	Value of Exports (Millions of $)	U.S. Share (Percent)
1986	5,329	27.8
1987	6,779	30.3
1989	10,310	33.2
1990	10,526	33.3

Source: JETRO *White Paper on International Trade, Japan*, various years.

In 1990, American commodities accounted for 33.3 percent of all Japanese agricultural and foodstuffs imports. American shares of Japan's agricultural imports were 73.3 percent of Japan's soybeans, 43.0 percent of feed grains, and 53.3 percent of wheat as well as 38.7 percent of meat and meat products, 51.8 percent of cotton, 37.9 percent of fruit, 84.7 percent of tobacco, and 21 percent of vegetables. American products also accounted for 19.7 percent of fish and shellfish imports, one of Japan's largest foodstuff import groups, as presented in Table 8A-5.

The United States has tended to be either the first- or second-ranked supplier for many of the major agricultural commodity groups imported by Japan. These commodity groups include soybeans, feed grains, wheat, meat and meat products, cotton, fruits, tobacco, vegetables, but not rice, as indicated in Table 8A-6.

Table 8A-5 U.S. Share of Selected Japan Agricultural Imports: 1986, 1990, 1992 (Given in Percent)

	1986	1990
Total imports	N/A	22.4
Total agricultural imports	27.8	33.3
Feed grains	46.5	43.0
Soybeans	89.4	73.3
Wheat	55.2	53.3
Meat and meat products	30.5	38.7
Vegetables	13.9	21.0
Fruits	38.9	37.9
Cotton	28.3	51.8
Tobacco	77.1	84.7
Rice	0.0	0.0

Source: JETRO *White Paper on International Trade, Japan*, various years.

Table 8A-6 Rankings of U.S. as a Supplier of Selected Japan Agricultural Imports: 1988, 1990, 1992

	1988	1990	1992
All agricultural products	1	1	1
Feed grains	1	1	1
Soybeans	1	1	1
Wheat	1	1	1
Meat and meat products	1	1	1
Vegetables	2	2	2
Fruits	1	1	1
Cotton	1	1	1
Tobacco	1	1	1
Rice	-	-	-

Source: JETRO *White Paper on International Trade, Japan*, various issues.

Concerning Japan's agricultural and foodstuffs exports, these accounted for only 3 percent of total Japanese exports to America, yet the United States was her third largest market for such goods in 1990, accounting for $276 million (16.8 percent of all such exports). The largest of these exports to the United States have been fish and seafood, specialty fruits, Japanese-style vegetables, and beer, all of which number among Japan's major exports of foodstuffs. Her 1990 American shares accounted for 17.3 percent, 16.0 percent, 13.9 percent, and 45.1 percent, respectively.[4]

The agricultural commodities trade between Japan and the United States has been, and continues to be, reciprocal but asymmetrical, with Japanese imports of U.S. agricultural products approximately 20 times greater in value than similar Japanese exports to America. The United States has consistently shown positive current accounts in agricultural commodities over the years, globally as well as bilaterally. Indeed, it is the single component of Japan-U.S. trade that has always registered in the black. Yet this relatively healthy component of the bilateral trade relationship is not without its share of contentiousness. Japan's system of trade barriers has limited sales of products such as foreign beef, citrus fruits, soybeans, wheat, barley, rice, and higher value, processed agricultural products.[5] As a result, most U.S. products shipped to Japan are bulk commodities rather than processed or semiprocessed products.

Trade Friction over Rice

Since Japan achieved self-sufficiency in rice in the mid-1960s, rice production has almost always exceeded consumption. Government-subsidized rice surpluses have been stored, exported as food aid (surplus disposal), used for industrial purposes (e.g., the making of sake and soy sauce), and placed in livestock feed mixtures.[6] The first of three recent American complaints concerning Japanese rice policies focused on the export sales of surplus government subsidized rice stocks.

When the Japanese government initiated a five-year disposal program in April 1979 to reduce its growing surplus rice stocks, then totaling approximately 6.5 million tons, exports at 250,000 tons a year were projected. In that same month, Korea suffered a shortfall in domestic rice production and announced its intention to purchase 500,000 tons of American rice. In May 1979, however, after contracting for 90,000 tons of U.S. rice, Korea canceled 55,000 tons of this amount and instead purchased 250,000 tons from Japan. The reasons given were price, shipping costs, and quality.[7] Indonesia also purchased about 350,000 tons, contributing to Japan's rice export sales that year of approximately 840,000 tons, or 640,000 tons more than the original estimate of 200,000 tons.

On April 4, 1980, the U.S. Rice Millers' Association (RMA) filed a complaint against Japan under Section 301 of the 1974 U.S. Trade Act. Japan was charged with violating Article 16 of the General Agreement on Tariffs and

Trade (GATT) as well as principles of the United Nations Food and Agricultural Organization, both of which stated that subsidized agricultural exports which displace another county's unsubsidized commercial sales were illegal. In short, the association accused the Japanese of 'dumping' subsidized rice at less than the going market rate, thereby threatening a 'disastrous market disruption and displacement of U.S. exports'.[8]

The U.S. Trade Representative's Office (USTR) delegated responsibility for negotiating a bilateral rice agreement to the Department of Agriculture (USDA). The result was a four-year agreement limiting Japanese rice exports to 1.4 million tons of subsidized rice and about 200,000 tons of grant rice over a four-year period. The only documentation was an exchange of letters in June 1980 between Under Secretary of Agriculture Dale Hathaway and Japanese Vice Minister Sawabe. The Hathaway letter detailed all pertinent aspects of the agreement but concluded with a statement calling for annual bilateral consultations to review world rice supply and demand situations and for emergency consultations in case of natural disasters, crop failures, or other events requiring food assistance. Sawabe's brief letter of compliance added that such emergency consultations should be addressed 'with swiftness and flexible attitudes'.[9]

As a result of this loophole, the U.S. government granted a one million ton exception for Korea in December 1980, dwarfing the terms of the actual agreement itself. Although Korea reaffirmed its intention to purchase 200,000 tons of U.S. rice in 1980 and 500,000 tons in 1981, American rice interests were angered over the results of an agreement with which they had expressed dissatisfaction even as they were withdrawing their complaint. The controversial agreement became the subject of a House of Representatives Subcommittee on Cotton, Rice, and Sugar hearing on February 26, 1981. Representative John Breaux of Louisiana, a rice-producing state, was one who expressed dismay at the outcome:

> April 12, 1980 long will be remembered by the U.S. rice industry. On that date our government signed a bilateral pact with the government of Japan which allows it to export surplus, subsidized rice into third country markets. Two of these markets, South Korea and Indonesia, which are termed *sensitive* in the agreement, are large importers of U.S. rice as a result of years of hard work in market development by our rice industry. No traditional rice exporting nation, which Japan is not, can compete with such unfair trade tactics. Exportation of these surplus, subsidized rice stocks, sold on concessional terms, have displaced U.S. rice sales to South Korea, forced down the US rice market price, caused a loss of interest in our domestic rice sales, distorted milling schedules, strained storage facilities, and imposed serious financial problems on farmers.[10]

Breaux recommended that no future emergency exceptions be granted until all available American rice supplies were exhausted.

Then, on September 10, 1986 the Rice Millers' Association (RMA) filed an unfair trade complaint against Japan for its quantitative limits on all rice imports and where only the state trading enterprise, the Japan Food Agency, was authorized to buy rice. In short, the RMA wanted access to the Japanese rice market. At the filing of this complaint, most rice bought from Japanese producers was selling at nearly 10 times the world market price, causing consumers to spend nearly $25 billion to insulate domestic rice production from world marketplace realities. Although Japan had allowed foreign rice imports in 1985, these had amounted to a mere 20,000 tons, representing less than two-tenths of 1 percent of Japan's total domestic consumption. The RMA estimated that, if Japan liberalized its rice market, Japan's rice price would fall by half, world prices would rise, the volume of American rice exports would double, and their value quadruple.[11]

The reaction to the Rice Millers' complaint among Japanese government and business leaders was largely negative. One of the milder criticisms came from Masaoki Kojima, chairman of the board of Keidanren (Federation of Economic Organizations), who pointed out that the RMAs' petition was 'too sudden' and 'not realistic'. After all, he said, the Japanese rice situation 'had long found bilateral acceptance'.[12] Yet there were those in the Japanese government and even the ruling Liberal Democratic Party (LDP) who were beginning to suggest that rice import restrictions were 'no longer valid', that it was 'about time that rice imports be liberalized'.[13]

In the end, the USTR decided against initiating an investigation, and the case was closed until 1988 when American rice processors (the RMA and American Rice Council) filed a similar complaint, this time under the Fair Trade and Competitive Act of 1988, arguing that Japan's rice policies violated international trade rules (GATT Article 11: General Elimination of Quantitative Restrictions) by denying fair and equitable market access. Soon after, the issue was brought to a vote before the Japanese Diet. Both Houses unanimously voted in favor of providing all rice domestically. Ruling LDP legislative leaders wrote the U.S. President a letter in which they predicted that if the matter were even discussed in bilateral talks, 'grave political problems would arise and cause serious anxiety and confusion among the Japanese people'. They added that they feared, should this happen, the long-standing friendship between the United States and Japan might be 'seriously impaired'.[14]

NOKYO, Japan's Association of Agricultural Cooperatives, also took action. Through ZENCHU, its political coordinating center, Washington lobbyists were hired to fight the Rice Millers' petition. A public relations campaign was mounted in the U.S. press and among American farm organizations. NOKYO's basic message was that, because rice farming played such an important role in Japanese culture, U.S. action on the rice issue would not be well received in Japan. Pointing out that Japan was already 'a very stable market' and 'the largest customer' for American farm products, NOKYO leaders warned that U.S. producers of other agricultural commodities exports might be adversely affected if Japan were forced to accept rice exports. Ultimately, major U.S. farm organizations did not support the petition, and leaders of the American Agricultural Movement, the North Dakota Wheat Commission, and the Colorado Wheat Administrative Committee publicly opposed it.[15] Finally in 1988, as in 1986, the USTR decided against initiating an investigation, and the case was closed.

Yet the issue of Japan's closed rice market remained very much alive. In March 1991 a highly-charged bilateral incident occurred at an international food fair outside Tokyo. A *New York Times* article referred to it as 'the latest twist in the continuing trade disputes between the U.S. and Japan' — a twist which began as 'an amusing standoff but turned serious as Japanese threats mounted'. The incident began when U.S. rice industry representatives displayed several sealed bags and plastic containers (totaling about 10 pounds) of different U.S. rice samples for Japanese consumers to view. Each day of the exhibition, officials from Japan's Food Agency ordered all rice removed from the American display, and each day the exhibitors listened politely but refused to comply.[16]

Japanese officials persisted, pointing out that displays of American rice violated Japan's Food Control Act and that anyone found guilty of importing foreign rice without the Ministry's permission could receive a prison term of up to two years or a fine of up to $22,000. Finally, Agriculture Minister Motoji Kondo called the U.S. Embassy to say that arrests would be made if the rice were not taken off display. Sometime later, U.S. Ambassador Michael Armacost together with other officials, visited the exhibition and 'armed' the American exhibitors with copies of Japan's Food Control Law, which allowed public educational displays of rice. Japan Food Agency Deputy Director Tetsuro Yakushiji, however, would not back down. He stated that the purpose of the exhibition was market development and sales promotion, that the Rice Council was in effect saying, 'Please buy American rice'. He added that 'if they say it is for education, it is education for sales promotion'.[17]

Some American and Japanese officials were critical of their respective nation's actions in the incident. One senior MITI official, Noboru Hatakeyama, said it would have been 'wise' for Japan to ignore the Rice Council's exhibit since it was 'strange to remove something which was not dangerous to national security'.[18]   Meanwhile, several U.S. officials criticized the Rice Council representatives for having gone too far in promoting rice in Japan. Yet David Graves, president of the Council, issued this statement:

> Having now been threatened with arrest, we will remove the rice on the last day of the exhibition to help publicize this very regrettable behavior by the Japanese government. . . . We intend to return to Washington and appeal directly to the Administration and to Congress for help. . . . We can no longer tolerate a Japan which has free access to the U.S. market for billions of dollars of automobiles and electronics but refuses to even discuss the possibility of importing a few tons of U.S. rice.[19]

The bilateral tug of war over Japan's rice market continued more quietly until July 1991 when NOKYO successfully organized the largest annual conference and demonstration in its history, bringing some 50,000 rice growers and demonstrators from all over Japan to protest any Diet motions to allow rice imports.[20] This was followed by another NOKYO-inspired protest in December 1992 when Frans Andriessen, vice president of the European Commission, met in Tokyo with Japan's trade minister to request the liberalization of Japan's rice market. Thousands of Japanese farmers and their supporters descended on Tokyo to demand that their government stand firm against foreign imports. Expressing his support for their position, LDP executive leader Hiroshi Mitsuzuka was quoted as saying, 'Rice is a symbol of our culture. It's only natural for a country to protect its culture'.[21]

The American Position on Rice

While U.S. agricultural trade issues with Japan are numerous and wide-ranging, recent rice complaints have concerned only three: the subsidization of rice production and rice consumption, the dumping of subsidized surplus rice into third world markets, and the maintenance of a closed domestic import market. The powerful Congressional Agricultural Committees, the USDA, USTR, and Departments of Commerce and State all oppose Japan's rice policies, generally pointing out that Japanese rice production is inefficient and that the United States is able to meet all of Japan's domestic rice needs.[22] These government agencies and U.S. farming interests advocate positions based on economic theories of free trade and comparative advantage. They support the idea that 'growth is best achieved in an open trading system where the market insures equal access to all trading partners'. They would like to see far less government and more market' in Japan, for as they typically point out,

'Japanese speak of the virtues of free trade, but practice protection'. Some express fear that American family farms are in jeopardy because of foreign trade barriers like those of Japan, which deny U.S. farmers the rightful benefits of comparative advantage.[23]   U.S. government officials argue that Japan's closed markets, of which the rice market is the most extreme example, are a major cause of bilateral trade imbalances.

Japan is perceived as moving slowly and ineffectually toward liberalizing her domestic agricultural markets, but, with rice, there had been no movement at all until 1994. In response to Japanese reasons based on cultural tradition and domestic requirements, American arguments are based on progress and meeting Japanese consumer needs more effectively. Americans like to point out that liberalization will lower Japan's consumer prices and cause real disposable incomes to rise. Although the primary USDA goal is long-term, sustainable export growth in volume and mix of commodities to Japan, the State Department has sometimes bypassed such goals if other treatment of Japan is deemed in the best security or diplomatic interests of the United States.

While rice has been a strictly bilateral issue for many Americans, the USDA is currently approaching the problem within the multilateral context of the General Agreement on Trade and Tariffs (GATT) where the basic argument put forth is that Japan's import barriers are inconsistent with her obligations under the GATT's international trading rules. Perhaps a more successful outcome might be expected within a multilateral (GATT) context than within a bilateral one, but as one U.S. trade economist has pointed out,

> In the politically sensitive case of rice, the U.S. government recognized a sector where the cost of obtaining concessions was disproportionate to any benefit.[24]

At the moment, it seems preferable to pursue a rational, low risk, and politically acceptable solution to opening Japan's rice trade rather than to cause unnecessary ill will in Japan.[25]

The Japanese Position on Rice

Japanese rice imports have almost always been relatively small, even in the years following Commodore Perry's visit. Only in the final months of World War I, when Japan faced acute rice shortages, was she forced to import large amounts of foreign rice. Even though domestic rice production steadily expanded, it could not totally meet Japanese demands. To make up the difference, Japan at first imported rice, mostly from Southeast Asia, but by the 1920s, Japan was developing rice production in Korea and Taiwan. By the

1930s, these two nations provided nearly all Japan's rice import requirements.[26]

The Great Depression and World War II created serious food shortages in Japan. Agricultural production dropped sharply in the late 1930s, and rice imports from Taiwan and Korea were eventually cut as war in the Pacific grew more intense.[27] Japanese suffered severe food shortages both during and after the war, memories forever etched in the minds of those who lived through it. Onc of the most urgent tasks of the Occupation (1945-1952) was to ensure that everyone had enough to eat. Even though Japan's goal of self sufficiency in rice was met by 1955, the government continued to subsidize rice farmers. This resulted in stock surpluses and export activities which led to the U.S. unfair trade petition of 1980.

Japan's agricultural power structure, composed of the powerful NOKYO, the JMAFF (Ministry of Agriculture, Forestry, and Fisheries), the LDP, and the Diet's agriculture committees generally defend Japan's rice self-sufficiency program and closed market policy. NOKYO, whose membership includes five million farming households, is a political base long associated with the LDP, Japan's most powerful political party. Since its founding in 1947, NOKYO has worked to maintain or increase government price supports on rice (and other agricultural crops) and to prevent or retard imports of less expensive agricultural products from abroad. Even though food prices have led to some national criticism, NOKYO's privileged position is assured by its generous contributions to LDP funds.

Organizations such as the powerful Keidanren and Keizai Doyukai (Japanese Association of Corporate Executives) generally advocate the liberalization of Japan's rice market as do many academics. Agricultural economist Yujiro Hayami, for example, argues that Japan's protection policies moderate the problem of needed agricultural adjustment in the short run, but lead to stalemate in the long run. He views Japan's agricultural protection advocacy groups, especially NOKYO, as barriers to needed policy reorientation and structural adjustment:

> (Japanese) agricultural policies are entrenched deeply in vested interests – above all, the powerful NOKYO organization with its alliance with JMAFF and LDP. . . . Probably, the greatest myth of Japanese agriculture today is the slogan that NOKYO is 'of the farmers, by the farmers, and for the farmers' . . . (NOKYO) as a whole is today a major seeker of 'institutional rent' arising from government regulation and control. . . .[28]

While Hayami predicts a loss of consumers due to high prices, many continue to support the self-sufficiency policy. Part of Japan's traditional sense of vulnerability is a fear that food might be used as a foreign policy instrument, so self-sufficiency in rice just makes good common sense.[29] Popular support is a major reason why Japan's rice policies are unlikely to change soon. At the GATT negotiations, Japanese diplomats represent the government's strong opposition to liberalizing the rice market and mirror the politically strong attitudes against rice imports. Typically, Japanese negotiators point out that Americans are inconsistent when they argue for free trade but maintain protectionist policies for agricultural products, like beef and dairy products.[30]

The Rice Sector in Japan and the United States

Bilateral disagreement over rice appears to be rooted in the fundamentally different roles which rice and the domestic rice industry have historically played in American and Japanese social and cultural life. Bilateral disagreement also appears to be fostered by national differences in rice production methods, marketing goals, and market organization. However, more important trade friction causes are probably the diverging national political scenes, especially the interplay of powerful farming interest groups and government agencies in national politics and policy-making.

Rice cultivation, brought to Japan from the Asian peninsula around the third century B.C., has played a crucial role throughout Japan's history.[31] Compared to the Japanese rice industry, the American industry is relatively young, having just marked its 300th anniversary in 1987.[32] While rice holds no special significance for Americans, it is rich with symbolic meaning for Japanese. The cultivation of rice shaped traditional Japanese village life and social organization and is generally considered the foundation of modern Japanese culture and social organization as well. Japan's irrigated rice-paddy system of rice cultivation, requiring close cooperation among villagers concerning water control and labor-sharing activities during planting and harvesting, fostered a collectivistic or group-oriented society in Japan.[33] The American single family farm system, which favored individual effort, contributed to the development of the United States as the individualistic society that it is today.[34] While rice has played a relatively minor role in the U.S. agricultural sector and, until recently, in the American national diet, it is considered the backbone of Japanese agriculture, accounting for approximately one-third of all agricultural production. In spite of a gradual decline in consumption, rice still accounts for about one-third of all Japanese per capita caloric intake. It is Japan's central staple food and leading agricultural crop.[35]

Because Japan's high population density, mountainous terrain, and postwar land reform favors small producers, the average Japanese farm has remained small in size (about 1.1 hectares or 2½ acres) and highly labor intensive. Japan's family farms are generally not as competitive as U.S. farms, many of which are large, mechanized business enterprises. Unlike Japan, the United States has abundant land resources, with the capacity to produce food far in access of domestic demand. Indeed, American rice production alone is more efficient and more cost-effective than Japanese rice production. While rice farms are located in the lowland rural areas across Japan, rice farming is primarily concentrated in four large rice-growing areas of the United States. Of all American milled rice output in 1988/1989, 40 percent came from Arkansas-Missouri, 12.5 percent from Louisiana-Florida, 25 percent from Texas-Mississippi, and 22 percent from California.[36] Unlike the Japanese rice industry, which is geared toward meeting domestic self-sufficiency needs, the American rice industry is, to a great extent, export-oriented. In fact, the United States is currently the world's second largest rice-exporter after Thailand.[37]

Even though farmers compose minority groups in both Japan (about 12 percent) and the United States (about 3 percent), their political clout greatly influences agricultural policies. Japanese farm policies in general, and the rice policy in particular, are highly protectionistic and geared toward self-sufficiency, while U.S. farm policies tend toward the supplementation of farm incomes when necessary, normally in return for voluntary supply controls or for promoting exports of excess production. Many of the U.S. rice export programs have been designed to counter EC export subsidies and Japanese import barriers.[38] Meanwhile, Japanese policies are not only designed to maximize food self-sufficiency for the sake of national security, but to maintain a viable and healthy farm sector with incomes at levels comparable to those in urban areas, and to develop secure, stable, and sufficient sources of staple foods, importing only those which can not be adequately produced domestically.[39] Even though food prices are generally higher in Japan than in most other countries, the Japanese view tends to be that stable prices and secure supplies of staple foods are benefits worth the extra cost.[40] Japan's current economic wealth and power have apparently not eradicated her traditional sense of vulnerability, perhaps because many of the contributing factors have not changed. With natural resources still extremely limited, Japan must depend heavily on imported raw materials.

In Japan the price of rice, which has long been considered one of the leading indicators on which the price of almost all other commodities and wage rates are based, is tightly controlled by the government. Consequently, consumer prices in Japan are still kept extremely high. In the United States, however, the market price of rice is allowed to fluctuate freely with little intervention, and rice imports are subject to only minor duties.[41] Concerning subsidies and subsidy-equivalents, Table 8A-7 reveals that Japanese agricultural subsidies in 1990 were higher than those in most other industrialized nations, except Switzerland, Finland, Norway, and Sweden. Yet national subsidy differences are a matter of degree, for even the United States, which takes issue with Japan on this matter, offers agricultural subsidies. In fact, the American public spends billions of dollars each year on agricultural commodity programs and trade restrictions to preserve the nation's ideal farm structure, the family farm.[42] Yet Japan spends far more than the United States does on agricultural commodity programs. As shown in Table 8A-7, Japan's producer subsidy-equivalents at 68 percent of producer incomes in 1990 and consumer subsidy-equivalents at 48 percent of consumer prices were more than double those of the United States at 30 percent and 19 percent, respectively.

Table 8A-7   Agricultural Producer Subsidy-Equivalents (PSEs) and Consumer Subsidy-Equivalents (CSEs) in Selected Industrialized Countries, 1990

	PSEs		CSEs	
Country	(Percent)a	(Billions $)	(Percent)b	(Billions $)
Australia	11	1.3	8	0.4
Austria	46	2.4	45	2.2
Canada	41	6.5	26	3.5
EC	48	81.6	41	63.8
Finland	72	5.3	71	3.5
Japan	**68**	**30.9**	**48**	**32.8**
New Zealand	5	0.2	7	0.1
Norway	77	3.1	64	1.7
Sweden	59	3.4	63	2.8
Switzerland	78	5.0	56	5.5
United States	**30**	**35.9**	**19**	**19.3**

Notes: a.   Percentages of total producer incomes accounted for by government policy.
   b.   Percentages of total consumer expenditures accounted for by government policy.
Source: OECD (1991) *Agricultural Policies, Markets, and Trade.*

Paradoxically, Japan is both the largest food importer and most protected food importer in the world.[43] A number of studies have calculated the economic impact of tariffs (formal trade barriers) and tariff-equivalents (informal trade barriers) on consumer prices in Japan. In one of the most recent, Yoko Sazanami and colleagues (1993) used Japanese import and producer unit price data to calculate tariff-equivalents for 51 of 500 products. Price differences on the fifteen items in Table 8A-8 are believed due largely to government policies rather than to consumer preferences. The tariff-equivalent for milled rice in 1989 was calculated to be 737.2 percent, the highest of all Japanese products analyzed.

Table 8A-8　Japan Tariffs and Estimated Tariff-Equivalents of Nontariff Barriers, 1989 (Percentages Ad Valorem)

Product	Tariff	Tariff-Equivalent
Milled rice	**0.0**	**737.2**
Citrus fruits	14.1	648.6
Oilseeds	0.0	625.8
Tea and Roasted Coffee	11.9	510.1
Wheat (domestic and import)	0.0	477.8
Soybeans (domestic and import)	0.0	423.6
Bread	6.5	346.5
Tobacco	0.0	316.8
Dairy products	17.6	242.0
Sparkling and still beverages	17.1	197.0
Beer	1.7	143.0
Confectionery	18.8	153.7
Leaf tobacco	0.0	119.7
Processed meat products	17.9	119.8
Canned and bottled vegetables/fruits	18.0	108.6

Source:　　Y. Sazanami, S. Urata, and H. Kuwai (1993) 'Trade Protection in Japan' in G. Huffbauer and K. Elliott (eds) *Comparing the Costs of Protection: Europe, Japan, and the United States.* Included are 15 of 51 products which Sazanami and her colleagues selected and analyzed from approximately 500 product categories.

Summary of Findings

In the case of trade friction over rice, the primary causal factor appears to be institutional differences rather than cultural differences or economic competition. Although defenders of Japan's rice policies like to use cultural factors to explain and justify the closed nature of Japan's domestic rice market, cultural factors turn out to be of substantially less importance than institutional and political factors in fostering trade friction. This appears to be true even though rice is rich in historical and cultural meaning for the Japanese and despite national rhetoric underlining that fact.

The institutional and political dynamics, including the agitation, pressure, and clout of Japanese agricultural interests and their supporters (e.g., NOKYO, ZENCHU, the LDP, JMAFF) kept Japan-U.S. contentiousness over rice alive in governmental processes and in the media. Meanwhile, American rice interests and their supporters (e.g., U.S. Rice Millers, USDA, USTR, Department of Commerce) used the large trade imbalance numbers and the fact of economic competition to buttress their arguments domestically and to effectively politicize the fact of Japan's closed rice markets. In reality, the liberalization of Japan's domestic rice market will affect the size of bilateral trade imbalances very little. Therefore, the economic competition factor is, in reality, of little importance in this case study of trade contentiousness. Because of the politicization of bilateral disputes and contentiousness over Japan's closed rice markets, bilateral perceptual differences have probably been the trade friction factor of secondary causal importance in this sector.[44]

B   The Automotive Sector

The automotive sector was chosen as the second of three case studies of Japan-U.S. trade friction because of four major reasons. First, trade in automobiles and automotive parts/accessories has been the focus of recent disputes and bilateral contentiousness. Second, the automotive sector is representative of the so-called heavy or mature industries in which the United States had enjoyed clear global dominance (e.g., steel, machine tools) until several decades ago. The automotive sector requires higher levels of technological sophistication than rice but lower levels than semiconductors; meanwhile, it is less labor intensive than rice production but more labor intensive than semiconductor production.

Third, the Japanese automotive industry has recently been more competitive than the U.S. industry. This fact is reflected in the large bilateral trade imbalances, of which automobiles and automotive parts/accessories together have accounted for substantially more than half of the total.[45] Although the automotive industry is one of centrality in the economies of both Japan and the United States, the large trade imbalance figures signify how highly effective the Japanese competition has been in challenging America's long-standing supremacy in this sector. These figures also symbolize the loss of American competitiveness relative to Japanese competitiveness and their apparent reversal of economic positions.

As a result, the fourth reason for selecting this sector as a case study was that the primary cause of trade friction has probably been strong bilateral economic competition. To explain the Japanese industry's success, Americans have tended to focus on Japan's relatively closed markets, 'unfair' trade practices, and differing government-business relations, while Japanese have tended to focus on Japan's superior product quality and America's declining competitiveness.[46] These tendencies suggest that differing bilateral perceptions also play a role of some importance in fostering trade friction. Whether or not these expectations are valid is determined in the subsequent set of discussions regarding the automotive sector.

Bilateral Automotive Production, Trade, and Consumption

The maintenance of a healthy automotive sector, the largest manufacturing activity in both Japan and the United States (the world's largest automobile producers) is crucial to the economies of both nations. Not only is this sector important, employing as it does a great number of workers and accounting for a substantial piece of GNP, but other industries depend on it for a goodly share of their profits as well. These include not only motor vehicle parts and accessories, composed of materials (e.g., steel, plastic, glass) and products (e.g., engines, chassis, electrical components), but also services (e.g., sales, service, finance).

There are those who suggest that the degree of development of a nation's automotive industry can be viewed as a reflection of its level of industrialization.[47] Partly as a result of its supremacy in automotive products, the United States had laid claim to the honor of being industrially the most highly developed nation in the postwar period. American supremacy in automotive production held until 1979 when Japanese automotive production first surpassed American production, a position Japan held throughout the 1980s. In Table 8B-1, the world's top ten motor vehicle-producing countries are listed with the numbers of vehicles each produced during the period 1988 to 1992.[48] During this five-year period, Japan maintained a substantial lead over the United States, whose own lead over Germany diminished. Japan's 1988 production of 12.7 million vehicles grew to 13.0 million in 1989 and 13.5 million in 1990, but dropped back to 13.2 million in 1991 and 12.5 million in 1992. U.S. motor vehicle production in 1988 was 11.2 million but slid to 10.9 million in 1989, 9.8 million in 1990, and 8.8 million in 1991. Beginning in 1992, however, U.S. production was on the rebound with a nearly 1 million vehicle increase, bringing the total to 9.7 million.

The substantial bilateral shift which took place in motor vehicle production between 1979 and 1980 is evident in the bilateral reversal of world shares presented in Table 8B-2. In 1979 the U.S. claimed a 27.6 share of world production, down slightly from 28.2 percent in 1970, whereas Japan claimed 23.2 percent, up from 18.0 percent in 1970. By 1980, U.S. production had fallen 6.8 points to 20.8 percent while Japanese production had risen 5.5 points to 28.7 percent. In 1992 Japan claimed 26.7 percent of the world's motor vehicle production, down from 28.5 percent in 1991, while the United States claimed 20.5 percent, up from 19.0 percent in 1991. From 1991 to 1992 the bilateral gap had narrowed from a 9.5 to a 6.2 percent difference.

Table 8B-1 Top Ten Motor Vehicle-Producing Countries, 1989-1992 (Millions of Vehicles*)

Country	1988	1989	1990	1991	1992
Japan	12.7	13.0	13.5	13.2	12.5
United States	11.2	10.9	9.8	8.8	9.7
West Germany	4.6	4.9	5.0	5.0	5.2
France	3.7	3.9	3.8	2.2	3.8
Spain	1.9	2.1	2.1	2.1	2.1
Canada	2.0	1.9	1.9	1.9	2.0
Italy	2.1	2.2	1.6	1.5	1.5
Great Britain	1.5	1.6	1.6	1.5	1.5
Belgium	1.2	1.2	.4	.3	.3
Sweden	.5	.6	.4	.3	.3
(Soviet Union)	(1.3)	(1.2)	(2.0)	(1.9)	(1.7)
TOTAL PRODUCTION	**49.1**	**50.3**	**46.9**	**44.6**	**47.7**

* Includes passenger cars, trucks, and buses.

Source: Automobile International *1990 World Automotive Market; Ward's Automotive Yearbook 1993.*

Table 8B-2 U.S. and Japan Shares of World Motor Vehicle Production (Given in Percent)

Country	1970	1979	1980	1989	1990	1991	1992
Japan	18.0	23.2	28.7	26.5	27.9	28.5	26.7
United States	28.2	27.6	20.8	22.1	20.2	19.0	20.5

Source: Calculations based on data compiled by AAMA from various sources and published in *Motor Vehicle Facts and Figures '93.*

The increase in American automotive production figures, however, was not due nearly as much to the efforts of the Big Three, whose overall production share continued to decline, as it was to the efforts of the recently established Japanese transplants. In 1982, Honda became the first Japanese automotive company to begin producing America-made automobiles. Nissan and NUMMI followed suit in 1985, as did Mazda in 1987, Toyota and Diamond-Star in 1988, and Subaru-Isuzu in 1989.[49] Table 8B-3, which presents U.S. automobile production share by company for 1990, 1991, and 1992, reveals that U.S. domestic production continued to be dominated by the Big Three, but that the transplants were increasing their shares. The Big Three claimed approximately 75 percent of U.S. domestic production in both 1991 and 1992, a five point drop from 1990, while Japanese transplants claimed approximately 25 percent, up from 20 percent in 1990.

Table 8B-3   U.S. Automobile Production Share by Company, 1990-1992

Company	1990	1991	1992
Big Three	**80.0**	**75.2**	**74.9**
General Motors	45.3	44.3	42.2
Ford	22.7	21.5	23.5
Chrysler	12.0	9.4	9.2
Transplants	**20.0**	**24.8**	**25.1**
Honda	7.2	8.3	8.1
Toyota	5.3	3.4	4.2
Nissan	1.6	2.5	3.0
Mazda	3.0	3.0	3.0
DSM (Diamond Star)	2.4	2.8	2.5
NUMMI	3.4	3.8	3.2
SIA (Subaru)	.5	1.0	1.1

Note: General Motors includes Opel and Vauxhall, Toyota includes Daihatsu, and Nissan includes Fuji (Subaru).
Source: *1993 Ward's Automotive Book.*

The 1991 world rankings of American and Japanese motor vehicle producers according to domestic and worldwide production levels is presented in Table 8B-4. Toyota ranked first in domestic production with 4,085.1 million vehicles, followed by General Motors with 3,720.5 million, Ford with 2,428.2 million, and Nissan with 2,391.5. As for worldwide production, General

Motors ranked first with 6,634.7 million vehicles followed by Ford with 5,138.4 and Toyota with 4,511.2 million. The ascendancy of the Japanese producers to their present high rankings, already in process in the late 1960s and 1970s, has largely occurred since the early 1980s.

Table 8B-4   World Rankings of the Top Eight Japanese and American Motor Vehicle Manufacturers, 1991

Rank by Domestic Production	Vehicles in Millions	Rank by Worldwide Production	Vehicles in Millions
(1) Toyota (J)	4,085.1	(1) General Motors (US)	6,634.7
(2) General Motors (US)	3,720.5	(2) Ford (US)	5,138.4
(3) Ford (US)	2,428.2	(3) Toyota (J)	4,511.2
(4) Nissan (J)	2,391.5	(5) Nissan (J)	3,025.8
(9) Mitsubishi (J)	1,405.6	(8) Honda (J)	1,908.8
(10) Mazda (J)	1,385.9	(10) Chrysler (US)	1,674.3
(11) Honda (J)	1,358.4	(11) Mitsubishi (J)	1,595.1
(12) Chrysler (US)	1,073.8	(12) Mazda (J)	1,551.3

Source: AAMA *World Motor Vehicle Data 1993.*

A major reason motor vehicle trade has drawn so much attention is that it accounts for a disproportionately large amount of the negative bilateral and global trade imbalances run by the United States over the past decade or so. Table 8B-5 reveals that U.S. automobile imports rose over time from 1970 until 1986 when they gradually declined. Also shown is Japan's increased share of U.S. automobile imports from 18.9 percent in 1970 to 63.9 percent in 1980 and a peak of 66.9 percent in 1981. A decline in Japan's share began to take place in 1982 and, by 1992, had dropped to 46.4 percent. This was not due to a decline in the popularity of Japanese automobiles, but to a decline in Japanese imports, for Japanese auto companies were in the process of establishing American production facilities from 1982 on. As shown in Table 8B-5, a large portion of Japan's American-made automobiles were purchased by Americans, while much of the remainder was exported to Japan.

Japan's automobile imports have been low compared to the auto imports of most other industrialized nations. As Table 8B-6 reveals, Japan's import market share remained at less than 2.0 percent until 1987 when it climbed to 3.6 percent in 1988 and 4.1 percent in 1989. Since then imports have continued to account for approximately four percent of the Japanese market.[50] Although government measures restricting access to the Japanese market were reduced in the late 1960s, and resulted in zero import duties, access continued to be

Table 8B-5   U.S. Automobile Imports from the World and Japan, 1970 and 1978-1992

	Total Imports (Thousands)	Imports from Japan (Thousands)	Japan's Share of Imports
1970	2,013.4	381.3	18.9%
1978	3,025.0	1,563.0	51.7%
1979	3,005.5	1,617.3	53.8%
1980	3,116.4	1,991.5	63.9%
1981	2,856.3	1,911.5	66.9%
1982	2,926.4	1,801.2	61.6%
1983	3,133.8	1,871.2	59.7%
1984	3,559.4	1,948.7	54.7%
1985	4,397.7	2,527.5	57.5%
1986	4,691.3	2,618.7	55.8%
1987	4,589.0	2,417.5	52.7%
1988	4,450.2	2,123.1	47.7%
1989	4,042.7	2,051.5	50.7%
1990	3,944.6	1,867.8	47.4%
1991	3,736.5	1,789.1	47.9%
1992	3,615.5	1,677.8	46.4%

Source: AAMA *Motor Vehicle Facts & Figures,* various years; AAMA *World Motor Vehicle Data 1993*; import share calculations are based on retail sales of new passenger automobiles as disclosed in *Ward's Automotive Report*, various issues.

Table 8B-6   Japan Automobile Imports from the World and the U.S., 1970 and 1978-1991*

	Total Imports (Thousands)	Total Import Share	Imports from U.S. (Thousands)	U.S. Share of Imports
1970	16.8	.7%	16.5	86.8%
1978	49.9	1.8%	13.3	24.4%
1979	60.2	1.2%	20.7	31.9%
1980	44.9	1.5%	10.5	22.7%
1981	38.1	1.3%	4.2	13.2%
1982	35.5	1.2%	3.1	8.8%
1983	35.3	1.1%	2.7	7.2%
1984	42.0	1.4%	2.3	5.2%
1985	50.2	1.6%	1.4	2.8%
1986	68.4	2.2%	2.8	4.5%
1987	97.8	3.0%	4.7	5.4%
1988	133.6	3.6%	21.7	14.0%
1989	180.4	4.1%	22.0	11.4%
1990	221.7	4.3%	39.2	14.2%
1991	197.2	4.1%	28.1	15.3%

* These statistics are based on Japanese new auto registrations.
Source: AAMA *Motor Vehicle Facts and Figures,* various issues; AAMA *World Motor Vehicle Data 1993*.

impeded until the late 1980s by discriminatory taxation, difficulty in obtaining safety and environmental certification, costly and time-consuming customs procedures, insurance rates discriminating against foreign cars, and lack of access to existing distribution networks.[51]

Except for some European luxury car producers that have been able to sell into a niche market, where Japanese competition was nonexistent until recently, most foreign producers have not enjoyed great success in selling their products in Japan. As shown in Table 8B-7, the United States, despite its domestic industry's size, comes up especially short. While American-made automobiles accounted for 15.3 percent of Japan's 4.1 percent import share in 1991 and 20.4 percent in 1992, the Big Three claimed an import share of 7.0 and 7.8 percent, while the Japanese transplants did substantially better with 8.3 and 12.7 percent. Therefore, less than half the U.S. import share was claimed by American domestic producers.

Table 8B-7 Japanese Imports of Automobiles by Country of Origin in 1991 and the Import Shares of Each

Country of Origin	1991	1992	1991	1992
Germany	119,048	104,680	60.4%	57.7%
United States	30,128	37,085	15.3%	20.4%
Big Three	13,711	14,093	7.0%	7.8%
Transplants	16,417	22,992	8.3%	12.7%
Great Britain	17,130	14,914	8.7%	8.2%
Sweden	12,363	10,494	6.3%	5.8%
France	10,854	7,906	5.5%	4.4%
Italy	5,754	4,573	2.9%	2.5%
Korea	688	762	.3%	.4%
Others	1,219	1,003	6.2%	5.5%
TOTAL	197,184	181,417	100.0%	100.0%

Source: Based on data from *Ward's Automotive Yearbook 1993*.

Japan's penetration of the world's largest automotive 1989 markets is shown in Table 8B-8. Approximately 20 percent of the U.S. market, 15 percent of the German market, and 11 percent of the British market went to Japanese imports, while the French and Italian markets remained largely closed to imports.[52] If transplants and imports are combined, Japan's total share of the U.S. market was about 30 percent.

Table 8B-8   **Japanese Automobile Import Penetration in Countries with the Most Motor Vehicles on the Road, 1989 (in percent)**

	U.S.	Germany	France	Italy	U.K.
1989	19.4	15.0	2.3	1.5	10.9

Source: AAMA *World Motor Vehicle Data 1993*, various issues.

In 1970, U.S. imports of Japanese automobiles were valued at $0.46 billion. By 1991, they amounted to $22.6 billion, while Japanese imports from the United States amounted to a mere $0.7 billion. These numbers from Table 8B-9a reveal that, even though U.S. global trade deficit in motor vehicles diminished by $5.7 billion from 1990 to 1992, the Japanese balance hardly budged.

Table 8B-9a   **Value of U.S. International Trade in Motor Vehicles, 1989-1992 (in billions of dollars)**

	Total Imports	Imports from Japan	Total Exports	Exports to Japan	Global Balance	Bilateral Balance
1989	54.5	23.0	13.3	0.5	-41.2	-22.4
1990	55.8	22.2	13.8	0.9	-42.0	-21.3
1991	55.3	23.3	16.5	0.7	-38.7	-22.6
1992	57.1	22.3	18.8	0.9	-38.3	-21.5

Note: The greater portion of these figures is claimed by passenger cars. In 1992, for example, Japan's $22.3 billion dollars worth of motor vehicle exports to the U.S. broke down into $20.8 billion for automobiles and $1.6 billion for trucks.

Source: U.S. Department of Commerce, International Trade Administration (ITA), Office of Automotive Industry Affairs (1993 September) *U.S. Motor Vehicle Trade Data Package 1989-1993*.

Japan's shares of the U.S. global and bilateral trade deficits from 1986 to 1992, as shown in Table 8B-9b, reveals this discrepancy more clearly. Japan's motor vehicle shares of the U.S. global deficit, rather than decreasing, actually increased from 19 percent in 1986 to 21 percent in 1989 and peaked at 34 percent in 1991 before it dropped back to 25 percent in 1992. Japan's motor vehicle exports accounted for 45 percent of the bilateral trade imbalance in

1986, rose to 52 percent in 1990 and 1991, and dropped to 43 percent in 1992. Once again, these figures do not take into account the transplants' shares of the American market, nor do they include the automotive parts and accessories' contributions to the bilateral trade deficit.

Table 8B-9b   U.S. Motor Vehicle Trade Deficit with Japan, 1986-1992 (in billions of dollars)

	Total U.S. Trade Deficit	Bilateral Trade Deficit	Bilateral Motor Vehicle Trade Imbalance	Japan Share of U.S. Deficit	Motor Vehicle Share of Bilateral Trade Imbalance
1986	138	58.6	-26.6	19%	45%
1987	152	59.8	-26.0	17%	43%
1988	119	51.8	-23.1	19%	45%
1989	109	49.1	-22.4	21%	46%
1990	102	41.1	-21.3	21%	52%
1991	67	43.4	-22.6	34%	52%
1992	85	49.4	-21.5	25%	43%

Source: U.S. Department of Commerce, International Trade Administration (ITA), Office of Automotive Industry Affairs (1993) *U.S. Automotive Parts Trade Statistics 1985-First Half 1993*.

Bilateral trade in automotive parts and accessories has followed the same general pattern as that of automobiles. Table 8B-10a once again reveals that American imports were greater than exports, both bilaterally and globally. However, from 1990 on, the U.S. global deficit in parts and accessories was entirely the product of bilateral trade with Japan. Indeed, the United States would have shown global surpluses from 1990 through 1992 had it not been for Japan.

A look at Japan's shares of U.S. automotive parts and accessories imports, exports, and consequent trade imbalances from 1990 through 1992, as presented in Table 8B-10b, once again reveals the same paradox. Japan's shares of the U.S. deficit in automotive parts were 110 percent in 1989, 109.5 percent in 1990, and 109.1 percent in 1991. If the Japanese shares were removed from the picture, the U.S. automotive parts and accessories balance would be running in the black.

Table 8B-10a   Value of U.S. International Trade in Automotive Parts and Accessories, 1988-1992 (in billions of dollars)

	Total Imports	Imports from Japan	Total Exports	Exports to Japan	Global Balance	Bilateral Balance
1988	31.0	9.3	17.4	0.5	-13.5	-8.8
1989	32.0	10.6	17.5	0.6	-14.6	-10.0
1990	31.7	10.4	22.9	0.9	-8.8	-9.6
1991	29.8	10.0	24.1	0.8	-5.7	-9.1
1992	33.5	10.8	28.5	1.0	-5.1	-9.8

Source: U.S. Department of Commerce, International Trade Administration (ITA), Office of Automotive Industry Affairs (1993) *U.S. Automotive Parts Trade Statistics 1985-First Half 1993.*

Table 8B-10b   U.S. Automotive Parts and Accessories Trade Deficit with Japan, 1986-1992 (in billions of dollars)

	Automotive Parts Deficit	Japan Share U.S. Deficit	Parts Share of Bilateral Deficit
1986	-6.0	4%	10%
1987	-7.3	5%	12%
1988	-8.8	7%	17%
1989	-10.0	9%	20%
1990	-9.5	9%	23%
1991	-9.1	14%	21%
1992	-9.8	12%	20%

Source: U.S. Department of Commerce, International Trade Administration (ITA), Office of Automotive Industry Affairs (1993) *U.S. Automotive Parts Trade Statistics 1985-First Half 1993.*

Figure 8B-1 highlights the central importance of the automotive sector in Japan-U.S. trade. It shows that, from 1986 to 1992, trade in motor vehicles, parts, and accessories produced between 55 percent and 75 percent of the annual bilateral trade imbalance. Not only have Americans been the Japanese automakers' best customers, the United States has also been, and continues to be, by far the world's largest national market for motor vehicles, claiming the greatest national share of automobiles, trucks, and buses on the road. In 1989, there were a total of 179 billion motor vehicles on the road, followed

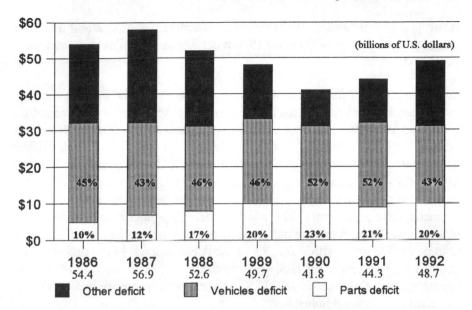

Figure 8B-1   The Motor Vehicle and Parts Share of the U.S.-Japan Merchandise Trade Imbalances, 1986-1992

Source: Based on U.S. Department of Commerce, International Trade Administration (ITA), Office of Automotive Industry Affairs (1993) *U.S. Automotive Parts Trade Statistics 1985-First Half 1993.*

by 50 billion in Japan, 30 billion in West Germany, and 25 billion in France.[53] The United States also continues to be the largest world market for automotive parts and accessories. In 1989 alone, Americans spent some $386 billion to purchase, operate, and maintain their motor vehicles, with one-fourth of this amount representing new car sales.

Automotive Trade Incidents, Complaints, and Agreements

Recent complaints brought by American automotive producers against Japanese producers have involved the dumping of Japanese vehicles into the U.S. market at below the going price in Japan, Japanese transplants' favoring of Japanese parts suppliers over American suppliers, and the relatively closed nature of Japan's automotive import market. Although Japanese producers have complied with U.S. requests on various issues, both Japanese and U.S. consumers have continued to purchase large numbers of Japanese automobiles, and U.S. shares of Japan's automotive parts and accessories market remain disproportionately small. What follows are summaries of bilateral incidents, complaints, and agreements since 1980 regarding automobiles and automotive parts/accessories.

Japanese Automobiles in the American Market With the first oil shock of 1973, motor oil prices doubled as lines formed at gasoline pumps around the world and fears of fuel shortages escalated. Japan's automobile producers took advantage of a worldwide shift in demand toward more fuel-efficient automobiles by increasing production and nearly doubling exports between 1970 and 1975. As gasoline prices fell, consumer demand shifted back toward larger, less fuel-efficient cars. However, with the second oil shock of 1979, a dramatic, more permanent shift toward smaller, high-mileage automobiles took place. Japanese auto makers met the challenge not met by the unprepared U.S. automobile industry, with a surplus of available exports; in the process, they claimed 66.9 percent of the U.S. import market in 1981.[54] This resulted in the unemployment of almost 300,000 U.S. auto workers and approximately double that number in related industries.

Consequently, on June 12, 1980, the United Auto Workers (UAW) and Ford Motor Corporation filed a petition with the U.S. International Trade Commission (USITC) under Section 201 of the Trade Act of 1974, claiming serious injury to domestic automotive production by imports; a USITC-initiated investigation quickly followed on June 30th.[55] On November 10, 1980, however, the USITC concluded that increased Japanese imports were not the major cause of the domestic producers' plight. Rather, they cited such factors as recessionary economic conditions and the structural shift toward smaller, more fuel-efficient vehicles.[56] In effect, the USITC had found Japanese imports 'innocent'.

Yet by early 1981, due to pressure from Ford and the UAW, legislation to restrict Japan's auto imports was gaining support. On February 5, 1981, Senators John C. Danforth (R-MO) and Lloyd Bentsen (D-TX) introduced legislation to limit Japanese automobile exports to 1.6 million units per year for three years beginning in 1981.[57] While the Carter Administration had avoided bilateralizing the situation, the new Reagan Administration eventually expressed its hope that Japan's government would voluntarily restrict their exports. In April 1981, in response to meetings with U.S. trade officials, Japan's Ministry of International Trade and Industry (MITI) presented a proposal for voluntarily restraining auto exports into the United States, a situation to be enforced by MITI through 'administrative guidance'. Even though Japanese auto makers were critical of this plan,[58] on May 1, 1981, MITI Minister Rokusuke Tanaka and Trade Representative William Brock agreed that Japan would restrict exports of passenger cars into the United States to 1.68 million vehicles per year. This would be a reduction of 7.7 percent for the period of April 1, 1981 through March 31, 1982. Later Japan announced that exports of four-wheel-drive station wagons and Jeep-type vehicles would be limited to 82,500 units, while exports to Puerto Rico would not exceed 70,000 units. Thus, total Japanese exports for 1981 were set at 1,832,500 units.[59] In effect, the problem had been solved by Japan's voluntary export restraints (VERs).[60]

Despite the VERs, Japan's share of the U.S. market continued to increase during 1981 and 1982.[61] On March 29, 1982, Japan renewed the VERs at the 1.68 million unit ceiling along with allowances for utility vehicles and exports to Puerto Rico. Once again, on February 1983, in response to Congressional pressure, Japan renewed the VERs for a third year at the existing levels. On November 1, 1983, the Japan announced that it would increase the export limit from 1.68 to 1.85 million automobiles during the period April 1, 1984 to March 31, 1985. In addition, it announced that the four-wheel-drive and Jeep-type vehicle limit would be increased to 90,848 units with 77,083 units to Puerto Rico, a 10.1 percent increase.[62]

In October 1984, Ford, Chrysler and the UAW urged the Reagan Administration to extend Japanese VERs for a fifth year, while General Motors and American International Automobile Dealers Association were opposed.[63] On January 30, 1985, high-level MITI officials disclosed that Japan's automotive VERs would not be renewed because of the record 1984 earnings posted by U.S. auto makers plus the sharp reduction in industry unemployment figures. They stressed, however, that 'administrative guidance' procedures would be used to prevent a sudden climb in Japanese auto shipments into the U.S. market.[64] Even so, key American Congressmen, organized labor, and auto makers, except for GM, pressed the White House to continue the VERs because of the record U.S. trade deficit with Japan.[65] Even though President Reagan decided not to ask Japan to continue the VERs, Japan announced that it would hold automobile exports to the United States to 2.3 million units in 1985, up 24 percent from the fiscal year of 1984. As a result, imports from Japan jumped to 19.2 percent of the U.S. market in May and 21.2 percent in June.

The VERs were still in effect by 1989 even though the U.S. auto industry appeared to have recovered.[66] Altogether, a large portion of the estimated $5.8 billion to $10.8 billion in quota rents had been transferred annually from American consumers to Japan's automobile producers, who in turn, had invested these earnings in new plants, equipment, and research and development, thereby making Japanese firms even more highly competitive. Japanese producers had also begun to upgrade into the luxury car market in order to maximize per unit profits. Finally, to further circumvent VER effects,

Japanese producers established American-based transplants which produced 1.7 million vehicles in 1992 alone. The single advantage for American producers was the probable accelerated diffusion of Japanese management and production techniques that helped American companies reorganize, retool, and improve their production and all-around competitiveness.[67]

The U.S. automobile industry once again filed antidumping cases against Japanese producers in 1988 and 1992 concerning profitable industry areas where Japan's producers had not yet established transplant production, namely, off-road vehicles and minivans. This time the USITC found Japanese exporters guilty as charged but declined to impose antidumping duties because the U.S. industry had not proved sufficient injury. In the minivan case of 1992, for example, the U.S. Commerce Department determined that Mazda had been charging 12.7 percent, Toyota 6.8 percent, and smaller Japanese producers 9.9 percent less for minivans in the States than they charged in Japan. However, the USITC concluded that Japanese dumping had not caused the domestic industry damage since it still controlled 88 percent of the minivan market; it also concluded that any market loss stemmed more from problems with American products than from Japanese pricing strategies. The Big Three continued to argue that Japanese minivan dumping reduced profits. However, new domestic products and a recovering economy together with Japanese domestic financial troubles and a rising yen had begun to shift momentum in Detroit's favor as the Big Three gradually recaptured market share from Japanese-brand vehicles.[68]

American Automobiles in the Japanese Market Selling Big Three produced automobiles in Japan's market has been difficult. Although Japan has comparative advantage in the automotive sector, the American companies have done poorly compared with other large foreign producers. Imports by Japanese transplants in America have even surpassed those of the Big Three, as shown in Table 8B-7. While Japanese claim that U.S. producers have not made a serious commitment to selling their automobiles in Japan, GM does ship a small number of right-hand steering Opels from Germany, and Ford uses its Japanese partner to produce cars for sale in the Japanese market. What is not explained is the Japanese consumers' apparent lack of interest in U.S. industry-produced automobiles.[69] The 1993 *National Trade Estimate Report on Foreign Trade Barriers* pointed out that:

> Informal business relationships between Japanese auto makers and their domestic dealers have effectively denied U.S automobile manufacturers the opportunity to market through existing dealer outlets. In addition certification

and homologation problems have complicated entry of U.S autos into the Japanese market.[70]

The report went on to say, however, that the Japanese government had taken steps to improve access to Japan's distribution system and had promised to further relax or eliminate barriers to dealership access. Additionally, both Japan and the United States had agreed to conduct a joint study on the problem.

Automotive Parts and Accessories One of the most contentious trade issues has been that of automotive parts and accessories, which alone accounts for approximately one-fifth of the U.S. bilateral trade deficit with Japan. Japan's low import levels of U.S. industry-produced automotive parts and Japanese practices of exclusive parts sourcing have hurt the American industry and threatened jobs of its sizable labor force of approximately 565,000 in 1991, a number considerably greater than the 351,000 involved in automobile assembly.[71] Contentiousness over automotive parts seems to have evolved out of unmet expectations of improvements in these areas. As U.S. complaints have escalated in frequency and pitch, Japanese have responded with growing irritation and resentment.

On September 21, 1982, Congressmen Richard L. Ottinger (D-NY) introduced the UAW-backed Fair Practices in Automotive Products Act. The proposed legislation would have required that vehicles sold in the American market be governed by a strict 'domestic content' formula. The larger a company's sales volume in the U.S. market, the greater the proportion of total value had to be produced in the United States. This meant that companies selling more than 900,000 cars in the United States would have been required to use 90 percent domestic content.[72] Auto-producers not meeting the requirement would have their American sales curtailed. Trade Representative William Brock set forth the Administration's position in a letter to the House Committee on Energy and Commerce. He wrote that, because passage of this bill would be devastating to U.S. economic health and employment, the Administration opposed it 'in the strongest possible terms'. Although the bill passed the House in December, Congress adjourned before the Senate's version of the bill could come to the floor.[73] Had the bill become law, imports of automobiles and automotive parts would have been slashed to a fraction of current levels.[74]

Yet the auto parts issue continued to be the subject of much ongoing debate. As Japanese automotive production in the United States expanded in the 1980s, critics increasingly complained that these assemblers were importing their *keiretsu* system and discriminating against established American parts suppliers by sourcing through their own long-standing supplier networks. Critics argued that this practice also affected access to the Japanese after-sales market because assemblers generally avoided certifying U.S. manufacturers' parts as *genuine*. As a result, dealers, garages, and other repair operations were reluctant to use them. Critics also blamed the *keiretsu* system for the closed nature of Japan's automotive parts market.[75]

Since 1986, both governments have been working together under the MOSS framework to improve market access for foreign parts suppliers. Although the U.S. government insists that the Japanese government encourage long-term relationships between U.S. and Japanese auto manufacturers, John LaFalce, Chairman of the House Committee on Small Business, pointed out at hearings in July, 1987 that very little change had taken place. In fact, he noted, the U.S. domestic auto parts industry had declined from 1978 to 1985, as evidenced by the 23 percent drop in industry employment figures and a 20 percent drop in real sales. He pointed out that U.S. products accounted for less than one percent of Japan's parts market and that only about $26 worth of U.S. parts were being used for each Japanese-made automobile. Meanwhile, he argued, great amounts of money were being spent on Japanese parts domestically for three main reasons: increases in imported Japanese cars containing mostly Japanese parts, the establishment of Japanese automobile and automotive parts plants in the United States, and foreign sourcing by U.S. automobile producers.[76] His was a powerful call for a halt to the 'bleeding' of the American industry.

As for Japan's market, the 1990 *National Trade Estimate Report on Foreign Trade Barriers* echoed Representative LaFalce's remarks by stating that, in 1988, U.S. suppliers accounted for less than a one percent market share of Japan's estimated $60 billion parts market for institutional and structural reasons:

> Auto parts is a sector frequently cited as illustrating structural barriers in the Japanese economy. Japanese auto companies are mainly assemblers of parts produced by other companies, but these companies are so tightly interlinked through long-standing business relationships that selling to the assemblers is as difficult as if the interlinked companies were one.

The 1991 *Report* noted that U.S. parts suppliers continued to account for less than one percent of Japan's auto parts market, estimated to be worth $102 billion in 1990. In spite of a June 1990 high-level bilateral agreement on a Market-Oriented Cooperation Plan (MOCP) to encourage the development of long-term business relationships between Japanese automobile manufacturers and American automotive parts suppliers, Senator Carl Levin from Michigan had this to say in an automotive hearing on June 20, 1991:

> We've got a competitive industry that's not being allowed to compete because of discriminatory Japanese trade policies. And the effect is devastating. Auto parts businesses, most of them small businesses, are going out of business at a record pace. The increased vehicle production by the Japanese auto 'transplant' factories has led to fewer, not more jobs, because these transplants have largely refused to buy from competitive traditional U.S. parts makers.[77]

Then on January 9, 1992, at the conclusion of a Presidential visit in Tokyo, Japan and the United States jointly issued an 'action plan' to help erase friction caused by the large bilateral trade imbalances. One plan included the procurement by Japanese automobile producers of $19 billion in auto parts from the United States by fiscal year 1994, (nearly double the 1990 procurement of $10 billion in parts).[78] Later that month, however, Prime Minister Kiichi Miyazawa and Toyota Motor Corporation Chairman Eiji Toyoda seemed to be edging away from what most U.S. government officials and industrial leaders present at the Tokyo meetings had thought firm. Apparently, the pledge was considered 'voluntary' by Japan's private sector and was not one government officials felt they had power to enforce. In fact, Prime Minister Miyazawa stated later that the pledges were 'a target rather than a firm promise'. Although GM spokesman John Pekarek agreed the Japanese had made no firm commitment, most members of the President's entourage thought they had.[79]

Adding fuel to the fire, Yoshio Sakurauchi, Speaker of Japan's House of Representatives, was quoted as saying that U.S. workers were lazy and unproductive, that their goods did not meet Japanese standards because 30 percent of them could not even read. The outspoken Sakurauchi criticized U.S. workers for demanding high pay when their productivity was so low. He added that if the United States did not watch out, it would be 'judged as finished by the world'.[80] Although Sakurauchi's opinions are widely held in Japan, they are not normally so forthrightly expressed by top leaders.

Then both the 1992 and 1993 *National Trade Estimate Reports* once again stated that the U.S. share of Japan's market was, depending on the measure, either less than one or two percent. They gave the following reason:

> Close and durable intercorporate relations make it difficult for foreign auto parts suppliers to compete with traditional Japanese suppliers for business from Japanese automotive manufacturers.[81]

By 1993, Japanese automobile assemblers continued to be under great pressure to increase purchases of U.S. parts to ease the $10 billion U.S. parts trade deficit with Japan. By August, a stronger yen aided them in doing so.[82] Even though many believe significant progress has been made, others remain critical, suggesting that the parts deficit will probably not shrink because most purchases are for Japanese transplant use and not for export. They also point out that Japan's market remains largely closed to U.S. suppliers even though the quality of U.S parts has improved substantially. The Japanese, meanwhile, continue to request patience, saying that business built on mutual trust takes a long time to develop.[83]

The American Position on Automotive Issues

Although the automotive industry continues to play a major role in the U.S. economy, the Big Three have been criticized for their lack of competitiveness and responsiveness to consumer preferences. In January 1992, following President Bush's trip to Tokyo with his entourage of government and industrial officials, including the Big Three's CEOs, an editorial cartoon depicted a huge, hulking football player with *DETROIT* across his jersey whining to the referee, a George Bush look-alike, 'No fair! He keeps hitting me!' The big guy pointed toward an undersized but trim player wearing a *JAPAN* jersey who had just run across the goal line and was triumphantly waving the ball. Typical of ridicule heaped on U.S. automobile leaders by the Japanese media, this particular piece came from the pen of a Chicago Tribune political cartoonist.[84] Indeed, editorial writers and commentators of all ideological persuasions lambasted the Big Three leadership during their Japan visit for their constant complaints of Japan's unfair competition. Still others criticized them for their million-dollar salaries and perks, while their companies were posting billions of dollars in losses and laying off thousands of workers. However, these attitudes are changing in the 1990s as American producers are making efforts to improve their competitiveness.[85]

Americans have also been critical of Japan's producers, even though they continue to purchase Japanese automobiles by the million. Perceptions of a monolithic Japanese auto industry, strengthened by governmental advice and economic support, flooding the American market with imports, are common. Imports have been sold at lower prices in the States than in Japan, while Japan's domestic market remains substantially closed to foreign-made vehicles. Finally Japanese auto makers are often perceived as contributing little to the U.S. economy even though they have benefited greatly from it. The Japanese tendency to purchase parts and accessories from Japanese rather than U.S.

producers has also elicited American charges of 'unfair'.

The Japanese Position on Automotive Issues

The Japanese tend to view Japan's automotive success as the result of effort, while they consider American problems as the result of U.S. industry shortcomings. Common Japanese complaints have included the following: American engines are too large; American quality is inferior; American prices are too high; Americans don't produce automobiles suited to Japanese roads, Japanese needs, or Japanese tastes; and Americans don't try hard enough to succeed in the Japanese market.[86] Because American producers were not prepared for either the quickness or the magnitude of the shift in consumer preference for smaller automobiles in 1979 and 1980, Japanese producers merely filled in the gap. Therefore, it was not 'a case of Japanese push, but rather of American pull'.[87]

Although it is generally acknowledged that Japan's earlier promotion policies, such as targeting automobiles as an industry of the future, restricting imports, promoting technology licensing, and awarding special depreciation allowances, have all fostered positive results, the automotive firms themselves are believed ultimately responsible for their own success.[88] Until recently, Japanese leaders tended to view Japan's domestic market as more open to foreign imports than most and that, if American auto makers had been willing to produce automobiles with right hand steering wheels, for example, they might have created a market for themselves in Japan. Moreover, Japanese often pointed out that tariffs and quantitative restrictions on imports had all but been eliminated and that the inspection and certification systems for foreign imports had been greatly simplified.

While it is sometimes acknowledged that the Japanese distribution system poses some difficulties for foreign imports, Japanese contend that this system has evolved over time and is rooted in custom rather than being a deliberate effort to exclude imports. They point out that overcoming distribution problems requires a sustained, long-term effort to sell vehicles that are adapted to the Japanese market. Concerning transplants, most Japanese believe these have made substantial contributions to the U.S. economy and to the training and employment of U.S. workers.[89]

The Automotive Sector in Japan and the United States

The American automotive sector of today features three producers, the Big Three: General Motors (GM), the American industry leader since 1920; Ford, the pioneer of mass production; and Chrysler. In the immediate postwar period, the Big Three accounted for 95 percent of the automotive market, a situation which many believe discouraged innovation and led to complacency. The U.S. industry, long considered a symbol of American industrial and economic strength, has been facing severe challenges from foreign competitors, especially the Japanese.

General Motors, the largest of the three, responded more quickly than either Ford or Chrysler to the change in consumer preference for smaller, more fuel-efficient cars. Yet, industry analyst Maryann Keller recounts how GM recognized the need for change during the 1980s but found implementation difficult within a complex corporate culture resistent to change. Keller identified four basic reasons for resistance: GM's overwhelming bigness which reflected an 'arrogant, risk-adverse philosophy', a parochial world view, leadership by numbers, and a 'contemptuous paternalism'.[90] Her views echo David Halberstam's conclusions concerning Ford and Chrysler in *The Reckoning*, a 752 page account of the American automotive industry's decline and the Japanese industry's rise.[91]

While the American automobile industry consists of the Big Three, the Japanese industry consists of multiple automobile firms. In rank order, the largest Japanese producers worldwide are Toyota, Nissan, and Honda, followed by Mitsubishi, Mazda, Suzuki, Daihatsu, Fuji, and Isuzu. Although Japanese firms had been producing automobiles on a relatively small scale since the turn of the century, GM and Ford, which had dominated the Japanese market from the late 1920s until 1936, were forced out by 1939 when the government introduced legislation to encourage Japanese-owned production. Then in the immediate postwar era, with Japan's industrial base destroyed, domestic automotive production was almost nonexistent. As Occupation authorities turned direct control of the government over to the Japanese, Japan's leaders were debating the future of their domestic automotive industry. Proponents of infant-industry nurturing, especially from MITI, eventually won out.[92]

Consequently, post-Occupation Japanese policies toward the automotive industry, the objectives of which had shifted from military to economic, involved economic support of domestic producers and protection from foreign competition. Policies included tariffs, a commodity tax system favorable to domestic autos, restrictions on the availability of foreign exchange for automobile importation, and restrictions on foreign direct investment. While these were highly effective in suppressing foreign imports and direct foreign investment, other policies successfully promoted domestic production. These included low-interest government loans, subsidies, special depreciation allowances, import tariff exemptions on crucial equipment, and approval of essential foreign technology.[93] With these policies in place from the early 1950s until 1969, Japan's automotive industry steadily grew from infant industry status to that of world-class competitor.[94] A large number of firms entered, or, as in Toyota's case, re-entered the Japanese automotive market, competing largely as equals. The Japanese automotive sector, then as now, is intensely competitive, with more independent manufacturers than any other industrialized country, yet with a market less than half the size of the American market. Because of the keen competition, Japanese producers have placed a high premium on product quality and marketing skills.[95]

Michael Cusumano's study of technology and management at Nissan and Toyota compares American and Japanese quality control in manufacturing and design. Unlike U.S. companies, Japanese firms began taking a broader approach to quality control early in the 1960s. This included carefully identifying consumer preferences, incorporating them into product designs, and instituting quality controls, from manufacturing and procurement to customer service. As competition and innovation spurred the development of a highly efficient industry, Japan's producers began exporting a significant number of small, low-cost passenger cars to America in the late 1960s. As the 1973 oil shock prompted a worldwide shift in demand toward fuel-efficient cars, Japanese automobile exports nearly doubled between 1970 and 1975.[96]

The most comprehensive study of the automobile industry, that of the International Motor Vehicle Program (IMVP) at Massachusetts Institute of Technology, concluded that contemporary Japanese automobile producers possess significant competitive advantages over American (and European) producers. These include higher productivity, superior quality, lower cost, and more efficient product development. Toyota Motor Corporation, for example, introduced a series of production innovations, such as continuous improvement circles (*kaizen*), the just-in-time (*kanban*) delivery system, and *keiretsu*-style relationships with suppliers. These innovations, collectively dubbed *lean production*, have revolutionized Japan's automotive industry.[97] They are now revolutionizing the American automotive industry as well.

It is generally agreed that restrictions placed on Japanese automotive products have had few positive effects on U.S. domestic competitiveness. To circumvent them, Japanese automotive firms simply built productive assembly plants in America. In 1982, Honda began assembling Accords in Ohio, while Nissan started producing trucks in Tennessee in 1983, expanding to automobiles two years later. Then Toyota formed a joint venture with General Motors in California and initiated an operation of its own in Kentucky. Mazda announced plans in 1984 to build an assembly plant in Michigan, and Mitsubishi said it would produce cars together with Chrysler in Illinois.[98]

While the Japanese industry has had a substantial, high profile in the United States, the American industry has had a minuscule one in Japan. In part this is the result of Japan's historical prohibition on direct foreign investment in the Japanese industry. In part, it is due to Japanese consumers' preference for German imports over American imports. Finally, it is also partly Japan's discriminatory taxation on imports, safety and environmental certification requirements, costly and time-consuming customs procedures, insurance rates discriminating against foreign cars, and lack of access to existing distribution networks.[99]

Summary of Findings

The trade friction causal factor of primary explanatory value in the automotive sector has clearly been the existence of strong bilateral economic competition. Although the American industry was slow to respond to the Japanese challenge during the 1970s and early 1980s, it is currently improving its competitiveness in an uphill battle to recapture lost market share and regain its former position of dominance. Recent improvements in the U.S. industry and a bilateral automobile accord signed in early 1996 are certain to have continued impact.

The trade friction factor of secondary explanatory importance can be considered the collection of differing Japan-U.S. institutional arrangements, policies, and practices. Japanese government policies, such as the earlier targeting of the automotive sector, aided the Japanese industry in achieving its present dominance; while policies, such as certification requirements, have helped prevent the penetration of the domestic automotive market by foreign imports. Meanwhile, Japan's *keiretsu*-style industrial structure has prevented foreign competitors from gaining access to the domestic distribution system. It has also hurt the competition with its collusive practices of purchasing parts/accessories from associated or member suppliers. At the same time, the American industry had, until recently, demonstrated inflexibility in responding to consumer preferences and unwillingness to tailor products to the Japanese market.

Factors of substantially less importance than strong bilateral economic competition and institutional differences are the existence of cultural and perceptual differences between Americans and Japanese. Regarding cultural differences, Japanese market requirements, such as right hand steering wheels, are probably more issues of U.S. competitiveness than issues of Japanese cultural uniqueness. Regarding perceptual differences, American consumers have lent strong support to the notion of superior Japanese product quality through their extensive purchases of Japanese vehicles. Additionally, recent government-sponsored studies and independent research efforts have examined the relative decline of U.S. competitiveness dynamic and identified causes. For these and other reasons, then, differing cultural and perceptual tendencies apparently have played relatively minor roles in causing friction over bilateral trade in automobiles and automotive parts and accessories.

C   The Semiconductor Sector

The semiconductor sector was selected as the third case study of Japan-U.S. trade friction for the following reasons.[100] First, semiconductors have been the focus of recent trade disputes and bilateral contentiousness.   Even the interpretation of content and intent of the mutually agreed upon Semiconductor Agreements of 1986 and 1991 have been issues of additional bilateral disagreement and friction.

Second, the semiconductor sector is representative of those high technology industries like computers, telecommunications equipment, and numerically-controlled machine tools, whose required levels of cutting-edge technological sophistication are extremely high but whose labor intensity requirements are quite low.

Third, the relative competitive strengths of the American and Japanese semiconductor industries are now considered relatively comparable, even though the Japanese industry had replaced the American industry as the front-runner for a short time several years ago.

Fourth, because the semiconductor sector is an industry of present and future technological and economic centrality, Japan-U.S. competition for supremacy in this sector has been intense. It can, therefore, be expected that the trade friction factor of greatest importance in this sector is the existence of strong bilateral economic competition.

While American and Japanese perceptual differences are expected to be of secondary explanatory importance in accounting for bilateral friction over trade in the semiconductor sector, the cultural factor is the least important or perhaps even a non-factor. Meanwhile, Japan-U.S. institutional differences were probably a more important factor in previous decades than they are at present. The following discussion regarding the semiconductor sector should indicate whether or not these expectations are valid.

Bilateral Semiconductor Production, Consumption, and Trade

The semiconductor sector is an integral part of the electronics industry whose total world market value in 1989 amounted to $740 billion and which has led all other U.S. sectors in production levels and employment figures. As shown in Figure 8C-1, electronics production in 1989 was valued at $295 billion, while automotive production, the nation's second largest industry, was worth $250 billion, aerospace $106 billion, and steel $61 billion.

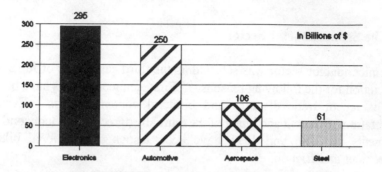

Figure 8C-1   The Largest U.S. Industrial Producers, 1989
Source: Based on Semiconductor Industry Association (1991) *The U.S. Electronics Industry: Facing the International Challenge* (from data furnished by U.S Department of Commerce, AEA).

As shown in Figure 8C-2, the U.S. electronics sector was also the largest American industrial employer in 1989, employing 2.6 million workers; whereas the automotive industry employed 0.9 million, aerospace 0.8 million, and steel 0.3 million.

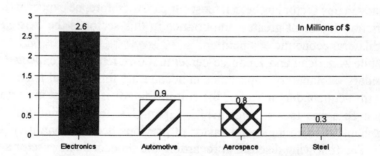

Figure 8C-2   The Largest U.S. Industrial Employers, 1989
Source: Based on Semiconductor Industry Association (1991) *The U.S. Electronics Industry: Facing the International Challenge* (from data furnished by U.S Department of Commerce, AEA).

Because so many other industrial sectors depend on semiconductor components, this sector is far more valuable than its $57 billion 1989 world market value, a 7.7 percent share, indicates.[101] As revealed in Figure 8C-3, semiconductor-dependent industries include aerospace, motor vehicles, computers, industrial robots, office equipment, consumer products, military equipment, medical instrumentation, and telecommunications. Semiconductors lie at the heart of the information-processing revolution which is transforming the global economy. The computer industry alone, whose products were worth $215 billion on the world market in 1989, is the largest semiconductor-dependent industry. For these reasons, semiconductors are often referred to as the DNA, petroleum, or rice of modern industry. Maintaining a competitive edge in semiconductors is not only a high priority for both the United States and Japan, but of special concern to the former because of crucial military applications.

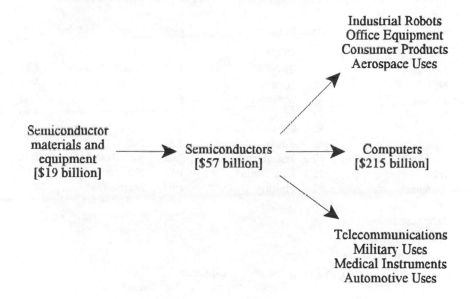

Figure 8C-3   **The Interdependence of the Electronics Industry and Breakdown of 1989's $740 Billion World Market**

Source: Based on Semiconductor Industry Association (1991) *The U.S. Electronics Industry: Facing the International Challenge* (from data furnished by AEA, VLSI Research and Rose Associated, Dataquest, Datamation, and SIA).

Both nations are currently competing for international leadership in the semiconductor sector. It was a race that had belonged entirely to Americans until a shift began to occur in the late 1970s. Table 8C-1 offers a comparison of the 1978 and 1990 production rates for the world's leading merchant semiconductor manufacturers. In a matter of twelve years, production had not only soared, but a tremendous shift had taken place in the rankings of the world's leading producers as well. In 1978 two U.S. firms, Texas Instruments and Motorola had ranked first and second, followed by Japan's NEC in third place, Holland's Philips in fourth, and America's National Semiconductor in fifth. By 1990, however, NEC had moved into first place, followed by Toshiba and Hitachi in second and third. Motorola, meanwhile, had dropped back to fourth place, while Intel had moved up to fifth.

Table 8C-1   Rankings of the World's Ten Leading Merchant Semiconductor Chip Firms (in billions of dollars)

Firm	1978	Firm	1990	Firm	1992
Texas Instruments	.99	NEC*	4.95	NEC*	5.24
Motorola	.72	Toshiba*	4.91	Toshiba*	4.93
NEC*	.52	Hitachi*	3.93	Intel	4.91
Philips+	.52	Motorola	3.69	Motorola	4.44
National	.50	Intel	3.14	Hitachi*	3.66
Fairchild	.50	Fujitsu*	3.02	Texas Instruments	3.08
Hitachi*	.46	Texas Instruments	2.57	Fujitsu*	2.68
Toshiba*	.40	Mitsubishi*	2.48	Mitsubishi*	2.46
Intel	.36	Matsushita*	1.95	Philips+	2.05
Siemens+	.27	Philips+	1.93	Matsushita*	2.02

*Japanese firm.
+European firm.
Those unmarked are U.S. firms.
Source: Based on Dataquest and VLSI data.

Figure 8C-4 reveals how volatile the competition in semiconductors was in the 1980s, not only between American and Japanese firms but among domestic firms as well. In 1980, five American firms and three Japanese firms were among the world's top-ranked producers. By 1989, only three U.S. firms remained among the world's top producers, while the number of Japanese firms had doubled to six, three of which captured the top three rankings. Texas Instruments, the leader in 1890 and 1984, fell to sixth place in 1989, while

Motorola fell from second to fourth place. Meanwhile, Japanese firms were more consistent in their national ranking configuration, with NEC, Toshiba, and Hitachi Japan's top three producers.

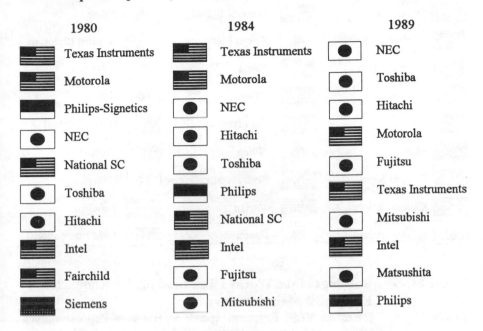

1980	1984	1989
Texas Instruments	Texas Instruments	NEC
Motorola	Motorola	Toshiba
Philips-Signetics	NEC	Hitachi
NEC	Hitachi	Motorola
National SC	Toshiba	Fujitsu
Toshiba	Philips	Texas Instruments
Hitachi	National SC	Mitsubishi
Intel	Intel	Intel
Fairchild	Fujitsu	Matsushita
Siemens	Mitsubishi	Philips

Figure 8C-4   Rankings of the World's Ten Leading Merchant Semiconductor Manufacturers
Source: Based on VLSI Research and Dataquest presentations.

An even greater shift had taken place in the worldwide rankings of the leading semiconductor equipment (chip-making machinery) manufacturers as shown in Figure 8C-5. In 1980, American firms had held all ten rankings except for the last. Four years later, while American firms still held seven of the ten top rankings, including first and second place, while Japan's firms had increased their numbers to three. Then, by 1989 only four U.S. firms remained among the top ten producers; Japan's firms numbered five and held the top two positions followed by an American firm, Applied Materials, in third place. The shift that had taken place in only nine years indicates just how volatile the semiconductor sector is and how quickly and impressively the Japanese firms have grown in competitive strength. This shift not only signaled a basic structural change in the global semiconductor industry, but it also offered further evidence of American economic decline.

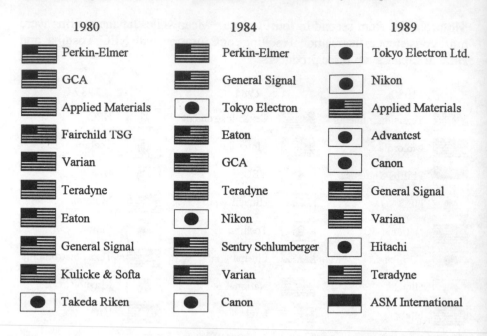

1980	1984	1989
Perkin-Elmer	Perkin-Elmer	Tokyo Electron Ltd.
GCA	General Signal	Nikon
Applied Materials	Tokyo Electron	Applied Materials
Fairchild TSG	Eaton	Advantest
Varian	GCA	Canon
Teradyne	Teradyne	General Signal
Eaton	Nikon	Varian
General Signal	Sentry Schlumberger	Hitachi
Kulicke & Softa	Varian	Teradyne
Takeda Riken	Canon	ASM International

Figure 8C-5   Rankings of the World's Ten Leading Semiconductor Equipment Manufacturers

Source: Based on VLSI Research and U.S. House of Representatives, Energy and Commerce Committee, Subcommittee on Commerce, Consumer Protection and Competitiveness (1990) *Decline of U.S. Semiconductor Infrastructure* (Hearing on May 9, 1990) p. 71.

A major reason for the shift in semiconductor producer rankings was the differing growth rates of capital investment by American and Japanese producers. From 1975 until 1982, as shown in Figure 8C-6, both American and Japanese capital spending grew, with U.S. firms consistently outspending Japanese firms. However, in 1983, Japanese capital spending surpassed that of the United States for the first time. From that year on, this trend continued. By 1988, the gap between the two nations in capital spending had widened to approximately $2.5 billion.

Table 8C-2 presents bilateral and world semiconductor trade statistics for 1982, 1985, and 1990. Although the world semiconductor market had increased in value from $14.2 billion in 1982 to $50.5 billion in 1990, the U.S. share of that market shrank from 56.7 percent in 1982 to 39.8 percent in 1990, while Japan's share expanded from 32.5 percent to 47.1 percent. As for the American market, valued at $6.3 billion in 1982 and $14.5 billion in 1990, the

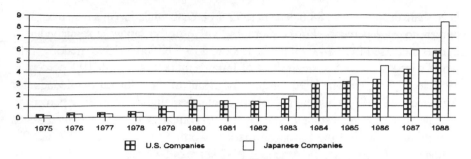

Figure 8C-6   **U.S. and Japanese Capital Spending in the Semiconductor Industry, 1975-1988**

Source: Dataquest.

Table 8C-2   **World Semiconductor Trade Statistics (in billions of dollars)**

	1982	1985	1990	1992
World Market	**$14.2**	**$21.8**	**$50.5**	**$132.0**
U.S.	56.7%	48.9%	39.8%	46.2%
Japan	32.5%	41.2%	47.1%	36.0%
Other	10.8%	9.9%	13.1%	17.8%
World Market (excluding Japan)	**$10.2**	**$14.2**	**$30.9**	**$97.8**
U.S.	74.4%	70.5%	57.2%	62.0%
Japan	10.8%	12.8%	22.2%	14.0%
Other	14.8%	16.7%	20.6%	24.0%
U.S. Market	**$6.3**	**$8.1**	**$14.5**	**$42.7**
U.S.	88.7%	85.7%	72.1%	67.6%
Japan	10.4%	11.8%	21.2%	19.0%
Other	0.9%	2.5%	6.7%	13.3%
Japanese Market	**$4.0**	**$7.6**	**$19.6**	**$34.2**
U.S.	10.1%	8.5%	12.3%	20.2%
Japan	89.9%	91.4%	86.5%	74.5%
Other	0.0%	0.1%	1.2%	5.3%
European Market	**$3.0**	**$4.5**	**$9.6**	**$27.6**
U.S.	54.6%	53.9%	46.2%	51.9%
Japan	7.1%	9.9%	14.8%	16.0%
Other	38.3%	36.2%	38.9%	32.1%

Note: The U.S. and Japan have no tariffs on semiconductors, while the EC maintains a 14 percent tariff on semiconductors.

Source: SIA data and U.S. House of Representatives, Committee on Foreign Affairs, Subcommittee on International Economic Policy and Trade (1991) *Prospects for a New United States Semiconductor Agreement* (Hearing on March 20, 1991), p. 69.

U.S. share dropped from 88.6 percent to 72.1 percent, while Japan's rose from 10.4 percent to 21.2 percent. Furthermore, the value of the Japanese semiconductor market increased from $4.0 billion in 1982 to $19.6 billion in 1990, making it the world's largest. The American share of Japan's market rose from 10.1 percent in 1982 to 12.3 percent in 1990, largely the result of the bilateral Semiconductor Agreement of 1986, while Japan's share diminished slightly from 89.9 percent to 86.5 percent. It is interesting to note, by way of comparison, that the United States claimed about half of the European market, worth $3.0 billion in 1982 and 9.6 billion in 1990. Even so, the American 1982 share of 54.6 dropped to 46.2 percent in 1990, while Japan's rose from 7.1 to 14.8 percent.

Thus far, the data show that Japanese firms always supplied more than 80 percent of their own market, while American firms have been dominant in markets at home and in Europe. Unfortunately for U.S. producers, however, Japan is the world's largest semiconductor market, accounting for 38 percent of worldwide sales in 1991; while the U.S. market accounted for 28 percent. American shares of the Japanese market from 1973 to 1990, are presented in Figure 8C-7 together with key bilateral semiconductor-related events. This figure shows that U.S. shares, which were on the decline before the 1986 Semiconductor Agreement, gradually moved upward after the Agreement to a high of 12 percent in 1990.

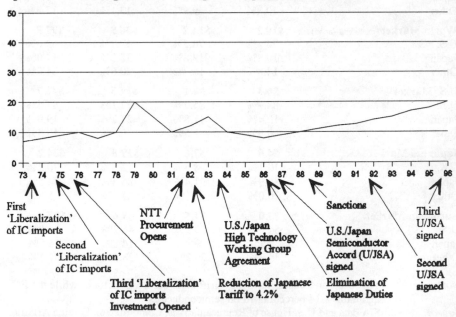

Figure 8C-7   **U.S. Share of Japan's Semiconductor Market**
Source: Based on Semiconductor Industry Association data.

As shown in Figure 8C-8, the foreign share of Japan's semiconductor market, the major portion of which was claimed by the United States, rose gradually over time until the renewal of the Semiconductor Agreement in 1991, after which it rose more steeply. Peaking in the fourth quarter of 1992 at 20.2 percent, it then declined throughout 1993 to a low of 18.1 percent in the third quarter.

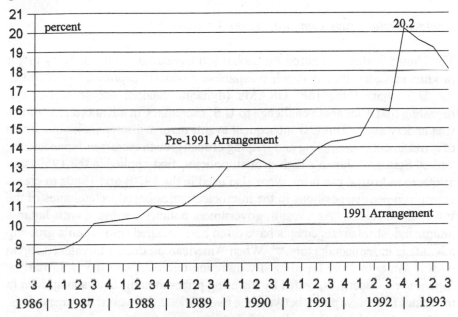

Figure 8C-8   **Foreign Shares of Japan's Semiconductor**
                  Market (quarterly report)

Note: World Semiconductor Trade Statistics (WSTS) were used for calculating foreign market share under the original 1986 U.S.-Japan Arrangement. For 3rd quarter 1991 and onward, Data Collection Program (DCP)/MITI-MOF is used, in accordance with the 1991 Arrangement.

Source: U.S. Commerce Department.

The preceding discussion of bilateral semiconductor production, consumption, and trade lends support to several key points. First, the semiconductor sector, which continues to show phenomenal growth, plays crucial roles in the technologically sophisticated industrial economies of Japan and the United States. Second, a crucial shift in semiconductor dominance has taken place since the late 1970s, as the U.S. position has weakened in relation to growing Japanese dominance. Third, the large, chronic discrepancy between American shares of Japan's semiconductor market and those of all other markets continues, despite some improvement. While the United States generally enjoys global trade surpluses in semiconductors, it continues to run deficits with Japan. In 1989 alone, this U.S. semiconductor deficit with Japan totaled $2.9 billion.

Semiconductor Trade Complaints and Agreements

The United States dominated the global semiconductor sector in every major product category until 1979 when Japanese producers captured 43 percent of the U.S. market for 16K DRAMs (dynamic random access memories), revealing that a Japanese challenge to U.S. supremacy in advanced electronics was underway.[102] This and subsequent events involve discrepancies in the role of government in promoting and shaping crucial growth sectors in Japan and the United States.[103] Japan's high-growth policies, first applied in the 1950s and 1960s to industrial catch-up, were also used in the 1970s and 1980s to create strong competitive positions in the microelectronics-based technologies of the Information Age.[104] As a result, government policies combined with Japan's unique industrial arrangements have often been credited with Japan's growing advantage in semiconductors.[105] When American producers threatened Japan with lawsuits in 1980 for allegedly dumping microchips in the U.S. market, Japanese producers responded by lowering prices at home and raising them in the States to achieve parity between the two markets. However, damage to U.S. producers had already been done.[106]

By 1981, some industry analysts were beginning to question whether, in the long run, the U.S. industry could effectively compete with the Japanese. Then, in the October 1981 issue of *Scientific American*, Japan's electronics industry, represented by seventeen of her most powerful electronics firms, placed their annual advertisement in the form of a lengthy article about the state of Japan's electronics sector. Essentially they claimed global supremacy in electronics and credited Japan's superior industrial system, cooperative relations between management and labor, high quality educational system, and management techniques for this success. The article closed with the claim that the center of world electronics and innovation was shifting to Japan.[107]

As U.S. critics have pointed out, no credit for Japan's newly won success was given to the roles played by adversarial pricing and closed domestic markets. Although U.S. companies held only ten percent of Japan's market, they claimed well over half of the market outside Japan.[108] Consequently, at the U.S. industry's urging, bilateral trade talks between the two governments were initiated primarily to prevent Japanese dumping and to open Japan's market. Former U.S. trade negotiator Clyde Prestowitz holds that selling more U.S. chips in Japan was particularly difficult because the closed market problem was far more subtle than formal barriers like tariffs and quotas:[109]

> (The problem) arose from several factors: the tight ties between Japan's manufacturers and their suppliers and distributors, which entail social obligations that go far beyond contractual dealings; the interlocking relations between major companies which enable them to ignore Western-style financial discipline; and the fact that, having long been encouraged by its government to displace foreign products, Japanese industry now did so as a kind of reflex action. In a word, the problem was structural. The whole industry was structured so as to reject, more or less automatically, penetration by outsiders or newcomers.[110]

Bilateral negotiations were almost continuous after 1981, as U.S. companies continued to complain of unfair trade practices and of having to compete not only with Japan's firms but with her government as well. Not surprisingly, these complaints did not find welcome reception in Japan.[111] After lengthy negotiations, an agreement was concluded in November 1982 which produced little change. Another year of negotiations yielded a second agreement in November 1983 which seemed to produce an increase of a few percentage points in the U.S. share of Japan's market in 1984, but this was to prove temporary. When the global demand for chips fell off later in the year, American sales in Japan fell 30 percent as Japanese demand fell 11 percent.[112] The U.S. industry viewed this as epitomizing their role in Japan's market as that of residual suppliers, to be used only when shortages produced a demand for additional products and the first to be cut when that demand dropped off.[113]

Despite ongoing assurances from the Japanese government, market access and dumping issues remained largely unresolved.[114] The Semiconductor Industry Association (SIA) and other industry representatives continued to pressure the U.S. government for further action. Various carefully defined and well-documented market access and dumping issues were then raised in the context of ongoing U.S.-Japan High Technology Working Group (HTWG) negotiations in 1984 and were eventually included in the Market Oriented Sector Specific (MOSS) talks, one of whose goals was the adequate protection of U.S. electronics technology. In the absence of such protection, many American semiconductor companies had seen their intellectual property rights in proprietary chip design dissipated by Japanese competition. Even before the talks began, Japan acquiesced to U.S. pressure for tougher intellectual property protection by adopting legislation providing 10-year protection for original semiconductor chip circuitry design.[115]

In 1985 and 1986, with trade deficits mounting despite a falling dollar, leading U.S. chip producers launched an increasingly sophisticated campaign for trade relief.[116] By January 1986, the U.S. government was pursuing a dumping case of its own on 256K DRAMs, a dumping petition from private industry on 64K DRAMs and another on EPROMs, as well as a 301 unfair trade case, all against Japan.[117] Each suit followed standard procedures prescribed by U.S. law. After a petition alleging dumping with consequent injury to a domestic industry was filed, the USITC investigated the claim of injury, while the Commerce Department simultaneously examined the extent of dumping. Each then issued both a preliminary finding, largely to eliminate frivolous legal suits, and a final determination.[118] Regarding semiconductors, findings would support U.S. industry claims.

Even as MOSS talks on electronics industries continued, America's Intel sued Japan's NEC in February 1985, charging copyright infringement of microprocessor microcoding. Then, in June 1985, the SIA filed a trade petition under Section 301 of the Trade Act of 1974, alleging that, for over a decade, Japan's government and six of its largest firms had acted to restrict the importation of foreign semiconductors. As evidence, the SIA argued that the 10 percent American share of Japan's market was far below that in other markets, which were typically over 50 percent.[119] The SIA basically asked the U.S. government to negotiate increased access for U.S. firms in Japan's market. If access were not forthcoming, retaliation in the form of trade restrictions on Japanese imports was requested.

Taking aim at Japan's electronics giants, the U.S. industry lobbied Congress extensively and continuously. These actions coincided with growing Congressional and Administration concern over the ever expanding, seemingly intractable, bilateral trade imbalances. Appealing to national sentiments, U.S. industry representatives successfully used legal and lobbying strategies to promote the concept that the U.S. semiconductor industry's troubles were the result of Japan's unfair practices, and this tactic afforded them unprecedented political clout.[120]

Shortly after the 301 petition was filed, Micron Technologies filed a $300 million antitrust suit against seven Japanese companies, charging them with conspiracy to monopolize the U.S. memory market by dumping 64K DRAM chips at below fair market value.[121] In August 1985, the USITC issued a preliminary finding that imports of 64K DRAMs from Japan were indeed injuring US producers. Consequently, the USTR began a Section 301 investigation of unfair Japanese trade practices. All issues involved in the

Section 301 investigation were removed from the MOSS talks as separate bilateral talks on semiconductor-related issues were initiated.[122]

Then in September 1985, Intel, National Semiconductor, and Advanced Micro Devices filed suit against eight Japanese firms for allegedly dumping EPROMs in the U.S. market.[123] To preserve their competitiveness in EPROMs, a memory device in which American producers still retained significant dominance, U.S. producers called for an embargo on Japanese imports. In the EPROM case, which opened before the USITC in October, 1985, a crucial but infamous piece of evidence was a memorandum circulated among Hitachi's EPROM distributors and sales staff in America challenging them to undercut competitors by offering to sell at 10 percent below any price, no matter how low. As an incentive, a 25 percent profit on all sales made was guaranteed. American industry officials charged that the Hitachi case was an example of Japan's pattern of 'sequential targeting' in which a few key, high-volume semiconductor components were picked and targeted for competitive success. As U.S. producers retreated under aggressive price-cutting tactics, Japanese companies extended the competition to other items until they had eliminated their competitors from the most profitable areas. As a result, Japan's producers had all but locked up the American memory chip market, acquiring 60 percent of the older RAM market, 70 percent of the overall DRAM market, and 90 percent of the most advanced (256K) DRAM market.[124] In an unprecedented move, the Commerce Department self-initiated a case in December, charging Japanese firms with dumping 256K DRAMs and 1M (megabyte) DRAMs.[125]

From late 1985 to mid-1986, a number of legal findings were announced. In November 1985, the USITC issued a preliminary finding that imports of EPROMs from Japan were indeed injuring U.S. producers. In late December, the Commerce Department issued preliminary findings Japan's firms guilty of dumping 64K DRAMs in the U.S. market. Nonetheless, by the year's end, after experiencing heavy losses, most U.S. producers of DRAMs had left the market.[126] Regardless, in March 1986, the Commerce Department issued preliminary findings that Japanese firms were dumping EPROMs and 256K DRAMs and set preliminary dumping margins. Then in April 1986, the Commerce Department issued a final ruling affirming that Japanese firms were indeed dumping 64K DRAMs. Finally, in May 1986, the USITC issued a final ruling affirming that imports of 64K DRAMs were injuring U.S. producers.

In response to these legal findings and in alarm over what was happening to the domestic semiconductor industry, the House of Representatives voted 408 to 5 to urge retaliation against Japan if a bilateral semiconductor agreement were not reached soon.[127] With this political mood as a backdrop, U.S. trade negotiators were well-positioned to achieve substantial results. The flurry of

U.S. legal activity alarmed Japan's trade officials, who finally acted to arrest the escalation of semiconductor related problems by reaching agreement with the United States.[128] After months of tedious negotiating sessions, the 1986 Semiconductor Agreement was completed on July 30, 1986 and signed on September 2, 1986.

This Agreement was a bilateral first in a number of respects. First, it was not only the first major agreement in a high-technology, strategic industry but also the first motivated by concern over the loss of national competitiveness rather than employment. Second, it was the first agreement dedicated to improving market access abroad rather than restricting it at home. Third, it was the first to attempt to regulate trade not only in the United States and Japan but in other global markets as well. Fourth, it was also the first time that the U.S. government had threatened Japan with trade sanctions for failure to comply with the terms of an agreement. Finally, the 1986 Semiconductor Agreement signalled major shifts in U.S. trade policy toward 'aggressive unilateralism, conditional reciprocity, and managing trade by results as well as by rules' that would characterize the rest of the decade.[129] The 1986 Agreement, together with the DRAM and EPROM antidumping agreements, had three basic parts. The first two addressed the issues of increased market access in Japan and the termination of dumping in all world markets. The third addressed the suspension of the Section 301 case, the two semiconductor chip dumping cases (DRAMs and EPROMs), and the estimated $2 billion in duties.[130]

In a confidential side letter to the official agreement, the Japanese government further clarified the market issue by stating that Japan 'understood, welcomed, and would make efforts to assist foreign companies in reaching their goal of a 20 percent market share within five years'.[131] Specifically, an organization would be established in Japan to help promote long-term relationships between Japanese and foreign firms and to help foreign producers increase sales in Japan. It would also ensure foreign firms full and equitable access to patents generated by government-sponsored research and development.[132] As for the dumping issues, the Japanese government agreed to monitor the prices of Japanese semiconductor exports to the United States and world markets. A 'fair market value' for most semiconductors would be calculated on a firm-specific basis in an attempt to preserve competition. If it appeared that dumping were taking place, the two governments would be allowed two weeks to engage in consultations before proceeding with any legal action.[133]

In late 1986, however, a different kind of troublesome event involving semiconductors occurred, indicating an escalating bilateral semiconductor battle. U.S. Defense and Commerce Department officials blocked the merger of Fairchild Semiconductor Corporation, the world's 13th ranked integrated circuits producer, with Fujitsu Microelectronics, a subsidiary of Japan's second largest computer and chip manufacturer. This merger would have involved the transfer of crucial cutting-edge integrated circuit technology and would have brought Fujitsu a means of circumventing limitations on Japanese semiconductor exports to the U.S. market.[134] The Japanese took issue with this move, particularly since Fairchild was no longer American-owned at the time of the proposed merger.[135]

Problems with semiconductor pricing also continued. Even though, MITI had established an agency which issued quarterly 'forecasts' of semiconductor demand and production, prices remained low. The United States warned that Japan was not adhering to her commitments under the 1986 Agreement. So, in February 1987, MITI requested production cutbacks. In spite of initial resistance, all Japanese producers, including Texas Instrument's subsidiary, fell into line. Unfortunately, however, OKI Electric's Hong Kong salesmen had already been lured into documenting sales at less than fair value, a situation which caused yet another flare-up in bilateral trade tensions. In an already tense atmosphere, the Defense Department issued an alarming report on the state of the U.S. semiconductor industry, as both the House and Senate voted to recommend retaliation against Japan for violating the price floor agreement. Finally, the Administration announced the imposition of $300 million in punitive tariffs on Japanese exports to the United States which had two apparent effects – the U.S. share of Japan's market increased, and semiconductor prices rose.[136]

By the fall of 1987, however, price increases were beginning to seriously hurt semiconductor users, especially U.S. computer firms. In response to pressure from computer manufacturers, the U.S. government did an about face and asked MITI to abandon production controls.[137] Semiconductor prices, however, continued to rise through 1988. There were reports that some Japanese firms were even demanding access to advanced technology in return for semiconductor sales.[138] As of 1989, practically no one was completely happy with the Agreement. The SIA and the American Electronics Association (AEA) continued to call for more Japanese market access, while U.S. computer makers were asking that the current floor price system be eliminated. Then, when the Administration complained in March 1989 that Japan was not living up to its commitment of a 20 percent foreign market share, Japan denied that the side letter existed, thereby denying any legally binding agreement regarding market share.

The perceptual and positional gaps concerning market share solidified as the Japanese argued that the Agreement's side letter merely acknowledged that they 'understood, welcomed, and would make efforts' to help foreign firms achieve 20 percent.   They also added that U.S. estimates of Japanese semiconductor imports excluded the sizable shares of IBM and AT&T, the two large U.S. captive producers. If these shares were included in the estimates, it was argued, Japan's foreign market share would be substantially higher. Japanese also pointed out that it was unrealistic to expect a strict linear progression in foreign market share growth. Rather, the growth pattern should show the same kinds of fluctuations over time that it had. Finally, Japan accused the United States of promoting managed trade, rather than trade based upon the *laissez-faire* principles Americans espoused and upon which the GATT was based.[139]

Americans viewed it differently, pointing out that the 20 percent market share figure was not an arbitrary decision by the U.S. government but a joint decision between trade negotiators from both countries. These negotiators had reviewed the data and identified some 55 submarkets for semiconductors before agreeing on 20 percent, a much lower figure than the 30 to 40 percent originally proposed by the Administration. Americans also pointed out that the 20 percent figure included shares of American-owned companies in Japan as well as imports from other countries. Finally, Americans pointed to the large discrepancy between U.S. shares in Japan and those in other markets. Even if allowance were made for the special historic and cultural problems facing exports to Japan, U.S. producers argued, it would be difficult to reconcile the fact that American companies accounted for about 70 percent of the global semiconductor market for automotive use while their Japanese market share was no more than one percent.[140] Responding to Japanese accusations of 'managed trade', U.S. producers argued that numerical figures offered an objective way of gauging the degree of market openness and the extent of Japanese compliance.   At hearings in March 1991 before the House of Representatives, Michael Maibach, representing both the SIA and Intel, maintained that a 20 percent foreign share of Japan's semiconductor market 'is not to manage trade, but rather to break the managed trade that we have seen since 1968 in Japan'.[141]

In short, most U.S. producers felt that the success of the 1986 Arrangement had been marred by Japan's non-compliance, estimating that the resulting U.S. loss was approximately $1 billion in sales, thousands of jobs, and reduced annual semiconductor R&D of over $100 million. The U.S. industry also accused MITI of using the antidumping provisions of the Agreement to impose production and export controls, which allowed Japan's producers, who now enjoyed a near monopoly in DRAMs, to raise prices and partially recover losses incurred from dumping penalties.[142] Finally, as in the automobile case, increased rents further improved Japan's competitive position, not only in semiconductors but in downstream products like computers and telecommunications equipment.[143]

Other difficulties resulted as well. American computer companies reported being adversely affected by difficulties in obtaining reasonably priced, Japanese state-of-the art DRAM semiconductors in 1987. Even though DRAM prices increased dramatically in 1988, most U.S. major chip consumers reported that they could finally obtain adequate supplies, with prices trending downward and regional price differentials all but disappearing by 1989.[144] American semiconductor producers also reported difficulties obtaining needed equipment, charging that Japanese firms were withholding crucial equipment.[145] A 1991 General Accounting Office (GAO) report verified that nearly half of 52 American firms surveyed had had difficulty obtaining advanced equipment and parts from Japanese suppliers and that seven of these firms had experienced pressure 'to take certain actions in order to obtain products'.[146]

In spite of disappointments and drawbacks, however, the U.S. industry generally felt that gains from the 1986 Agreement far outweighed losses. By the time the Agreement expired in July 1991, U.S. producers' total share of Japan's market had risen from 8.5 percent to over 12 percent, an increase to be sure, but one falling short of the expected 20 percent. At a House International Economic Policy and Trade Subcommittee hearing on March 20 1991, an industry representative who spoke in favor of renewing the Agreement, stressed that the U.S. industry had made great efforts to increase sales in Japan. He reported that, since the 1986 Agreement's signing, more than thirty new sales offices, 16 new design centers, and 10 new test, quality, and failure analysis centers had been opened up in Japan. He stressed that the U.S. industry preferred sales and pleasant relations with the Japanese industry to trade sanctions.[147]

Once an agreement between U.S. computer manufacturers, represented by the Computer Systems Policy Project (CSPP), and semiconductor manufacturers, represented by the SIA, was reached, the way was made clear for the government to pursue an Agreement renewal. The joint CSPP-SIA position recommended an agreement that addressed market access and dumping in ways beneficial to both industries' immediate and long term needs.[148] Shortly thereafter, the Administration and Congress also settled their differences as they prepared to use industry recommendations as the basis for a new agreement. In a hearing on March 22, 1991 before the International Subcommittee of the Senate's Finance Committee, Chairman Max Baucus insisted that the new agreement include quantifiable indicators of progress to ensure that Japan's market was really open to U.S. semiconductors, guarantee that trade sanctions then in place against Japan not be lifted until the 1986 Agreement's 20 percent market share target was met, and include expedited dumping enforcement provisions.[149] The Japanese, however, objected to a fixed quota of 20 percent and wanted all sanctions on semiconductors since 1986 lifted. In the end, a compromise was reached. The 20 percent indicator would remain in some form, but sanctions would be lifted.

In June 1991, the two governments agreed on an extension of the Agreement for another five years, specifying that sales of foreign-made semiconductors should reach at least 20 percent of the Japanese market by the end of 1992. However, in the same ambiguous wording as that used in the side letter of 1986, the Agreement specified that the 20 percent figure was only a goal, not a quota.[150] Additionally, it was agreed that no penalties would be generated if the goal were not reached.[151] Only days after signing the 1991 Agreement, Americans and Japanese were once again disagreeing over its meanings. On the one hand, W. J. (Jerry) Sanders III, chief executive of Advanced Micro Devices, echoed the sentiments of many U.S. semiconductor leaders when he was quoted as saying, 'We have an agreement that says we should have a 20 percent market share by the end of 1992'.[152] On the other hand, Eichi Hasegawa, director of MITI's North American Trade Policy Planning Section, typified the Japanese inclination to place far less importance on the 20 percent figure, saying, 'We consider the (20 percent) figure not as a target but as a recognition of expectations by the U.S. semiconductor industry. Even if the 20 percent is not reached, it doesn't mean that Japan contravened the agreement'.[153] The problem apparently lay not only in both parties' inclinations to continue the same pattern of disagreement, but also in the ambiguity of the Agreement's language itself. One U.S. executive close to the negotiations predicted that this ambiguity would undercut the aims of the Agreement and sow the seeds of continued trade friction. As he remarked, 'If you look at the Agreement, it just looks like the two sides have agreed to disagree'.[154]

While most Americans were pleased with the Agreement's renewal, many Japanese were not. Japanese newspapers came out with editorials against the agreement using unusually strong language. The *Nihon Keizai Shimbun*, Japan's largest business daily, charged that it was 'utterly incomprehensible' that an attempt had been made to set a figure to control market share in a free market, while the *Asahi Shimbun*, Japan's most prestigious daily criticized U.S. companies for using the treaty to increase sales without making efforts of their own when Japan's industries 'spend day and night developing better products'.[155]

By June 1992, both sides were once again disagreeing over unmet goals. Although the foreign market share in Japan had increased to 14.6 percent, it was 5.4 percent short of the goal, even while the U.S. share in markets outside Japan stood at 56 percent. U.S. trade officials were beginning to show impatience with Japan's pledges, which appeared sincere but produced few results, while Japanese officials felt that the United States should be more appreciative of Japan's efforts. Setuo Iiuchi, deputy director of MITI's America Division, emphasized that both the government and industry of Japan had 'made great efforts to increase access to the market'.[156] At the same time, Japan's industry leaders were increasingly expressing defiance, saying that there was no reason why MITI's demands should be listened to. Some Japanese industry leaders blamed the shortfall on U.S. manufacturers' failure to provide the kind and quality of products that Japanese users required, while most U.S. industry leaders blamed Japan's unfair discrimination against foreign firms.[157] Some American executives believed that the fundamental problem was simply Japanese reluctance to depend on foreign companies for crucial components.[158] Said Norman Neureiter, director of Texas Instrument's Asia office in Tokyo,

> The whole history of Japan's technical development has been the effort to achieve technological independence. As soon as they can make something, they don't want to buy it.[159]

A short time later, third quarter results for 1992 revealed that foreign market share in Japan had climbed to 16 percent, four percentage points short of the goal. Then, shortly before the new semiconductor talks commenced in March 1993, Japanese computer companies accused U.S. semiconductor suppliers of failing to honor their contracts, charging that orders from Japanese customers were diverted to U.S customers when a boom in the U.S. personal computer market resulted in a flood of orders for a limited supply of semiconductors. Tamotsu Harada, a spokesman for Japan's Electronic Industries Association (EIAJ), was quoted as saying,

> There have been many cases of cancellations, reductions and delays in deliveries from big American chip makers since demand picked up in America. When you can't even fill your orders, is it fair to stand up and complain about Japan not buying enough?[160]

However, American industry officials quickly dismissed the charges. Roger Mathus, executive director of SIA's Tokyo office, was reported as saying,

> This sounds like a panic move on the eve of the (bilateral semiconductor) talks. There are always shortfalls in some product areas. I could come up with a list of Japanese companies that aren't filling American orders for products.[161]

When results of the fourth quarter of 1992 were announced, showing that foreign share of Japan's semiconductor market had actually reached 20.2 percent, U.S. producers were elated. Throughout 1993, as the U.S. total world market share (41.9 percent) moved ahead of Japan's (41.1 percent) for the first time since 1985, foreign market share in Japan gradually declined.[162] By the third quarter, it had dropped to 18.1 percent, and the Administration's response was quick as U.S. Trade Representative Mickey Kantor called for emergency talks under the 1991 Semiconductor Agreement.[163] Japanese government officials, however, pointed out that the 1991 Agreement had not stipulated improved access would only be measured by market share, but measures like increased sales figures over recent quarters would also be used. Furthermore, Japanese officials stated, the 20 percent market share goal had only applied until the end of 1992. They also added that imports of U.S. semiconductors had not kept pace with Japan's increased demand as Japanese officials stressed that continued U.S. pressure could only backfire. One MITI official was quoted as saying,

> The more the U.S. side overemphasizes this decline in the market share, the more we are convinced that we will never again negotiate a semiconductor-type arrangement.[164]

Although conventional wisdom among economists is that the 1986 and 1991 Semiconductor Trade Agreements have been unmitigated failures, they were successful with respect to certain objectives. The U.S. share of the global DRAM market stabilized, the precipitous decline in the U.S share of the global EPROM market was reversed, and shares of U.S. and foreign companies in the Japanese market reached new highs.[165] However, concerning trade friction, not only had contentiousness not been reduced, it had continually been triggered by the ongoing semiconductor competition, trade disputes, rhetorical battles, and perceptual differences between American and Japanese government and industry leaders.

The American Position on Semiconductor Issues

American leaders tend to believe that, if the United States loses the semiconductor competition, the technological and economic consequences will be serious. For many, the U.S. semiconductor industry represents the very best of American entrepreneurship and embodies the highly esteemed American values of individualism, self-sufficiency, and hard work. The perception of Japan as a monolithic competitor appears to be common among U.S.

semiconductor producers, government leaders, and the public-at-large. The commonly used term, *Japan Inc.*, implicitly promotes the idea that current bilateral trade discrepancies are largely the result of Japan's industrial policies, collusive business and government arrangements, adversarial business practices, and closed markets.[166] At a 1991 Senate hearing to review the 1986 Agreement's renewal prospects, one U.S. industry representative summarized the basic U.S. attitude as follows:

> The 1986 Agreement recognized that limited market access and dumping are two sides of the same coin. The protected Japanese market assured its producers of market share and profits. This assurance minimized the risk of engaging in capacity expansion races at home and enabled Japanese companies to sell at a loss abroad. Japanese companies, sheltered from risk in their home market – the world's largest – by anticompetitive practices and financed by the deep pockets of their affiliated and parent companies, engaged in tremendous capacity expansion races that resulted in the sale of semiconductors at prices far below the cost of production during the mid-1980s. The Agreement was intended to instill competition and market forces in Japan – in other words, to break Japan's semiconductor 'managed trade'.[167]

The Japanese Position on Semiconductor Issues

Japanese leaders tend to view Japan's success in the semiconductor industry as resulting from long hours of hard work and meticulous, painstaking attention to product quality on the part of competent management teams, and a highly trained work force. They often point out that American-made semiconductor chips, like many U.S. products, do not meet Japan's standard of excellence and, therefore, they prefer Japanese-made components.[168] Furthermore, the term 'Japan basher' continues to be used to describe those who criticize Japan's technological and commercial successes. It is also used to discount anyone who focuses unduly on industrial policy and the *keiretsu* to account for her success. Much current criticism is considered 'a demagogic, unjustified assault on Japan, the blameless victor in bilateral trade rivalry'.[169] Similarly, unrelenting U.S. demands over semiconductor quotas are viewed as unwarranted, aggressive, and inflammatory in content and style.

The Semiconductor Sector in Japan and the United States

The Japan-U.S. competition for supremacy in the semiconductor sector as well as the apparent perceptual differences concerning causes of trade disputes and interpretations of agreements are ultimately rooted in each nation's distinctive structural, institutional, and cultural dynamics. A company's relationships with other companies and with government agencies are both shaped by, and help shape, a nation's political, economic, and technological environment. The semiconductor industry, like other industries, develops and functions within a particular national political economic system whose structural and fundamental characteristics ultimately affect productive capability and international competitiveness.[170]

The semiconductor sector in both Japan and the United States have benefited greatly from government investment. In the American case, most funding was awarded for military and space exploration purposes and targeted specific end products (e.g., the NASA moonshot and Minuteman missile programs of the 1960s). Although these investments accelerated the industry's development, American entrepreneurs, steeped in the cultural values of individualism, self-sufficiency, and hard work, created the domestic semiconductor industry without government guidance or intervention. It all began when three U.S. scientists at AT&T's Bell Laboratories invented the transistor in 1948. Because AT&T, as a regulated monopoly under U.S. antitrust law, was required to share its inventions with all other companies, transistor technology was quickly disseminated, thereby becoming the foundation for both the American and Japanese semiconductor industries.[171]

Then, in 1959, Robert Noyce at Fairchild and Jack Kilby at Texas Instruments simultaneously invented integrated circuitry. This led to a host of new products, one of which was the hand-held calculator. In 1968, Robert Noyce left Fairchild to found Intel Corporation whose early success would be based on DRAMs and microprocessors. DRAMs, on the one hand, were to become the memory bank for all electronics products and would establish the industry's fundamental technological direction for the next two decades. They would dramatically increase the computer's power and reduce costs. The microprocessor, on the other hand, often referred to as a 'computer on a chip', was an Intel invention that put all of the power of a room-sized machine on a sliver of silicon the size of a postage stamp. In 1973, Intel introduced the 4K DRAM. Two years later, the 4K chip gave way to 16K chips, as Mostek Corporation took the lead, followed soon after by Intel, Motorola, Texas Instruments, and others. Through most of the decade, the United States maintained its global leadership role.[172]

Factors responsible for the U.S. industry's early success included proximity to a major research university, a well-developed infrastructure, a pleasant climate and quality of life, and American-style entrepreneurship.[173] The industry gradually spread, from Silicon Valley, California to other parts of the country, from Oregon to New York. The more quickly a semiconductor firm got on the learning curve, the greater advantage it had over its competitors. The company best exemplifying this learning curve ideal is Intel, famous for its continuous innovations. Intel's fast early start and continued success has been due largely to the quality of its staff, its personal management style, its long-range planning, and its ability to build on its strengths.[174] Intel's staff is composed of people of diverse cultural and ethnic backgrounds, starting with its current CEO, Hungarian-born Andrew Grove. Intel continues to effectively combine a 'nimble product strategy with a barrage of lawsuits to keep competitors at bay'.[175] Even though Intel captured the global lead in semiconductor production and sales in 1993, surpassing Japan's NEC, Toshiba, and Hitachi, it is not resting on its laurels. Rather, it is using its huge profits to invest heavily in R&D and capital equipment for the next generation of leading edge technologies and products.

Most American companies, however, have not enjoyed the security of a financially stable, supportive environment. Most firms were relatively small, independent 'merchant producers' whose principal business was designing, producing, and marketing semiconductor products. Of the top ten American semiconductor producers, only IBM, Motorola, and RCA were significantly diversified enterprises, while two of the largest, IBM and AT&T, were captive producers whose output was used exclusively for their own products. Smaller companies suffered most from shortages of available capital for investment, research, and development. Although venture capitalists often invested in these firms, helping foster their early success, most funds evaporated in the 1980s, as competition grew more intense. Many smaller companies failed as a result of insufficient capital, scale-up problems, and management difficulties, while larger companies were particularly vulnerable to shareholders' demands for profits.[176] These companies often sold their technology to Japanese companies for much needed capital.[177] Not only did their best employees often leave to start up companies of their own, but individual companies also did not typically work together due to cultural and legal constraints.[178] This combination of factors resulted in a substantially fragmented American industry.[179]

More recently, many firms have converted from a strictly competitive mode to a more collaborative one, as the U.S. government has begun to play a more supportive role. One government boost came in the form of Sematech, a research and development project established by Congress in 1987. This group, whose purpose was the development of manufacturing technology for new generations of chips, was financed on a fifty-fifty basis by the Pentagon and a group of twelve American electronics firms, including Intel, Motorola, and IBM. Its major underlying goal is the restoration of U.S. dominance in advanced chip-making equipment. The American domestic industry is making a comeback.[180] The chairman of Silicon Valley Group, the second largest U.S. chip-equipment supplier, recently commented, 'It would be an understatement to say Sematech saved the (American) industry'.[181]

Today various U.S. government agencies are actively involved in protecting and promoting the American semiconductor industry and related high technology sectors. The Department of Defense, has actively supported information technology sectors since early times, providing the funding for the Very High Speed Integrated Circuit (VHSIC) Project. In addition to the Department of Defense and the National Aeronautics and Space Administration, Federal government agencies supporting the national industry's competitiveness include the Justice Department, Federal Trade Commission (FTC), Department of Commerce, Federal Bureau of Investigation (FBI), and Internal Revenue Service (IRS).[182]

In Japan's case, the national government took a strong leadership role in the industry's development from the very beginning. Funding was made available for commercial applications and national competitive purposes rather than for defense or space programs. The Japanese government's early commitment to semiconductors is understandable considering their economic appeal, small size, value-added intensity, strategic importance in world industrial and social development, and minimal raw material requirements.[183] American companies attempting to enter Japan's market in the early 1960s were rebuffed by MITI, whose efforts were instrumental in launching Japan's industry in 1963.[184] Texas Instruments (TI), which had applied to establish a wholly-owned subsidiary in Japan as early as 1964, was refused. TI continued pressing its case, emphasizing that a patent infringement suit would be brought against any firm exporting products to the U.S. market with its technology. Under pressure from Japanese firms who wanted access to TI's technology, MITI finally agreed in 1968 to allow the company to establish a subsidiary in the form of a joint venture with Sony Corporation. TI also had to agree to license its technology to Japanese firms at concessional rates and to submit production and market share data to MITI.[185]

By 1971, MITI had adopted a policy aimed at gaining greater control of world sales of computers. Officials had recognized that, to be a leader in computers, Japan would first have to achieve a dominant position in semiconductors. Through administrative guidance, MITI gave priority to semiconductor and computer firms, establishing a national 'vision' for the future and providing capital, tax breaks, and R&D assistance. Unlike the Americans, the Japanese invested heavily even when markets were depressed, thereby creating capacity for greater market share in the next market upswing. Also unlike Americans, they ran their plants at maximum capacity, even if excess production resulted in sales that yielded losses. They cross-licensed technology to other Japanese firms and bought microchips from them, especially affiliates, rather than from foreign firms. Four major factors for Japan's semiconductor success have been MITI's guidance, a collectivistic management style, an emphasis on quality, and access to American technology. Popular Japanese sayings such as 'the pheasant that flies gets shot' and 'the nail that protrudes gets pounded down' reflect the Japanese emphasis on group-oriented values. These values permeate the various institutions and companies involved in semiconductor production, even shaping the manner in which innovations and improvements are made.[186]

Japan's top ten semiconductor producers are all structurally large, vertically integrated electronics firms, not unlike the prewar *zaibatsu*, with extensive non-semiconductor businesses. Together they account for more than 90 percent of Japan's semiconductor production.[187] They also account for most of Japan's consumption, with the top six claiming more than 60 percent of the total.[188] These firms have tended to source internally and produce high volumes to minimize uncertainty with regard to price and supply availability. Outside producers typically find it difficult to sell semiconductors to Japanese users, and the greater diversification of Japanese firms, with their *keiretsu* links, reinforce this tendency. The six Japanese electronics giants manufacturers are Fujitsu, Hitachi, Mitsubishi, Matsushita, NEC, and Toshiba.[189] Table 8C-3 offers information concerning their strengths in semiconductor production and sales. Semiconductor sales accounted for between 4 and 20 percent of all company sales, whereas semiconductors are for most U.S. firms their sole product.

Japan's six large captives are backed by the huge financial resources of their parent corporations as well as by the national government's banking system, in bad times and good. As a result, Japanese semiconductor enterprises have not suffered the shortages of available capital and consequent investment restraints that American firms have.[190] Table 8C-4 lists the *keiretsu* affiliations of the six leading Japanese semiconductor producers with their national rankings.

Although the U.S. industry dominated the world market throughout the 1970s, by 1985 Japanese firms had supplanted American firms as marketplace leaders, especially in DRAMs. U.S. firms began to stage a comeback later in the decade by concentrating on more specialized logic chips, microprocessors, and EPROMs, while Japanese continued to excel in DRAMs and process/production technologies. Because of skyrocketing requisite investment, research, and development costs, American and Japanese firms have both begun to form a variety of joint venture arrangements in which research resources and efforts are shared for mutual gain. Even so, Americans and Japanese continue to hold distinctly different views on semiconductor trade issues, and the rhetoric of blame shows little sign of abating any time soon.

Table 8C-3   Dominant Firms in Japan's Semiconductor Industry, 1986 (in billions of dollars)

Firm	Total Sales	SC Sales	SC Sales (Percent)	SC Strength	Systems Market Segments
NEC	13	2.5	20%	MOS memory and microprocessors, ECL bipolar, linear and discretes	Leader in ICs, telecommunications, computers
Hitachi	28	2.3	7%	MOS memory and microprocessors, digital bipolar, linear and discretes	Leader diversified systems in computers, communications, consumer, heavy industrial, and electrical machinery
Fujitsu	9	1.3	14%	MOS memory, gate arrays, bipolar logic	Leader in computers, audio products, communications
Toshiba	22	2.2	10%	CMOS logic, MOS memory, gate arrays, microprocessors, linear	Diversified systems esp. consumer, industrial, instrumentation, and electrical equipment
Mitsubishi	12	1.1	9%	MOS memory, discrete and linear	Diversified systems for small business, computers, industrial and heavy equipment
Matsushita	27	1.2	4%	Consumer linear microprocessors	Leader in consumer and appliances, home computers

Source: Based on M. Borrus (1988) *Competing for Control: America's Stake in Microelectronics*, p. 105.

Table 8C-4   The *Keiretsu* Affiliations of Japan's Leading Semiconductor Producers

Producer Name	*Keiretsu* Affiliation and Ranking
NEC	Sumitomo Group (3)
Hitachi Ltd.	Hitachi Group (10) and others
Fujitsu	Dai-Ichi-Kangyo Bank (DKB) Group (5)
Toshiba Corporation	Mitsui Group (2)
Mitsubishi Electric Corporation	Mitsubishi Group (1)
Matsushita Electronics Industrial	Matsushita Group (13)

Source: Based on M. Borrus (1988) *Competing for Control: America's Stake in Microelectronics*, p. 106; rankings from M. Eli (1991) *Japan Inc.: Global Strategies of Japanese Trading Corporations*, p. 2.

Summary of Findings

The competitive strengths of the American and Japanese semiconductor industries are now relatively comparable, even though the Japanese industry had, at one point, temporarily moved ahead of the American industry as the global front-runner. Due to the strategic nature of the semiconductor industry, the technological and economic stakes in bilateral competition continue to be high. At risk is each nation's overall competitiveness in the high technology cutting-edge industries of the Information Age. As expected, the competition between Japan and the United States in this volatile sector continues to be fierce. Consequently, the trade friction factor of greatest explanatory importance in this sector is the existence of strong bilateral economic competition.

As early as 1979, U.S. government officials were beginning to worry that Japan's industrial policies and business practices in the high technology sectors were hurting U.S. global competitiveness. Involved were Japan's alleged mercantilistic policies (e.g., industrial targeting), adversarial business practices (e.g., dumping), collusive institutional and business arrangements (e.g., *keiretsu*), and relatively closed domestic markets. Also involved were U.S. relative economic decline issues.[191] Even former Foreign Affairs Minister Saburo Okito credited Japan's targeting of future-oriented, high-technology, high-value industries in which the United States was dominant, for a goodly share of recent bilateral trade friction.[192] Bilateral semiconductor rivalry also contributed to an American environment increasingly friendly to the idea of a national industrial policy and system of managed bilateral trade as a means of 'containing' the Japanese economic threat.

Regarding Japan-U.S. institutional differences, these were profoundly influential in the past. Several decades ago, the Japanese had targeted the computer sector and related industries; they had offered guidance and financial assistance in research and development endeavors and encouraged collaborative government-industry efforts; they had also created policies which curtailed the success of foreign companies in Japan, like IBM and TI, and required the licensing of their technology. Additionally, *keiretsu* ties reinforced the collusive activities of Japanese semiconductor enterprises and fostered the practice of dumping semiconductors in foreign markets. Consequently, the Japanese industry grew in competitive strength, while the American semiconductor industry was unable to respond to the Japanese challenge and grew increasingly fragmented and weak.

However, it now appears that the American industry has successfully addressed many of its institutional and structural weaknesses and is currently holding its own in the keen competition with the Japanese. The American semiconductor industry has gained strength and increased solidarity through the U.S. government-sponsored semiconductor industry consortium, Sematech, and through well-organized industry organizations like the Semiconductor Industry Association (SIA). These organizations represent the industry's interests and concerns in government hearings and the media. Although institutional differences probably were once an important explanatory factor, they had diminished in importance by the mid-1990s because of U.S. government participation and changes in the American industrial structure and function. Meanwhile, the cultural factor appears to be a minimal contributor to trade friction in the semiconductor case.

The preceding discussion also verifies the importance of perceptual differences in aggravating bilateral trade friction over trade in the semiconductor sector. The U.S. issues of contention in this sector have been Japan's closed markets, 'unfair' or adversarial trade practices, and differing institutional structures and functions regarding the semiconductor sector, while the Japanese issues of contention have been inferior U.S. product quality and declining U.S. competitiveness. In the past decade, both sides grew increasingly polarized as Americans and Japanese laid blame at the other side's doorstep.

An objective, dispassionate look at the facts indicates that both sets of views express partial truths and are, by themselves, misleading.[193] Research has tended to confirm the veracity of both national positions. On the one hand, the Japanese market has been significantly more closed to foreign exports than markets of most other industrial nations, and while the means of blocking access have changed, the goal has not.[194] On the other hand, a major factor in the U.S. industry's competitive troubles during the 1980s lay with the fragmented nature of the industry and the instability of its funding sources which prevented crucial levels of R&D, capital investment, and production. Yet neither side has seemed to hear the arguments of the other or comprehend its underlying logic. When successive bilateral negotiations and agreements continued to yield paltry results, mutual recriminations only increased. Hopefully, the signing of a new agreement in 1996 between the two industries (SIA, EIAJ) as well as the two governments, will reduce these dynamics.

Conclusions

What conclusions might be drawn concerning the relative importance of factors causing bilateral friction over trade in each of these three sectors? In the case of trade friction over rice, the primary causal factor appears to have been institutional differences, rather than cultural differences or economic competition. Governmental policies and political actions on the part of agricultural interests and their supporters kept bilateral contentiousness over rice alive in both countries, but especially in Japan. Although defenders of Japan's rice policies liked to use a cultural argument to justify the closed nature of Japan's domestic rice market, cultural factors turned out to be of substantially less importance than political factors in fostering trade friction over rice. Even though U.S. rice interests and their supporters used the bilateral trade imbalance numbers and the fact of economic competition to politicize the issue of Japan's closed rice market, bilateral economic competition was actually of minor relevance in creating and supporting rice-related trade contentiousness. Bilateral perceptual differences appear to have been the factor of secondary explanatory importance in the case of rice sector trade friction. This was largely the result of the politicization of rice issues in both nations and the symbolic value of 'closed Japanese markets' for the Americans.

The primary trade friction causal factor in the automotive sector has been the existence of strong economic competition between Japan and America. With the recent improvements in the U.S. industry's competitiveness and the Japanese automotive sector's continued dominance, bilateral competition in this sector will remain strong. The trade friction factor of secondary explanatory importance, especially in the 1980s, was the collection of differing Japan-U.S. institutional arrangements, policies, and practices. The existence of cultural and perceptual differences between Americans and Japanese have been of comparatively little importance. Japanese market problems have probably been more issues of U.S. competitiveness and Japanese institutional dynamics than issues of Japanese cultural uniqueness. Meanwhile, large automotive trade imbalance figures, U.S. government-sponsored studies, and independent research efforts verify the decline of U.S. competitiveness relative to Japan during that period. It can be concluded that cultural and perceptual differences have played relatively minor roles in causing friction over bilateral trade in automobiles and automotive parts and accessories, while institutional factors were secondary to the primary factor of strong competition between the two national industries.

The trade friction factor of greatest explanatory importance in the semiconductor sector has once again been the existence of strong bilateral economic competition. Although Japan-U.S institutional differences were important bilateral trade friction factors in the past, it appears that these are of less importance now in trade friction over semiconductors than perceptual factors, which appear to be of secondary causal importance in causing semiconductor trade friction. The U.S. issues of contention in this sector have been Japan's closed markets, 'unfair' or adversarial trade practices, and differing institutional structures and functions regarding the semiconductor sector; Japanese issues of contention have been inferior U.S. product quality and declining U.S. competitiveness. Meanwhile, cultural differences appear to be non-factors in bilateral friction over trade in semiconductors.

What conclusions might be reached concerning the relative importance of factors in causing and supporting the overall Japan-U.S. trade friction dilemma? Each of the three sectoral accounts tells a substantially different trade friction story, and the proportional mix of causal factors varies from sector to sector. Yet, on the basis of the discussion above, tentative conclusions can be drawn. The trade friction factor of greatest overall causal importance is the existence of strong bilateral economic competition. This was especially true for the automotive and semiconductor sectors, although this issue was used by American rice interests to muster domestic support for their position on Japan's closed rice market.

The secondary trade friction factor is probably Japan-U.S. institutional differences. It has been found to be the second most important factor in bilateral friction over trade in the automotive sector, but the first factor over trade in the rice sector. Meanwhile, it currently ranks after perceptual differences in the semiconductor sector, although a decade ago it would probably have ranked a strong secondary position. The perceptual differences factor probably follows next in explanatory importance for overall bilateral trade friction, while the cultural factor contributes only minimally to the Japan-U.S trade friction dilemma. Yet, bilateral perceptual dynamics exacerbate the effects of the other factors.

Notes

1   USDA, Economic Research Service *FATUS*, January/February 1993.
2   USDA, Economic Research Service *FATUS*, January/February 1989, 1993, 1995.
3   JETRO *White Paper on International Trade, Japan*, various issues. Japan External Trade Organization (JETRO) and the USDA Economic Research Service import and export statistics differ. JETRO groups imports and exports by use or application whereas USDA groups by mode of production (e.g., JETRO's *Foodstuffs* and USDA's *Agricultural Commodities*). While JETRO includes fish and shellfish as *foodstuffs*, it classifies cotton as a *textile raw material* and soybeans as *other raw material*. The USDA includes cotton and soybeans as *agricultural commodities* but not fish and shellfish.
4   JETRO (1992) *White Paper on International Trade, Japan 1991*.
5   In response to pressure from the U.S., Japan liberalized its markets for grains and lemons in the 1960s, grapefruit in the 1970s, and its beef and citrus quotas in 1977 and 1978. In April 1992, Japan's tariffs on beef imports dropped from 70% to 60% as specified in

the 1988 U.S.-Japan Beef and Citrus Agreement.

6 Vogt, D. (1986) 'Japanese Import Barriers to U.S. Agricultural Exports' in *Studies Prepared for the Use of the Republican Members of the Joint Economic Committee*, prepared by the Congressional Research Service, Library of Congress, October 1, 1986.

7 U.S. House of Representatives, Subcommittee on Cotton, Rice, and Sugar (1981) *Review United States-Japan Rice Agreement* (Hearing on February 26 1981) (USDA Serial No. 97-B). This document also explains how Korea went from being a Title I rice recipient beginning in 1955 to being the most important commercial U.S. rice customer in 1980. Although she had continued to accept American rice under Title I off and on again until 1978, Korea had already begun to move into the commercial U.S. rice market around 1967, buying American rice both commercially and under Public Law 480 for many years. At the time, Korea was the number one market for U.S. rice.

8 See pp. 129-146 of *Review United States-Japan Rice Agreement* (1981) for a detailed discussion of this complaint against Japan in the prepared remarks of J. Stephen Gabbert, Executive Vice President of The Rice Millers' Association.

9 See *Review United States-Japan Rice Agreement* (1981) for copies of the letters of U.S. Undersecretary of Agriculture Dale Hathoway and Japanese Vice Minister Sawabe which together constitute the bilateral rice agreement.

10 Ibid.

11 For more details, see the following documents: U.S. House of Representatives, Committee on Agriculture (1987) *Review of Japan's Policy Concerning the Importation of Rice, Including a Petition Filed by the U.S. Rice Millers' Association* (Hearing held on October 1, 1986); U.S. Senate, Committee on Agriculture, Nutrition, and Forestry (1987) *U.S.-Japan Rice Trade* (Hearing held on October 21, 1986).

12 *Japan Economic Journal* (1986 September 20) 'Japan Shocked by U.S. Protests against Rice Import Restrictions'.

13 Ibid.

14 Letter from Shintaro Abe, Masayoshi Ito, Michio Watanabe and others to President Ronald Reagan, September 29, 1988.

15 Choate, P. (1990) *Agents of Influence*, pp. 11-12.

16 Most of the details and all of the quotations for the discussion of this incident come from D. Sanger (1991 March 18) 'Japan Shuts U.S. Rice Exhibition', *The New York Times*.

17 Ibid.

18 Ibid.

19 *The Los Angeles Times* (1991 November 12) 'Japan Forces Removal of U.S. Rice Sample'.

20 Yamaji, S. and S. Ito (1993) 'The Political Economy of Rice in Japan' in L. Tweeten, et al (eds) *Japanese and American Agriculture: Tradition and Progress in Conflict*, pp. 345-355.

21 Helm, L. (1992 December 17) 'Japanese Rice Farmers Steam: Thousands Rally to Demand Government Keep Import Ban', *The Los Angeles Times*.

22 Childs, N. (1990b) *The World Rice Market: Government Intervention and Multilateral Policy Reform* (USDA, Economic Research Service, Commodity Economics Division, Document # AGES 9060). California, accounting for 99% of all U.S. short grain rice exports, grows the type of rice Japanese consumers prefer.

23 Tweeten, L. (1993b) 'Overview' in L. Tweeten et al (eds) *Japanese and American Agriculture: Tradition and Progress in Conflict*.

24   Cohen, S. (1991) *Cowboys and Samurai: Why the U.S. Is Losing the Battle with the Japanese, and Why It Matters*, p. 47.

25   Wailes, E. et al (1993) 'Rice and Security in Japan: An American Perspective' in L. Tweeten et al (eds) *Japanese and American Agriculture: Tradition and Progress in Conflict*.

26   Hayami, Y. (1972) 'Rice Policy in Japan's Economic Development', *American Journal of Agricultural Politics*, vol. 54, pp. 19-31; Yamaji, S. and S. Ito (1993) 'The Political Economy of Rice in Japan' in L. Tweeten et al (eds) *Japanese and American Agriculture: Tradition and Progress in Conflict*. Major rice shortages in Japanese urban areas due to increased rice demand during the First World War culminated in Japan's infamous Rice Riots of 1918 and 1920. In response to this situation, the Rice Law of 1921 was enacted. This law was replaced by the Rice Control Law of 1933. These laws permitted the government to *indirectly* intervene in the rice market by establishing means of purchasing, selling, storing, and restricting imports so that market prices would be maintained between floor and ceiling prices. However, these measures were insufficient to stabilize production, consumption, and prices.

27   Hayami, Y. (1972), vol. 54, pp. 19-31. As Japan became increasingly involved in World War II, the Rice Distribution Control Act was enacted in 1939 to allow the government to *directly* influence the rice supply and distribution. This law was eventually replaced by the Food Control Act of 1942, which made direct government intervention permanent. This act included nearly all other food commodities in addition to rice.

28   Hayami, Y. (1988) *Japanese Agriculture Under Siege: The Political Economy of Agricultural Policies*, p. 125.

29   Moore, R. H. (1990) *Japanese Agriculture: Patterns of Rural Development*, p. 266.

30   Yamaji, S. and S. Ito (1993) 'The Political Economy of Rice in Japan', p. 355, in L. Tweeten et al (eds) *Japanese and American Agriculture: Tradition and Progress in Conflict*.

31   JETRO (1974) *The Rice Cycle: The Grain That Created a Culture*. This publication, prepared for the 1974 Spokane World Exposition in Spokane, Washington, offers an historical overview of Japan's rice culture with photographs of rice-influenced Japanese cuisine, packaging, materials, festivals, crafts, and fine arts.

32   Shannon, A. (1987) 'The U.S. Rice Industry Celebrates 300 Years', *American Foodservice Journal*, vol. 41, 3, pp. 60-61.

33   Moore, R. H. (1990) *Japanese Agriculture: Patterns of Rural Development*, pp. 4-8. For a detailed historical account of Japanese agriculture from its earliest beginnings to the present and an analysis of the impact it has had on contemporary Japan, see T. Smith (1959) *The Agrarian Origins of Modern Japan*. For an intimate account of a Japanese rural hamlet, see D. Dore (1978) *Shinohate: A Portrait of a Japanese Village*.

34   Tweeten, L. (1993) 'Overview', p. 3 in L. Tweeten et al (eds) *Japanese and American Agriculture: Tradition and Progress in Conflict*.

35   Oga, K. (1993) 'Impacts of Trade Arrangements on Farm Structure and Food Demand: A Japanese Perspective', p. 400. In L. Tweeten et al (eds) *Japanese and American Agriculture: Tradition and Progress in Conflict*.

36   Childs, N. (1990a) *U.S. Rice Distribution Patterns 1988/89* (USDA, Economic Research Service, Statistical Bulletin #836).

37 Childs, N. (1990b) *The World Rice Market: Government Intervention and Multilateral Policy Reform* (USDA, Economic Research Service, Commodity Economics Division, Document # AGES 9060).

38 Childs, N. (1990b) Approximately 40 percent of all U.S. rice exports are shipped under some form of credit assistance or as bona fide food aid.

39 Goto, J and N. Imamura (1993) 'Japanese Agriculture: Characteristics, Institutions, and Policies' in L. Tweeten et al (eds) *Japanese and American Agriculture: Tradition and Progress in Conflict*. For a detailed historical account and critical evaluation of Japanese agricultural policy measures from 1945 to 1979, see F. Egaitsu (1982) 'Japanese Agricultural Policy: Present Problems and Their Historical Background' in E. Castle and K. Hemmi (eds) *U.S.-Japanese Agriculture: Tradition and Progress in Conflict*. See also Y. Hayami (1988) *Japanese Agriculture Under Siege: The Political Economy of Agricultural Policies* for a survey of the various policy tools of Japanese agricultural protection and their consequences; the mechanism of rice support is analyzed as a typical example.

40 OECD (1987) *National Policies and Agricultural Trade: Japan.*

41 Wailes, E. et al (1993) 'Rice and Security in Japan: An American Perspective', p. 380 in L. Tweeten et al (eds) *Japanese and American Agriculture: Tradition and Progress in Conflict*; OECD (1987) *National Policies and Agricultural Trade: United States.*

42 Tweeten, L. (1993) 'American Agriculture: Organization, Structure, Institutions, and Policy' in L. Tweeten et al (eds) *Japanese and American Agriculture: Tradition and Progress in Conflict*.

43 Tweeten, L. (1993) 'Overview', p. 4 in L. Tweeten et al (eds) *Japanese and American Agriculture: Tradition and Progress in Conflict*.

44 The GATT's Uruguay Round of talks was concluded on December 15, 1993 following seven years of negotiations. For the rice sector, the major results were increased market access, reduced export subsidies, and reduced internal support. Japan, as well as Taiwan and South Korea, are expected to increase rice imports according to their GATT commitment. Japan's increases in rice imports will mean major changes in her rice policy.

45 Automotive trade accounted for 63 percent of the $49.4 billion 1992 bilateral trade deficit, 43 percent of which was due to motor vehicles (predominantly automobiles) and 20 percent to automotive parts and accessories. In 1991 automotive trade had accounted for 73 percent of the bilateral deficit, with 52 percent claimed by motor vehicles and 21 percent by parts and accessories. These figures are from U.S. Department of Commerce, International Trade Administration, Office of Automotive Affairs (1993) 'U.S. Automotive Parts Trade Statistics, 1985-First Half 1993' (compiled from U.S. Bureau of Census statistics).

46 See Tables 7.1a and 7.1b in the preceding chapter.

47 Mutoh, H. (1988) 'The Automotive Industry', chapter 12 in R. Komiya, M. Okuno, and K. Suzumura (eds) *Industrial Policy of Japan*, p. 307.

48 Figures for each country include the production of domestic companies as well as that of transplants. Noteworthy is the lack of foreign transplant production in Japan.

49 *1993 Ward's Automotive Yearbook*, p. 17, NUMMI, it should be noted, is a joint venture between Toyota and General Motors. It should also be noted that, although bilateral trade issues and trade balances are increasingly affected by transplants, joint ventures, and international sourcing, these issues are not directly dealt with in this research

project. For a more detailed account of the effects of internationalization, see USITC (1985) *Internationalization of the Automobile Industry and Its Effects on the U.S. Automobile Industry.*

50   Other calculations arrive at between two and three percent; see, for example, F. Bergsten, and M. Noland (1993) *Reconcilable Differences?   United States-Japan Economic Conflict*, p. 114.

51   Bergsten, F. and M. Noland (1993), pp. 113-114.

52   These nations were selected because, according to Automobile International's *World Automotive Market* (1989), they had the most vehicles on the road in 1988. The U.S. had 179.0 billion, Japan 49.9 billion, West Germany 30.1 billion, France 24.9 billion, Italy 24.7 billion, and the U.K. 23.5 billion. For more on EC restrictions on Japanese imports, see D. Halberstam (1986) *The Reckoning*, p. 630.

53   Automobile International (1986) *World Automotive Market.*

54   Refer to Tables 2 and 5 in Appendix B.   Other calculations arrive at a 75 percent Japanese share of the U.S. import market.

55   Winham, G. and I. Kabashima (1982) 'The Politics of U.S.-Japanese Auto Trade', Chapter 3 in I.M. Destler and H. Sato (eds) *Coping with U.S.-Japanese Economic Conflicts*, pp. 73-74. For two other accounts, see USITC (1980) *Certain Motor Vehicles and Certain Chassis and Bodies Therefor* (USITC Publication No. 1110); and K. Mutoh (1988) 'The Automotive Industry', Chapter 12 in R. Komiya, M. Okuno, and K. Suzumura (eds) *Industrial Policy of Japan.*

56   USITC (1980) *Certain Motor Vehicles and Certain Chassis and Bodies Therefor* (USITC Publication No. 1110), pp. 34-35.

57   Nanto, D. (1983) *Automobiles Imported from Japan* (U.S. Congressional Research Service Brief No. IB 80030), p. 14.

58   Winham, G. and I. Kabashima (1982) 'The Politics of U.S.-Japanese Auto Trade', Chapter 3 in I.M. Destler and H. Sato (eds)   *Coping with U.S.-Japanese Economic Conflicts*; Feenstra, R. (1984) 'Voluntary Export Restraints in Autos, 1980-1981: Quality, Employment, and Welfare Effects' in R. Baldwin and A. Krueger (eds) *The Structure and Evolution of Recent U.S. Trade Policy*, p. 37.

59   USITC (1985) *A Review of Recent Developments in the U.S. Automobile Industry Including an Assessment of the Japanese Voluntary Restraint Agreements* (USITC Publication 1648), p. 2.

60   For an account of this issue from U.S. trade policy concerns, see chapter 3 in S. D. Cohen and R. I. Meltzer (1982) *United States International Economic Policy in Action.*

61   Refer back to Tables 2 and 5 in Appendix B.

62   See U.S. House of Representatives, Committee on Ways and Means, Subcommittee on Trade (1985) *Japanese Voluntary Restraints on Auto Exports to the United States* (Hearings on February 28 and March 4, 1985) Serial 99-1.

63   See U.S. Congress, Joint Economic Committee, Subcommittee on Trade, Productivity, and Economic Growth (1986) *The Legacy of the Japanese Voluntary Restraints* (Hearing on June 24, 1985).

64   Cullison, A. (1985 January 31) 'Japan Won't Renew U.S. Car Export Ceiling', *Journal of Commerce.*

65   Auerbach, S. and D. Hoffman (1985 February 20) 'Car Quotas to Be Left Up to Japan', *Washington Post.*

66 See S. Okita (1990) *Approaching the 21st Century: Japan's Role* for a high level Japanese government official's views on the auto VER issue. Saburo Okita was Minister of Foreign Affairs during this time.

67 Bergsten, F. and M. Noland (1993) *Reconcilable Differences? United States-Japan Economic Conflict*, p. 106; see also J. Womack (1989) 'The U.S. Automobile Industry in the Era of International Competition: Performance and Prospects' in *the Working Papers of the MIT Commission on Industrial Productivity*, Vol. 1.

68 Harmon, A. (1992 May 20) 'Japanese Car Firms Found to Be Dumping', *Los Angeles Times*; Woutat, D. (1992 June 25) 'Big Three Lose Round on Minivans', *Los Angeles Times*.

69 Bergsten, F. and M. Noland (1993) point out in *Reconcilable Differences? United States-Japan Economic Conflict*, pp. 114-115.

70 USTR, *1993 National Trade Estimate Report on Foreign Trade Barriers*, p. 163.

71 Bergsten, F. and M. Noland (1993) *Reconcilable Differences? United States-Japan Economic Conflict*, p. 112.

72 *The Congressional Digest* (1983 February) 'Proposed Automobile 'Domestic Content' Legislation', Vol. 62 (2): 34, 39-41. A committee report issued in September 1982 contained data on 1982 domestic sales and how the required 'domestic content' percentage formula would apply to each manufacturer: General Motors, 4,673,000 vehicles (90 percent required domestic content); Ford, 2,148,000 vehicles (90 percent); Chrysler, 883,000 (88.3 percent); Nissan (Datsun), 736,000 (73.6 percent); Toyota, 719,000 (71.9 percent); Honda, 371,000 vehicles (37 percent); VW/Audi/Porsche, 340,000 vehicles (34 percent); Toyo/Kogyo (Mazda), 247,000 (24.7 percent); AMC/Renault, 231,000 vehicles (23.1 percent); and Mitsubishi, 145,000 vehicles (14.5 percent).

73 Ibid., p. 34; Destler I. M. (1986) *American Trade Politics: System under Stress*, p. 72.

74 Bergsten, F. and M. Noland (1993) *Reconcilable Differences? United States-Japan Economic Conflict*, pp. 116-117.

75 Ibid., pp. 112-113.

76 House of Representatives, Committee on Small Business (1987) *Global Competition in the Auto Parts Industry* (Hearings on July 21 and 22, 1987): pp. 1-2; for comprehensive information on Japanese auto components supplier groups, see Dodwell Consultants (1987) *The Japanese Automotive Components Industry*, 3rd edition.

77 U.S. House of Representatives, Committee on Small Business, Subcommittee on Innovation, Technology, and Productivity, *United States-Japan Auto Parts Trade* (Hearing on June 20, 1991) pp. 1-3.

78 *The Congressional Quarterly* (1992 January 11) 'Trade Talks: Outline of Mutual Agreement To End U.S.-Japan Discord', p. 72.

79 Watanabe, T. (1992 January 21) 'Japan Hedges Commitments on U.S. Cars', *Los Angeles Times*.

80 Ibid.

81 Office of the U.S. Trade Representative (1993) *National Trade Estimate Report on Foreign Trade Barriers*, p. 163.

82 Templin, N. (1993 August 24) 'Japan Auto Makers Buy More U.S. Auto Parts', *The Wall Street Journal*.

83 Nauss, D. (1988 May 9) 'Japan Shaving the Trade Gap in Auto Parts', *Los Angeles Times*; an interview with several Japanese transplant managers during July, 1993.

84 Associated Press (1992 January 13) 'Not Much Sympathy at Home for Big Three: Many Think Detroit Makes Its Own Trouble', *Star-News*.

85 Miller, K. and J. Mitchell (1993 March 4) 'Stalling Out: After Years in U.S. Market, Japanese Surge Is Over', *The Wall Street Journal*; Nauss, D. (1993 March 9) 'Big 3's Trade Gripe Gets More Attention', *Los Angeles Times*; McWhirter, W. (1993 December 13) 'Back on the Fast Track', *Time*.

86 Ono, Y. and J. Schlesinger (1993 October 5) 'Japan's Auto Makers Fault Big Three for Not Doing Enough to Boost Exports', *The Wall Street Journal*.

87 Suzuki, Y. (1981) 'U.S.-Japan Trade Relations: Reaching Accommodations' in R. Cole (ed) *The Japanese Automobile Industry: Model and Challenge for the Future?* (Michigan Papers in Japanese Studies, No. 3), p. 19.

88 Mutoh, K. (1988) p. 330.

89 Ono, Y. and J. Schlesinger (1993 October 5).

90 Keller, M. (1989) *Rude Awakening: The Rise, Fall, and Struggle for Recovery of General Motors*.

91 Ibid.; Keller, M. (1993) *Collision: GM, Toyota, Volkswagen and the Race to the 21st Century*; Halberstam, D. (1986) *The Reckoning*. Both Halberstam and Keller view the U.S. auto industry as a paradigm of what was occurring in U.S. manufacturing industries across the board. Their analyses also lend support to recent research findings concerning relative U.S. economic decline. See also M. Moritz and B. Seaman (1981) *Going for Broke: The Chrysler Story* and S. Yates (1987) *The Decline and Fall of the American Automobile Industry*.

92 Bergsten, F. and M. Noland (1993) p. 105.

93 Mutoh, H. (1988) 'The Automotive Industry', chapter 12 in R. Komiya, M. Okuno, and K. Suzumura (eds) *Industrial Policy of Japan*, pp. 312-313.

94 Ibid., p. 314.

95 Ibid., p. 316.

96 For a comparison of American and Japanese approaches to quality control, see Chapter 6 of M. Cusumano (1985) *The Japanese Automobile Story: Technology and Management at Nissan and Toyota* (Harvard East Asian Monographs 122). This study recounts how Japan began manufacturing motor vehicles and eventually passed the U.S. in productivity while matching the Europeans in small-car design. This study covers the decades prior to World War II through the early 1980s. The central focus of this story is the rivalry between Nissan and Toyota – the two firms that accounted for 50 to 85 percent of Japan's automobile production during those years. See also Y. Monden (1983), *The Toyota Production System*.

97 Womack, J. et al (1990) *The Machine That Changed the World*.

98 Bergsten, F. and M. Noland (1993) pp. 108-111; Crandall, R. (1984) 'Import quotas and the Automobile Industry: The Costs of Protection', *Brookings Review*, vol. 2, 4, pp. 8-16.

99 Ibid., pp. 113-114.

100 Semiconductors are materials containing both insulating and conducting properties; consequently, they conduct electrons about half as efficiently as materials having only conducting properties. The most common semiconductor materials are silicon, germanium, and gallium arsenide. The term 'semiconductors' also refers to tiny 'chips' composed of silicon on which thousands of individual transistors, diodes, and resistors are densely placed. These chips serve various memory or logic functions in a variety of

industrial and consumer products.

101 Cohen, S. D. (1991) *Cowboys and Samurai: Why the U.S. Is Losing the Battle with the Japanese and Why It Matters*, p. 53.

102 Borrus, M. (1988) *Competing for Control: America's Stake in Microelectronics*, p. 143. For accounts of how the Japanese accomplished higher productive yields and higher quality at lower prices, see also pp. 139-143 in M. Borrus (1988) and pp. 39-41 in F. Weinstein, M. Uenohara, and J. Linvill (1984) 'Technological Resources' (Chapter 3) in D. Okimoto, T. Sugano, and F. Weinstein (eds) *Competitive Edge: The Semiconductor Industry in the U.S. and Japan*.

103 Borrus, M., J. Millstein, and J. Zysman (1982) *U.S.-Japanese Competition in the Semiconductor Industry: A Study in International Trade and Technological Development*, p. 111; Okimoto, D. (1989) *Between MITI and the Market: Japanese Industrial Politic for High Technology*, pp. 56-57.

104 Borrus, M. et al (1982) pp. 112-113; Okimoto, D. (1984) 'Political Context' (chapter 6) in D. Okimoto, T. Sugano, and F. Weinstein (eds) *Competitive Edge: The Semiconductor Industry in the U.S. and Japan*, pp. 220-226.

105 As noted French science adviser, Jean Claude Derian (1990), writes in *America's Struggle for Leadership in Technology*: 'Japan is one of the few countries whose leaders have been able to articulate a long-term strategy for industrial development, including an important international dimension, and to implement it via close cooperation between industry and government. The example of semiconductors (highlights) the nature of this relationship and the true reasons for Japan's superiority in this field. . . . The Japanese strategy for penetrating the world's semiconductor markets only repeats the well-rehearsed scenario that enabled Japan to emerge during the 1960s as an industrial power with worldwide ambitions in sectors such as steel, shipbuilding, and automobiles.'

106 Prestowitz, C. (1988) pp. 38-39.

107 Referenced in C. Prestowitz (1988) p. 39; for the entire advertisement, see G. Gregory and A. Etori, 'Japanese Technology Today', *Scientific American*, pp. 15-46.

108 M. Dertouzas et al (1989) point out in *Made in America: Regaining the Productivity Edge*, pp. 248-249, that in the mid-1970s, when the American industry was at the height of its success, it held 60 percent of the world market, 95 percent of the domestic market, and half of the European market, but only a fourth of the Japanese market.

109 Prestowitz, C. (1988) p. 50.

110 Ibid., pp. 50-51.

111 Ibid., pp. 46-50.

112 Ibid., p. 54.

113 Semiconductor Industry Association (1993) 'Materials for Academics on Japanese Semiconductor Market Access', p. 1.

114 Borrus, M. (1988) p. 185.

115 Tyson, L. (1992) *Who's Bashing Whom? Trade Conflict in High Technology Industries*, pp. 58-59; for more detail on the MOSS talks in electronics, see C. Prestowitz (1988) pp. 296-299; E. Lincoln (1990) *Japan's Unequal Trade*, pp. 148-151; and U.S. General Accounting Office, National Security and International Affairs Division (1988) 'U.S.-Japan Trade: Trade Data and Industry Views on MOSS Agreements'.

116 Borrus, M. (1988) pp. 185-186.

117 Prestowitz, C. (1988) p. 61.

118 Pugel, T. (1987) 'Limits of Trade Policy toward High Technology Industries: The Case of Semiconductors' in R. Sato and P. Wachtel (eds) *Trade Friction and Economic Policy: Problems and Prospects for Japan and the United States*, p. 192.
119 Bergsten, C. F. and W. Cline (1987) *The United States-Japan Economic Problem*, p. 67.
120 Borrus, M. (1988) pp. 183-186.
121 Ibid., p. 186.
122 Bergsten, C. F. and M. Noland (1993) *Reconcilable Differences? United States-Japan Economic Conflict*, pp. 129-130.
123 EPROMs (erasable programmable read only memories) are important because their programs can be erased and replaced with new ones, thereby affording great flexibility.
124 Marshall, E. (1985 November) 'Fallout from the Trade War in Chips', *Science,* vol. 230, p. 918; Bergsten, C. F. and M. Noland (1993) p. 129.
125 Tyson, L. (1992) pp. 107-108.
126 Wolff, A. Wm. and T. Howell (1992) 'Japan' (chapter 2) in A. Wm. Wolff and T. Howell (eds) *Conflict among Nations: Trade Policies in the 1990s*, p. 109.
127 *Congressional Record* (1986 May 21) U.S. House of Representatives Resolution 4800.
128 Bergsten, C. F. and M. Noland (1993) p. 129; Clyde Prestowitz, a former U.S. negotiator contends that the semiconductor case is a classic example of Japanese negotiating tactics. In *Trading Places: How We Allowed Japan to Take the Lead*, p. 64, he writes: 'Negotiations with Japan are always drawn out as the Japanese wait for division or personnel changes on the U.S. side to weaken its position. . . . (The Japanese) made a great effort to divide and conquer'.
129 Tyson, L. (1992) p. 109.
130 Semiconductor Industry Association (1993) pp. 1-3.
131 Tyson, L. (1992) p. 109.
132 Bergsten, C. F. and M. Noland (1993) p. 130.
133 Ibid., pp. 129-130.
134 *Aviation Week and Space Technology* (1986 November 10) 'Integrated Circuit Technology Concerns U.S. Officials', p. 31.
135 C. F. Bergsten and M. Noland (1993) point out, in a footnote on p. 95 of *Reconcilable Differences? United States-Japan Economic Conflict*, that Fairchild, which had been owned by Schlumberger NV, a European firm, was eventually taken over by National Semiconductor Corporation in 1987 and no longer exists as a separate operation.
136 Tyson, L. (1992) p. 114; Bergsten, C. F. and M. Noland (1993) pp. 130-131.
137 Gilder, G. (1988 June 13) 'How the Computer Companies Lost Their Memories', *Forbes*, pp. 79-84.
138 Choate, P. (1990) *Agents of Influence*, pp. 20-21.
139 Cohen, S. D. (1991) p. 59.
140 Ibid., p. 60.
141 House of Representatives, Committee on Foreign Affairs, Subcommittee on International Economic Policy and Trade (1991) 'Prospects for a New United States-Japan Semiconductor Agreement' (Hearing on March 20, 1991) p. 26.
142 Ibid., p. 13.
143 Bergsten, C. F. and M. Noland (1988) p. 131; Cohen, S. D. (1991) pp. 64.
144 House of Representatives, Committee on Foreign Affairs, Subcommittee on International Economic Policy and Trade (1991) pp. 13-14; Tyson (1992) pp. 114-115.

145 Lachica, E. and J. Bartimo (1991 May 6) 'U.S. Claims Japanese Firms Withhold Equipment from American Chip Makers', *The Wall Street Journal.*

146 Referenced in A. Wm. Wolff (1992) 'The Failure of American Trade Policy' (Chapter 8) in *Conflict among Nations: Trade Policies in the 1990s*; see General Accounting Office (1991) *U.S. Business Access to Certain Foreign State-of-the-Art Technology* (September).

147 House of Representatives, Committee on Foreign Affairs, Subcommittee on International Economic Policy and Trade (1991) pp.4-5.

148 Ibid., p. 15.

149 U.S. Senate, Committee on Finance, Subcommittee on International Trade (1991) 'Renewal of the United States-Japan Semiconductor Agreement' (Hearing on March 22, 1991) p. 28.

150 Pollack, A. (1991 May 30) 'Chip Trade Talks Fail to Set Measure for Market Share', *The New York Times.*

151 Schlesinger, J. and C. Chipelo (1991 May 22) 'U.S., Japan Close to Chip Trade Pact Setting Targets, Not Quotas, for Sales', *The Wall Street Journal.*

152 Helm, L. (1991 June 10) 'Japanese, U.S. Differ on Intent of Chip Accord', *Los Angeles Times.*

153 Ibid.

154 Ibid.

155 Ibid.

156 Helm, L. (1992, June 3) 'U.S., Japan on a Collision Course over Chip Trade', *Los Angeles Times.*

157 *The Economist* (1992 May 30) 'Chip Trade: Worthless Target', p. 68.

158 Helm, L. (1992 June 3).

159 Ibid.

160 Helm, L. (1993 March 15) 'U.S., Japan Swap Insults before Chip Talks Open', *Los Angeles Times.*

161 Ibid.

162 These figures are based on U.S. calculations. Japanese figures, which show greater market share, include chips that foreign-based companies (e.g., IBM) sell to their own Japanese subsidiaries, while U.S. figures do not.

163 Groves, M. (1993 December 28) 'Kantor Calls for Emergency Talks with Japanese', *Los Angeles Times.*

164 Nomani, A. (1993 December 28) 'U.S. Seeks Talks with Tokyo on Chip Accord', *The Wall Street Journal.*

165 Tyson, L. (1992) p. 132.

166 See L. Tyson (1992) pp. 82-83.

167 House of Representatives (1991) p. 11.

168 Gregory, G. (1986) p. 198.

169 Tyson. L. (1992) pp. 82-83.

170 Okimoto, D. (1984) 'Conclusions' (chapter 6) in Okimoto, D., T. Sugano, and F. Weinstein (eds) *Competitive Edge: The Semiconductor Industry in the U.S. and Japan*, p. 177.

171 Prestowitz, C. (1988) p. 29.

172 Ibid., pp. 31-32.

173   Rogers, E. and J. Larsen (1984) *Silicon Valley Fever: Growth of High-Technology Culture*, pp. 230-251.

174   Ibid., pp. 96-136.

175   *The Economist* (1993 July 3) 'The Coming Clash of Logic'.

176   Dietrich, W. (1991) *In the Shadow of the Rising Sun: The Political Roots of American Economic Decline*, pp. 28-29; Rogers, E. and J. (1984) pp. 96-136.

177   MITI also played an important role in this process. In the early 1960s, when Texas Instruments (TI), the world's largest semiconductor producer, applied for permission to begin production in Japan, MITI permitted TI to do so only if it agreed to license its patents to Japanese companies and to take no more than ten percent of the Japanese domestic market. See Clyde Prestowitz (1988) *Trading Places: Howe We Allowed Japan to Take the Lead*, pp. 26-70, for a U.S. trade negotiator's account of how the U.S. industry went into decline.

178   Prestowitz, C. (1988) p. 44.

179   Borrus, M. (1988) pp. 26-32.

180   Schlender, B. (1991 May 6) 'Chipper Days for U.S. Chipmakers', *Fortune*, pp. 90-96; McCarroll, T. (1992 November 23) 'Chips Ahoy!', *Time*, 62-63; Butler, S. (1993 March 1) 'Winning Chip Shots', *U.S. News & World Report*, pp. 53-54.

181   McCarroll, T. (1992 November 23) p.63.

182   Davidson, W. (1984) *The Amazing Race: Winning the Technorivalry with Japan*, pp. 222-225.

183   Davidson, W. (1984) p. 98.

184   Bergsten, C. F. and M. Noland (1993) p. 128.

185   For more extensive accounts of Texas Instruments' experience, see M. Anchordoguy (1989) *Computers Inc: Japan's Challenge to IBM*, and D. Encarnation (1992) *Rivals beyond Trade: America versus Japan in Global Competition*.

186   Rogers, E. and J. Larsen (1984) pp. 205-229.

187   Steinmuller, W. (1988) 'Industry Structure and Government Policy in the U.S. and Japanese Integrated-Circuit Industries' in J. Shove (ed) *Government Policy towards Industry in the United States and Japan*, p. 85.

188   Bergsten, C. F. and M. Noland (1993) pp. 128-129.

189   Borrus, M. (1988) p. 105; Dietrich, W. (1991) p. 28.

190   Ibid., pp. 28-29.

191   These have been major topics in widely-read works by so-called Japan-bashers, Chalmers Johnson (1982) *MITI and the Japanese Miracle: The Growth of Industrial Policy*, Clyde Prestowitz (1988) *Trading Places: How We Allowed Japan to Take the Lead*, and Karl van Wolferen (1987) *The Enigma of Japanese Power*, which have further inflamed trade tensions.

192   Okita, S. (1990) *Approaching the 21st Century*, p. 46.

193   Tyson, L. (1992) pp. 82-83.

194   Ibid., p. 83.

9 Conclusions and Recommendations

Conclusions Concerning the Causes of the Japan-U.S. Trade Friction Dilemma

This research effort has only begun to explore the nature of diverging Japan-U.S. perceptual dynamics and their role in exacerbating the bilateral trade friction dilemma. Primary reasons for currently high levels of trade friction are the existence of real bilateral economic competition and conflicting national purposes, as evidenced by large intractable trade imbalances. These trade imbalances are both symptomatic and symbolic of the rapid changes in relative economic power and competitive strength between the two nations and their apparent reversal of national fortunes. However, the competition between the two national economies goes deeper. At a more fundamental level, it can be said to be a competition between two quite different political economic systems and their respective governmental institutions, industrial arrangements, economic policies, and business practices as well as between two quite different national cultures. Indeed, this study has argued that the sources of bilateral trade friction are complex, multifaceted, and impossible to comprehend if not viewed holistically. A model of these complexities was presented in Figure 1.1.

Aggravating the effects of bilateral economic competition and structural, institutional, and cultural differences are Japan-U.S. perceptual discrepancies on issues ranging from the causes of large trade imbalances to the negotiation and interpretation of sectoral agreements. These perceptual differences are believed to exacerbate the already negative affective and cognitive dynamics occurring as a result of the keen economic competition occurring between the two national groups. A mutually negative Japan-U.S. perceptual differential ultimately fosters counterproductive attitudes, actions, and reactions between the two national governments and their constituents. As each group perceives bilateral trade problems in different terms, each tends to blame the other for these problems. This dynamic impedes the resolution of real issues by means of mutually agreeable solutions, thereby aggravating bilateral trade friction in the process.

257

This study has examined the evolution of Japan-U.S. trade friction in the following ways. Chapter Two reviewed the early beginnings of the trade relationship when cross-cultural perceptual patterns and communication/negotiation dynamics similar to those observed today first became established. Americans today, as they did then, tend to initiate the bilateral negotiation process by presenting the Japanese with a directly stated set of demands. Japanese now, as they did then, have tended to respond to these demands with resistance, evasiveness, and foot-dragging tactics. In response, Americans generally resort to the application of both implicit and explicit forms of pressure and threats. As the Japanese continue to resist American demands, Americans more aggressively and confrontationally insist, pressure, and use threats. This relational process continues until the last hour when the Japanese make some concessions. In the late 1930s and early 1940s, during a period of conflicting national goals, this pattern of American pressure, threats, and economic sanctions in combination with Japanese resistance, evasiveness, and implicit refusal to change expansionist behavior grew increasingly counterproductive to the point where political and diplomatic contentiousness escalated into military conflict. The overview of bilateral trade relations, the growth of trade-related complaints and cross-purposes, showed the evolution of postwar bilateral economic competition, while the summary of generic American and Japanese trade positions on contemporary bilateral trade problems revealed the enormity of the perceptual gap between the two national groups.

Chapter Three offered an interpretive essay on the ways in which cultural factors have shaped American and Japanese national life, normative values, and behavioral patterns. It was shown how these cultural differences fostered uniquely American and Japanese approaches to work-related activities as well as uniquely American and Japanese styles of communication, decision-making, and negotiation. Such differences have fostered and supported the evolution of institutional, structural, and sectoral issues of bilateral trade contention. They continue to complicate and impede American and Japanese communication and negotiation processes and bilateral efforts at finding mutually acceptable solutions and compromises. Indeed, the relative success or failure of bilateral trade negotiations has been complicated, at times undermined, by these differing Japan-U.S. behavioral patterns and communication/negotiation styles. In the process, they have further fostered the development of bilateral misperceptions, biased perceptions, and misunderstandings. It has been argued that these culturally based differences have contributed, and continue to exacerbate problems in the relational interface between Americans and Japanese.

Chapter Four continued the discussion on cultural factors by describing how these have structurally and functionally informed most aspects of each nation's political-economic system, from government institutions to industrial arrangements, from organizational structure to organizational function, from producers to consumers, and from managers to workers. These culturally flavored institutional factors have contributed to the creation and entrenchment of current bilateral structural asymmetries. These asymmetries include national savings rate and macroeconomic policy differentials as well as the relative U.S. economic decline-Japan rise dynamic. Institutional factors have also helped foster perceptual differences between American and Japanese opinion leaders regarding trade imbalance causal factors and other issues of contention.

Finally, it was the social psychological theory explored in Chapter Five that began to shed light on the development of Japan-U.S. perceptual discrepancies and their adverse impact on bilateral trade relations. Of all the factors involved in the bilateral trade friction dilemma, the Japan-U.S. perceptual differential is arguably the most volatile, least predictable component in the calculus of factors determining future outcomes. In this research effort, the ingroup-outgroup tendency toward diverging perceptions and attributions was treated not as a competing causal variable, but as an intervening variable standing between the primary causal variables (structural discrepancies, sectoral competition, large trade imbalances) and outcomes (high levels of bilateral trade friction). The causal model shown in Figure 1.2 suggested how perceptual differences might aggravate the affective and cognitive effects of structural tensions and sectoral issues of contention, and frustrate efforts at finding mutually agreeable solutions to these problems.

The hypothesized Japan-U.S. perceptual differential was developed as a major component of the research methodology and design discussion in Chapter Six, in which eighteen hypotheses based on Chapter Five's discussion of realistic conflict theory, attribution theory, and contributions from cross-cultural research were developed. These were then tested and evaluated in Chapter Seven. American and Japanese perceptual differences regarding various aspects of the bilateral trade relationship were identified by means of a survey instrument and quantified. Questionnaires sent to 460 opinion leaders (230 from America, 230 from Japan) yielded a 70 percent response rate, with 61 percent of the sample actually completing questionnaires. Respondents included government officials, academics, media specialists, and agricultural/industrial leaders representing the rice, automotive, and semiconductor sectors. Surveyed topics included: (1) the relative importance of 14 commonly cited causes of the bilateral trade imbalances; (2) the country bearing greater responsibility for these imbalances; (3) the degree of domestic market openness to imports in Japan and the United States; (4) the quality of current trade relations; (5) the probable effects of a breakdown in bilateral trade relations on the prosperity of each nation; (6) the degree of expected structural change addressed in the 1989-1990 Structural Impediments Initiative occurring in each nation by the year 2000; and (7) the national negotiation styles of Japan and the United States. Differences in American and Japanese perceptions on these topics were generally found to be statistically significant. In addition to perceptual differences related to nationality were those affected by academic training and career choice. Such differences are believed to further complicate the already difficult task of effectively diagnosing and addressing the causes of trade imbalances.

In addition to the quantification and analysis of statistically significant perceptual differences, Chapter Eight examined how perceptual differences over issues of bilateral contention regarding three quite different trade sectors were played out over the course of a decade beginning in the early 1980s. The first set of sectoral disputes concerned Japan's severely restricted rice market, her rice sufficiency policy, her subsidization of rice production and consumption, and her exportation of subsidized rice surpluses for profit. It also addressed the existence of diverging Japan-U.S. economic ideologies and political-economic institutions, and the confrontive posturing of American rice interests while in Japan.

The second set of sectoral disputes concerned automobiles and automotive parts/accessories. This set of disputes involved such issues as the loss of U.S. competitiveness, superior Japanese product quality, relatively closed Japan import markets, and Japan's distribution system. It also included Japanese firms' collusive purchasing of automotive parts and accessories and dumping of vehicles into the American market at below market prices.

The third and final set of sectoral disputes concerned semiconductors. These disputes involved such issues as the decline of U.S. competitiveness and superior Japan product quality as well as differences in the structure and functions of the American and Japanese political-economic systems and their industrial arrangements. They also involved Japanese adversarial pricing and collusive purchasing practices as well as Japan's relatively closed domestic markets.

The evolution of these three sectoral disputes demonstrated the existence of real (objective) and perceived (subjective) competition between two quite different national political-economic systems, government policies, political realities, financial arrangements, technologies, policies, and practices in quite tangible ways. Just as these three sectors must be viewed as interdependent parts of the two national economic systems, so must they also be viewed as major actors in the unfolding postwar bilateral trade friction drama as well. The three sectoral disputes have also demonstrated the existence of a variety of differing Japan-U.S. perceptions and positions regarding national culpability, causes and remedies, policies and practices, and the interpretation of negotiated agreements.

Recommendations for Reducing Bilateral Trade Friction

The reduction of potentially harmful bilateral perceptual tendencies regarding Japan-U.S. trade relations and the enhancement of stronger *win-win* relational characteristics and constructive approaches to conflict management are the topic of this section. Although proposals for bilateral structural convergence are touched on, it is the convergence of bilateral perceptions and creative problem-solving that receive greatest attention. The economic interdependence of Japan and the United States is now deeply entrenched. Japan is one of the largest markets for American goods, and the United States is still the largest market for Japanese goods. As many have said, divorce is not a viable option; therefore, efforts to improve the relationship by diminishing currently high levels of trade friction through creative conflict resolution approaches and problem-solving techniques are the most viable options. They are also the most practical.

Much of the real change that is needed will ultimately take place only as a result of appropriate forms of domestic initiative, commitment, and action. Although it has been said that asking Japan and the United States to change internal institutional structures within their respective political-economic systems, to reshape economic ideologies, to modify national decision-making or negotiating styles, or to change basic standard operating procedures is to ask Americans and Japanese to stop being who they are. Yet American and Japanese leaders are well advised to pursue deeper understandings of their respective country's contributions to real as well as subjective bilateral issues of contention. In this way, both sets of leaders can work toward developing a national consensus in their respective countries for change even as they begin to address the internal obstacles preventing it.

If the United States is to face the challenge of its enormous national budget debt, its eroding national economic competitiveness, and its unresolved trade deficits, Americans themselves must determine which uniquely American attributes to apply in the development of domestic resolve and constructive action to reverse contemporary national trends. Until recently, American government and business leaders have often appeared incapable, perhaps unwilling, to do what is necessary to counter the loss of U.S. national competitiveness. Japanese SII prescriptions for the United States are an ideal place to begin, but all indications are that the American political-economic system is slow in providing the needed impetus or motivation for national change. Nor do Japanese leaders, on the whole, seem substantially more able or willing to pursue fundamental domestic change than American leaders. In the short run, Japan stands to lose less than the United States by not making changes of the type identified during the SII process. However, in the long run, both nations conceivably have much to lose by not addressing these issues with meaningful domestic change in their respective countries.

Not only did the SII lay important groundwork for change in both Japan and the United States by contributing an agenda for constructive change, but it also worked to increase mutual awareness and understanding of the difficulties each side faced in implementing such changes. For the health of the bilateral relationship as well as for the general health of the global trade system, both sides are well advised to continue to work together in the continuation of an SII-type process, which economists C. Fred Bergsten and Marcus Noland propose be called Structural Convergence Talks (SCT).[1] The name itself would be a positive step forward, for it would be a move away from focusing on problems (impediments) to focusing on solutions (convergence). Bergsten and Noland propose that the goal of SCT would be to select and address structural issues that meet a number of criteria. One criterion would be that each issue discussed would importantly affect the two nations' economic performance and interaction with trade and investment. A second criterion would be that the issues be susceptible to remedial action which, in most cases, would mean policy changes by one or both governments.[2] The SCT process should also be expanded to include the institutions and practices of the private sectors of both countries since these contribute substantially to structural differences and business practices. (e.g., Japanese *keiretsu*, short-term orientation of American businesses). Inclusion of the private sector in the SCT process would not only help the talks address the key issues, but they would also enhance the prospects for a meaningful convergence or harmonization of practices and outcomes.[3]

Whether or not an SCT-type process is initiated, both Americans and Japanese need to gain substantially more comprehension of each other's historical, cultural, institutional, and political realities, including the ways in which problems are framed and solutions proposed and negotiated. In addition to the effects of U.S. trade deficits with Japan, bilateral deficits of understanding cause the trade deficit to grow more menacing. Such deficits in understanding undermine the potential success of trade talks, negotiations, and agreements. In other words, a cognitive/perceptual convergence is also proposed. However, this does not mean a meltdown of what it means to be American or Japanese. It does mean, however, that both sides need to modify counterproductive aspects of their respective communication and negotiation styles. On the one hand, Americans need to develop greater patience and skill in ameliorating difficulties less bluntly and confrontationally. On the other hand, Japanese need to develop greater skill in addressing difficulties more directly and assertively. Another means of attacking the problem of misperception is for both sides to gain deeper, more accurate understanding of the other nation's political-economic system and cultural tendencies as well as how their political-economic system and cultural tendencies are perceived by the other side. One way to do this is through the various bilateral exchanges of ideas and information, including an SCT-type process.

Successful efforts to alleviate trade problems must be rooted in good faith and mutual confidence and trust that each is making legitimate efforts to cooperate. Such a process can only contribute to better informed negotiating agendas and more realistic expectations on both sides of the Pacific. This can be facilitated by employing various negotiating techniques and tactics. Some of the sources for these are Roger Fisher and colleagues.[4] Another approach might be Robert Axelrod's bargaining strategy, in which issues of equivalent value are used as bargaining chips rather than issues of the same categories.[5] In the process, Japan and the United States might establish a higher platform for negotiation, agreement, and cooperation – one that rises above and beyond national pride and unresolved trade irritations.

Another highly considered approach is to increasingly multilateralize the bilateral dialogue over trade imbalance causal factors and sectoral issues of contention, while continuing bilateral efforts to address structural impediments and convergence. Multilateralizing the dialogue within the context of the GATT negotiations as well as G-5 and G-7 summit proceedings would serve to diffuse tensions aroused within the bilateral context and provide a stronger impetus for productive changes in the domestic policies and practices of both nations through the mechanism of group consensus. The GATT negotiations and G-5/G-7 summits might prove to be environments conducive to achieving greater bilateral understanding, commitment, and resolve to effectively pursue the kinds of domestic and bilateral changes that are needed.[6]

Concerning methods to increase perceptual convergence and mutual understanding, Morton Deutsch writes that change can take place either through a process of confrontation, which is costly to the conflicting groups, or through a process of problem solving, which is mutually rewarding to both.[7] He notes that the major features of productive conflict resolution processes are similar to the processes involved in creative thinking. Such processes are generally described as consisting of several overlapping phases in a sequence. The key psychological elements in this process are: (1) the experiencing and recognition of a problem that is sufficiently arousing to motivate efforts to solve it; (2) the development of conditions that permit the reformulation of the problem once an impasse has been reached; and (3) the concurrent availability of diverse ideas that can be flexibly combined into novel and varied patterns.[8] Regarding the Japan-U.S trade friction dilemma, it is clear that the first element in the process has been accomplished; hopefully, the second and third are currently in the process of being developed. What is needed is a little more 'water logic' and a little less 'rock logic' in bilateral trade negotiation processes. As creative (lateral) thinking guru Edward Debono (1990) writes,

> In a conflict situation both sides are arguing that they are right. This they can show logically. Traditional thinking would seek to discover which party was 'right'. Water logic [as opposed to rock logic] would acknowledge that both parties were right but that each conclusion was based on a particular aspect of the situation, particular circumstances and a particular point of view.[9]

At that point, the two sides could move on to solve the real issues more effectively.

Recommendations for Future Research

The role of perception in the creation and aggravation of conflictual bilateral dynamics needs to be further explored. Additional hypotheses based on ingroup-outgroup and cross-cultural approaches to attribution theory should be developed and tested using the data collected for this study. At a later date, a replication of the present study, using a slightly revised version of the current questionnaire, should be conducted. The research staff would ideally be composed of a small team of American and Japanese political economists, preferably with backgrounds in social psychological and cultural content theory.

The survey instrument would use the same basic format as the questionnaire of this study, and it would be administered to an equivalent sample of American and Japanese opinion leaders. However, some of the questions in Part B would be revised slightly. For example, the question concerning the extent to which the Japan-U.S. trade relationship was perceived as *win-win* or *win-lose* (B11) would have the terms cooperative and competitive dropped. This would eliminate confusion, and the data collected could better be used as a measure of bilateral trade contentiousness. Also questions specifically eliciting perceptions concerning the rice, automotive, and semiconductor disputes might be included. The question concerning national negotiation styles would also be revised so that the question would yield ordinal rather than nominal data. Osgood's semantic differential would be a good model for the revision of this question.[10] Furthermore, a set of questions whose purpose would be to tap into the relationship of cognition and emotion in creation of trade friction could be developed. For this, Bernard Weiner's attributional theory of motivation and emotion would be the likely model. Future research might also focus on the development of effective solutions to minimize the bilateral perceptual discrepancies exacerbating Japan-U.S. trade friction. Furthermore, respondents would be asked to offer their own suggestions for reducing trade friction levels.

Epilogue

The national leaders of Japan and the United States have yet to mutually agree on the diagnoses of chronic bilateral structural and trade disequilibria and effective policies to address the causes. Additionally, the patchwork of bilateral trade agreements do not appear to have resolved underlying problems of Japan-U.S. trade relations. Nor do they seem to have bridged the perceptual gap between the two national groups. Negative rhetoric, recriminations, and confrontations are likely to continue, perhaps escalate in the future unless mutual agreement can be reached concerning the causes, consequences, and cures of the trade imbalances. To accomplish this, both nations must acknowledge and address their part in the problem and undertake effective remedial actions on their domestic fronts. For as one scholar has recently written:

> The war of words about U.S.-Japan trade continues to escalate. . . . A spate of books describing Japan as an international outlaw nation has become popular in America, while Japanese mutter about Asian trading blocs. It all might be dismissed as rhetoric and posturing were it not so frighteningly reminiscent of the run-up to the 1930s.[11]

Over the years, Japan and the United States have faced a number of crises in their relationship, but today they grapple not only with trade imbalances and major sectoral disputes but with the implications these have for the greater health of the bilateral relationship. The preceding chapter examined three politicized trade disputes during the 1980-1992 period over rice, automobiles and automotive parts, and semiconductors. During the course of these disputes, various bilateral relational continuities could be observed. Moreover, Japan-U.S. perceptual differences concerning the causes of these disputes, their consequences and cures, not to mention the assignment of blame and counterproductive rhetoric, were evident. Hopefully, these perceptual patterns and relational continuities might be modified in sufficiently positive, results-oriented ways so that historians in future years will not be writing these words:

> The coming of the Japan-U.S. *[trade war]* still evokes an overwhelming sense of sadness that two nations whose *[economics]* and cultures were so intertwined could find no escape from the impasse that they reached. Neither government wanted a *[trade war]*, but neither could, in the end, conceive of a way to achieve its aims without one.[12]

Notes

1   Bergsten, C. F. and M. Noland (1993) *Reconcilable Differences? United States-Japan Economic Conflict*, p. 212.
2   Ibid., pp. 212-213.
3   Ibid. This began to occur when, in 1996, the two industries joined the two governments in signing a new Japan-U.S. semiconductor agreement.
4   See R. Fisher (1969) *International Conflict for Beginners*; F. Fisher and W. Ury (1981) *Getting to Yes: Negotiating Agreement without Giving In*; and R. Fisher and S. Brown (1988) *Getting Together: Building Relationships as We Negotiate*.
5   R. Axelrod (1984) *The Evolution of Cooperation*.
6   See R. Putnam and N. Bayne (1987) *Hanging Together: Cooperation and Conflict in the Seven-Power Summits and Bayne*, for more detailed discussion concerning the effect of summit meetings and summit proposals on the domestic policies of the participants' respective governments. Indeed, it was in a multilateral setting, the GATT Uruguay talks, that the bilateral rice issue was brought to resolution.
7   Deutsch, M. (1973) *The Resolution of Conflict*, pp. 359-360.
8   Ibid., p. 360.
9   DeBono, E. (1990) *I Am Right--You Are Wrong: From Rock Logic to Water Logic*, p. 291.
10 Osgood, C., G. Suci, and P. Tannenbaum (1957) *The Measurement of Meaning*; Osgood, C. (1965) 'Cross-Cultural Comparability in Attitude Measurement via Multilingual Semantic Differentials' in I. Steiner and M. Fishbein (eds) *Current Studies in Social Psychology*.
11 Abegglen, J. (1989 July) 'U.S.-Japan Trade: Hot Words, Cold Facts', *TOKYO Business Today*, p. 8.
12 See footnote 33 in Chapter Two. [Bracketed words in italics are my substitutions for words in the original quote.]

Appendix A

Questionnaires

The Japan-U.S. Trade Friction Dilemma

Part A (Trade Imbalance)

Directions: Please rate the following factors below as to their relative importance in causing the enormous bilateral trade imbalances of the 1980s and early 1990s.

Not a factor 1
Minor factor 2
Somewhat important factor 3
Very important factor 4
Unfamiliar . . . . U

1.	Currency misalignment	1	2	3	4	U
2.	Superior Japanese product quality	1	2	3	4	U
3.	Differing political-economic ideologies	1	2	3	4	U
4.	Low U.S. national savings rate	1	2	3	4	U
5.	Differing government/business relations	1	2	3	4	U
6.	U.S. national budget deficit	1	2	3	4	U
7.	Global economic conditions	1	2	3	4	U
8.	Unfair Japan trade practices	1	2	3	4	U
9.	Japan macroeconomic policies	1	2	3	4	U
10.	Relatively closed Japan domestic markets	1	2	3	4	U
11.	Differing negotiating styles	1	2	3	4	U
12.	High Japan national savings rate	1	2	3	4	U
13.	Declining U.S. competitiveness	1	2	3	4	U
14.	U.S. macroeconomic policies	1	2	3	4	U
15.	_____	1	2	3	4	U

(Insert your own/topic/idea here)

Part B (Perceptions)

Directions: Please place an *X* in a blank along the continuum underneath each question which best represents your *personal* opinion. Then place an *A* and a *J* in the blanks which you believe best represent the opinions of most Americans and Japanese, respectively.

1. Which country is more responsible for the bilateral trade imbalance?

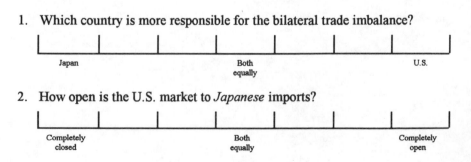

    Japan   Both   U.S.
                                  equally

2. How open is the U.S. market to *Japanese* imports?

    Completely   Both   Completely
    closed   equally   open

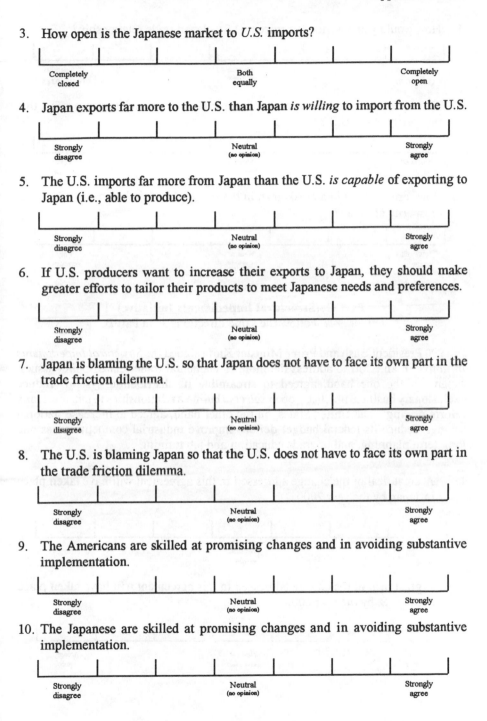

3. How open is the Japanese market to *U.S.* imports?

Completely closed — Both equally — Completely open

4. Japan exports far more to the U.S. than Japan *is willing* to import from the U.S.

Strongly disagree — Neutral (no opinion) — Strongly agree

5. The U.S. imports far more from Japan than the U.S. *is capable* of exporting to Japan (i.e., able to produce).

Strongly disagree — Neutral (no opinion) — Strongly agree

6. If U.S. producers want to increase their exports to Japan, they should make greater efforts to tailor their products to meet Japanese needs and preferences.

Strongly disagree — Neutral (no opinion) — Strongly agree

7. Japan is blaming the U.S. so that Japan does not have to face its own part in the trade friction dilemma.

Strongly disagree — Neutral (no opinion) — Strongly agree

8. The U.S. is blaming Japan so that the U.S. does not have to face its own part in the trade friction dilemma.

Strongly disagree — Neutral (no opinion) — Strongly agree

9. The Americans are skilled at promising changes and in avoiding substantive implementation.

Strongly disagree — Neutral (no opinion) — Strongly agree

10. The Japanese are skilled at promising changes and in avoiding substantive implementation.

Strongly disagree — Neutral (no opinion) — Strongly agree

11. How would you describe the current U.S. - Japan trade relationship?

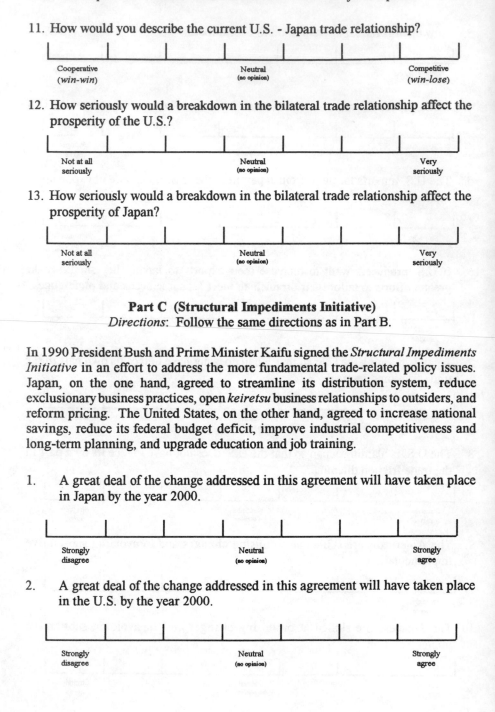

Cooperative   Neutral   Competitive
(*win-win*)   (no opinion)   (*win-lose*)

12. How seriously would a breakdown in the bilateral trade relationship affect the prosperity of the U.S.?

Not at all   Neutral   Very
seriously   (no opinion)   seriously

13. How seriously would a breakdown in the bilateral trade relationship affect the prosperity of Japan?

Not at all   Neutral   Very
seriously   (no opinion)   seriously

Part C (Structural Impediments Initiative)
Directions: Follow the same directions as in Part B.

In 1990 President Bush and Prime Minister Kaifu signed the *Structural Impediments Initiative* in an effort to address the more fundamental trade-related policy issues. Japan, on the one hand, agreed to streamline its distribution system, reduce exclusionary business practices, open *keiretsu* business relationships to outsiders, and reform pricing. The United States, on the other hand, agreed to increase national savings, reduce its federal budget deficit, improve industrial competitiveness and long-term planning, and upgrade education and job training.

1.   A great deal of the change addressed in this agreement will have taken place in Japan by the year 2000.

Strongly   Neutral   Strongly
disagree   (no opinion)   agree

2.   A great deal of the change addressed in this agreement will have taken place in the U.S. by the year 2000.

Strongly   Neutral   Strongly
disagree   (no opinion)   agree

Part D (Trade Negotiations)

Directions: Answer the questions below, and write in any words or items not mentioned which you believe should be included.

1. Circle the words which best describe *American* negotiation styles. Write in any other words you would like to add.

1. Direct	2. Indirect	3. Legalistic	4. Vague
5. Detailed	6. Fair	7. Unfair	8. Honest
9. Deceptive	10. Flexible	11. Rigid	12. Effective
13. Ineffective	14. Cooperative	15. Uncooperative	16. Confrontational
17. Modest	18. Arrogant	19. Goal-oriented	

2. Circle the words which best describe *Japanese* negotiation styles. Write in any other words you would like to add.

1. Direct	2. Indirect	3. Legalistic	4. Vague
5. Detailed	6. Fair	7. Unfair	8. Honest
9. Deceptive	10. Flexible	11. Rigid	12. Effective
13. Ineffective	14. Cooperative	15. Uncooperative	16. Confrontational
17. Modest	18. Arrogant	19. Goal-oriented	

Part E (Miscellaneous)

1. What is your current occupation? _____

2. If you would like to receive a summary of research results, please fill out your name and address below.

   Name_____

   Address_____

   City, State, Zip_____

3. If you have any comments you would like to make, please use the following space.

   _____

   _____

   _____

   _____

THANK YOU

日米両国間の貿易摩擦問題に関する質問状

質問　A（貿易の不均衡に関して）

<u>質問への回答方法</u>：下記各項目と、1980年代および1990年代に入ってからの両国間貿易の膨大な不均衡を生じるに至った要因との関連について、貴方ご自身の評価を丸で囲んで下さい。

要因とは思わない…………………………… 1
些細だが要因と思う………………………… 2
やや重要な要因と思う……………………… 3
極めて重要な要因と思う…………………… 4
よくわからない……………………………… U

1)　通貨の不適正評価	1	2	3	4	U
2)　日本製商品の高品質性	1	2	3	4	U
3)　政治・経済に関するイディオロギーの相違	1	2	3	4	U
4)　米国人の低貯蓄性向	1	2	3	4	U
5)　政府・企業間の関係の相違	1	2	3	4	U
6)　米国政府の財政赤字	1	2	3	4	U
7)　世界経済の条件	1	2	3	4	U
8)　日本の不公正な貿易	1	2	3	4	U
9)　日本のマクロ経済政策	1	2	3	4	U
10)　日本国内市場の相対的な閉鎖性	1	2	3	4	U
11)　交渉スタイルの相違	1	2	3	4	U
12)　日本人の高貯蓄性向	1	2	3	4	U
13)　米国の競争力低下	1	2	3	4	U
14)　米国のマクロ経済政策	1	2	3	4	U

15)　その他、貴方ご自身が考えられる
　　要因があれば、下欄にご記入ください

_____　1　2　3　4　U

質問　B　（認識の仕方に関して）

<u>質問への回答方法</u>：下記の各質問について、左右に分けた７つの枠のうち、貴方自身の
ご意見に最も近いと思われる箇所に『X』印をご記入下さい。次に、日本人およびアメ
リカ人が一般的に持っているであろう意見に最も近いと貴方が思われる枠に、それぞれ
『J』および『A』印をご記入下さい。

1．２国間貿易不均衡の責任はどちらの国に帰せられると思うか。

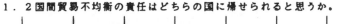

　　日本　　　　　　　　　　両国平等　　　　　　　　米国

2．日本からの輸入についての米国市場の開放性。

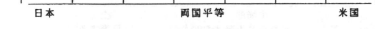

　　完全に　　　　　　　　その中間　　　　　　　　完全に
　　閉鎖的　　　　　　　　　　　　　　　　　　　　開放的

3．米国からの輸入についての日本市場の開放性。

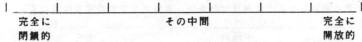

　　完全に　　　　　　　　その中間　　　　　　　　完全に
　　閉鎖的　　　　　　　　　　　　　　　　　　　　開放的

4．日本が希望する米国からの輸入量よりはるかに多くの量を、日本は米国に対して輸
　　出している。

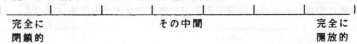

　　少しも　　　　　　　　中間的　　　　　　　　　全く
　　そう思わない　　　（どちらとも言えない）　　　同意する

5．米国から日本への輸出可能量（つまり生産可能量）よりはるかに多くの量を、米国
　　は日本から輸入している。

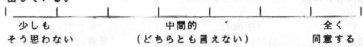

　　少しも　　　　　　　　中間的　　　　　　　　　全く
　　そう思わない　　　（どちらとも言えない）　　　同意する

6．もし、米国の生産会社が日本への輸出を増やしたければ、その製品を日本人の必要
　　性や好みに合うように改造すべく、より大きな努力を払うべきである。

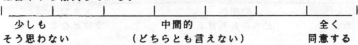

　　少しも　　　　　　　　中間的　　　　　　　　　全く
　　そう思わない　　　（どちらとも言えない）　　　同意する

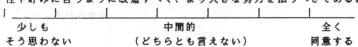

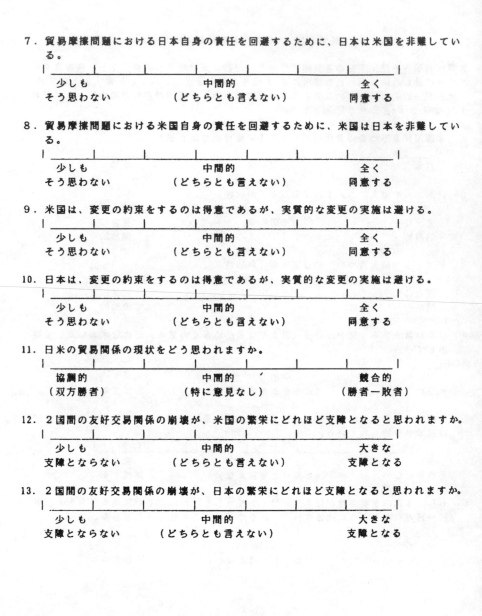

7．貿易摩擦問題における日本自身の責任を回避するために、日本は米国を非難している。

少しも　　　　　　　　　　　　中間的　　　　　　　　　　全く
そう思わない　　　　（どちらとも言えない）　　　同意する

8．貿易摩擦問題における米国自身の責任を回避するために、米国は日本を非難している。

少しも　　　　　　　　　　　　中間的　　　　　　　　　　全く
そう思わない　　　　（どちらとも言えない）　　　同意する

9．米国は、変更の約束をするのは得意であるが、実質的な変更の実施は避ける。

少しも　　　　　　　　　　　　中間的　　　　　　　　　　全く
そう思わない　　　　（どちらとも言えない）　　　同意する

10．日本は、変更の約束をするのは得意であるが、実質的な変更の実施は避ける。

少しも　　　　　　　　　　　　中間的　　　　　　　　　　全く
そう思わない　　　　（どちらとも言えない）　　　同意する

11．日米の貿易関係の現状をどう思われますか。

協調的　　　　　　　　　　　中間的　　　　　　　　競合的
（双方勝者）　　　　　（特に意見なし）　　　（勝者一敗者）

12．2国間の友好交易関係の崩壊が、米国の繁栄にどれほど支障となると思われますか。

少しも　　　　　　　　　　　　中間的　　　　　　　　大きな
支障とならない　　　　（どちらとも言えない）　　　支障となる

13．2国間の友好交易関係の崩壊が、日本の繁栄にどれほど支障となると思われますか。

少しも　　　　　　　　　　　　中間的　　　　　　　　大きな
支障とならない　　　　（どちらとも言えない）　　　支障となる

質問　C　（構造障害指針に関して）

<u>質問への回答方法</u>：下記の質問に対し、質問Bと同じ要領でお答え下さい。

　1992年に、海部総理大臣とブッシュ大統領との間で、基本的な交易政策問題の解決の手始めとして、「構造障害指針」に関しての調印がなされました。そのなかで、日本側は流通システムの近代化、排他的な業務手続の減少、「系列」的業務関係の第三者への公開、価格制度の改善に同意しました。米国側は、貯蓄の増大、政府負債の削減、国際競争力と長期計画の改善、教育と職業教育の高度化に同意しました。

1. 日本において、この協定にうたわれた施策の多くの部分が2000年までに実行される。
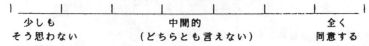
　　　少しも　　　　　　　　　　中間的　　　　　　　　　全く
　　そう思わない　　　　　（どちらとも言えない）　　　　同意する

2. 米国において、この協定にうたわれた施策の多くの部分が2000年までに実行される。
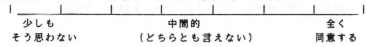
　　　少しも　　　　　　　　　　中間的　　　　　　　　　全く
　　そう思わない　　　　　（どちらとも言えない）　　　　同意する

質問　D　（貿易交渉関連）

<u>質問</u>：以下の質問に答えてください。また、その回答欄には書いてはないが、含まれるべきであると思われる語句があれば、括弧内に自由にご記入下さい。

1．米国側の交渉スタイルをよく表していると思われる語句の数字を丸で囲んで下さい。それ以外に、加えたい言葉があれば括弧内に自由に記述してください。
　　　1:直接的、　2:間接的　3:法律にこだわる　4:あいまい　5:細かい　6:公正
　　　7:不公正　8:正直　9:誤解させやすい　10:柔軟　11:硬直的　12:効果的
　　　13:非効果的　14:協力的　15:非協力的　16:対決的　17:謙遜　18:傲慢
　　　19:目標志向的
　　（_____）

2．日本側の交渉スタイルをよく表していると思われる語句の数字を丸で囲んで下さい。それ以外に、加えたい言葉があれば括弧内に自由に記述してください。

    1:直接的、　2:間接的　3:法律にこだわる　4:あいまい　5:細かい　6:公正
    7:不公正　8:正直　9:誤解させやすい　10:柔軟　11:硬直的　12:効果的
    13:非効果的　14:協力的　15:非協力的　16:対決的　17:謙遜　18:傲慢
    19:目標志向的
    （_____）

質問　E　（その他）

  依頼文にも書きましたが、今後の本調査結果に関する要約の送付のためにも必要となりますので、お差し支えなければ、下記項目にご記入いただけると幸いです。

1．お職業：（英文または日本文のいずれでも結構です）。
    _____

2．ご芳名とご住所とを下記にローマ字でご記入いただければ幸いです。

    ご芳名：_____　_____
             Givent name　　　　　　Family name

    連絡先ご住所：_____
                _____
                _____
                _____

3．何かコメントがございましたら、日本語で結構ですから下欄にご記入いただけたら幸いです。
_____
_____
_____
_____
_____
_____

  ご多忙のなか、この質問状にご回答下さいましたことに対して、厚くお礼申上げます。有難うございました。

Appendix B

Cover Letters

April 25, 1993

Name
Title
Corporation
Address
City

Dear :

Quite rare is the American two dollar bill. Far more rare is the enduring friendship between two nations.

Although the United States and Japan have enjoyed this rarity over the past 50 years, current levels of trade-related friction are poised to do irreparable damage to the relationship. Most American and Japanese academic, business, and government leaders do not want to see this happen. They want to find solutions to the problem, as do we. That is the reason for our study.

Would you help us in our search for solutions by filling out the enclosed questionnaire? This should take you no more than 15 minutes to complete. Please return the questionnaire by *May 10th* in the self-addressed envelope.

Your responses will remain confidential unless you give us written permission to cite you by name. In return for your cooperation, we will be happy to send you a brief summary of our research results several months from now.

In sincere gratitude,

Karen M. Holgerson
Director of Research

KMH:tbc

Enclosures

1993年4月15日

謹啓

　最初に、不躾けな質問状を直接にお送りする失礼をお許しください。

　私は、近くの大学で、教授として教職をとるかたわら、ピータ・ドラッカー先生が在籍・ご活躍されていますクレアモント大学院大学での博士課程の受講を終了し、目下、博士論文の執筆に取掛かっております。

　私の博士論文の課題が日米貿易摩擦を如何に減少させるかということでありますので、論文を完成するのに、同封のような調査が必要で、ご多忙のなか恐縮に存じますが、ご回答を依頼申上げている次第です。この質問に対する回答所要時間が15分以内で済むように、この質問状を作成したつもりです。

　日米両国は、過去、５０年近く友好的な関係を保持して参りましが、現状の両国間の貿易摩擦は、両国間の関係に回復困難な障害を与えかねない状況にさえあると思えます。日米両国の学会、実業界、政界の指導的立場の多くの方々は、このような事態が起こらないことを望んで、その解決策を探索されていると存じます。

　貴方も、そのような指導的立場のお一人と存じます。そこで、お願いなのですが、貴方ご自身（または、この件に関して貴方に代るどなたか）から、同封の質問状にご回答たまわり、勝手に期日を指定して恐縮ですが、論文の完成上、私宛ての送付先記入済みで返送切手を貼った同封の封筒にて、５月15日までに貴地よりご発送いただけないでしょうか。ご返答に基づき、２国間の貿易摩擦に内在する原因とその影響に関する何等かの合意点を、私なりに見出すてだてにしたいと存じます。

　ご回答は、日本語または英語のどちらででも結構です。また、貴方のご返信に関するプライバシは厳重にお守りしますので、もし貴方の御住所、お名前を記入いただけるようでしたら、数ヵ月後に私の研究結果の要約を、両国政府の関係先と貴方様とにお送りすることで、ご協力に対するお礼の一部に代えさせていただきたく存じます。

敬具

Karen M. Holgerson

Appendix C

Sources Used to Develop Mailing List

Government

Congressional Directory
Congressional Index
Congressional Staff Directory
JETRO *STEP: The Business Person's Guide to the Japanese Market*
Who's Who In Japanese Government

Academic

Japanese Colleges and Universities: A Guide to National and Public Institutions of Higher Learning in Japan
International House of Japan *List of Members*
Various American professional membership lists

Media

Broadcasting Yearbook
International Directory of Corporate Affiliations
Ward's Business Directory of U.S. Private and Public Corporations
Ward's Business Directory of U.S. Private and Public Companies

Industry

Directory of Corporate Affiliations Domestic Edition
Encyclopedia of Associations
JETRO *Japanese Affiliated Companies in North America*
JETRO *STEP: The Business Person's Guide to the Japanese Market*
Ward's Business Directory of U.S. Private and Public Companies

Japanese Telephone Directories

English Telephone Directory: Tokyo, Yokohama, Narita
The Japan Times Directory
Japan Yellow Pages
The Japanese Telephone Directory and Guide: Southern California
Yellow Pages Japan in USA

Appendix D

Mailing Codes, Questionnaires Sent and Returned

Sector	Code	U.S. Sent/Returned	Code	Japan Sent/Returned
Government Totals	**AG**	**83/71**	**JG**	**83/44**
Executive branch	AGex	10/4	JGex	10/0
Legislative branch	AGle	15/13	JGle	15/5
National bureaucracies				
Agriculture/JMAFF	AGag	8/6	JGag	8/3
Commerce/MITI	AGcm	18/17	JGcm	18/11
State/Foreign Affairs	AGfa	12/12	JGfa	12/10
Miscellaneous*	AGms	10/10	JGms	10/6
State/prefecture bureaucracies	AGst	10/9	JGst	10/9
Academic Totals	**AA**	**32/30**	**JA**	**32/22**
Political Scientists	ACps	13/13	JAps	13/5
Economists	ACec	11/9	JAec	11/12
Area specialists	ACas	8/8	JAas	8/5
Media Totals	**AM**	**32/18**	**JA**	**32/22**
Newspaper	AMnp	13/12	JAnp	13/8
Magazine	AMmg	11/4	JAmg	11/8
Television	AMtv	8/2	JAtv	8/6
Industry Totals	**AI**	**83/61**	**JI**	**83/55**
Rice	AIri	25/18	JIri	25/14
Automotive	AIau	25/17	JIau	25/19
Semiconductor	AIsc	25/19	JIsc	25/15
Miscellaneous**	AIms	8/7	JIms	8/7
TOTALS		**230/180**		**230/143**
Return Rate		**(78%)**		**(62%)**

Legend   *   Includes various national government agencies/organizations.
           **   Includes various trade-related private organizations.

Appendix E

Preliminary Summary of Results

The Japan-U.S. Trade Friction Dilemma
SUMMARY OF RESEARCH RESULTS

Research Goals and Survey Response Data

This study identifies and quantifies perceptual differences of Japanese and American leaders regarding (1) causes of the chronic trade imbalance; (2) country bearing more responsibility for the imbalance; (3) bilateral trade relations; (4) plausible solutions to the trade friction dilemma; (5) probable outcomes if the dilemma is not resolved; and (6) national negotiating styles. The sample population included 460 leaders and officials in government, academe, media, and three industries – rice, autos, and semiconductors. The 70 percent response rate (61 percent actually completing questionnaires) was gratifying – as were results – considering respondents' heavy work schedules and responsibilities. Those adding comments included 46 percent of the Japanese and 23 percent of the American respondents, with 87 percent and 53 percent, respectively, asking for research summaries. In Table 1 and subsequent tables, statistically significant perceptual differences are marked with asterisks (*).

Research Findings

Tables 2a and 2b reveal significant differences in perceptions regarding factors causing the enormous bilateral trade imbalances of the 1980s and early 1990s. The American respondents' first ranked factor for "relatively closed Japanese domestic markets" (3.33) was followed by "differing government/business relations" (3.29), and "Japan macroeconomic policies" (3.21). The Japanese

Table 1   Sample Population and Response Data

	Americans		Japanese		Total	
Total questionnaires sent	230		230		460	
Government	83		83		166	
Academic	32		32		64	
Media	32		32		64	
Industry	83		83		166	
Total response rate	180	(78%)	143	(62%)	323	(70%)
Government	71	(39%)	44	(31%)	115	(35%)
Academic	30	(17%)	19	(13%)	49	(15%)
Media	18	(10%)	22	(15%)	40	(13%)
Industry	61	(34%)	58	(41%)	119	(37%)
Completed questionnaires	147	(64%)	135	(59%)	282	(61%)
Additional comments	41	(23%)*	66	(46%)*	107	(33%)
Requests for summary	96	(53%)*	125	(87%)*	221	(68%)

Table 2a   Relative Importance of Trade Imbalance Causal Factors with Americans (results in ranked order)

Causal Factors	Americans		Japanese	
Relatively closed Japan domestic markets	(1)	3.33*	(11)	2.31*
Differing government/business relations	(2)	3.29*	(9)	2.39*
Japan macroeconomic policies	(3)	3.21*	(7)	2.53*
Differing political-economic ideologies	(4)	3.09*	(12)	2.25*
U.S. macroeconomic policies	(5)	3.08	(4)	3.10
Unfair Japanese trade practices	(6)	3.08*	(14)	1.83*
U.S. national budget deficit	(7)	3.06	(3)	3.19
Superior Japanese product quality	(8)	3.05*	(1)	3.57*
Low U.S. national savings rate	(9)	2.96	(5)	3.07
High Japan national savings rate	(10)	2.85	(6)	2.67
Currency misalignment	(11)	2.82*	(10)	2.34*
Declining U.S. competitiveness	(12)	2.59*	(2)	3.33*
Global economic conditions	(13)	2.41	(8)	2.47
Differing negotiating styles	(14)	2.25	(13)	2.08

Legend: 4 = Very important factor
3 = Somewhat important factor
2 = Minor factor
1 = Not a factor

Table 2b **Relative Importance of Trade Imbalance Causal Factors with Japanese (results in ranked order)**

Causal Factors	Americans		Japanese	
Superior Japanese product quality	(1)	3.57*	(8)	3.05*
Declining U.S. competitiveness	(2)	3.33*	(12)	2.59*
U.S. national budget deficit	(3)	3.19	(7)	3.06
U.S. macroeconomic policies	(4)	3.10	(5)	3.08
Low U.S. national savings rate	(5)	3.07	(9)	2.96
High Japan national savings rate	(6)	2.67	(10)	2.85
Japan macroeconomic policies	(7)	2.53*	(3)	3.21*
Global economic conditions	(8)	2.47	(13)	2.41
Differing government/business relations	(9)	2.39*	(2)	3.29*
Currency misalignment	(10)	2.34*	(11)	2.82*
Relatively closed Japan domestic markets	(11)	2.31*	(1)	3.33*
Differing political-economic ideologies	(12)	2.25*	(4)	3.09*
Differing negotiating styles	(13)	2.08	(14)	2.25
Unfair Japanese trade practices	(14)	1.83*	(6)	3.08*

Legend: 4 = Very important factor
3 = Somewhat important factor
2 = Minor factor
1 = Not a factor

respondents' first ranked factor of "superior Japanese product quality" (3.57) was followed by "declining U.S. competitiveness" (3.33) and "U.S. national budget deficit" (3.19). The American top ranked factor (3.33) was ranked eleventh (2.31) by Japanese, while the top-ranked Japanese factor (3.57) was ranked eighth (3.05) by Americans. Of 14 factors, 8 showed statistically significant differences between the two groups.

Tables 3 to 7 present various group perceptions regarding the bilateral trade relationship. Respondents were asked to indicate their personal opinions as well as the opinions they believed most Americans and Japanese held. For the most part, both groups view public perceptions as more polarized than their own or those of the other group. Generally, however, the American group's personal opinions and perceived American opinions showed substantially more divergence than the Japanese group's personal opinions and perceived Japanese opinions.

Table 3 reveals that American respondents hold Japan more responsible for the trade imbalance, while Japanese respondents tend to place slightly more responsibility with the U.S.

Table 3   Country More Responsible for Bilateral Trade Imbalance

Respondents	Own Personal Opinion	Perceived American Opinion	Perceived Japanese Opinion
Americans	3.20*	1.88	5.49
Japanese	4.43*	1.81	5.13

Legend: 1 = Japan
           4 = Both equally
           7 = U.S.

Table 4 shows significant disagreement over degree of domestic market openness. While both Japanese and American respondents perceive the American market as inclining toward openness and the Japanese market toward closure, each group perceives their respective domestic market as being more open than the other group perceives it to be.

Table 4   Degree of Domestic Market Openness to Imports

Respondents	Own Personal Opinion	Perceived American Opinion	Perceived Japanese Opinion
Openness of the U.S. market to Japanese imports:			
Americans	5.73*	6.31	4.33*
Japanese	5.22*	6.51	5.30*
Openness of the Japanese market to U.S. imports:			
Americans	2.77*	2.02	5.16*
Japanese	4.05*	1.99	4.44*

Legend: 1 = Completely closed
           4 = Both equally
           7 = Completely opened

Table 5 reveals both significant differences of opinion and varying degrees of agreement on seven statements regarding bilateral trade relations. For example, Americans believe more strongly than Japanese respondents that Japan exports far more to the U.S. than Japan is willing to import, whereas Americans disagree, and Japanese only slightly so, that the U.S. imports far more from Japan than the U.S. is capable of exporting. However, both groups believe that if American producers want to export more to Japan, they should make greater efforts to meet Japanese needs and preferences.

Table 5   Degree of Agreement with Various Statements Regarding Bilateral Trade Relations

Respondents	Own Personal Opinion	Perceived American Opinion	Perceived Japanese Opinion
"Japan exports far more to the U.S. than Japan is willing to import from the U.S."			
Americans	5.40*	6.38	3.02*
Japanese	4.89*	6.37	4.63*
"The U.S. imports far more from Japan than the U.S. is capable of exporting to Japan."			
Americans	2.62*	2.33*	4.65
Japanese	4.24*	5.13*	4.18
"If U.S. producers want to increase their exports to Japan, they should make greater efforts to tailor their products to meet Japanese needs and preferences."			
Americans	5.63*	4.64*	6.64
Japanese	6.40*	3.59*	6.60
"Japan is blaming the U.S. so that Japan does not have to face its own part in the trade friction dilemma."			
Americans	5.07*	6.07*	2.29
Japanese	2.42*	5.71*	2.08
"The U.S. is blaming Japan so that the U.S. does not have to face its own part in the trade friction dilemma."			
Americans	4.58*	2.74*	6.04
Japanese	5.50*	2.19*	5.92
"The Americans are skilled at promising changes and in avoiding substantive implementation."			
Americans	3.68	2.75	5.69*
Japanese	3.70	2.61	4.06*
"The Japanese are skilled at promising changes and in avoiding substantive implementation."			
Americans	5.68*	6.35*	2.41*
Japanese	3.75*	5.81*	3.42*

Legend: 1 = Strongly disagree
            4 = Neutral
            7 = Strongly agree

In Table 6 American respondents, to a significantly higher degree than Japanese respondents, perceive bilateral trade relations as competitive (win-lose) rather than cooperative (win-win).

Table 6   Perceptions of Current U.S.-Japan Trade Relations

Respondents	Own Personal Opinion	Perceived American Opinion	Perceived Japanese Opinion
Americans	5.07*	6.14	4.29
Japanese	4.22*	6.06	4.53

Legend: 1 = Cooperative *(win-win)*
             4 = Neutral
             7 = Competitive *(win-lose)*

Table 7 reveals that both groups believe Japan would be more adversely affected by a breakdown in bilateral trade relations than would the U.S.

**Table 7   Effects of Breakdown in Bilateral Trade Relations
                on the Prosperity of Each Country**

Effects on prosperity of:	Respondents	Own Personal Opinion	Perceived American Opinion	Perceived Japanese Opinion
U.S.	Americans	5.38*	4.00	5.60
	Japanese	5.92*	4.35	5.60
Japan	Americans	6.09*	5.67	5.64*
	Japanese	6.49*	5.70	6.27*

Legend: 1 = Not at all serious
             4 = Neutral
             7 = Very serious

Table 8 shows that, despite statistically significant responses, both groups believe less change (of the type addressed by the 1990 Structural Impediments Initiative) will take place in the U.S. by the year 2000 than in Japan.

Table 9 reveals how Japanese and Americans perceive national negotiating styles. While styles have little to do with causing trade imbalances, they have much to do with the maintenance of cordial bilateral relations and effective problem-solving. Respondents were asked to circle words best describing the

Table 8   Degree of Agreement with the Following Statements

Statements	Respondents	Own Personal Opinion	Perceived American Opinion	Perceived Japanese Opinion
"A great deal of the change addressed in this agreement will have taken place in Japan by the year 2000."				
	Americans	4.08*	2.71*	5.26*
	Japanese	4.89*	3.31*	4.56*
"A great deal of the change addressed in this agreement will have taken place in the U.S. by the year 2000."				
	Americans	3.63	4.38	2.68
	Japanese	3.28	4.19	3.00

Legend: 1 = Strongly disagree
4 = Neutral
7 = Strongly agree

Table 9   Words Best Describing Negotiation Styles (Percentage of Times Chosen)

Words	American style		Japanese style	
	American Response	Japanese Response	Japanese Response	American Response
Direct	77.5%	80.6%	2.2%	7.1%
Indirect	2.1%	.0%	59.0%*	75.2%*
Legalistic	59.2%*	37.3%*	17.2%	17.7%
Vague	9.2%*	2.2%*	54.4%*	45.6%*
Detailed	39.4%*	20.9%*	14.2%*	22.7%*
Fair	31.0%*	11.2%*	4.5%	7.1%
Unfair	.0%*	11.2%*	2.2%*	10.6%*
Honest	32.4%*	9.7%*	8.2%	7.8%
Deceptive	2.1%*	9.0%	64.2%*	29.8%*
Flexible	30.3%*	1.5%*	23.1%	14.9%
Rigid	8.5%*	39.6%*	14.9%*	27.7%*
Effective	11.3%	9.0%	2.2%*	33.3%*
Ineffective	29.6%*	6.7%*	17.9%*	5.0%*
Cooperative	21.8%*	2.2%*	31.3%*	14.2%*
Uncooperative	.0%*	6.0%*	2.2%*	19.9%*
Confrontational	40.1%*	75.4%*	.7%	4.3%
Modest	9.2%*	.0%*	23.1%	17.0%
Arrogant	17.6%*	46.3%*	3.0%*	17.0%*
Goal-oriented	57.7%	59.7%	6.0%*	31.9%*

negotiating style of Americans and Japanese. The percentages given below indicate how often respondents chose or didn't choose a given word. On the one hand, Americans chose direct (77.5 percent), legalistic (59.2 percent), goal-oriented (57.7 percent), confrontational (40.1 percent), and detailed (39.4 percent) for the American negotiating style, while Japanese chose direct (80.6 percent), confrontational (75.4 percent), goal-oriented (59.7 percent), arrogant (46.3 percent), and rigid (39.6 percent). On the other hand, Japanese chose deceptive (64.2 percent), indirect (59.0 percent), vague (54.4 percent), and cooperative (31.3 percent) for the Japanese negotiating style, while Americans chose indirect (75.2 percent), vague (45.6 percent), effective (33.3 percent), goal-oriented (31.9 percent), and deceptive (29.8 percent).   Concerning "deceptive", the Japanese concept (unlike the American concept) suggests nothing about motive.

Application of Research Findings

Various psychological dynamics underlying perceptual differences will be identified and described upon completion of comprehensive data analysis. Recommendations based on recent research in conflict resolution will then be made.

Bibliography

General

Abegglen, J. (1984) *The Strategy of Japanese Business*, Cambridge, Massachusetts: Ballinger.

Abegglen, J. (1989 July) 'U.S.-Japan Trade: Hot Words, Cold Facts', *Tokyo: Business Today*.

Abegglen, J. and G. Stalk (1985) *Kaisha: The Japanese Corporation*, Tokyo: Charles E. Tuttle.

Allen, G. C. (1978) *How Japan Competes: An Assessment of International Trading Practices with Special Reference to 'Dumping'*, London: Institute of Economic Affairs.

Allen, G. C. (1981) *A Short Economic History of Modern Japan* (fourth edition), New York: St. Martin's.

Aoki, M. (1987) 'The Japanese Firm in Transition' in K. Yamamura and Y. Yasuba (eds), *The Political Economy of Japan, vol. 1, The Domestic Transformation*, Stanford, California: Stanford University.

Asahi Shimbun (eds) (1972) *The Pacific Rivals: A Japanese View of Japanese-American Relations*, New York: Weatherhill.

Balassa, B. and M. Noland (1988) *Japan in the World Economy*, Washington, D.C.: Institute for International Economics.

Baldwin, R. (1984) 'The Changing Nature of U.S. Trade Policy since World War II' in R. Baldwin and A. Krueger (eds), *The Structure and Evolution of Recent U.S. Trade Policy*, Chicago: University of Chicago.

Barnhart, M. (1987) *Japan Prepares for Total War: The Search for Economic Security, 1919-1941*, Ithaca, New York: Cornell University.

Beasley, W. G. (1973) *The Modern History of Japan*, New York: Praeger.

Bergsten, C. F. and W. R. Cline (1987) *The United States-Japan Economic Problem*, Washington, D.C.: Institute for International Economics.

Bergsten, C. F. and M. Noland (1993) *Reconcilable Differences? United States-Japan Economic Conflict*, Washington D.C.: Institute for International Economics.

291

Borg, D. and S. Okamoto (eds) (1973) *Pearl History as History: Japanese-American Relations, 1931-1941*, New York: Columbia University.

Bousquet, N. (1980) 'From Hegemony to Competition: Cycles of the Core?' in T. Hopkins and I. Wallerstein (eds), *Processes of the World System*, Newbury Park, California: Sage.

Boyd, R. (1987) 'Government-Industry Relations in Japan: Access, Communication, and Comparative Collaboration' in S. Wilks and M. Wright (eds), *Comparative Government-Industry Relations: Western Europe, United States, and Japan*, Oxford: Clarendon.

Caves, R. and M. Uekasa (1976) *Industrial Organization in Japan*, Washington, D.C.: The Brookings Institution.

Choate, P. (1990) *Agents of Influence: How Japan's Lobbyists in the United States Manipulate America's Political and Economic System*, New York: Alfred A. Knopf.

Cipolla, C. M. (1970) *The Economic Decline of Empires*, London: Methuen.

Clark, R. (1979) *The Japanese Company*, London: Yale University.

Cohen, J. B. (1949) *Japan's Economy in War and Reconstruction*, Minneapolis: University of Minnesota.

Cohen, J. B. (ed) (1972) *Pacific Partnership: United States and Japan*, Lexington, Massachusetts: Lexington.

Cohen, S. D. (1990) 'United States-Japanese Trade Relations, *Proceedings of the Academy of Political Science*, vol. 37, 4, pp. 122-136.

Cohen, S. D. (1991) *Cowboys and Samurai: Why the U.S. Is Losing the Battle with the Japanese and Why It Matters*, New York: Harper Business.

Cohen, S. D. and R. Meltzer (1982) *United States International Economic Policy in Action*, New York: Praeger.

Conybeare, J. (1985) 'Trade Wars: A Comparative Study of Anglo-Hanse, Franco-Italian, and Hawley-Smoot Conflicts', *World Politics* (October), pp. 147-172.

Conybeare, J. (1987) *Trade Wars: The Theory and Practice of International Commercial Rivalry*, New York: Columbia University.

Council of Economic Advisers (various years) *Economic Report of the President*, Washington, D. C.

Destler, I. M. (1986) *American Trade Politics: System under Stress*, Washington, D.C.: Institute for International Economics.

Destler, I. M., H. Fukui, and H. Sato (1979) *The Textile Wrangle*, Ithaca, New York: Cornell University.

Destler, I. M. and M. Nacht (1990/91) 'Beyond Mutual Recrimination: Building a Solid U.S.-Japan Relationship in the 1990s', *International Security*, vol. 15, 3, pp. 92-119.

Destler, I. M. and H. Sato (eds) (1982) *Coping with U.S.-Japanese Economic Conflicts*, Lexington, Massachusetts: Lexington.

Destler, I. M., H. Sato, P. Clapp, and H. Fukui (1976) *Managing an Alliance: The Politics of U.S.-Japanese Relations*, Washington, D.C.: The Brookings Institute.

Diebold, W. (1972) *The United States and the Industrial World: American Foreign Economic Policy in the 1970s*, New York: Praeger.

Dietrich, W. (1991) *In the Shadow of the Rising Sun: The Political Roots of American Economic Decline*, University Park: Pennsylvania State University.

Dore, R. P. (1986) *Flexible Rigidities*, London: Athlone.

Dore, R. P. (1987) *Taking Japan Seriously: A Confucian Perspective on Leading Economic Issues*, Stanford, California: Stanford University.

Dower, J. (1986) *War without Mercy: Race and Power in the Pacific War*, New York: Pantheon.

Drucker, P. (1992) *Managing for the Future: The 1990s and Beyond*, New York: Plume.

Duus, P. (1976) *The Rise of Modern Japan*, Boston: Houghton & Mifflin.

Encarnation, D. (1992) *Rivals beyond Trade: America versus Japan in Global Competition*, Ithaca, New York: Cornell University.

Fallows, J. (1989) 'Containing Japan', *The Atlantic Monthly*, vol. 263, 5, pp. 40-54.

Frost, E. (1987) *For Richer For Poorer: The New U.S.-Japan Relationship*, New York: Council on Foreign Relations.

Gerlach, M. (1989) '*Keiretsu* Organization in the Japanese Economy: Analysis and Trade Implications' in C. Johnson, L. Tyson, and J. Zysman (eds), *Politics and Productivity: How Japan's Development Strategy Works*, Cambridge, Massachusetts: Ballinger.

Gerschenkron, A. (1962) *Economic Backwardness in Historical Perspective*, Cambridge, Massachusetts: Belknap.

Gilpin, R. (1975) *U.S. Power and the Multinational Corporation: The Political Economy of Foreign Direct Investment*, New York: Basic.

Gilpin, R. (1981) *War and Change in World Politics*, Cambridge: Cambridge University.

Gilpin, R. (1987) *The Political Economy of International Relations*, Princeton: New Jersey: Princeton University.

Hadley, E. (1970) *Antitrust in Japan*, Princeton, New Jersey: Princeton University.

Halliday, J. (1975) *A Political History of Japanese Capitalism*, New York: Pantheon.

Hart, J. (1992) *Rival Capitalists: International Competitiveness in the United States, Japan, and Western Europe*, Ithaca, New York: Cornell University.

Higashi, C. (1982) *U.S.-Japanese Trade Policy Formulation and Friction in Trade Relations: 1978-1979* (unpublished dissertation), George Washington University.

Higashi, C. (1983) *Japanese Trade Policy Formulation*, New York: Praeger.

Holland, H. (1992) *Japan Challenges America: An Alliance in Crisis*, Boulder, Colorado: Westview.

Howell, T. and A. Wm. Wolff (1992) 'Introduction' in A. Wm. Wolff and T. Howell (eds), *Conflict among Nations: Trade Policies in the 1990s*, Boulder, Colorado: Westview.

Hunsberger, W. (1964) *Japan and the United States in World Trade*, New York: Harper & Row.

Hunsberger, W. (1972) 'Japan-United States: Patterns, Relationships, Problems' in J. B. Cohen (eds), *Pacific Partnership: United States-Japan Prospects and Recommendations for the Seventies*, Lexington, Massachusetts: Lexington.

Ibe, H. (1992) *Japan Thrice-Opened: An Analysis of Relations between Japan and the United States* (translated by L. Riggs and M. Takechi), New York: Praeger.

Ike, N. (ed) (1967) *Japan's Decision for War: Records of the 1941 Policy Conferences* (translation, editing, and 'Introduction' by N. Ike), Stanford, California: Stanford University.

Impoco, J. and C. Work (1990 April 15) 'The Trade War Gets Personal', *U.S. News & World Report*, vol. 108, pp. 38-40.

Inoguchi, T. and D. Okimoto (eds) (1988) *The Political Economy of Japan, vol. 2: The Changing International Context*, Stanford, California: Stanford University.

Ishihara, S. (1991) *The Japan That Can Say No: Why Japan Will be First among Equals*, New York: Simon and Schuster.

Ito, K. (1990) 'Trans-Pacific Anger', *Foreign Policy*, vol. 78, pp. 131-153.

Itoh, M. (1991) 'The Japanese Distribution System and Access to the Japanese Market' in P. Krugman (ed), *Trade with Japan*, Chicago: University of Chicago.

Japan Economic Institute (various) *Yearbook of United States - Japan Economic Relations*, Washington: JEI.

Japan External Trade Organization (various) *White Paper on International Trade: Japan*, Tokyo: JETRO.

Johnson, C. (1982) *MITI and the Japanese Miracle: The Growth of Industrial Policy, 1925-1975*, Stanford, California: Stanford University.

Karatsu, H. (1990) *Tough Words for American Industry*, Cambridge, Massachusetts: Productivity.

Kash, D. (1989) *Perpetual Innovation: The New World of Competition*, New York: Basic.

Keizai Koho Center (1988) *Japan 1989: An International Comparison*, Tokyo: Japan Institute for Social and Economic Affairs.

Keohane, R. (1984) *After Hegemony: Cooperation and Discord in the World Political Economy*, Princetown, New Jersey: Princeton University.

Kindleberger, C. P. (1981) 'Dominance and Leadership in the International Political Economy: Exploiting Public Goods, and Free Rides', *International Studies Quarterly*, vol. 25, pp. 242-254.

Kindleberger, C. P. (1983) 'On the Rise and Decline of Nations', *International Studies Quarterly*, vol. 27, pp. 5-10.

Kindleberger, C. P. (1986) *The World in Depression, 1929-1939* (originally published in 1973), Berkeley: University of California.

Koh, B. C. (1989) *Japan's Administrative Elite*, Berkeley: University of California.

Komiya, R. and M. Itoh (1988) 'Japan's International Trade and Trade Politics, 1955-1984' in T. Inoguchi and D. Okimoto (eds), *The Political Economy of Japan, vol. 2, The Changing International Context*, Stanford, California: Stanford University.

Krasner, S. (1976) 'State Power and the Structure of International Trade', *World Politics*, vol. 28, pp. 317-347.

Krasner, S. (1978) 'United States Commercial and Monetary Policy: Unravelling the Paradox of External Strength and Internal Weakness' in P. Katzenstein (ed), *Between Power and Plenty: Foreign Economic Policies of Advanced Industrial States*, Madison: University of Wisconsin.

Kreinin, M. (1988) 'How Closed Is Japan's Market?', *World Economy*, vol. 7, pp. 529-541.

Kumon, S. (1987) 'The Theory of Long Cycles Examined' in G. Modelski (ed), *Exploring Long Cycles*, Boulder, Colorado: Lynne Rienner.

Laumer, H. (1986) 'The Distribution System: Its Social Function and Import-Impeding Effects' in M. Schmiegelow (ed), *Japan's Response to Crisis and Change in the World Economy*, London: M. E. Sharpe.

Lawrence, R. (1987) 'Imports in Japan: Closed Markets or Closed Minds?', *Brookings Papers on Economic Activity*, vol. 2, pp. 517-554.

Lawrence, R. (1991) 'How Open is Japan?' in P. Krugman (ed), *Trade with Japan*, Chicago: University of Chicago.

Lincoln, E. (1988) *Japan: Facing Economic Maturity*, Washington, D.C.: The Brookings Institution.

Lincoln, E. (1990) *Japan's Unequal Trade*, Washington, D.C.: The Brookings Institution.

Lockwood, W. W. (1954) *The Economic Development of Japan: Growth and Structural Change, 1868-1938*, Princeton, New Jersey: Princeton University.

Miyoshi, M. (1979) *As We Saw Them: The First Japanese Embassy to the United States, 1860*, Berkeley: University of California.

Miyoshi, M. (1991) *Off Center: Power and Culture Relations Between Japan and the United States*, Cambridge, Massachusetts: Harvard University.

Morishima, M. (1978 June) 'The Power of Confucian Capitalism', *The Observer*.

Morita, A. (1987) *Made in Japan*, London: Collins.

Naitoh, M. (1980a) 'American and Japanese Industrial Structures: A Sectoral Comparison' in D. Tasca (ed), *U.S.-Japanese Economic Relations: Cooperation, Competition, and Confrontation*, New York: Pergamon.

Naitoh, M. (1980b) 'Overview: The Bases for Conflict and Cooperation in U.S.-Japanese Relations' in D. Tasca (ed), *U.S.-Japanese Economic Relations: Cooperation, Competition, and Confrontation*, New York: Pergamon.

Neu, C. (1975) *The Troubled Encounter: The United States and Japan*, New York: John Wiley & Sons.

Neumann, W. (1963) *America Encounters Japan: From Perry to MacArthur*, Baltimore, Maryland: The Johns Hopkins University.

Ogura, K. (1982) *Trade Conflict: A View from Japan* (first seven chapters of K. Ogura *Nichi-bei Keizai Imasatsu* [U.S.-Japan Economic Conflict]), Washington, D.C.: Japan Economic Institute.

Okimoto, D. (1987) 'Outsider Trading: Coping with Japanese Industrial Organization', *Journal of Japanese Studies*, vol. 13, 2, pp. 383-414.

Okimoto, D. (1989) *Between MITI and the Market: Japanese Industrial Policy for High Technology*, Stanford, California: Stanford University.

Okimoto, D. and T. Rohlen (1988) *Inside the Japanese System: Readings on Contemporary Society and Political Economy*, Stanford, California: Stanford University.

Okita, S. (1990) *Approaching the 21st Century: Japan's Role*, Tokyo: University of Tokyo.

Pempel, T. J. (1987) 'The Unbundling of 'Japan Inc.': The Changing Dynamics of Japanese Policy Formation', *Journal of Japanese Studies*, vol. 13, 2, pp. 271-286.

Petri, P. (1991) 'Japanese Trade in Transition: Hypotheses and Recent Evidence' in P. Krugman (ed), *Trade with Japan*, Chicago: University of Chicago.

Pineau, T. (1968) *The Japan Expedition 1852-1854: The Personal Journal of Commodore Matthew C. Perry*, Washington: Smithsonian Institution.

Prestowitz, C. (1988) *Trading Places: How We Allowed Japan to Take the Lead*, New York: Basic.

Pugel, T. (ed) (1986) *Fragile Interdependence: Economic Issues in U.S.-Japanese Trade and Investment*, Lexington, Massachusetts: Lexington.

Putnam, R. and N. Bayne (1987) *Hanging Together: Cooperation and Conflict in the Seven-Power Summits*, Cambridge, Massachusetts: Harvard University.

Rapp, W. (1986) 'Japan's Invisible Barriers to Trade' in T. Pugel (ed), *Fragile Interdependence: Economic Issues in U.S.-Japanese Trade and Investment*, Lexington, Massachusetts: Lexington.

Rasler, K. and W. Thompson (1988) 'Consumption and Decline', unpublished paper presented at the annual meeting of the American Political Science Association, September 1988, in Washington, D. C. (a later version of this paper, 'Relative Decline and the Overconsumption-Underinvestment Hypothesis' was published in *International Studies Quarterly* (1991), vol. 35, pp.273-294).

Reischauer, E. (1965) *The United States and Japan*, third edition, Cambridge, Massachusetts: Harvard University.

Reischauer, E. (1988) *The Japanese Today*, Cambridge, Massachusetts: Harvard University.

Saito, S. (1990) *Japan at the Summit: Its Role in the Western Alliance and in Asian Pacific Co-operation*, London: Routledge.

Sansom, G. (1963) *A History of Japan, 1615-1867*, Stanford, California: Stanford University.

Sato, R. and D. Wachtel (eds) (1987) *Trade Friction and Economic Policy: Problems and Prospects for Japan and the United States*, Cambridge: Cambridge University.

Saxonhouse, G. (1986) 'Japan's Intractable Trade Surpluses in a New Era', *World Economy*, vol. 61, 3, pp. 239-258.

Saxonhouse, G. (1988) 'Comparative Advantage, Structural Adaptation, and Japanese Performance' in T. Inoguchi and D. Okimoto (eds), *The Political Economy of Japan, vol. 2, The Changing International Context*, Stanford, California: Stanford University.

Saxonhouse, G. (1993) 'Economic Growth and Trade Relations: Japanese Performance in Long-Term Perspective' in T. Ito and A. Krueger (eds), *Trade and Protectionism*, Chicago: University of Chicago.

Saxonhouse, G. and K. Yamamura (eds) (1986) *Law and Trade Issues of the Japanese Economy: American and Japanese Perspectives*, Seattle: University of Washington.

Sazanami, Y., S. Urata, and H. Kuwai (1993) 'Trade Protectionism in Japan' in G. Hufbauer and K. Elliott (eds), *Comparing the Costs of Protectionism: Europe, Japan, and the United States*, Washington, D.C.: Institute for International Economics.

Schwantes, R. (1972) 'American Relations with Japan, 1853-1895: Survey and Prospect' in E. May and J. Thompson (eds), *American - East Asian Relations: A Survey*, Cambridge, Massachusetts: Harvard University.

Smith, A. (1937) *An Inquiry into the Nature and Causes of the Wealth of Nations*, New York: Modern Library.

Tasca, D. (ed) (1980) *U.S.-Japanese Economic Relations: Cooperation, Competition, and Confrontation*, New York: Pergamon.

Tsurumi, Y. (1989-90) 'U.S.-Japan Relations: From Brinkmanship to Statesmanship', *World Policy Journal*, vol. 7, 1, pp. 1-33.

U.S. Congress House of Representatives Foreign Affairs Committee, Subcommittees on Asian and Pacific Affairs and on International Economic Policy and Trade (1991) 'United States-Japan Economic Relations: Structural Impediments Initiative' (Hearings on February 20 and April 19, 1990), Washington, D.C.

U.S. Congress Joint Economic Committee (1990) 'The Japanese Market: How Open Is It?' (Hearing on October 11, 1989) Washington, D.C.

U.S. Department of Commerce News (1991) 'Results of the 1991 DOC/MITI Price Survey' (ITA 91-32, May 20) Washington, D.C.

U.S. Tariff Commission (1936) *Recent Developments in the Foreign Trade of Japan*, Washington, D.C.

U.S. Trade Representative (various) *National Trade Estimate Report on Foreign Trade Barriers*, Washington, D.C.

Vogel, D. (1987) 'Government-Industry Relations in the United States: An Overview' in S. Wilks and M. Wright (eds), *Comparative Government-Industry Relations: Western Europe, United States, and Japan*, Oxford: Clarendon.

Vogel, E. (1979) *Japan as Number One: Lessons for America*, Cambridge, Massachusetts: Harvard University.

Vogel, E. (1986) 'Pax Nipponica?', *Foreign Affairs*, vol. 64, pp. 752-767.

Wada, M. (1986) 'Selling in Japan: Behavior and Distribution as Barriers to Imports' in T. Pugel (ed), *Fragile Interdependence: Economic Issues in U.S.-Japanese Trade and Investment*, Lexington, Massachusetts: Lexington.

Whitman, M. (1975) 'The Decline in American Hegemony', *Foreign Policy*, vol. 20, pp. 138-160.

Wilks, S. and M. Wright (eds) (1987) *Comparative Government-Industry Relations: Western Europe, United States, and Japan*, Oxford: Clarendon.

Wolferen, K. van (1989) *The Enigma of Japanese Power: People and Politics in a Stateless Nation*, New York: Alfred A. Knopf.

Wolff, A. Wm. (1992) 'The Failure of American Trade Policy' (Chapter 8) in A. Wm. Wolff and T. Howell (eds), *Conflict among Nations: Trade Policies in the 1990s*, Boulder, Colorado: Westview.

Wolff, A. Wm. and T. Howell (1992) 'Japan' (Chapter 2) in A. Wm. Wolff and T. Howell (eds), *Conflict among Nations: Trade Policies in the 1990s*, Boulder, Colorado: Westview.

Yamamura, K. and Y. Yasuba (eds) (1987) *The Political Economy of Japan, vol. 1: The Domestic Transformation*, Stanford, California: Stanford University.

Yoshino, M. (1976) *Japan's Multinational Firms*, Cambridge, Massachusetts: Harvard University.

Yoshino, M. and T. Lifson (1986) *The Invisible Link: Japan's Sogo Shosha and the Organization of Trade*, Cambridge, Massachusetts: MIT.

Zysman, J. and L. Tyson (1984) *U.S. and Japan Trade and Industrial Policies* (BRIE Working Paper #2), Berkeley, California: Berkeley Roundtable on the International Economy, University of California.

Culture and Political Culture

Austin, L. (1975) *Saints and Samurai: The Political Culture of the American and Japanese Elites*, New Haven: Yale University.

Barnlund, D. C. (1989) *Communicative Styles of Japanese and Americans*, Belmont, California: Wadsworth.

Bellah, R. (1957) *Tokugawa Religion: The Cultural Roots of Modern Japan*, New York: Free.

Bellah, R. et al (1985) *Habits of the Heart: Individualism and Commitment in American Life*, New York: Harper & Row.

Benedict, R. (1970) *The Chrysanthemum and the Sword*, New York: Meridian.

Blaker, M. (1977a) *Japanese International Negotiating Style*, New York: Columbia University.

Blaker, M. (1977b) 'Probe, Push, and Panic: The Japanese Tactical Style in International Negotiations' in R. Scalapino (ed), *The Foreign Policy of Modern Japan*, Berkeley: University of California.

Caudill, W. (1973) 'The Influence of Social Structure and Culture on Human Behavior in Modern Japan', *Journal of Nervous and Mental Disorders*.

Caudill, W. and H. Weinstein (1974) 'Maternal Care and Infant Behavior in Japan and America' in T. S. Lebra and W. Lebra (eds), *Japanese Culture and Behavior*, Honolulu: University of Hawaii.

Condon, J. and M. Saito (eds) (1974) *Intercultural Encounters with Japan: Communication-Contact and Conflict*, Tokyo: Simul.

Doi, T. (1974) 'Some Psychological Themes in Japanese Human Relationships' in J. Condon and M. Saito (eds), *Intercultural Encounters with Japan: Communication-Contact and Conflict*, Tokyo: Simul.

Doi, T. (1981) *The Anatomy of Dependence* [English translation by J. Bester of *Amae No Kozo*, 1971], Tokyo: Kodansha International.

Doi, T. (1985) *The Anatomy of Self: The Individiual Versus Society* [English translation by M. Harbison of *Omote To Ura*, 1985], Tokyo: Kodansha International.

Eckstein, H. (1988) 'A Culturalist Theory of Political Change', *American Political Science Review*, vol. 82, 3, pp. 789-804.

Elkins, D. and E. Simeon (1979) 'A Cause in Search of an Effect, or What Does Political Culture Explain?', *Comparative Politics*, vol. 11, pp. 127-145.

Evan, W. (1975) 'Culture and Organizational Systems', *Organization and Administrative Services*, vol. 5.

Fallows, J. (1989) *More Like Us: Making America Great Again*, Boston: Houghton Mifflin.

Fisher, G. (1980) *International Negotiation: A Cross-Cultural Perspective*, Chicago: Intercultural.

Fisher, G. (1988) *Mindsets: The Role of Culture and Perception in International Relations*, Yarmouth, Maine: Intercultural.

Fukutake, T. (1989) *The Japanese Social Structure: Its Evolution in the Modern Century*, second edition [English translation and Foreword by R. Dore, *Nihon Shakai no Kozo*, 1981], Tokyo: University of Tokyo.

Graham, J. L. and Y. Sano (1984) *Smart Bargaining: Doing Business with the Japanese*, Cambridge, Massachusetts: Ballinger.

Hall, E. T. (1959) *The Silent Language*, New York: Doubleday.

Hall, E. T. and M. R. Hall (1983) *Hidden Differences*, New York: Doubleday.

Hendry, J. (1987) *Understanding Japanese Society*, New York: Croom Helm.

Hendry, J. (1988) *Becoming Japanese*, Honolulu: University of Hawaii.

Hofstede, G. (1978) 'Culture and Organization: A Literature Review Survey', *Enterprise Management 1*.

Hofstede, G. (1984) *Culture's Consequences: International Differences in Work-Related Values*, Beverly Hills, CA: Sage.

Hofstede, G. (1991) *Cultures and Organizations: Software of the Mind*, New York: McGraw-Hill.

Imai, M. (1975) *Never Take Yes for an Answer*, Tokyo: Simul.

Imai, M. (1981) *16 Ways to Avoid Saying No*, Tokyo: Nihon Keizai Shimbun.

Inoue, K. (1991) *MacArthur's Japanese Constitution: A Linguistic and Cultural Study of Its Making*, Chicago: University of Chicago.

Keesing, R. (1974) 'Theories of Culture', *Annual Review of Anthropology*, vol. 3, pp. 73-97.

Kluckhorn, C. (1951) 'The Study of Culture' in D. Lerner and H. Lasswell, (eds), *The Policy Sciences*, Stanford, California: Stanford University.

Krauss, E., T. Rohlen, and P. Steinhoff (1984) 'Conflict and Its Resolution in Postwar Japan' in E. Krauss, et al (eds), *Conflict in Japan*, Honolulu: University of Hawaii.

Krauthammer, C. (1983 August 15) 'Deep Down, We're All Alike, Right? Wrong', *Time*.

Lane, R. (1992) 'Political Culture: Residual Category or General Theory?', *Comparative Political Studies*, vol. 25, 3, pp. 362-387.

Lebra, T. S. (1976) *Japanese Patterns of Behaviour*, Honolulu: University of Hawaii.

Marsella, A., G. DeVos, and F. Hsu (eds) (1985) *Culture and Self: Asian and Western Perspectives*, New York: Tavistock.

Maruyama, M. (1969) *Thought and Behavior in Modern Japanese Politics* (edited by I. Morris), Oxford: Oxford University.

Matsumoto, M. (1989) *The Unspoken Way*, Tokyo: Kodansha International.

Mitchell, D. (1976) *Amaeru: The Expression of Reciprocal Dependency Needs in Japanese Politics and Law*, Boulder, Colorado: Westview.

Mizutani, O. (1981) *Japanese: The Spoken Language in Japanese Life* (translated by J. Ashby), Tokyo: *Japan Times*.

Murakami, Y. et al (1985) *Bunmei to shite no ie sha kai* (The Ie Society as a Civilization), Tokyo: Chuo Koronsha.

Nakamura, H. (1964) *Ways of Thinking of Eastern Peoples*, Honolulu: University of Hawaii.

Nakane, C. (1973) *Japanese Society*, Berkeley: University of California.

Potter, D. (1954) *People of Plenty: Economic Abundance and the American Character*, Chicago: University of Chicago.

Rohlen, T. (1974) *For Harmony and Strength: Japanese White-Collar Organization in Anthropological Perspective*, Berkeley: University of California.

Singer, M. (1968) 'The Concept of Culture', *International Encyclopedia of the Social Sciences*, vol. 3, pp. 527-543.

Stewart, E. (1972) *American Cultural Patterns: A Cross-Cultural Perspective*, Chicago: Intercultural.

Stewart, E. and M. Bennett (1991) *American Cultural Patterns: A Cross-Cultural Perspective*, revised edition, Yarmouth, Maine: Intercultural.

Thayer, N. and S. Weiss (1987) 'Japan: The Changing Logic of a Former Minor Power' in H. Binnendijk (ed), *National Negotiating Styles* (U.S. Department of State, Foreign Service Institute), Washington, D.C.

Tocqueville, A. de (1945) *Democracy in America*, vols. 1 & 2, New York: Vintage.

Ueda, K. (1974) 'Sixteen Ways to Avoid Saying 'No' in Japan' in J. Condon and M. Saito (eds), *Intercultural Encounters with Japan: Communication-Contact and Conflict*, Tokyo: Simul.

Walker, R. B. J. (1990) 'The Concept of Culture in the Theory of International Relations' in J. Chay (ed), *Culture and International Relations*, New York: Praeger.

Social and Political Psychology (including Negotiation)

Allison, S. and D. Messick (1985) 'The Group Attribution Error', *Journal of Experimental Social Psychology*, vol. 21, pp. 563-579.

Allport, G. (1954) *The Nature of Prejudice*, Reading, Massachusetts: Addison-Wesley.

Amir, Y. (1969) 'Contact Hypothesis in Ethnic Relations', *Psychological Bulletin*, vol. 71, pp. 319-342.

Austin, W. G. and S. Worchel (eds) (1979) *The Social Psychology of Intergroup Relations*, Monterey, California: Brooks/Cole.

Axelrod, R. (1976) *Structure of Decision: The Cognitive Maps of Political Elites*, Princeton, New Jersey: Princeton University.

Axelrod, R. (1984) *The Evolution of Cooperation*, New York: Basic.

Betancourt, H. (1990) 'An Attributional Approach to Intergroup and International Conflict' in S. Graham and V. Folkes (eds), *Attribution Theory: Applications to Achievement, Mental Health, and Intergroup Conflict*, Hillsdale, New Jersey: Erlbaum.

Bochner, S. (1982) 'The Social Psychology of Cross-Cultural Relations' in S. Bochner (ed), *Cultures in Contact: Studies in Cross-Cultural Interaction* (International Series in Experimental Psychology, vol. 1), New York: Pergamon.

Bond, M. (1983) 'A Proposal for Cross-Cultural Studies of Attribution' in M. Hewstone (ed), *Attribution Theory: Social and Functional Extensions*, Oxford: Basil Blackwell.

Bond, M. (ed) (1988) *The Cross-Cultural Challenge to Social Psychology* (Cross-Cultural Research and Methodology Series, vol. 11), Newbury Park, California: Sage.

Brewer, M. (1979) 'The Role of Ethnocentrism in Intergroup Conflict' in W. G. Austin and J. Worchel (eds), *The Social Psychology of Intergroup Relations*, Monterey, California: Brooks/Cole.

Chilstrom, G. (1984) 'Psychological Aspects of the Nuclear Arms Race', *Journal of Humanistic Psychology*, vol. 24, pp. 12-29.

Cooper, J. and R. H. Fazio (1979) 'The Formation and Persistence of Attitudes that Support Intergroup Conflict' in W. G. Austin and S. Worchel (eds), *The Social Psychology of Intergroup Relations*, Monterey, California: Brooks/Cole.

DeBono, E. (1990) *I am Right — You are Wrong: From Rock Logic to Water Logic*, New York: Viking.

Deutsch, M. (1969) 'Conflicts: Productive and Destructive', *Journal of Social Issues*, vol. 25, 1, pp. 8-9.

Deutsch, M. (1973) *The Resolution of Conflict: Constructive and Destructive Processes*, New Haven: Yale University.

Deutsch, M. (1983) 'The Prevention of World War III: A Psychological Perspective', *Political Psychology*, vol. 4, pp. 3-31.

Deutsch, M. and S. Schichman (1986) 'Conflict: A Social Psychological Perspective' in M. Hermann (ed), *Political Psychology: Contemporary Problems and Issues*, San Francisco: Jossey-Bass.

Fisher, R. (1969) *International Conflict for Beginners*, New York: Harper & Row.

Fisher, R. and S. Brown (1988) *Getting Together: Building Relationships as We Negotiate*, New York: Penguin.

Fisher, R. and W. Ury (1981) *Getting to Yes: Negotiating Agreement without Giving In*, New York: Penguin.

Fiske, S. and S. Taylor (1984) *Social Cognition*, first edition, Reading, Massachusetts: Addison-Wesley.

Fiske, S. and S. Taylor (1991) *Social Cognition*, second edition, New York: McGraw-Hill.

Fletcher, G. and C. Ward (1988) 'Attribution Theory and Processes: A Cross-Cultural Perspective' in M. Bond (ed), *The Cross-Cultural Challenge to Social Psychology*, Newbury Park, California: Sage.

George, A. (1979) 'The Causal Nexus between Cognitive Beliefs and Decision-Making Behavior: The 'Operational Code' Belief System' in L. Falkowski (ed), *Psychological Models in International Politics*, Boulder, Colorado: Westview.

Gudykunst, W. (1988) 'Culture and Intergroup Processes' in M. Bond (ed), *The Cross-Cultural Challenge to Social Psychology*, Newbury Park, California: Sage.

Hamilton, D. (1979) 'A Cognitive-Attributional Analysis of Stereotyping' in L. Berkowitz (ed), *Advances in Experimental Social Psychology*, vol. 12, New York: Academic.

Hamilton, D. (ed) (1981) *Cognitive Processes in Stereotyping and Intergroup Behavior*, Hillsdale, New Jersey: Erlbaum.

Harvey, J. and G. Weary (1984) 'Current Issues in Attribution Theory and Research', *Annual Review of Psychology*, vol. 35, pp. 427-459.

Heider, F. (1944) 'Social Perception and Phenomenal Causality', *Psychological Review*, vol. 51, pp. 358-374.

Heider, F. (1958) *The Psychology of Interpersonal Relations*, New York: John Wiley & Sons.

Heradsveit, D. (1979) *The Arab-Israeli Conflict: Psychological Obstacles to Peace* (Norwegian Foreign Policy Studies, vol. 28), Oslo: Univeritetsforlaget.

Hewstone, M. (1985) 'Social Psychology and Intergroup Relations: Cross-Cultural Perspectives', *Journal of Multilingual and Multicultural Development*, vol. 6, 3-4, pp. 4, pp. 209-216.

Hewstone, M. (1988) 'Attributional Biases of Intergroup Conflict' in W. Stroebe, A. Kruglanski, D. Bar-Tal and M. Hewstone (eds), *The Social Psychology of Intergroup Conflict: Theory, Research, and Applications*, New York: Springer-Verlag.

Hewstone, M. (1989) *Causal Attribution: From Cognitive Processes to Collective Beliefs*, Oxford: Basil Blackwell.

Hewstone, M. (1990) 'The 'Ultimate Attribution Error'?, A Review of the Literature on Intergroup Causal Attribution', *European Journal of Social Psychology*, vol. 20, pp. 311-335.

Hewstone, M. and R. Brown (1986) 'Contact Is Not Enough: An Intergroup Perspective on the 'Contact Hypothesis' in Intergroup Encounters' in M. Hewstone and R. Brown (eds), *Contact and Conflict*, Oxford: Basil Blackwell.

Hewstone, M. and J. Jaspars (1982) 'Intergroup Relations and Attribution Processes' in H. Tajfel (ed), *Social Identity and Intergroup Relations*, Cambridge: Cambridge University.

Hewstone, M. and C. Ward (1985) 'Ethnocentrism and Causal Attribution in Southeast Asia', *Journal of Personality and Social Psychology*, vol. 48, pp. 614-623.

Holsti, O. (1962) 'The Belief System and National Images: A Case Study', *Journal of Conflict Resolution*, vol. 6, pp. 244-252.

Holsti, O. (1976) 'Foreign Policy Formation Viewed Cognitively' in R. Axelrod (ed), *Structure of Decision: The Cognitive Maps of Political Elites*, Princeton, New Jersey: Princeton University.

Horai, J. (1977) 'Attributional Conflict', *Journal of Social Issues*, vol. 33, pp. 88-100.

Horrocks, J. (1966) 'Editor's Foreword' to M. Sherif, *Intergroup Conflict and Cooperation: Their Social Psychology*, London: Routledge & Kegan Paul.

Janis, I. (1982) *Groupthink: Psychological Studies of Policy Decisions and Fiascoes* (revised and enlarged edition of *Victims of Groupthink*, 1972), Boston: Houghton Mifflin.

Jaspars, J. and M. Hewstone (1982) 'Cross-Cultural Interaction, Social Attribution and Intergroup Relations' in S. Bochner (ed), *Cultures in Contact: Studies in Cross-Cultural Interaction* (International Series in Experimental Psychology, vol. 1), New York: Pergamon.

Jaspars, J. and M. Hewstone (1990) 'Social Categorization, Collective Beliefs, and Causal Attribution' in C. Fraser and G. Gaskell (eds), *The Social Psychology of Widespread Beliefs*, Oxford: Clarendon.

Jaspars, J., M. Hewstone, and F. Fincham (1983) 'Attribution Theory and Research: The State of the Art' in J. Jaspars, F. Fincham, and M. Hewstone (eds), *Attribution Theory and Research: Conceptual, Developmental and Social Dimensions*, London: Academic.

Jervis, R. (1976) *Perception and Misperception in International Politics*, Princeton, New Jersey: Princeton University.

Jones, E. E. (1979) 'The Rocky Road from Acts to Dispositions', *American Psychologist*, vol. 34, pp. 107-117.

Jones, E. E. and K. Davis (1965) 'From Acts to Dispositions: The Attribution Process in Person Perception' in L. Berkowitz (ed), *Advances in Experimental Social Psychology*, vol. 2, New York: Academic.

Jones, E. E. and V. Harris (1967) 'The Attribution of Attitudes', *Journal of Experimental Social Psychology*, vol. 3, pp. 1-24.

Jones, E. E. and R. Nisbett (1972) 'The Actor and the Observer: Divergent Perceptions of the Causes of Behavior' in E. E. Jones et al (eds), *Attribution: Perceiving the Causes of Behavior*, Morristown, New Jersey: General Learning.

Kahn, R. and R. Kramer (1990) 'Untying the Knot: De-Escalatory Processes in International Conflict' in R. Kahn and M. Zold (eds), *Organizations and Nation-States: New Perspectives on Conflict and Cooperation*, San Francisco: Jossey-Bass.

Kashima, Y. and H. Triandis (1986) 'The Self-Serving Bias in Attributions as a Coping Strategy: A Cross-Cultural Study', *Journal of Cross-Cultural Psychology*, vol. 17, pp. 83-97.

Kelley, H. (1967) 'Attribution Theory in Social Psychology' in D. Levine (ed), *Nebraska Symposium on Motivation*, vol. 15, pp. 192-240, Lincoln: University of Nebraska.

Kelley, H. and J. Michela (1980) 'Attribution Theory and Research', *Annual Review of Psychology*, vol. 31, pp. 457-501.

Kelman, H. and S. D. Cohen (1986) 'Resolution of International Conflict: An Interactional Appraisal' in W. Worchel and W. Austin (eds), *Psychology of Intergroup Relations*, Chicago: Nelson-Hall.

Kruglanski, A. (1979) 'Causal Explanation, Teleological Expansion: On the Radical Particularism in Attribution Theory', *Journal of Personality and Social Psychology*, vol. 37, pp. 1447-1457.

Kruglanski, A. (1983) 'Bias and Error in Human Judgement', *European Journal of Social Psychology*, vol. 44, 1, pp. 1171-1181.

Larson, D. (1985) *Origins of Containment: A Psychological Explanation*, Princeton, New Jersey: Princeton University.

Lebow, R. (1981) *Between Peace and War: The Nature of International Crisis*, Baltimore, Maryland: The Johns Hopkins University.

Leventhal, H. (1980) 'Toward a Comprehensive Theory of Emotion' in L. Berkowitz (ed), *Advances in Experimental Social Psychology*, vol. 13, New York: Academic.

Mack, J. (1985) 'Toward a Collective Psychopathology of the Nuclear Arms Competition', *Political Psychology*, vol. 6, pp. 291-321.

McArthur, L. (1981) 'What Grabs You? The Role of Attention in Impression Formation and Causal Attribution' in E. Higgins et al (eds), *Social Cognition: The Ontario Symposium*, vol. 1, pp. 201-246, Hillsdale, New Jersey: Erlbaum.

Morley, I., J. Webb and G. Stepenson (1988) 'Bargaining and Arbitration in the Resolution of Conflict' in W. Stroeb, A. Kruglanski, D. Bar-Tal and M. Hewstone (eds), *The Social Psychology of Intergroup Conflict*, New York: Springer-Verlag.

Nisbett, R. and L. Ross (1980) *Human Inference: Strategies and Shortcomings of Social Judgment*, Englewood Cliffs, New Jersey: Prentice-Hall.

Park, B. and M. Rothbart (1982) 'Perception of Out-Group Homogeneity and Levels of Social Categorization: Memory for the Subordinate Attributes of In-Group and Out-Group Members', *Journal of Personality and Social Psychology*, vol. 42, pp. 1051-1068.

Pettigrew, T. (1979) 'The Ultimate Attribution Error: Extending Allport's Cognitive Analysis of Prejudice', *Personality and Social Psychology Bulletin*, vol. 5, pp. 461-476.

Pruitt, D. G. (1971) 'Indirect Communication and the Search for Agreement in Negotiation', *Journal of Applied Psychology*, vol. 1, pp. 205-239.

Pruitt, D. G. (1981) *Negotiation Behavior*, Orlando, Florida: Academic.

Pruitt, D. G. and J. Z. Rubin (1986) *Social Conflict: Escalation, Stalemate, and Conflict*, New York: Random House.

Pyszczynski, T. and J. Greenberg (1981) 'Role of Disconfirmed Expectancies in the Instigation of Attributional Processing', *Journal of Personality and Social Psychology*, vol. 40, pp. 31-38.

Ross, L. (1977) 'The Intuitive Psychologist and His Shortcomings: Distortions in the Attribution Process' in L. Berkowitz (ed), *Advances in Experimental Social Psychology*, vol. 10, pp. 173-220, New York: Academic.

Ross, M. and G. Fletcher (1985) 'Attribution and Social Perception' in G. Lindzey and A. Aronson (eds), *The Handbook of Social Psychology*, Reading, Massachusetts: Addison-Wesley.

Sherif, M. (1958) 'Superordinate Goals in the Reduction of Intergroup Conflict: An Experimental Evaluation', *The American Journal of Sociology*, vol. 3, 4, pp. 349-356.

Sherif, M. (1966) *Intergroup Conflict and Cooperation: Their Social Psychology*, London: Routledge & Kegan Paul.

Stephan, W. (1977) 'Stereotyping: Role of Ingroup-Outgroup Differences in Causal Attribution of Behavior', *Journal of Social Psychology*, vol. 101, pp. 255-266.

Sumner, G. (1906) *Folkways*, New York: Gunn.

Tajfel, H. (1978) 'Social Categorization, Social Identity and Social Comparison' in H. Tajfel (ed), *Differentiation between Social Groups: Studies in Intergroup Behavior*, London: Academic.

Taylor, D. and V. Jaggi (1974) 'Ethnocentrism in a South Indian Context', *Journal of Cross-Cultural Psychology*, vol. 5, pp. 162-172.

Taylor, D. and F. Moghaddam (1987) *Theories of Intergroup Relations: International Social Psychological Perspectives*, New York: Praeger.

Taylor, S. and S. Fiske (1975) 'Point-of-View and Perceptions of Causality', *Journal of Personality and Social Psychology*, vol. 32, pp. 439-445.

Taylor, S. and S. Fiske (1978) 'Salience, Attention, and Attribution: Top of the Head Phenomena' in L. Berkowitz (ed), *Advances in Experimental Social Psychology*, vol. 11, New York: Academic.

Tetlock, P. and C. McGuire (1986) 'Cognitive Perspectives on Foreign Policy' in S. Long (ed), *Political Behavior Annual*, vol. 1, pp. 147-179, Boulder, Colorado: Westview.

Turner, J. C. (1981) 'The Experimental Social Psychology of Intergroup Behaviour' in J. C. Turner and H. Giles (eds), *Intergroup Behaviour*, Oxford: Blackwell.

Tversky, A. and D. Kahneman (1973) 'Availability: A Heuristic for Judging Frequency and Probability', *Cognitive Psychology*, vol. 5, pp. 207-232.

Tversky, A. and D. Kahneman (1982) 'Judgment under Uncertainty: Heuristics and Biases' in D. Kahneman, P. Slovic, and A. Tversky (eds), *Judgment under Uncertainty: Heuristics and Biases*, Cambridge: Cambridge University.

Weiner, B. (1982) 'The Emotional Consequences of Causal Attributions' in M. Clark and S. Fiske (eds), *Affect and Cognition: The 17th Annual Carnegie Symposium on Cognition*, Hillsdale, New Jersey: Erlbaum.

Weiner, B. (1985) 'An Attributional Theory of Achievement Motivation and Emotion', *Psychological Review*, vol. 92, pp. 548-573.

Weiner, B. (1986) *An Attributional Theory of Motivation and Emotion*, New York: Springer-Verlag.

White, R. (ed) (1986) *Psychology and the Prevention of Nuclear War*, New York: New York University.

Worchel, S. (1986) 'The Role of Cooperation in Reducing Intergroup Conflict' in S. Worchel and W. G. Austin (eds), *Psychology of Intergroup Relations*, Chicago: Nelson-Hall.

Zartman, I.W. (1989) 'In Search of Common Elements in the Analysis of the Negotiation Process' in F. Mautner-Markhof (ed), *Processes of International Negotiations*, Boulder, Colorado: Westview.

Zartman, I.W. and M. R. Beeman (1982) *The Practical Negotiator*, New Haven: Yale University.

Zartman, I.W. and S. Touval (1985) 'International Conflict and Power Politics', *Journal of Social Issues*, vol. 41, 2, pp. 527-45.

The Rice Sector (Agriculture)

Bateman, M. (1988) *Economic Efforts of Japan's Rice Policy on the U.S. and*

World Rice Economies, Orem, Utah: Commodity Information.

Castle, E. and K. Hemmi (eds) (1982) *U.S.-Japanese Agricultural Relations*, Washington, D.C.: Resources for the Future.

Childs, N. (1990a) *U.S. Rice Distribution Patterns, 1988/89* (USDA, Economic Research Service – Statistical Bulletin # 836), Washington, D.C.: Government Printing Office.

Childs, N. (1990b) *The World Rice Market: Government Intervention and Multilateral Policy Reform* (USDA, Economic Research Service, Commodity Economics Division, Document # AGES 9060), Washington, D.C.: Government Printing Office.

Davis, B. (1993 October 15) 'Japan Offers to Allow Some Importing of Rice, but U.S. Remains Unsatisfied', *The Wall Street Journal*.

Dore, R. (1978) *Shinohata: A Portrait of a Japanese Village*, New York: Pantheon.

Egaitsu, F. (1982) 'Japanese Agricultural Policy: Present Problems and Their Historical Background' in E. Castle and K. Hemmi (eds), *U.S.-Japanese Agricultural Relations*, Washington, D. C.: Resources for the Future.

Goto, J. and N. Imamura (1993) 'Japanese Agriculture: Characteristics, Institutions, and Policies' in L. Tweeten et al (eds), *Japanese and American Agriculture: Tradition and Progress in Conflict*, Boulder, Colorado: Westview.

Hayami, Y. (1972) 'Rice Policy in Japan's Economic Development', *American Journal of Agricultural Economics*, vol. 54, pp. 19-31.

Hayami, Y. (1988) *Japanese Agriculture under Siege: The Political Economy of Agricultural Policies*, New York: St. Martin's.

Helm, K. (1992 December 17) 'Japanese Rice Farmers Steam: Thousands Rally to Demand Government Keep Imports Ban', *The Los Angeles Times*.

Hemmi, K. (1982) 'Agriculture and Politics in Japan' in E. Castle and K. Hemmi (eds), *U.S.-Japanese Agricultural Relations*, Washington, D.C.: Resources for the Future.

Houck, J. (1982) 'Agreements and Policy in U.S.-Japanese Agricultural Trade' in E. Castle and K. Hemmi (eds), *U.S.-Japanese Agricultural Relations*, Washington, D.C.: Resources for the Future.

Japan Economic Journal (1976 September 20) 'Japan Shocked by U.S. Protests against Rice Import Restriction'.

Japan External Trade Organization (various) *White Paper on International Trade, Japan*, Tokyo: JETRO.

Japan External Trade Organization (1974) *The Rice Cycle: The Grain That Created a Culture*, Tokyo: JETRO.

Kamegai, K. (1990) *An International Comparative Study of Rice Economy and Policy among the United States, Thailand, and Japan* (A Report of the Japanese Ministry of Education, Science and Culture, International Scientific Research Program), Tokyo.

The Los Angeles Times (1991 March 18) 'Japan Forces Removal of U.S. Rice Samples'.

Moore, R. H. (1990) *Japanese Agriculture: Patterns of Rural Development*, Boulder, Colorado: Westview.

Nomani, A. (1992 November 12) 'Rice Industry to Seek Sanctions on Japan', *The Wall Street Journal*.

OECD (1987) *National Policies and Agricultural Trade: Japan*, Paris: OECD.

OECD (1987) *National Policies and Agricultural Trade: United States*, Paris: OECD.

Oga, K. (1993) 'Impacts of Trade Arrangements on Farm Structure and Food Demand: A Japanese Perspective' in L. Tweeten et al (eds), *Japanese and American Agriculture: Tradition and Progress in Conflict*, Boulder, Colorado: Westview.

Sanger, D. (1991 March 18) 'Japan Shuts U.S. Rice Exhibition', *The New York Times*.

Shannon, A. (1987) 'U.S. Rice Industry Celebrates 300 Years', *American Foodservice Journal*, vol. 41, 3, pp. 60-61.

Smith, T. C. (1959) *The Agrarian Origins of Modern Japan*, Stanford, California: Stanford University.

Tweeten, L. (1993a) 'American Agriculture: Organization, Structure, Institutions, and Policy' in L. Tweeten et al (eds), *Japanese & American Agriculture: Tradition and Progress in Conflict*, Boulder, Colorado: Westview.

Tweeten, L. (1993b) 'Overview' in L. Tweeten et al (eds), *Japanese and American Agriculture: Tradition and Progress in Conflict*, Boulder, Colorado: Westview.

U.S. Department of Agriculture (1990) *The Basic Mechanisms of Japanese Farm Policy* (USDA Miscellaneous Publication # 1478), Washington, D.C.

U.S. Department of Agriculture, Economic Research Service (various) Foreign Agricultural Trade of the United States (FATUS), Washington, D.C.

U.S. Department of Agriculture, Economic Research Service (1992) *Rice Situation and Outlook Yearbook* (USDA Publication # RS-64), Washington, D.C.

U.S. House of Representatives, Committee on Agriculture, Subcommittee on Cotton, Rice, and Sugar (1981) *Review United States-Japan Rice*

Agreement (Hearing on February 26, 1981), Washington, D.C.

U.S. House of Representatives, Committee on Agriculture, Subcommittee on Cotton, Rice, and Sugar (1987) *Review of Japan's Policy Concerning the Importation of Rice, Including the Petition Filed by the U.S. Rice Millers' Association* (Hearing on October 1, 1986), Washington, D.C.

U.S. Senate, Committee on Agriculture, Nutrition, and Forestry (1987) *U.S.-Japan Rice Trade* (Hearing on October 21, 1986 in Sacramento, California), Washington, D.C.

Vogt, D. (1986) 'Japanese Import Barriers to U.S. Agricultural Exports' included in *Report for the Republican Members of the Joint Economic Committee* (prepared by the Congressional Research Service, Library of Congress, October 1, 1986), Washington, D.C.

Wailes, E. et al (1993) 'Rice and Food Security in Japan: An American Perspective' in L. Tweeten et al (eds), *Japanese and American Agriculture: Tradition and Progress in Conflict*, Boulder, Colorado: Westview.

Wailes, E., S. Ito, and G. Cramer (1991) *Japan's Rice Market: Policies and Prospects for Trade Liberalization* (Report Series 319), Fayetteville: Arkansas Agricultural Experiment Station.

Watanabe, T. (1991 June 3) 'Rice an Emotional Agriculture Issue in Japan and U.S.', *The Los Angeles Times*.

Yamaji, S. and S. Ito (1993) 'The Political Economy of Rice in Japan' in L. Tweeten et al (eds), *Japanese and American Agriculture: Tradition and Progress in Conflict*, Boulder, Colorado: Westview.

The Automotive Sector (Heavy Industry)

American Automobile Manufacturers Association (various) *Motor Vehicle Facts and Figures*, Washington, D.C.: AAMA.

American Automobile Manufacturers Association (1993) *World Motor Vehicle Data 1993*, Washington, D.C.

Associated Press (1992 January 13) 'Not Much Sympathy at Home for Big Three: Many Think Detroit Makes Its Own Trouble', *Star-News*.

Auerbach, S. and D. Hoffman (1985 February 20) 'Car Quotas to be Left Up to Japan', *Washington Post*.

Automobile International (various) *World Automotive Market*, New York: Johnston International.

Congressional Digest (1983 February) 'Proposed Automobile 'Domestic Content' Legislation', vol. 62, 2.

Congressional Quarterly (1992 January 11) 'Trade Talks: Outline of Mutual

Agreement to End U.S.-Japan Discord', vol. 72.

Crandall, R. (1984) 'Import Quotas and the Automobile Industry: The Costs of Protection', *Brookings Review*, vol. 2, 4, pp. 8-16.

Cullison, A. (1985 January 31) 'Japan Won't Renew U.S. Car Export Ceiling', *Journal of Commerce*.

Cusumano, M. (1985) *The Japanese Automobile Industry: Technology and Management at Nissan and Toyota* (Harvard East Asian Monographs 122), Cambridge, Massachusetts: The Council of East Asian Studies, Harvard University.

Dodwell Consultants (1987) *The Japanese Automotive Components Industry*, 3rd edition, Hong Kong: Dodwell Consultants.

Feenstra, R. (1984) 'Voluntary Export Restraint in U.S. Autos, 1980-81: Quality, Employment, and Welfare Effects' in R. Baldwin and A. Krueger (eds), *The Structure and Evolution of Recent U.S. Trade Policy* (National Bureau of Economic Research Conference Report), Chicago: University of Chicago.

Halberstam, D. (1986) *The Reckoning*, New York: William Morrow.

Harmon, A. (1992 May 20) 'Japanese Car Firms Found 'Dumping'', *Los Angeles Times*.

Keller, M. (1989) *Rude Awakening: The Rise, Fall, and Struggle for Recovery of General Motors*, New York: William Morrow.

Keller, M. (1993) *Collision: GM, Toyota, Volkswagen and the Race to Own the 21st Century*, New York: Doubleday.

McWhirter, W. (1993 December 13) 'Back on the Fast Track', *Time*.

Miller, K. and J. Mitchell (1993 March 4) 'Stalling Out: After Years of Growth in U.S. Car Market, Japanese Surge Is Over', *The Wall Street Journal*.

Monden, Y. (1983) *The Toyota Production System*, Atlanta: Institute of Industrial Engineers.

Moritz, M. and B. Seaman (1981) *Going for Broke: The Chrysler Story*, Garden City, New York: Doubleday.

Motor Vehicle Manufacturers Association: See American Automobile Manufacturers Association.

Mutoh, H. (1988) 'The Automotive Industry' (chapter 12) in R. Komiya, M. Okuno, and K. Suzumura (eds), *Industrial Policy of Japan*, Tokyo: Academic.

Nanto, D. (1983) 'Automobiles Imported from Japan' (U.S. Congressional Research Service, Issue Brief No. IB 80030), Washington, D.C.

Nauss, D. (1988 March 9) 'Big 3's Trade Gripe Gets More Attention', *Los Angeles Times*.

Nauss, D. (1988 May 9) 'Japan Shaving the Trade Gap in Auto Parts', *Los Angeles Times*.

Ono, Y. and J. M. Schlesinger (1993 October 5) 'Japan's Auto Makers Fault Big Three for Not Doing Enough to Boost Exports', *The Wall Street Journal*.

Suzuki, Y. (1981) 'U.S.-Japan Trade Relations: Reaching Accommodations' in R. Cole (ed), *The Japanese Automobile Industry: Model and Challenge for the Future?* (Michigan Papers in Japanese Studies, No. 3), Ann Arbor, Michigan: University of Michigan.

Templin, N. (1993 August 24) 'Japan Auto Makers Buy More U.S. Parts', *The Wall Street Journal*.

U.S. Congress, Joint Economic Committee, Subcommittee on Trade, Productivity, and Economic Growth (1986) *The Legacy of the Japanese Voluntary Export Restraints* (hearing on June 24, 1985), Washington, D.C.

U.S. Council of Economic Advisers (1982 May 24) 'Domestic Content Requirements for U.S. Auto Sales: An Economic Assessment', Washington, D.C.

U.S. Department of Commerce, International Trade Commission, Office of Automotive Industry Affairs (1993) 'U.S. Automotive Parts Trade Statistics: 1985 - First Half 1993', Washington, D.C.

U.S. Department of Commerce, International Trade Commission, Office of Automotive Industry Affairs (1993 September) 'U.S. Motor Vehicle Trade Data Package 1989-1993 (Qtr 2)', Washington, D.C.

U.S. House of Representatives, Committee on Small Business (1987) *Global Competition in the Auto Parts Industry* (hearings on July 21 and 22, 1987), Serial 100-17, Washington, D.C.

U.S. House of Representatives, Committee on Small Business, Subcommittee on Innovation, Technology, and Productivity (1991), *United States-Japan Auto Parts Trade* (hearing on June 20, 1991), Washington, D.C.

U.S. House of Representatives, Committee on Ways and Means, Subcommittee on Trade (1985) *Japanese Voluntary Restraints on Auto Exports to the United States* (hearings on February 28 and March 4, 1985), Serial 99-1, Washington, D.C.

U.S. International Trade Commission (1980) *Certain Motor Vehicles and Certain Chassis and Bodies Therefor*, USITC Publication No. 1110 (December, 1980), Washington. D.C.

U.S. International Trade Commission (1985) *Internationalization of the Automobile Industry and Its Effect on the U.S. Automobile Industry*, Washington, D.C.

U.S. International Trade Commission (1985) *A Review of Recent Developments in the U.S. Automobile Industry Including an Assessment of the Japanese Voluntary Restraint Agreements*, USITC Publication 1648,

Washington, D.C.

Ward's Automotive Yearbook 1993 (1993) Detroit: Ward's Communications.

Watanabe, T. (1992 January 21) 'Japan Hedges Commitments on U.S. Cars', *Los Angeles Times*.

Winham, G. and I. Kabashima (1982) 'The Politics of U.S.-Japanese Auto Trade', Chapter 3 in I.M. Destler and H. Sato (eds), *Coping with U.S.-Japanese Economic Conflicts*, Lexington, Massachusetts: Lexington.

Womack, J. (1989) 'The U.S. Automobile Industry in an Era of International Competition: Performance and Prospects' in *The Working Papers of the MIT Commission on Industrial Productivity*, vol. 1, Cambridge, Massachusetts: MIT.

Womack, J. (1990) *The Machine That Changed the World*, New York: Macmillan.

Woutat, D. (1992 June 25) 'Big Three Lose Round on Minivans', *Los Angeles Times*.

Yates, S (1987) *The Decline and Fall of the American Automobile Industry*, New York: Empire.

The Semiconductor Sector (High Technology)

Anchordoguy, M. (1989) *Computers Inc: Japan's Challenge to IBM*, Cambridge, Massachusetts: Harvard University.

Aviation Week And Space Technology (1986 November 10) 'Integrated Circuit Technology Concerns U.S. Officials'.

Borrus, M. (1988) *Competing for Control: America's Stake in Microelectronics*, Cambridge, Massachusetts: Ballinger.

Borrus, M., J. Millstein and J. Zysman (1982) *U.S.-Japanese Competition in the Semiconductor Industry: A Study in International Trade and Technological Development*, Berkeley: Institute of International Studies, University of California.

Borrus, M., L. Tyson, and J. Zysman (1988) 'Creating Advantage: How Government Policies Shape International Trade in the Semiconductor Industry' in P. Krugman (ed), *Strategic Trade Policy and the New International Economics*, Cambridge, Massachusetts: MIT.

Butler, S. (1993 March 1) 'Winning Chip Shots: America Has Surged Ahead of Japan in the Global Semiconductor Wars', *U.S. News & World Report*.

Congressional Record (1986 May 21), 'U.S. House of Representatives Resolution 4800', Washington, D.C.

Davidson, W. (1984) *The Amazing Race: Winning the Technorivalry with Japan*, New York: John Wiley & Sons.

Derian, J.C. (1990) *America's Struggle for Leadership in Technology* (translated from French by S. Schaeffer), Cambridge, Massachusetts: MIT.

Dertouzos, M. et al (1989) *Made in America: Regaining the Productivity Edge* (MIT Commission on Industrial Productivity), Cambridge, Massachusetts: MIT.

The Economist (1992 May 20) 'Chip Trade: Worthless Target'.

The Economist (1993 July 3) 'The Coming Clash of Logic'.

Gilder, G. (1988 June 13) 'How the Computer Companies Lost Their Memories', *Forbes*, pp. 79-84.

Gregory, G. (1986) 'Semiconductors' (Part IV) in *Japanese Electronics Technology: Enterprise and Innovation*, New York: John Wiley & Sons.

Gregory, G. and A. Etori (1981 October) 'Japanese Technology Today', *Scientific American*, pp. 15-46.

Groves, M. (1993 December 28) 'Kantor Calls for Emergency Talks with Japanese', *Los Angeles Times*.

Helm, L. (1991 June 10) 'Japanese, U.S. Differ on Intent of Chip Accord', *Los Angeles Times*.

Helm, L. (1992 June 3) 'U.S., Japan on a Collision Course over Chip Trade', *Los Angeles Times*.

Helm, L. (1993 March 15) 'U.S., Japan Swap Insults before Chip Talks Open', *Los Angeles Times*.

Hills, C. (1993 June 11) 'Targets Won't Open Japanese Markets', *The Wall Street Journal*.

Lachica, E. and J. Bartimo (1991 May 6) 'U.S. Claims Japanese Firms Withhold Equipment from American Chip Makers', *The Wall Street Journal*.

Marshall, E. (1985 November) 'Fallout from the Trade War in Chips', *Science*, vol. 230, pp. 917-919.

McCarroll, T. (1992 November 23) 'Chips Ahoy!', *Time*.

Nomani, A. (1993 December 28) 'U.S. Seeks Talks with Tokyo on Chip Accord', *The Wall Street Journal*.

Okimoto, D. (1984) 'Political Context' (Chapter 4) and 'Conclusions' (Chapter 6) in D. Okimoto, T. Sugano, and F. Weinstein (eds), *Competitive Edge: The Semiconductor Industry in the U.S. and Japan*, Stanford, California: Stanford University.

Pollack, A. (1991 May 30) 'Chip Talks Fail to Set Measure for Market Share', *The New York Times*.

Pugel, T. (1987) 'Limits of Trade Policy toward High Technology Industries: The Case of Semiconductors' in R. Sato and P. Wachtel (eds), *Trade Friction and Economic Policy: Problems and Prospects for Japan and the United States*, Cambridge: Cambridge University.

Rogers, E. and J. Larsen (1984) *Silicon Valley Fever: Growth of High-Technology Culture*, New York: Basic.

Schlender, B. (1991 May 6) 'Chipper Days for U.S. Chip Makers', *Fortune*.

Schlesinger, J. and C. Chipelo (1991 May 22) 'U.S., Japan Close to Chip Trade Pact Setting Targets, Not Quotas, for Sales', *The Wall Street Journal*.

Semiconductor Industry Association (1993) 'Materials for Academics on Japanese Semiconductor Market Access' [unpublished].

Steinmueller, W. (1988) 'Industry Structure and Government Policy in the U.S. and Japanese Integrated-Circuit Industries' in J. Shoven (ed), *Government Policy towards Industry in the United States and Japan*, Cambridge: Cambridge University.

Tyson, L. (1992) *Who's Bashing Whom? Trade Conflict in High Technology Industries*, Washington, D.C.: Institute for International Economics.

U.S. Department of Commerce, Office of Microelectronics, Medical Equipment, and Instrumentation (1993) 'Electronic Components, Equipment, and Superconductors' (Chapter 15) in *U.S. Industrial Outlook 1993*, Washington, D.C.

U.S. General Accounting Office (1991) 'U.S. Business Access to Certain State-of-the-Art Technology', Washington, D.C.

U.S. General Accounting Office, National Security and International Affairs Division (1988) 'U.S.-Japan Trade: Trade Data and Industry Views on MOSS Agreements' (Fact Sheet for the Honorable Lloyd M. Bentsen, U.S. Senate), Document GAO/NSIA-88-120FS, Washington, D.C.

U.S. House of Representatives, Energy and Commerce Committee, Subcommittee on Commerce, Consumer Protection and Competitiveness (1990) 'Decline of U.S. Semiconductor Infrastructure' (Hearing on May 9, 1990), Washington, D.C.

U.S. House of Representatives, Foreign Affairs Committee, Subcommittee on International Economic Policy and Trade (1991) 'Prospects for a New United States-Japan Semiconductor Agreement' (Hearing on March 20, 1991), Washington, D.C.

U.S. Office of the Trade Representative (1986) 'Arrangement between the Government of Japan and the Government of the United States of America Concerning Trade', Washington, D.C.

U.S. Senate, Banking, Housing, and Urban Affairs Committee, Subcommittee on International Finance and Monetary Policy (1985) 'Semiconductor Trade

and Japanese Targeting' (Hearing on July 30, 1985), Washington, D.C.
U.S. Senate, Finance Committee, Subcommittee on International Trade (1991) 'Renewal of the United States-Japan Semiconductor Agreement' (Hearing on March 22, 1991), Washington, D.C.
Weinstein, F., M. Uenohara and J. Linville (1984) 'Technological Resources' (Chapter 3) in D. Okimoto, T. Sugano and F. Weinstein (eds), *Competitive Edge: The Semiconductor Industry in the U.S. and Japan*, Stanford, California: Stanford University Press.

Research Methods

Babbic, E. (1986) *The Practice of Social Research*, fourth edition, Belmont, California: Wadsworth.
Babbie, E. (1990) *Survey Research Methods*, second edition, Belmont, California: Wadsworth.
Bradburn, N. and S. Sudman (1988) *Polls and Surveys: Understanding What They Tell Us*, San Francisco: Jossey-Bass.
Dillman, D. (1978) *Mail and Telephone Surveys: The Total Design Method*, New York: John Wiley & Sons.
Himmelweit, H. (1990) 'The Dynamics of Public Opinion' in C. Fraser and G. Haskell (eds), *The Social Psychological Study of Widespread Beliefs*, Oxford: Clarendon.
Judd, C., E. Smith, and L. Kidder (1991) *Research Methods in Social Relations*, sixth edition (Chapters 7, 10, 11), Fort Worth, Texas: Holt, Reinhart, and Winston.
Kojima, K. (1977) 'Public Opinion Trends in Japan', *Public Opinion Quarterly*, vol. 41, pp. 206-216.
Labaw, Patricia (1980) *Advanced Questionnaire Design*, Cambridge, Massachusetts: Abt.
Nisihira, S. (1983) 'Political Opinion Polling in Japan' in R. M. Worcester (ed), *Political Opinion Polling: An International Review*, New York: St. Martin's.
Oskamp, S. (1991) *Attitudes and Opinions*, Eaglewood Cliffs, New Jersey: Prentice Hall.
Payne, S. (1951) *The Art of Asking Questions*, Princeton, New Jersey: Princeton University.
Zimbardo, P. and M. Leippe (1991) 'Measuring Attitudes and their Components' in *The Psychology of Attitude Change and Social Influence*, New York: McGraw-Hill.

Index

Abe, Shintaro 247f
Abegglen, James 85f, 266f
'administrative guidance' 76, 206-207,
    240
Advanced Micro Devices 229, 234
adversarial trade 30-32, 244, 246
affect 92-93, 112f
agricultural commodities, trade in
    beef 31, 184, 191, 246-247f
    beer 184, 194
    citrus fruits 184, 194, 246-247f
    cotton 21-22, 27, 182-185, 246f,
        247f
    feed grains 181-184
    foodstuffs 25, 31, 76, 179, 182-184,
        246f
    fruits 181-184, 194
    meat and meat products 181-183,
        194
    soybeans 181-184, 194, 246f
    tobacco 181-183, 194
    vegetables 181-184
    wheat 181-184, 187, 194
Allen, G. C. 36f, 37f, 86f
Allport, Gordon 102, 112f, 113f
amae 49, 52-53, 60f, 62f
American Automobile Manufacturers
    Association (AAMA) 197, 199-
    200, 202
American Complaints 13, 15, 22, 29-33,
    35, 40, 79, 99, 184, 188, 205-
    206, 209
American Electronics Association
    (AEA) 218-219, 231
American International Auto
    Dealers 207
American Occupation (1945-1952) 1, 13,
    21, 24, 37f, 53, 71, 190, 214

American Rice Council 186-188
Amir, Yehuda 94, 112f
Anchordoguy, Marie 256f
Andriessen, Frans 188
antidumping 72, 208, 230, 232
antitrust laws
    Japan 24, 36f, 71-72, 78, 228
    U.S. 21, 71, 155, 238
Applied Materials 221-222
Armacost, Michael 187
AT&T 232, 238-239
attribution theory 8-9, 14, 88-92, 100-
    106, 110f, 111f, 112f, 113f, 114f,
    119, 142, 259, 264-265
    actor-observer fallacy 103
    fundamental attribution error
        (FAE) 102-103
    group-serving attribution 147, 175
    ingroup-outgroup 5, 13, 14-15, 42,
        57, 60f, 94, 100, 103-104, 106,
        108, 112f, 118, 142, 173, 259,
        264
    internal-external 67, 151-152, 101,
        103, 120, 123, 134, 147, 167
    schema theory 42, 100, 105
    self-serving bias 102, 106, 114f
    ultimate attribution error (UAE) 103,
        104, 108, 113f, 114f, 120, 123,
        124
attributional theory of motivation and
    emotion 92, 112f, 265
automobile sector 195-217
    agreements 206-208
    consumption 196
    employment in 209-210, 213
    VERs 207

318